THE RISE OF
MULTICULTURAL
AMERICA

THE
RISE
OF

Multi

AME

The University of North Carolina Press :: CHAPEL HILL

cultural

RICA

ECONOMY AND

PRINT CULTURE

1865–1915

SUSAN L. MIZRUCHI

© 2008

THE UNIVERSITY OF

NORTH CAROLINA PRESS

Designed by Courtney Leigh Baker
Set in Dante by Keystone Typesetting, Inc.
Manufactured in the United States of America

The paper in this book meets the guidelines for
permanence and durability of the Committee
on Production Guidelines for Book Longevity
of the Council on Library Resources.

The University of North Carolina Press has been
a member of the Green Press Initiative since 2003.

Library of Congress Cataloging-in-Publication Data
Mizruchi, Susan L. (Susan Laura)
The rise of multicultural America : economy
and print culture, 1865–1915 / Susan L. Mizruchi.
p. cm.
Includes bibliographical references and index.
ISBN 978-0-8078-3250-9 (cloth: alk. paper) —
ISBN 978-0-8078-5912-4 (pbk.: alk. paper)
1. Pluralism (Social sciences)—United States—History—
19th century. 2. Pluralism (Social sciences)—United
States—History—20th century. 3. Pluralism (Social
sciences)—Economic aspects—United States—History.
4. United States—Economic conditions—1865–1918.
5. Capitalism—Social aspects—United States—
History. 6. United States—Emigration and immigration
—History. 7. United States—Race relations—History.
8. United States—Intellectual life—1865–1918. 9. American
literature—19th century—History and criticism.
10. American literature—20th century—History and
criticism. I. Title.
E184.A1M585 2009
305.800973—dc22

2008023201

Excerpts from pp. 413–740,
*Becoming Multicultural:
Culture, Economy, and the
Novel, 1860–1920,* by Susan
L. Mizruchi, in Cambridge
History of American
Literature, Volume 3, *Prose
Writing, 1860–1920,* edited
by Sacvan Bercovitch.
Copyright © Cambridge
University Press 2005.
Reprinted with permission.

CLOTH   12 11 10 09 08   5 4 3 2 1
PAPER   12 11 10 09 08   5 4 3 2 1

TO

Saki,

Sascha,

AND

Eytan

CONTENTS

ILLUSTRATIONS

ACKNOWLEDGMENTS

It is a pleasure to thank the friends and family who contributed to this book.

My brother Mark provided invaluable advice on the book's social scientific and historical aspects as well as on the writing. Eytan Bercovitch offered a rich fund of knowledge and debate on all aspects of my research. Julia Brown and Maurice Lee read drafts of the introduction and made very helpful suggestions. Daniel Aaron, Nancy Bentley, Thomas Ferraro, Gordon Hutner, Jeanne Follansbee Quinn, Werner Sollors, John Tessitore, and audiences at Syracuse University, the University of California–Irvine, and Washington University prodded me to clarify my terms and arguments and supplied stimulating forums for rehearsing earlier versions of the book. I want to thank my parents, Ephraim and Ruth Mizruchi, my brother, David Mizruchi, and my sisters-in-law, Sylvia Ary, Gail Mizruchi, Marcia Mizruchi, and Ninel Segal, for their encouragement and support. Sian Hunter was a marvelously engaged editor, and the staff at the University of North Carolina Press, especially my copyeditor, John K. Wilson, offered expert help at all stages of the production process. I also want to acknowledge fellowship support from the John Simon Guggenheim Foundation and to thank Philip Fisher, Giles Gunn, and Barbara Packer for their confidence in my work. Sascha Bercovitch contributed significantly to this book, advising me on the title, reading different sections, and inspiring many improvements. Above all, I am grateful to Saki Bercovitch for his criticism and generosity, for his humor, warmth, and devotion, and for sustaining a life full of so many good things.

INTRODUCTION

In 1899 Mark Twain published an essay, "Concerning the Jews," that is rarely considered today because it confronts an embarrassing topic: the commercial expertise of the Jews. Responding to a letter from a Jewish lawyer seeking an explanation for anti-Semitism, Twain highlighted "the average Christian's inability to compete successfully with the average Jew in business."[1] It was not that Jews were uninterested in other pursuits; they cultivated money-getting, according to Twain, because in country after country they were systematically expelled from other trades. Now in America at the turn of the twentieth century, Jews had a strategic advantage in the financial and entrepreneurial activities that preoccupied everyone. They comprised such a social presence, Twain observed, that he was convinced their number was at least twice that confirmed by population figures. His essay was unusual in minimizing the religious causes of anti-Semitism and in attributing Jewish commercial aptitude to historical rather than essential factors. He was tentative about how far Jews as Jews might go in America but was confident that they would continue to thrive within limits.

This was not the first time that Twain had probed connections between ethnicity and economy.[2] The sign that the slave Jim in *The Adventures of Huckleberry Finn* is prepared for citizenship is Jim's interest in capital and monetary speculation. Twain saw that blacks' mastery of finance would be required in the turbulent years ahead, and he was one of the few who anticipated, after the broken promise of "forty acres and a mule" and the failure of the Freedmen's Bureau Bank, that some of the most profitable opportunities for blacks in the post-Emancipation era would derive from the effects of racism. W. E. B. Du Bois called this "the advantage of the disadvantage" in describing how some blacks made fortunes in the funeral industry by exploiting the prohibition against whites burying blacks.[3]

For these two quintessential groups of outsiders, Jews and blacks, capitalism provided the road to survival, however rocky, but by constituting them as aliens, or "others," capitalism also circumscribed their relationship to society. The interplay between capitalism and ethnicity at this crucial point in the nation's history, as Twain understood it, is dynamic: racial-ethnic others are defined through their economic behavior, which assists but also limits their social integration. Thus Twain sanctioned one of American capitalism's conventions by codifying a Jewish propensity for commerce. But he remained critically aware of how American capitalism operated in relation to racial-ethnic others. Twain seemed to recognize that ethnicity and race would persist and be utilized by a capitalist system rather than be gradually erased by it.

While it has often been assumed that social mobility required giving up ethnic attachments, I will demonstrate that there was in fact much productive fusion of ethnic identities and economic aspirations. The pursuit of material bounty that inspired so many migrants and immigrants in America often demanded their toleration of demeaning stereotypes. But American capitalist energies also sponsored nuanced and creative conceptions of cultural difference. This was most obvious in advertising, "capitalism's way," in one commentator's notorious phrase, "of saying I love you to itself."[4] Ethnic figures in ads of the era were often represented with the sort of complexity that invited admiration and imitation: an ad for Waterman Pens featured Pocahontas and John Smith as mutual representatives of Indian and British aristocracies, while Sapolio hawked the cleansing powers of its soap by identifying it (in Hebrew lettering) with Judaic laws of kashrut.[5]

This book tells the story of a remarkable convergence of forces. Between 1865 and 1915, America underwent the most rapid corporate capitalist development in history and at the same time unparalleled rates of immigration.[6] The result was the first multicultural modern capitalist society. Cultural diversity and the ever-growing awareness of it provided one of the conditions of capitalist America that distinguished it from all other modern capitalist countries—such as Britain, France, and Germany.[7] Different aspects of the story have been recounted in such books as *Strangers in the Land*, *The Incorporation of America*, and *Creating Modern Capitalism*.[8] But the story has never been told in the terms set out here. This book explores and analyzes a momentous and enduring national metamorphosis through the lens of literary writers. I refer to authors, popular and elite, who played pivotal roles in articulating the stakes of these enormous cultural and economic changes. Because this was a period of widespread literacy, when best-selling works of literature and magazines reached vast readerships and immigrants could find newspapers and magazines in their native languages, writers themselves assumed an unparalleled cultural authority.[9] They became mediators of modernization who were experiencing firsthand the dramatic historical transformations they were representing for others. Henry James, for instance, joined fellow writers in recognizing the need for international copyright protections for literature, even testifying before the United States Congress prior to the 1891 passage of the International Copyright Act. But he was equally alert to inadvertent opportunities in the modern marketplace, noting how the "pirating" of his *Art of Fiction* (originally published in London) in Boston accrued to his benefit by having "advertised my fictions."[10]

The extraordinary interdependence between literature and other vocations in this period explains why this book is a literary-*cultural* study, also concerned with essays, memoirs, biographies, journalism, works of social reform, photography, and advertising. Corporate heads explaining their philosophy of business, novelists portraying financiers, advertisers selling soap to "ethnics," and civil servants distinguishing Indian notions of property all joined a conversation about the effects of capitalist development and the role of racial and ethnic others. It was a dynamic and contradictory economic-literary-cultural conversation. On the one hand, an expanding capitalist industry, far from being inimical to cultural difference, welcomed it, taking advantage of the tremendous diversity of American society to identify and pitch products to consumer groups.[11] On the other hand, American capitalism aggressively manipulated racial hostility, fanning the flames of nativism, devaluing and excluding through various means blacks and ethnic others, and defending the social Darwinism that legitimated claims of Anglo-Saxon superiority.

My use of the term "multicultural" is deliberately anachronistic. The term was not coined until the 1940s, and most historians place the advent of multiculturalism in the 1960s.[12] But hindsight can provide a valuable perspective for analysis. It allows us to see what in its own time was underappreciated. Racial and ethnic others, including immigrants, were not simply subsets of the native population; their numbers were equivalent to, and in some places higher than, those of the "natives," whose feelings of embattlement paralleled similar attitudes today. I invoke "multiculturalism," then, both to identify a certain historical moment and to underscore continuities between past and present.[13] Finally, this perspective serves to confirm the homegrown characteristics of American multiculturalism. These have been seen as a direct reaction against modern European fascism, where intolerance toward racial and ethnic others began with stereotypes and ended in genocide.[14] But American multiculturalism did not need an external catalyst for its formation; it emerged, I will be arguing, in the late nineteenth century as the extremes of social diversity met an accelerating capitalist system.

The depth and range of the migrant and immigrant roles in American society during this period would be hard to overestimate. Whether one lived in an urban area, in the countryside, or in a small oil or mining town, places where immigrants were most numerous relative to other groups, it was impossible to avoid confronting a variety of languages and cultures. It was not simply that immigrants and former slaves and their offspring comprised increasingly significant percentages of the population. These "minorities" were responsible for some of the most important social transformations, they wrote significant works of literature, they founded schools, they launched magazines and industries, they framed the national discourse of incorporation, and they helped to formulate the interests of labor.

While most mainstream Americans resented immigrants, it was possible for the Irish-born Andrew Carnegie to come penniless to America and within forty years build a fortune through steel manufacturing. So, too, the Scottish-born Samuel McClure, by editing a magazine he identified with American ideals of justice, became one of the country's most influential figures. Samuel Gompers immigrated to the United States from England with his Dutch-Jewish parents when he was thirteen years old and within twenty-three years had become president of the American Federation of Labor, a post he held for almost forty years. There were less happy experiences, of course.[15] Ely S. Parker, a Seneca Indian, contributed so substantially to anthropologist Lewis Henry Morgan's book on the Iroquois that he was attributed with coauthorship. Later, as secretary to Ulysses S. Grant, Parker drafted Robert E. Lee's surrender at Appomattox. Then in 1871, he was unjustly dismissed as the first Indian commissioner of the Bureau of Indian Affairs and later died in obscurity. The unorthodox prosecution methods used to convict eight anarchists, most of them German immigrants, of the murder of a police officer in Chicago's 1886 Haymarket Affair aroused worldwide furor. The controversy that ensued following the execution of four of them foreshadowed the Sacco and Vanzetti case forty years later.[16]

Major American writers bore witness to the problem of national solidarity; they highlighted the fissures in society and staged conflict among cultural groups. American literature consistently exposed the divisions that prevented the country from dealing with the worst effects of industrial capitalism. Some of the literary works discussed in the following pages, such as John Hay's *The Bread-Winners* (1884) and Upton Sinclair's *The Jungle* (1906), reinforced these divisions, either by depicting them as irreparable or by excoriating a particular class. Other literary works, for example, Marie Ruiz de Burton's *Who Would Have Thought It?* (1872) and Albion Tourgée's *A Fool's Errand* (1879), challenged these divisions by showing that they served to weaken social ties, allowing for more general exploitation. Still others, like Mark Twain's *Extract from Captain Stormfield's Visit to Heaven* (1909) and Charlotte Perkins Gilman's *Herland* (1915), depicted the reconciliation of such divisions through settings that were literally out of this world.

But whether they sought to enhance, redress, or reconcile, all these writers confirmed widespread perceptions of America as a nation of many cultures that were increasingly set against one another. As the economist Simon Patten observed in 1895, "Each class or section of the nation is becoming conscious of an opposition between its standards and the activities and tendencies of some less developed class. The South has its negro, the city has its slums. . . . Everyone is beginning to differentiate those with proper qualifications for citizenship from some class or classes which he wishes to restrain or to exclude from society."[17] This picture of an embattled social and economic system finds full expression in an expanding novelistic tradition, in the pages of widely circulating magazines, in best-selling works of social reform, in the new art of photography, and in the science of advertising. Some of these artists and social observers were themselves distrustful of racial and ethnic "strangers," others were deeply pessimistic about American society and its capacity for forging solidarity, and most worried about the nation's future even as they pursued the opportunities afforded both by capitalism and by cultural diversity.

In particular, the periodicals industry profited from these factors—from the availability of capital as well as from an increasingly diverse society.[18] Magazines revolutionized books and their marketing. They were critical arbiters of literary wares, and many writers contributed to them as often as they could, worked on them, and even started their own. Many American novelists serialized their works in magazines before publishing them in book form. This process not only supplied an important source of revenue for authors, who could earn large sums for serialization well before book profits accrued; it also enabled them to advertise to readers, who often bought the books after reading them serialized or excerpted in magazines.

As moneymaking enterprises, magazines pitched their contents at their largest possible specified audience. General-interest magazines like the *Saturday Evening Post* and *McClure's* were most ambitious in their pursuit of readers, but more focused periodicals like *Atlantic Monthly* and *Crisis* were also eager to preserve and extend their circulation base. Magazines helped to define classes and cultures with sets of interests that they both anticipated and shaped, and advertisers adjusted their promotions accordingly. Thus magazines reflected and helped create America's great cultural variety. In some cases they presented racial and ethnic others through familiar stereotypes in ads and illustrations. In other cases they sought publications from writers of "different" backgrounds, including Paul Laurence Dunbar, who published in *Century* and *Harper's Weekly*, and Abraham Cahan, who published in *Atlantic Monthly* and *McClure's*. In still other cases, they openly confronted the favorable and unfavorable aspects of American multiculturalism.

The development of the American novel in this period is an intrinsic part of the multicultural laboratories created by magazines. Indeed, novels may be said to have functioned as advertisements themselves, locating and also creating a market for their goods. In selling their stories and novels to magazines, ambitious authors such as William Dean Howells, Mary Wilkins Freeman, Jack London, and Henry James were entering a continuum of promotion. At the same time that they were representing the world of business to consumers, they were also representing their insights into their consumer audiences and into American attitudes toward cultural multiplicity. For as William Dean Howells perceived, the attempt to sell cultural commodities, like magazines and the literature they featured, confronted the reader with the deep stratification of American society. The pursuit of markets implicated the pursuer, as a matter of course, in class and cultural analysis. American novelists were helping to shape attitudes toward cultural others, and they were well aware of this fact.

The challenge of this book is to convey the breadth and complexity of these developments, while at the same time capturing the variety of ways in which American writers responded. To this end, I have divided my narrative into eight chapters, each of which encompasses a large cross-section of cultural and economic activity. Chapters 1 (Remembering Civil War) and 4 (Indian Sacrifice in an Age of Progress) focus on the national confrontation of mass death during and especially after the Civil War and the forced migration and annihilation of Indian tribes. Chapter 2 (Racism as Opportunity in the Reconstruction Era) explores the economic and legal institutions that extended the subordination of American blacks well beyond the era of enslavement while offering, inadvertently, opportunities for personal advancement. Chapter 3 (Cosmopolitanism) examines the migration and immigration that accompanied the late nineteenth-century experience of capitalist expansion. Chapters 5 (Marketing Culture) and 7 (Corporate America) trace the rise of advertising and media forms and the revolution in business methods, including the establishment of corporations and trusts. Chapters 6 (Varieties of Work) and 8 (American Utopias) represent different reactions (economic, political, religious) to capitalist growth.

Thus the book's early chapters cover the destruction initiated or sanctioned by the expanding nation in this period, while later chapters tell a largely triumphant story of economic progress, an arc that suggests the dependence of this progress on human casualties—casualties that were neither inevitable nor necessary. One of my principal claims in this study is that Americans at the time were dramatically engaged in debating the proposition that sacrifice was essential to rapid cultural and economic development. When W. E. B. Du Bois declared in *The Souls of Black Folk* (1903) that during Reconstruction blacks—whose social and political exclusion after the war overshadowed their emancipation during it—had been "sacrificed in [their] swaddling clothes on the altar of national integrity," he was challenging the doctrine (adapted from Darwinian science and all major religions) that sacrifice was both indispensable and beneficial.[19] Yet despite the uses of sacrificial beliefs to rationalize the victimization of their peoples during this period, black and Indian intellectuals also confirmed the central place of sacrificial rites in their cultures. Du Bois outlined a "Gospel of Sacrifice" that obligated black elites to support their weaker brethren, and Charles Alexander Eastman described in his autobiography, *Indian Boyhood*, the Sioux initiation ceremony where he makes an offering of his beloved dog.

Moreover, Du Bois emphasized what *was* accessible to blacks at the time. And in another famous declaration from *Souls*, he claimed the ongoing vitality of a cultural inheritance at odds with more local prejudices. "I sit with Shakespeare and he winces not. Across the color line I move arm in arm with Balzac and Dumas."[20] Du Bois's choice of British and European writers was undoubtedly a rebuke to his own country. But as one of the first genuinely global thinkers in history, Du Bois was familiar with the dismal records of these other empires in encounters with people of color. And his use of epigraphs from popular American writers like John Greenleaf Whittier and James Russell Lowell throughout his book, like his insistence on the African American roots of a considerable portion of *American* culture, confirms that he saw just as much untapped potential at home.[21]

In such optimistic moments, Du Bois might have found support in an unexpected source: advertising. For in their efforts to articulate the ambitions of entrepreneurs in ever more sophisticated form, advertising professionals drew increasingly on the prospects of a genuinely multicultural society. Hence my second principal claim: that capitalism's romance with the exceptional diversity of American society dates back to this historical period. Like the culture industries I have described, American business from 1865 to 1915 capitalized on the nation's growing multiculturalism. This resourcefulness took many forms, including the incorporation of vast numbers of immigrants into the American workforce at low wages. At the same time, these immigrant populations provided a critical mass of new consumers, eager to spend their earnings on the magical commodities of the American marketplace, a development that became a generic trope in novels about immigrants. Advertisers directed their appeals to immigrant populations, sometimes even adopting foreign scripts. But they also exploited widespread nervousness about this immigrant influx by filling their ads with assorted racial and ethnic "aliens." By constantly invoking the source of anxiety and fascination, they sought to capture the attention of Americans by familiarizing what they feared.

Some of the most incisive responses to the spectacular turbulence of the period came from the American utopian novel. Acutely aware of widespread suffering, and just as aware of the excessive profits accruing to some, utopian and dystopian novelists, such as Edward Bellamy, Ignatius Donnelly, and Charlotte Perkins Gilman, set out renovation schemes that sought to equalize the proceeds of progress. Significantly, however, in these works and in others like them, the first step en route to a welfare system is the purification of the body politic. There are no aliens in the social worlds of these novels; Indians, blacks, and Jewish and European immigrants have disappeared. I argue, and this is my third principal claim, that these works register a key facet of American resistance to a full-fledged welfare system: that it was spurred by the threat of cultural diversity. At a time when other Western countries (England, Germany, France) were instituting extensive welfare systems—old-age pensions, workers compensation, and health coverage— American efforts lagged far behind. A powerful and persistent ideology of individualism, which throughout American history has energized antipathy toward taxation and "big government," was no doubt partly responsible. But the attractions of populism confirm that other stakes were involved. America's extreme cultural diversity was a critical barrier to welfare measures; most Americans were reluctant to support benefits for peoples unlike themselves who, they believed, were most likely to qualify for them. As my final chapter on utopian novels reveals, a theory long recognized by historians and social scientists had been for even longer embedded in a key literary genre of the period.[22] Thus, in one American literary utopia after another, radical redistribution of wealth is accompanied by eugenicist measures designed to homogenize the citizenry. Alexander Craig's *Ionia* (1898), for instance, features a harmonious Anglo-Saxon socialist state where Jews are forbidden to marry and are sterilized if charged with a crime and where Asian invaders are exterminated.

The pages that follow tell the story of a literary culture that reflects a great economic transformation and represents a newly formed multiculturalism in all its variety and complexity—a literary culture that demonstrated a remarkable sense of obligation to bear witness and a remarkable capacity to predict both the perils and the possibilities of American capitalist expansion.

REMEMBERING CIVIL WAR

The Civil War initiated a publishing industry. The war between the northern Union and the southern Confederacy inspired chronicles—photographic, historical, journalistic, and literary—at a rate unmatched by previous wars. Dime novels written for soldier audiences and run in series—"Dawley's Camp and Fireside Library" and Redpath's "Books for the Camp Fires"—sold in the hundred thousands. As one soldier noted of his appetite for "cheap literature . . . I, certainly, never read so many such before or since." More conventional novels—Metta Victor's *The Unionist's Daughter* (1862); Charles Alexander's *Pauline of the Potomac* (1862); John Trowbridge's *The Drummer Boy* (1863); Edward Willett's *The Vicksburg Spy* (1864); and Sarah Edmonds's *Unsexed: or, The Female Soldier* (1864)—provided those at home and at war, on both sides, with a steady stream of courageous soldiers, wartime courtships, and cross-dressed spies. Newspapers and magazines featured dramatic war testimonials, such as Oliver Wendell Holmes Sr.'s account (in *Atlantic Monthly*) of his frantic search for Oliver Jr. (the future Supreme Court justice), who was wounded at Antietam. Editors like Joseph Medill of the *Chicago Tribune*, Horace Greeley of the *New York Tribune*, and Henry J. Raymond of the *New York Times* assumed the role of elder statesmen as they reviewed military and diplomatic strategies, while one Alabama editor warned those corresponding with soldiers to avoid news "that will embitter their thoughts or swerve them from the path of duty."[1]

The most significant Civil War writing was retrospective. The literary surge of Civil War remembering began, it seems, with the drying of the ink on General Robert E. Lee's April 9, 1865, surrender. This prodigious production continued to the end of the decade and beyond. Indeed, the need for imaginative recollection of this momentous event was intensified by historical distance, so that a writer in 1998 could describe the Civil War as still "unfinished."[2] In this sense, the chief cultural effect of the Civil War was to keep Americans permanently fixed in the four years (1861–65) of traumatic conflict. The array of novels and memoirs published in the decades after the war by such varied and prominent authors as Elizabeth Stuart Phelps, Ellen Glasgow, Frances Harper, Paul Laurence Dunbar, Henry James, and Ulysses S. Grant lend support to this view. At the same time, however, the war played a critical role in accelerating capitalist development and modernization (in part through its eradication of the antiquated institution of slavery) and thus seemed to all who witnessed it to speed the nation rapidly into the future.

Before the war, the country was largely rural and agrarian, with only the railroads qualifying as a "big business." Between 1865 and 1895, most competitive industries—from textiles, oil, iron, and steel, to glass, paper, liquor, and sugar—entered into forms of cooperation that led to their formation as trusts. The need for managing and transmitting information both within and between growing business networks required ever more complex and efficient systems. The development in this period of new methods for typing and copying, filing and storage, spurred a communications revolution extending to the computer in the twentieth century. The most revolutionary invention of the antebellum era was the telegraph, an advance in communications technology unrivaled even by the telephone (introduced in 1876 by Alexander Graham Bell). The telegraph, like other industries, profited greatly from the war, emerging at its end as a monopoly of Western Union. Many financiers made fortunes through bond purchase and speculation. And wartime investing prompted renewed calls for a national banking system and currency, which was instituted by the National Banking Act of 1863.[3]

On the eve of the war, the North was considerably more advanced than the South: more industrialized and urbanized, with twice the amount of cultivated land and a vast and well-consolidated railroad network. Because southern secession eliminated a key legislative barrier to economic development, President Lincoln was able during the war to usher various modernizing measures through Congress and sign them into law. These included the 1862 Homestead Act, which expedited western development, tariff legislation to advance northern industry, and the Pacific Railway Act, facilitating construction on the transcontinental railroad. The South's great military resource was slave labor, which kept their lead, salt, and iron mines as well as agriculture fully productive. Slave labor also enabled an astonishing 80 percent conscription rate among the Confederacy's white male population. Yet this resource proved unreliable (as fictionalized by Harper in *Iola Leroy*). Over time slaves became increasingly identified with the Union campaign when emancipation was embraced as its purpose. Frederick Douglass had predicted this in 1861: "The American people and the Government at Washington may refuse to recognize it for a time, but the 'inexorable logic of events' will force it upon them in the end; that the war now being waged in this land is a war for and against slavery." On January 1, 1863, Lincoln signed the Emancipation Proclamation, a measure that resulted in a major escalation of what had been a limited conflict. Ulysses S. Grant called it "the heaviest blow yet given the Confederacy."[4] In all, over 180,000 blacks served in the Union army. The desperate Confederate decision near the war's end to arm slaves and grant them freedom in exchange for military service nullified the very principle upon which the South had staked its rebellion.

The end of the Civil War plunged America into a double-edged mourning—for catastrophic losses, personal and public, and for a way of life. While the war itself could hardly have provided the impetus to an industrial and technological transformation at once so complex and so rapid, the Civil War and modernization remained intertwined for many. The literature that was produced in the postwar years registered a view of an American society that had grown increasingly diverse and splintered. It was as if the great rift between North and South had yielded a series of aftershocks, resulting in many smaller cleavages and separations. Thus, in novels, memoirs, biographies, even in photographs, the war was portrayed as a highly particularized experience rather than a nationally definitive event.[5] Stephen Crane's *The Red Badge of Courage* was typical: it focused on the working-class men who either volunteered or were forced to fight because they, unlike their wealthier counterparts, could not hire substitutes. Crane's war fiction was not the record of a nation but of a class, the class that in his view gave the most. This perspective was characteristic of many literary works that foreground the experiences in turn of free blacks in Ohio (Dunbar's *The Fanatics*) the genteel poor in New England (Louisa May Alcott's *Little Women*), subversive slaves in the South (Harper's *Iola Leroy*), and northern war heroes (Owen Wister's *Ulysses S. Grant*).

Thus, despite the complex combination of forces—social, political, economic—that set the long nineteenth-century process of modernization in motion, the Civil War was commonly understood in its own time and well after as *the* cause of modern social change. As Henry James famously characterized it in his 1879 biography of Nathaniel Hawthorne, "four long years of bloodshed and misery, and a social revolution as complete as any the world has seen . . . the Civil War marks an era in the history of the American mind."[6] The challenge for the series of narratives explored in the following pages was to represent that social revolution. As a catalyst of change, whose impact was ongoing, the war for those who sought to capture its deepest implications remained truly "unfinished." Each example discussed below is an effort to frame an image of a Civil War world that is remembered as traumatically continuous with the present. Indeed, these examples are most accurately viewed as sustained meditations on historical continuity in its own right. Among the Civil War effects most consistently remarked upon are the shift to a commercial ethos, the prevailing concern with capital and accumulation; the alteration of work, accompanied by a growing divide between owners, managers, and laborers; and scientific progress and the consumption it fosters. Through them all runs the ongoing drama of American diversity—the global reach of innovation and commerce; the immigrant backgrounds of key participants in the arts and sciences, in trade and industry, in education and government; and the reckoning with racial and cultural difference that resulted from slavery's abolition—a drama whose script was the emergence of a uniquely heterogeneous nationality.

WAR STILLS

Perhaps no single late nineteenth-century device was more indicative of the changes the Civil War came to symbolize than the camera. Photography was pivotal in distinguishing both how the war differed from previous ones and how it helped to bring about a modern nation-state and industrial power.[7] Moreover, the camera provided Americans with a distinct perspective on war in the abstract; it afforded a detached outlook on the carnage, as a spectacle devised with a viewer in mind. All the narratives discussed below, which represent the most popular and critically acclaimed late nineteenth-century works about the war, exploit the aesthetic prospects of mass death and mourning. The story of remembering the Civil War begins with Mathew Brady and Alexander Gardner, two photographers who apprehended the dramatic possibilities of this fraternal strife and sought to memorialize it while it was still being waged. Brady's beginnings are swathed in mystery, so only his immigrant origins (Irish) help to account for his driving ambition. Raised near Lake George, New York, Brady worked in Albany for portrait artist William Page before relocating to the more expansive urban environment of New York

City. In 1840 Brady became a disciple of Samuel F. B. Morse, who was pivotal in establishing both telegraphy and daguerreotypes in the United States. By 1844 Brady had his own daguerreotype studio and in 1850 published a collection of portraits entitled *The Gallery of Illustrious Americans*. Brady's title confirmed his success in identifying his studio with distinction; he made a point of profiling celebrities from Tom Thumb and Jenny Lind to Daniel Webster and Abraham Lincoln, who claimed that "Brady made me president." Brady's forte was entrepreneurship, and he reigned supreme in his time as a commercial emissary of photography who was quick to embrace technological advances.

Brady's associate and ultimate rival, Alexander Gardner, was born in Scotland in 1821 and trained as a scientist but worked in a variety of professions, including bookkeeping and journalism. Employed by a savings and loan company, Gardner developed skills in business management that proved indispensable to his career in Civil War photography. Gardner appears to have met Mathew Brady in 1851 at the Crystal Palace Exhibition in London, where Brady was awarded a prize for his *Gallery of Illustrious Americans*. By 1855, Gardner was earning praise for his own photography in the *Glasgow Sentinel*, to which he also contributed editorials in support of the laboring poor. The next year he immigrated to New York with his family, sought out Brady, and became his assistant, working in all areas of Brady's operation.

Brady and Gardner anticipated the profitability of a monopoly on Civil War photography and took steps to make Brady's name synonymous with it. Exploiting an acquaintance with Allan Pinkerton, head of what would become the secret service, Brady secured a pass from President Lincoln in 1861 that allowed him to travel with Union troops. Meanwhile, Gardner, as manager of their Washington offices, ordered quantities of four-tube carte de visite cameras, to satisfy another market niche—soldiers seeking to be photographed in uniform. He also signed a contract with a commercial photography establishment to reproduce images of major war personalities and mass distribute them as trade cards. Given their mutual aptitude for the technical and business ends of their enterprise, Brady and Gardner were probably destined to be rivals. Both claimed credit for the idea of photographing the war, and both petitioned Congress separately and almost simultaneously in February 1869 to sell their collections of negatives to the government.

Because he suffered from severe myopia and was content to handle social and financial matters, Brady relied increasingly on others to take pictures for his studio. In a review of his 1861 collection, *Incidents of the War*, the *New York Times* accurately confirmed Brady's essential preeminence, while noting his penchant for delegating work. "Mr. Brady was the first to make photography the Clio of war. . . . His artists have accompanied the army on nearly all its marches, planting their sun batteries by the side of our Generals' more deathful ones, and taking town, cities, and forest with much less noise, and vastly more expedition. The result was a series of pictures christened, 'Incidents of the War,' and nearly as interesting as the war itself: for they constitute the history of it, and appeal directly to the great throbbing heart of the north."[8] The subjects that predominated in the Civil War scenes of Brady's photographers were respites, conferences, battle sites, and corpses. This was partly because photography at this early stage was unable to depict motion and also because photographers were barred from live combat. Yet there was a deeper limitation to Civil War photography: its inability to bridge the chasm created by a war whose effects were pervasive, but whose experience and meaning remained widely inaccessible.

Consider Gardner's "The Burial Party," dated April 15, 1865, at Cold Harbor, Virginia, the day after Lincoln's assassination and less than a week after Lee's surrender at Appomattox (Fig. 1). The top of the photograph is framed by a dark row of trees, so lush that it looks like a beard or ruff for the horizon; and just below the trees, four black men, dressed in white shirts, darker pants, and hats, holding shovels, dig or stand poised to dig in the sandy, grassy soil. In the foreground, another black man, dressed in a coat and wool seaman's cap, poses deliberately beside a stretcher upon which five skulls are neatly arranged. The nearest skull is straight up and grinning. There are no corpses in this image of burial, only the hint of one—a shoed foot, protruding rather ghoulishly from the middle of the stretcher. Details subtle as well as explicit establish correspondence between the living and dead: the white skulls echo the white shirts of the laborers; the shoed foot that provides the photograph's central axis completes the body of the laborer on a direct line with it, whose feet appear buried in the grassy surface where he digs; the shoulder of the posed man grazes the closest skull, a contiguity reinforced by the equal number of skulls (five) and laborers (five). The monumental import of *this* picture taken presumably at *this* moment suggests that its memorializing effect is both particular and collective. A particular group fulfills the ritual obligation to bury the dead, while also symbolizing a larger collective will to bury the war.

Yet this elaborately orchestrated image raises more questions than it answers. Are these former soldiers, collecting the remains of their comrades, and if so, why aren't they in uniform? Are they local inhabitants providing a proper burial for martyrs fallen far from the families who might

F I G U R E   I ::   "Burial Party. Cold Harbor, Virginia, April 15, 1865." From *Photographic Sketch Book of the War* by Alexander Gardner (1865).

have performed this function? Or are they professional grave diggers, hired to roam the country interring corpses still above ground ten months after the battle that took place June 1864? These men might as easily be exhuming for scientific purposes as burying for hygienic or spiritual ones, because dead bodies and their effects were viewed as keys to human diversity in the nineteenth century by natural philosophers (e.g., John William Draper) and anthropologists (e.g., Lewis Henry Morgan) alike. Whatever their identity and function, these men recall what most representations of the war assiduously repress: the economic transformation of black slaves into free laborers. The very difficulty of pinpointing exactly who these men are and what they are doing—do they serve the past (burying the bodies?) or the future (digging them up for science?)—signals the dynamic nature of this still life and of the war it represents.

The Gardner photograph affords a critical distinction between universal and historically specific understandings of death. In all cultures, death rituals negotiate the ultimate experience of estrangement—the conversion of intimates (parents, spouses, children, friends) into others. But in post–Civil War America such rituals also distinguished relative states of kinship and alienation among native, migrant, and immigrant. To the extent that this highly composed scene stages an affinity between black Americans and the dead, it confirms social Darwinist views of their culture as obsolete or moribund.[9] In keeping with dominant theories on the plural origins of humankind, death was understood increasingly in this period as an expression of prevailing class and racial hierarchies as well as of religious and cultural differences. For ethnologists, skulls and bones provided an encyclopedia of knowledge about human diversity. Scientists measured craniums and compared the immune systems of racial and ethnic groups. Social scientists studied mortality rates and the vast array of mourning customs. Philosophers and theologians explored contrasting views of the afterlife. Literary authors, painters, photographers, and advertisers sought to represent death as well as human difference in aesthetic and commercial terms. Making sense of death in this era required multidisciplinary approaches, which is one reason why Stephen Crane reviewed the Brady-Gardner archive while writing his secondhand account of the Civil War.

Indeed, Crane's best seller, *The Red Badge of Courage: An Episode of the American Civil War* (1895), seems situated squarely in an era of mechanical reproduction. The novel depicts a common soldier, Henry Fleming, who enlists in the Union army, eager to prove his "manhood" by displaying courage in battle. Henry flees from his first encounter with Confederate troops, however, and rejoins his regiment to discover that others have fought intensely and been killed or wounded. Rage and guilt fuse the subsequent near-hysterical pitch into battle that transforms Henry into a "true hero." Crane's persistent irony toward military ideals (courage, manliness, heroism) undermines the novel's closing suggestion that war is the making of men. The mind of Crane's protagonist works at times like a camera, alternately distancing and intense.

> It seemed to the youth that he saw everything. Each blade of the green grass was bold and clear. He thought that he was aware of every change in the thin, transparent vapor that floated idly in sheets. The brown or gray trunks of the trees showed each roughness of their surfaces. And the men of the regiment, with their starting eyes and sweating faces, running madly, or falling, as if thrown headlong, to queer, heaped-up corpses—all were comprehended. His mind took a mechanical but firm impression, so that afterward everything was pictured and explained to him, save why he himself was there.[10]

The passage conveys the subject position of photography, which is represented throughout the novel as competitive with writing. The emphasis on focus, on color and texture, details of piercing sight cataloged for the sake of retrospective contemplation, all serve to expose what this "mechanical" art cannot apprehend: the "why" of things. In other instances, the written word displays the pithiness and oddity of captions: "He was the picture of an exhausted soldier after a feast of war."[11] It is as if Crane set his novel in dialogue with photography—appreciatively, but more often critically—over the meaning of war and the problem of how to recall its events.

Brady and Gardner appear not to have considered the metaphysical or ethical consequences of careers spent photographing war's effects. Such questions absorb Crane. The Red Badge of Courage is haunted by the ethical predicament of representation, which is heightened where the representation concerns a bloody war that has not been suffered firsthand. Representing the Civil War is an ethical dilemma because, as the novel's beginning makes clear, it is a war fought largely by a class whose idiom sets it apart from Crane's bourgeois and elite readers. Crane joins many contemporaries in hinting at a distinctly modern aspect of the Civil War: its reputation as a "poor man's fight" regularly avoided by the propertied and by others who could afford $300 to hire a substitute. The business titans whose careers were launched in the flush war economy and who built immense fortunes in the years after it—Andrew Mellon, John D. Rockefeller, Pierpoint Morgan, Philip Armour, or Jay Gould—relied, in the words of Mellon's father, on "lives less valuable or others ready to serve for the love of serving."[12] In keeping with this, the novel's ninth chapter, which ends with the notorious sun simile, invokes the "ultimate substitute," the Christian God who died for the sins of humanity. The chapter opens with Henry, whole and wandering "amid wounds," which stand metonymically for the injured men overtaken by them. Henry himself stands for everyone who has either deliberately evaded or missed the Civil War, including Stephen Crane. Henry is uninjured and therefore stigmatized by shame that he imagines as visible to all: "the letters of guilt . . . burned into his brow." While each death in the novel is exquisitely prolonged, like a sacrament, the death of Jim Conklin is even more so, as his bleeding body is converted into the "red sun pasted in the sky like a wafer."[13]

Tenuous and childlike, this Eucharistic image suggests what has become of religion in the modern age. A symbol that announces its own uncertain ground, the "pasted" sun implies a workmanlike or pragmatic aspiration to believe, rather than a conviction that true faith is viable. Indeed, The Red Badge of Courage is pervaded with nostalgia for religion that is expressed in an antiquarian spirituality. References to soldiers as "sheep for slaughter," destined for "a blood-swollen God," depict a war machine with appetites at once murderous and divine. Crane displays a profound understanding of sacrifice as a ritual that stages the distance between humans and their gods, as well as the dependence of social ideologies on live bodies. His portrayal of the Union army as composed principally of men from the working classes likewise confirms how the spiritual economies of sacrifice that were so prevalent in Crane's time served to reinforce divisions between the fortunate and the bereft. For all these reasons, there is no redemption in *The Red Badge of Courage*. Technology (in the form of the camera) and art (in the form of Crane's distinctive style and theatrical scenes) predominate in the absence of the religious solutions demanded by this spectacle of death.[14]

The novel is preoccupied with the questions of how to tell a war story in the modern era and how to capture in language the experience of historical change. One method perfected by the narrative, to the consternation of many critics, is the rigorous repudiation of historical specificity. There are no place names, no recognizable battlefields or battles, no references to leading personages or events. The narrative's persistently narrow focus, sensuality, and abstractness, serve to emphasize the war's impact on working-class soldiers, on religious belief, even on black Americans. Highly charged symbols confirm an overriding interest in what the Civil War left behind and ushered in. The novel's lone black, a "Negro teamster . . . dancing upon a cracker box," is introduced, it seems, for the sake of establishing his insignificance. Blacks, whether enslaved or free, this passing mention suggests, were incidental to the war and its aftermath. Yet this figure holds a symbolic significance that surpasses his limited role in the narrative. It is critical that the man is portrayed as a worker, not a slave, at the same time that he performs a stereotypical dance entertainment for the soldiers. Like the social history it encompasses, the symbol takes away with one hand what it offers with the other: blacks have entered the labor force as free workers, but the price of their liberation is the group's containment through stereotype. The dancing "Negro teamster" achieves the status of a cultural myth, as defined by Roland Barthes: "constituted by the loss of the historical quality of things . . . the world enters language as a dialectical relation between activities, between human actions; it comes out of myth as a harmonious display of essences."[15] The threat of black laborers post-Emancipation is here defused through a familiar image of a "Negro" entertainer doing an obliging "it's jes me folks" dance.

The representation of the "Negro teamster," whose trade would be unionized less than a decade after the publication of Crane's novel, is consistent with one of the novel's most prominent concerns: the changing nature of work in the post–Civil War era. When they aren't lolling on hillsides like cattle, waiting for orders from an inefficient military command, the soldiers are identified with wholesome, rural labor. One soldier recalls "a carpenter who has made many boxes," while another sweats "like a laborer in a foundry."[16] The chief purpose of the war, it seems, is to transform these skilled workers into cogs in a "mighty blue machine." Crane's understanding of war as the most extreme form of worker objectification, whereby the worker becomes inextricably bound up with the materials of his labor—indistinguishable from his environment (for the sake of survival)—is especially relevant to the 1890s context of the novel's writing.[17] Like the working classes of the 1890s who were increasingly employed in factories, the soldiers are represented as alienated from their labor. This is a world in which objects ("weapons") are "confident," not the men who hold them. Moreover, the contemporary handbook on principles of management for the modern factory described the making of the industrial labor class as war in its own right. The novel is pervaded by management rhetoric as Henry Fleming internalizes his superiors' supervision of himself. Corpses are key agents of this administrative control: in one scene, a particularly gruesome yet vigilant corpse drives the guilt-ridden Henry back to battle.[18]

Thus, in *The Red Badge of Courage* the dead become messengers of the nation's future, inadvertent prophets of a modern industrial workplace. Crane's corpses tell the future in confirmation of the corporeal sacrifices that help to make that future possible. There were many literary methods for relaying the future by way of the past and recognizing soldiers' bodies as vehicles of modernization. Where *The Red Badge of Courage* forecast the prospects for working-class men during and after the war, best-selling Civil War novels by New Englanders Elizabeth Stuart Phelps and Louisa May Alcott anticipated the transformed circumstances of women. What these novels shared with *The Red Badge of Courage* was their particularistic treatments of national trauma as well as a commitment to capturing the trials of the insignificant. These novels too were engaged with history in the abstract, with the emotional losses suffered by, and the opportunities made available to, women by mass casualties of men. Published soon after the war, Phelps's *The Gates Ajar* (1868) and Alcott's *Little Women* (1868) gave substance, respectively, to a heaven where President Lincoln presided to greet soldiers upon arrival and to the myriad sacrifices required of the genteel poor on the home front. The great popularity of *The Gates Ajar* and *Little Women* were due, in no small part, to what they omitted. Written on behalf of the spheres their authors knew, the most successful portraits of wartime love and domesticity avoided the problems of race, slavery, and emancipation.[19] Civil War novels that foregrounded race and went so far as to represent the prospects of interracial romance and marriage were far less enthusiastically received. Lydia Maria Child's *The Romance of the Republic* (1867), Rebecca Harding Davis's *Waiting for the Verdict* (1868), and Anna Dickinson's *What Answer* (1868) resolved their risky plots in various ways. Child married her beautiful and multitalented octoroon heroines to a German (whose nationality freed him from American-bred racism) and a Boston abolitionist. Davis emphasized the strong bonds between white and black matriarchs, while withholding marriage between the mulatto doctor, John Broderip, and his white beloved, Margaret Conrad. Dickinson married her mulatto heroine, Francesca Ercildoune, to the white officer, William Surrey, whose parents disown them. Prejudice against blacks, the Surreys assert, "is a feeling that will never die out, and ought never to die out, so long as any of the race remain in America,"[20] a judgment underlined by the deaths of Francesca and William at the hands of racists in the New York Draft Riots.

WAR CURES

The Civil War novels of Phelps and Alcott were influential because they affirmed convention while subtly undermining it, searching within familiar territory for therapeutic remedies to war. They did not challenge readers to look outside themselves as a way of mapping the future. They did not ask them to imagine, for instance, how black people, whose status had been radically altered by the war, might be accommodated socially, economically, or politically. Instead, they depicted worlds of women in specific cultures and regions—white, Anglo-Saxon, Protestant New Englanders—shaping their Christian beliefs into coping strategies. In both novels, the Civil War is remote, but its effects are felt keenly, through the traumatic death of a brother (in Phelps's novel) and the debility of a father (in Alcott's). The power of these books lies in their claims for the ongoing vitality of certain traditional American legacies whose principles were tested and strengthened by the trials of wartime. At the same time, both books manage to expand the ground of both Protestant piety and literary production to accommodate the growing economic needs and ambitions of their women characters.

Elizabeth Stuart Phelps (1844–1911) was a pivotal cultural figure of the post–Civil War era, immersed in its most important religious developments. She was a feminist who protected her career by delaying marriage (to a much younger man) until the advanced age of forty-four, by which time she had produced a voluminous body of fiction, poems, and essays.[21] Her father, Austin, a minister, married Elizabeth Stuart in 1842 and joined the faculty of Andover in 1848 as a professor of sacred rhetoric and homiletics, a post he held until his retirement in 1870. The author of many books on religion, Austin Phelps appears in his daughter's 1891 autobiography, *Chapters from a Life*, as a tormented figure with a morbid sense of guilt and various physical ailments. Her mother, Elizabeth Stuart Phelps, was a popular writer whose novel about a parsonage, *Sunny Side* (1851), brought her fame just before her death. Phelps's maternal grandfather, Moses Stuart, believed that if Andover was to become "the sacred West Point," its students needed powerful modern methods at their disposal. While Andover from its founding in 1808 was known for orthodox Calvinism, its curriculum combined Calvinist doctrine—predestination, the total depravity of humankind, the limited atonement of Christ—with Unitarianism and Methodism and included Common Sense, Kantian, and Hegelian philosophies, German Romanticism, and Darwinism. Despite her gender, Phelps was integrated into the Andover community, where intellectual seriousness was a way of life. Inspired to pursue writing by the example of her mother, Phelps invested it with a theological rigor she associated with her father. Yet Phelps's inheritance also featured idiosyncratic strains that found their way into her thought. Her paternal grandfather, Eliakim Phelps, a Congregational minister in Stratford, Connecticut, became famous when official investigators of spirit possession confirmed that his parsonage was overrun by poltergeists, an incident that profoundly affected his granddaughter. Phelps followed the research of the Psychical Society to the end of her life, seeking evidence of clairvoyance and communication with the dead. While Phelps insisted in *Chapters from a Life* that no "candlestick ever walked an inch for me," she was, like many intellectuals of her time, drawn to the holistic vision of spiritualism, which seemed in the post–Civil War era a uniquely powerful means of reuniting the living with the dead.[22]

The Gates Ajar is a work of religious protest that seeks to reform Christianity by highlighting its reserves of psychic and spiritual nourishment.[23] At the novel's end, the clergy, recognizing historical necessity, succumb rather feebly to the more responsive and fulfilling interpretations of female parishioners. Emotional and supple in their approaches to the Bible, the women prove to be especially suited to fashioning a loving religion with wide appeal. Phelps spent years reading up on mourning and eschatology before beginning *The Gates Ajar*, which she saw in part as a means for making the liturgy amenable to the human suffering issuing from war. To this end, the novel synthesizes philosophy and theology while devising its own therapeutic psychology. Joseph Butler's inductive rationale for the probability of life after death, Schleiermacher's Romantic interpretation of faith, and liberal Christianity's emphasis on God's immanence and human perfectibility are combined with methods of counsel and comfort, both traditional and new. In keeping with the novel's effort to model a type of mental healing, diary and dialogue forms predominate, intermixed with sermons, poems, and hymns. The heroine, Mary, is an afflicted soul, an everywoman, plunged by the loss of her beloved soldier-brother Roy into a morass of doubt. She is rescued by a long lost aunt, an enormously learned woman who is also practiced in modern strategies of emotional repair. According to the classic allegory that is masterfully reconciled with the novel's more innovative dimensions, Aunt Winifred stands for the heartfelt reason that guides Mary's return to Faith (the name of Winifred's soon-to-be motherless daughter). As a spokesperson for Phelps's own extensive scholarship, Aunt Winifred allows Phelps to earn theological respect for her therapeutic Christianity.

The materiality of Phelps's heaven has long been a source of critical debate: disparaged as "a Biedermeier paradise," "a Gilded-Age heaven," a "celestial retirement village," and admired as "a carefully crafted argument for the literal interpretation of the Bible." What has often been overlooked, however, are the subtle distinctions between literal and figurative language in Phelps's account.[24] Every description of heaven in *The Gates Ajar* is conveyed in qualified, provisional terms. Hence the novel's title, as parsed by Aunt Winifred: God "has obviously not *opened* the gates which bar heaven from our sight, but he has as obviously not *shut* them; they stand ajar, with the Bible and reason in the way, to keep them from closing."[25] The Bible remains accessible to successive generations of interpreters, a living document, renewed by everyone who draws inspiration from it.

In this context, the directness and simplicity of Mary's mourning makes for the novel's extraordinary accessibility. Her grief is so vast that it nullifies the rhythms of the sun, converting a familiar domestic space into a sterile cell. Mary responds only to authentic comfort—the comfort of Aunt Winifred's dialogistic talking-cure, which is the channel for her divinely inspired imagination. Aunt Winifred herself proves as mortal as Roy and the other unnamed family members (mother, father), whose deaths can be inferred by their absence. It is only a matter of time before Aunt Winifred dies as well, of breast cancer, leaving her daughter in Mary's care. But her cure has fulfilled its purpose: Mary's liberation from the prison of mourning is signaled by her apprehension of "Faith," as an objective entity. Mary describes how "the picture that she made sitting there on the short, dying grass—the light which broke all about her . . . has photographed itself into my thinking."[26] What makes this passage noteworthy is the way it conflates a standard religious motif—the light of faith—with a modern technology—photographic light—in their common triumph over death and loss. In the service of eternity as well as modernity, the sun's renewed rhythms reconcile distinct methods for keeping the dead: faith and photography.

Phelps's conflation also confirms contemporary ideas about the interdependency of spiritual and technological mediums. Both are mysterious in proffering ties to the dead: photography in hinting that some human remnant lingers over the flat surface of an albumen image; spiritualism in suggesting that those lost lurk in hidden recesses of this world. These assumptions share a fantasy of ghostly spectatorship: that the dead are watching the living. Indeed, spiritualism, which Phelps explored throughout her life, was committed to the prospect of communication from the other world. These are the subjects of the subsequent novels in Phelps's trilogy, *Beyond the Gates* (1883) and *The Gates Between* (1887), which feature, in turn, a woman who experiences heaven firsthand in her illness but returns somewhat bitterly to earth at the book's end, and a deceased physician who writes regretfully from heaven, where he learns charity and is then happily reunited with his family.

Longings for the afterlife and for those who were believed to populate it were exploited by the fad of spirit photography. The practice became notorious in 1869 when William Mumler, who published his first spirit photographs in 1862, was charged with fraud in a New York City courtroom, a charge that proved impossible to substantiate. Bolstered by a collective will to believe, the technique involved photographing clients in the company of ghosts that were detectable only in developed photographs. It is telling that spirit photography, whose commercial vogue extended from the end of the Civil War through the 1870s, experienced another strong revival in England as well as America during World War I when mass death renewed appetites for the now largely discredited medium.[27]

The recurring story of Civil War death concerns a mass event that could never be brought close enough, but never completely put away. One of the most remarkable articulations of this predicament was Walt Whitman's poem, "Vigil Strange I Kept on the Field One Night" (1865), which recounts the poet's nightlong communion with the body of a dead soldier, possibly his lover ("vigil for boy of responding kisses"). The poem's vigil is variously described: "vigil strange," "vigil wondrous," "vigil sweet," "vigil of silence, love, and death," "vigil for you my son and my soldier," "vigil final." The poet serves watch on behalf of wonder, pleasure, devotion (secular and sacred), but above all on behalf of a boundary, which is the subject of the poem's closing lines. Detailing how he "envelop'd well his form," "folded the blanket well," "folded my soldier well," marking with his grave, the spot "where he fell"—the ending presents through rhyme and repetition the forceful containment ("well") required by death ("fell"). Whitman's poetic caretaking in "Vigil Strange" recalls his work as a nurse in Washington, D.C., military hospitals where he went in 1862 to find his brother George who had been wounded at the battle of Fredericksburg, Virginia. Whitman's friend John Burroughs characterized him in this role as "a great tender mother-man," and Whitman duly bemoaned "the dead, the dead, our dead—or South or North, ours all," whose sacrifices had contributed to the redemptive unification achieved by war. Whitman could be terribly graphic in letters home, about the wounds on the men who poured into Union hospitals, but he seldom wavered in his conviction of the war's purposefulness.[28] The poet might well have encountered another famous author, Louisa May Alcott, tending the casualties of Fredericksburg, had her own nursing sojourn in Washington lasted longer. They could have found much to talk about: their views of the war, their experiences as nurses, their efforts to express in letters and literature the tomblike quiet of suffering and death. They might also have discussed their shared identification with the soldiers they aided, for Alcott was her father's virtual son (called "Louy" by her family).[29]

More practical than her cerebral counterpart Elizabeth Stuart Phelps, Louisa May Alcott experienced the Civil War directly when she enlisted at the age of thirty as a military nurse. Callous physicians, derelict clergy, and squalid conditions at the Union Hotel Hospital in Washington, D.C., were the subject of a subsequent book, *Hospital Sketches* (1863), in which she took the Union to task for careless treatment of the wounded and dying on both sides. Alcott herself caught typhoid during her six weeks of work and never fully recovered from the poisonous mercury treatments she received. Portions of *Hospital Sketches* are devoted to the curiosities of the nation's capital, including the types of animals and people that filled the streets. Despite her fervent abolitionism, Alcott's response to the "colored brothers and sisters" she observes suggests how far the nation had to go in liberating itself from a demeaning race-consciousness. They were, she writes, "the sort of creatures generations of slavery have made them: obsequious, trickish, lazy and ignorant, yet kind-hearted, merry-tempered, quick to feel and accept the least token of brotherly love."[30] Alcott stresses, to her credit, the impact of institutions and remains open to the possibilities of religious and educational uplift. Yet there is no recognition of the ties between these newly freed blacks and the suffering casualties around her. Her sympathy for her patients remains relentlessly abstracted from the war's moral and political dimensions. She feels pride in her instinctive ability to support the "relations and friends by the bedsides of the dead or dying," who are "not near enough to know how best to comfort, yet too near to turn their backs upon the sorrow."[31] While fresh encounters of the kind Alcott experiences as a Civil War nurse cannot alleviate significant rifts in the culture, they do kindle compassion for familiar suffering. Social bonds, according to Alcott, are strengthened by shared sacrifice.

Alcott shared Phelps's rich theological legacy, though hers was less formal and institutional, as befitted the daughter of a transcendentalist. The self-educated son of a poor Connecticut farmer, Bronson Alcott gained renown for his radical theories about nutrition and pedagogy (implemented in his brief utopian experiment, Fruitlands) while failing to earn a living as a peddler, factory worker, or teacher. Abba May Alcott was the principal breadwinner for her four daughters, pursuing the occupations available to women of her day (including social work among the Boston Irish) while her husband wrote and lectured. Though Abba May's wealthy relatives provided some support, poverty always threatened, and there were repeated crises in her marriage. During the family's sojourn at Fruitlands, for instance, after the other starving disciples had deserted the snowbound utopia, Abba forced Bronson to choose between his relations and his ideals. Bronson preferred the agreeable family of theory, described in his book *Concord Days* (1872), to the needy family of fact, invariably clamoring for food and shelter. While Alcott adored her mother, immortalizing her in *Little Women's* Marmee, she was always ambivalent toward her father.

Among Abba's gifts to her daughter was the encouragement of her writing. Alcott wrote from an early age, and her oeuvre eventually expanded to include fairy tales, gothic thrillers, personal sketches, and sentimental fiction, all of them united by a common subject, women's experiences in work, love, and marriage, and a common perspective on those experiences, feminist. Her writing seems from the first to have been a means of complicating cultural norms about gender in terms that were widely acceptable. This helps to explain the astonishing professional success that allowed her to assume her mother's role as the financial supporter of the family. It was this success itself that appeared to raise the ire of a male-dominated cultural establishment exemplified by *Atlantic Monthly* editor Thomas Wentworth Higginson's remark that Alcott's "muse was sociable; the instinct of art she never had."[32] Higginson's effort to rationalize her powerful bond with readers represents a persistent strain in literary criticism, which Alcott dismissed but struggled not to internalize. Alcott's most prominent commercial achievement, *Little Women*, was an immediate best seller and among *the* most popular books ever published. The novel has never been out of print and continues to cross cultural and national boundaries in attracting new generations of readers. While its status as *the* novel about female initiation makes for a women-centric readership, the novel has also appealed broadly to men.

Little Women represented a major breakthrough in Alcott's career; it brought fame, fortune, and a set of characters, the Marches, that the public could not get enough of. As a domestic account of women during the Civil War, the novel showed how life at home among the genteel poor required its own form of valor. The novel opens at Christmas, and the holiday is presented as an opportunity for sacrifice. The March sisters' modest celebration proves an inadequate trial; their mother, Marmee, insists that they bestow their meager meal and gifts upon a more unfortunate family. Sacrifice, according to the novel, is essential to initiation: the initiation of women as well as men, of regions as well as nations. This can be explicit at times, with references to burnt offerings, cross bearing, and the like. As each March daughter endures a series of sacrificial rites of passage, denying her desires and quelling her resentment, she is compensated in some self-completing way. Meg attains domestic bliss, Jo finds an appropriate husband and vocation, Amy marries Laurie, as virtuous as he is rich, and Beth goes to heaven. The novel promises that renunciation will be rewarded and counsels a spirit of gratitude. Learn to appreciate the small, good things, and you will enjoy the bigger things more when you get them. The commodities purchased by Laurie for Meg and John's new home either break or disappoint, in contrast to the handmade gifts of Meg's industrious sisters. It is mistaken however to take such moments as disdain for the modernist aspirations of novelty and consumption, for they amount to a different kind of instruction, in how to be a wise consumer. The novel manages to endorse consumption largely through its portrayal of possessions, whether Bibles, drawing pencils, or damask tablecloths, as the preoccupation of women's lives, no matter how poor they are. Like its sentimental predecessor, *The Wide, Wide World*, *Little Women* prepares its characters in the deepest patriotic sense for their future roles in a developing consumer economy.

The wounds of the war years are healed by consumption in the postwar years. If this were Alcott's only message, her novel would have been far less powerful and popular. For novels become popular by confronting, not by avoiding, social conflicts. While there are many sources of social unity in the Marches' world, the novel emphasizes divisions, most prominently divisions of class. No one questions the divergent obligations of the poor tutor John Brooke (to go to war) and his wealthy tutee Laurie (college). Meg experiences a variety of humiliations at the home of the Moffats, though Alcott underscores the crudity that "all their gilding could not quite conceal."[33] The novel distinguishes throughout between those who are truly genteel and those who just have money. Such distinctions, however, reinforce a larger class system that was expanding at an intense rate as the century wore on.

Alcott's ideals of Christian renunciation, inner fortitude, and modesty sanction a society of increasing economic differentiation. Coping with the loss of her beloved Beth, Jo curbs her literary aspirations, renouncing the type of writing she finds empowering and financially rewarding. Her savior (and husband) is Professor Bhaer, who adheres to his Christian faith with a military dedication. When he convinces Jo of the worthlessness of her saleable fiction, she pitches it into the fire in a gesture of self-mastery. Yet Jo does achieve commercial success. In the manner of her creator "Louy," Jo manages to write a story that is moral as well as "popular," addressed "straight to the hearts of those who read it."[34] Jo and Professor Bhaer transform the estate she inherits from her aunt into a school, an inclusive place serving rich as well as poor, "slow boys . . . feeble boys . . . and a merry little quadroon."[35] The collective sacrifice of Beth yields a considerable "harvest" for Marmee and Father March: a nest of happily married daughters and grandchildren. Hence the novel's ultimate creed: in giving up, all is gained, which turned out to be a highly appropriate gloss for the Civil War and the development that followed it.

Alcott's very public domestic drama supports a society in which aspirations are as essential as the limits upon them. The heroes of post–Civil War America were not the wealthy titans whose economic ambitions knew no bounds, but those who accepted whatever glory fate thrust upon them in the name of progress. This is what made Ulysses S. Grant, the Union general and subsequent president, one of the most admired men of his generation. Indeed, Grant's best-selling *Personal Memoirs of U. S. Grant* (1885, 1886), which liberated his family from debt following his death from throat cancer, echoes Alcott's particular reconciliation of virtue and ambition. Grant had turned down requests by the *Century* magazine to write for their Battles and Leaders of the Civil War series, but the financial collapse precipitated by his postpresidency career as a bank head and investor changed his mind. The *Century* articles (November 1884 to February 1886) were so popular that editors clamored to publish them in book form. The ailing Grant chose Mark Twain's short-lived publishing house, and the two-volume book appeared after his death on July 23, 1885. A fundamental argument of *Personal Memoirs* was that the sacrifices of war "begot a spirit of independence and enterprise."[36] Grant acknowledged slavery as the war's cause, insisting that the North could not accept "the role of police for the South" instituted by the Fugitive Slave Law. But the main thrust of his conclusion was the value of these national losses. "It is probably well that we had the war when we did. We are better off now than we would have been without it, and have made more rapid progress than we otherwise should have made."[37]

Owen Wister's redaction of *Personal Memoirs* for his biography in the Beacon Biographies of Eminent Americans series presents such submission to fate as key to Grant's character. Wister's *Ulysses S. Grant* (1900) follows the account of war and peace in *Personal Memoirs* but adds a crucial psychological dimension to Grant's solemn "facts." The air of inevitability that marks Grant's life before the Civil War, Wister argues, enables his transformation into a war hero. At thirty-nine years old, Grant is overlooked by his family, which he can barely support (despite his efforts at farming, real estate, and clerking in his father's leather goods store), and is hardly known in his provincial hometown. At forty-three, his picture hangs in homes across the country. His subsequent presidency is beset by scandal, and he leaves office in disgrace: the *Nation* (which had endorsed his first presidential candidacy) lamented his "entire ignorance of the intellectual and political life of modern society."[38] But he is redeemed yet again, this time posthumously, by his *Personal Memoirs*. In all of these instances, according to Wister, Grant's genius is his resignation in the face of destiny. Grant's great accomplishments—planning and executing battles, handling his men, negotiating with the opposition, defining the terms of Lee's surrender—are simple manifestations of character, humbly carried out and humbly regarded by Grant himself. This case for the man's essential passivity allows Wister to minimize Grant's responsibility for the scandals—both military and political—that shadow his historical profile: stories about his drinking, his responsibility for some of the war's ugliest and most costly battles (including the battle of Cold Harbor, Virginia), and the reputation for corruption as president.

Wister's Grant finds his element in war: reading the prospects for battle in a landscape, intuiting how to penetrate southern strongholds by conquering rivers that extend from northern borders in Ohio deep into southern territory. Grant at war becomes an actor in his ultimate role. Wister's account is overtly theatrical, and he invokes and even embellishes the apocryphal story (discounted by Grant himself in *Personal Memoirs*) of Lee on the point of surrender, under an apple tree contemplating the Virginia sky. More important, Grant's generous treatment of Lee and his troops demonstrate his careful recognition of the war's ultimate purpose—reunion. In war Grant displayed a capacity for innovation that eluded him in the occupational and presidential roles that preceded and followed it. Grant understood "the progressive nature of warfare," exploiting northern resources —men, food, transportation—systematically against southern resources, launching relentless, coordinated assaults upon southern strongholds that built momentum for the Union army from one victory to the next.[39] In the business and political realms, Grant's determination disappeared, but his reflections upon his moment in the sun, and the development that it enabled, proved a lasting monument to the costs and rewards of the Civil War. There were many ways of memorializing war, however, and dignified acceptance and celebration was only one of them. The next section explores a pair of works whose recollections of the Civil War and the modernization precipitated by it were aggressively critical.

WAR SATIRES

The Civil War novels of Maria Ruiz de Burton and Henry James were satires that highlighted the foibles of generals and presidents and the greed of capitalist entrepreneurs. In contrast to the respectful treatments by Phelps and Alcott of Christianity's valuable therapeutic role during and after the war, Maria Ruiz de Burton portrays New England Protestantism as punitive and racist, with a clergy that ruthlessly exploits its flock. Women suffering nobly back home in Phelps and Alcott become perverse martyrs in James. For all their differences, both Ruiz de Burton and James abandoned the fictional deference typically accorded the war. This was perhaps attributable to their marginality—one, a Mexican who had become a U.S. citizen through marriage to an American army officer, the other, a homosexual expatriate. In any case, they shared a conviction that satire was the most reliable route to a realist account of the Civil War. Ruiz de Burton and James offered critiques of an American war machine that they understood as ongoing, linked as it was to persistent social policies, colonial conquest, and gender socialization.

While Phelps qualified religious orthodoxy in highly controversial terms, she did so as a member of that orthodoxy. Maria Amparo Ruiz de Burton was a stranger to the eastern religious and cultural establishment that provided the setting for her first novel, *Who Would Have Thought It?* (1872). Published anonymously because of its biting content, the novel was the product of the author's sojourn on the East Coast, where her husband was stationed. Ruiz de Burton was as hostile in this novel to the nation's war effort, North and South, as she was in a subsequent novel to its colonization policy. *Who Would Have Thought It?* exposed the corruption of the Union military establishment, the pursuit of wealth by those who avoided enlistment, the racism of the genteel North, and the hypocrisy of its clergy.

Ruiz de Burton's focus on economic development in the context of colonialism provides a rare novelistic approach to the Civil War. The acceleration of industrialization, investment, and speculation is explored through the conquest of gold and silver in the West and Southwest. The novel's plot hinges on the theft of a theft of a theft: the gold of the Mohave Indians is stolen by the female protagonist's mother, a Mexican national, and is stolen in turn from the female protagonist by the New England family that adopts her, and then is stolen a third time by the treacherous minister who befriends them. The initial theft by Maria Medina is justified by the fact that the Apaches have kidnapped her and her daughter Lola and sold them to the Mohaves, who have kept them hostage for ten years, dyeing their skin black to prevent their escape. Ruiz de Burton features another side of the war that was rarely represented: Confederate prison camps, where Union soldiers died regularly from cold, starvation, and disease. She emphasizes the Union army's complicity in these deaths through its repudiation of prisoner exchanges with the Confederacy. Reputedly Grant's brainchild, the policy was designed to reduce southern manpower, since returned Confederate prisoners typically reenlisted, while their Union counterparts went home. This was one consequence of the standard northern practice among eligible recruits, who could afford to, of hiring substitutes to fight in their place.

Ruiz de Burton is blunt about war profiteering. The conflict, as she portrays it, unleashes a range of schemes, from the proceeds accrued through government contracts for literal "fat" ("salt pork and lard") to private monopolies on essential services, like the telegraph.[40] In the war's aftermath, these shady riches are fortified and expanded through shrewd trading on the stock exchange and real estate investment in a hot New York City market. The Union government is portrayed as a well of corruption. The executive branch exploits the war by expanding its powers: suspending the writ of habeas corpus, issuing the Emancipation Proclamation, and instituting the first military draft in American history. President Lincoln appears as coarse and also vain, his dedication to "the people" a sham pretense.

The Civil War in *Who Would Have Thought It?* is an assault in its own right upon whatever values—free speech, democracy, opportunity—the American nation was thought to stand for. In one scene, the hero, Julian Norval, comes to the War Department to appeal his dismissal and wonders, as he looks around, how many injustices will stand due to the poverty and insignificance of the supplicants. The war on the battlefield is echoed throughout the novel in the war waged by government against its citizens. Julian is admitted to a hearing with the president and pardoned, only because of his wealth and connections. The greatest war casualty, according to Ruiz de Burton, is the principles of the nation, which, she strongly implies, were never secure to begin with. No wonder that Julian Norval, in the company of his bride, Lola Medina, opts for an expatriate life in Mexico.

Ruiz de Burton's description of an embattled East Coast manages to establish ties between the seventeenth-century colonization of New England and the nineteenth-century colonization of Mexico. In her account, the American nation rolls self-righteously along, expanding its wealth and territory from conquest to conquest, fueled by the rhetoric of a Protestant clergy with its hand in the till. But satires, as is well known, tend toward conservatism, often in the form of some imagined golden age. In *Who Would Have Thought It?* the golden age represents a direct critique of capitalism—Ruiz de Burton evokes an aristocratic, civilized, moral Mexico before America's Mexican War. But her critique is highly problematic. Julian Norval and Lola Medina return to Mexico with their wealth restored, prepared to take their place among a ruling elite, which had its own violent record of handling Indian affairs. Satire here betrays a familiar contradiction. It offers as a solution what elsewhere (and more fundamentally) it treats with contempt. Ruiz de Burton condemns northern racism and ridicules the class snobbery of a supposedly democratic nation, only to join the pure aristocratic line of a white-skinned Mexican with a New England blue blood. In keeping with satire's effort at social preservation, she forecasts a complex form of capitalist development—at once elite and multicultural.

Henry James's *The Bostonians* (1886) is equally steeped in the rhetoric and agendas of the Civil War and its aftermath and equally pessimistic about the state of the Union. Despite the greater subtlety of James's satire, commercial success eluded his novel. Editors of *Century* magazine, which ran *The Bostonians* in thirteen installments (1884–85), complained that no serial they had *ever* published had fared so badly. There was apparently little public appetite at the time for a Civil War novel that belittled the war's ideologies and the business ethic it ushered in. James highlights a prevailing cultural obsession with commerce and commodities, the purchase and sale of everything and anything, and suggests how this impacts on gender relations, including norms of "compulsory heterosexuality."[41] The novel transforms the war into a melodramatic love contest between Basil Ransom, the heterosexual ex-Confederate, and his distant cousin, Olive Chancellor, a northern lesbian loyalist, as they battle over the working-class girl. Verena Tarrant is beautiful and talented but profoundly naïve, which makes her the ideal female commodity. "There's money for someone in that girl," says Matthias Pardon, the hyperprofessionalized "reporter, interviewer, manager, [and] agent."[42] That prospect is soon realized by Verena's father, a spiritual healer who "sells" his daughter to Olive on the condition that Verena come to live with her. From James's dark perspective, the country is dominated by hypocritical idealists prepared to part with their daughters for cash, greedy capitalists, and political ideologues—ranging from rabid conservative (Ransom) to radical feminist (Chancellor). The social developments that defined the Reconstruction era—changing conventions of gender and sexuality, the rise of consumerism, the growth of a publicity culture, conspicuous poverty, and conspicuous wealth—make for endless distinctions, small and large. Thus, James dwells on the ways in which different forms of mobility (carriages, streetcars, walking) serve to mediate class relations while depicting feminist speeches that attribute the state of the world, "wars, wars, always more wars," to male governance.[43]

Regional warfare continues in the postwar phase; the novel opens with Olive, the northerner, exercising control over her distant cousin Basil, the southerner, by making him wait. And regional differences are only the beginning. Social multiplicity is a fact of modern life, and reading difference is a necessity for those who seek to understand as well as to triumph in society. Hence, characters struggle to classify each other as types—through region, gender, culture, religion, race, class. Olive and Verena in their first private encounter perceive each other as, respectively, elite Bostonian and poverty-stricken Bohemian. In another scene two ladies from New York's cultivated class anticipate an upcoming lecture by Professor Gougenheim on the Talmud, while Miss Birdseye has to satisfy her nostalgia for the Underground Railroad by saving political émigrés from Europe. America is teeming with Jews, Germans, Dutch, Africans, Irish, Poles, and Italians, and The Bostonians emphasizes how besieged its "natives" feel, a sentiment that gives rise to a general preoccupation with reproduction.

For James, sexual preference and its impact on marriage and procreation rates is a major focus. Homoeroticism in The Bostonians is represented as a valid alternative to heterosexuality. There is a pervading awareness of the threat this poses to society. Fears that white Anglo-Saxons were losing the population battle to less desirable races and ethnicities fueled anxiety about deviations from heterosexuality. America in the 1880s had a vibrant eugenics movement, which warned that "native" groups were committing "race suicide" and promoted large families among these groups. Reformers who endorsed "family values" felt particularly wary of the women's rights movement and the homoerotic behavior associated with it.

It is a sign of James's ambivalence toward such values that the heavily satirized Basil and Olive are, respectively, hostile and beholden to them. Olive is a guilt-ridden bourgeois whose northern family has preserved and even enhanced its wealth. This inspires a predatory socialist-feminism, marked by her generosity with money and her "desire to know intimately some *very* poor girl."[44] Basil is a mediocre lawyer and penniless intellectual. Hoping that he might "make a living through his opinions," he is drawn to journalism, but conservative magazines with names like the *Rational Review* keep rejecting his heartfelt submissions.[45] His sense of injustice as a southerner, whose family fortune was lost in the war, is expressed in a martial masculinity. That intensifies the stakes represented by Verena, the daughter of New England. At the novel's end, Ransom embodies a kind of reactionary hysteria as he stalks Verena in the guise of John Wilkes Booth (combination actor-assassin). Against these compromised idealists, James sets Henry Burrage, a New Yorker of the new moneyed class who desires the precious girl for his collection. He likes her, we read, "for the same reason that he liked old enamels and old embroideries."[46] Which is to say, he doesn't think enough of her to engage in battle with the likes of Olive and Basil.

James ultimately rewards Basil, the magazine writer, with a budding career *and* the girl. It's a conclusion consistent with James's own investments in magazines and, more reluctantly, "compulsory heterosexuality." Financial contradictions were for him more readily overcome than sexual ones. James had no difficulty lamenting a culture of letters beholden to crass commercialism while managing his own fictional enterprises with entrepreneurial zeal. The novel closes with a classic purgation: Olive the scapegoat rushes onto a stage expecting to be "hissed and hooted," as the heterosexual couple destined for marriage and reproduction beats a hasty retreat. It amounts to a partial accommodation to the culture.[47] By contrast, James's satire presents, as its golden-age alternative, a New England in the days when social reform had more to do with principles than publicity. By qualifying the future happiness of his heterosexual couple and by limiting his faux-hero's success to a tepid academic register (an accepted article), James balances conservatism and critique. He manages to have his cake and eat it too. James is suspicious of the immigrant hordes, as *The American Scene* (1907) will emphatically confirm, and he recognizes the authentic homoerotic love between Olive and Verena as a necessary sacrifice to offset that reproductive threat. Yet he remained, to the end of his life, an ambitious author, in "the great army of constant producers,"[48] entranced by the possibilities of a vast literary marketplace.

WAR MIGRATIONS

Like all wars, the Civil War displaced people, but it also enabled voluntary migration of various kinds, including tourism. Before the war, noted Ulysses S. Grant, "the great mass of people were satisfied to remain near the scenes of their birth," but after it, a new feeling arose, "that a youth must cut loose from his old surroundings to enable him to get up in the world."[49] European travel increased significantly among the middle and upper classes. *Appleton's Journal* reported in 1873 an annual rate of 25,000 Americans touring Europe, while *Scribner's Monthly* declared "All Americans . . . by nature 'Passionate Pilgrims.'"[50] Travel writings became abundant, as few major writers failed to record their experiences of the wonders and snares awaiting Americans abroad.[51] Equally prevalent were the accounts of northerners who ventured south after the war to confront the mythic ground of fraternal conflict. Among the most successful and unusual of these explorers was James's confidant, Constance Fenimore Woolson, a great-niece of James Fenimore Cooper and a significant author in her own right whose popular success James envied. Like James, Woolson was a New Englander who had resigned herself to the life of a wanderer, a "curious fate," she mused, for "the most domestic woman in the world."[52] While she wrote, as did James, about expatriated Americans, she also produced compelling fictions about northerners seeking intimacy with the scarred South. James envied this too. He had always planned, he confessed to Woolson, to visit the Florida plantation purchased after the war by his younger brothers, Wilky and Bob. He compared his prospective writings on the postwar South to the unrealized commodities of his notoriously unsuccessful siblings, "material wasted, my material not being in the least the crops unproduced or unsold but the precious store of images ungathered."[53] Woolson's southern works resemble the fiction she and James set in Europe. They feature similar ethnographic positions, observers in places that are foreign but familiar, and similar ethical dilemmas, the apparently unavoidable complicity of outsiders. Indeed, what Woolson captures most powerfully in her original portraits of the region's characters and scenes is a lingering northern passion for southern prejudices and myths.

The title story in *Rodman the Keeper: Southern Sketches* (1880), which first appeared in magazines of the 1870s, is an extended meditation on the word "keep." What does it mean to keep a body after death? How is the honor of the dead best kept? What are acceptable proprieties for the keeper of the dead? John Rodman is an ex-colonel from New England appointed guardian of the national cemetery in Florida, an Aunt Ophelia come to order the dilapidated land where the Union dead are buried. His days are spent cataloging the names of dead soldiers, mowing the grass, and smoothing the gravel paths near his bare cottage. The primary obligation of the living to the dead, he believes, is to satisfy their presumed needs while negating his own, a task suitable to a New Englander. Rodman takes pleasure in self-denial: the companionship of a dog (barking might disturb them); a pipe (selfish—the dead can't smoke); minimal cooking (so they won't resent his meals). Nothing threatens his imagined community: the appearance of an ailing former Confederate and his servant intensifies the keeper's quiet. Taking stock of each other's respective losses, the ex-soldiers find peace in silence.

In the inadvertent domesticity that grows up around these ruins of war—Union keeper, Confederate, freedman—a former southern belle, Miss Bettina Ward, provides a note of antagonism. Women, it appears, are the keepers of rebel wrath, ardently opposed to everything northern and national. The keeper insists that Pomp, the freedman, can only wait upon his "master" if he learns to read via cemetery placards. This governmental poetry anticipates northerners coming to honor their dead, but the grave-yard's only visitors are a solemn parade of freed slaves on Memorial Day. Attired in their Sunday best, these designated mourners sing "Swing Low, Sweet Chariot" while showering the graves with flowers in gratitude for their freedom. Rodman achieves a measure of victory when the still slavish Pomp steals out at night to place his own flowers on the graves. Meanwhile, the visitor registry remains blank, signaling the anonymity of the war's unclaimed dead and the persisting illiteracy of the former slaves.

David King, a young man from New Hampshire who goes south after the war to teach in the story "King David," shares Rodman's ambitions. Yet the sketch, from the title on, is full of irony at David's expense. He romanticizes the old cotton fields and throws away every leftover from a meal he dutifully cooks for two freedmen to reveal himself as hardly more enlightened than those he desires to reform. A northern merchant who plies the black students with alcohol and a southern aristocrat who undermines David's loyalty to them further impair his efforts. Like Albion Tourgée, Woolson insists that North and South are equally responsible for the state of postwar race relations. More particularly, David King's abrupt departure represents the northern cultural elite's abandonment of downtrodden southern blacks.

Among Woolson's most enduring works on the South, *For the Major* (1883) might be described as an antimobility novel whose central characters reject all forms of movement, historical progress especially. The novel dramatizes a triangulated love affair between a daughter, her young stepmother, and her aged father, an ex-Confederate major. The community of the small mountain town of Edgerley, Virginia, distrusts anyone from outside, including natives who have been elsewhere. The daughter, Sara, who has been exiled (by her stepmother) to school in New England, is considered dangerously advanced, while the stepmother, Marion Carroll, is revered for upholding the courtly rituals still central to town life. The major, who is going blind, lives in the past, preferring European papers because they don't cover contemporary America. Everyone is threatened when Marion's repressed past returns in the form of her son, a musician, who comes to the isolated mountain town looking for her. To recognize him would expose Marion's tainted past, and she responds with anxiety to the offspring she has so missed. Dupont is an alluring yet suspect presence, and his songs (Indian, African, Gypsy) are identified with cultures viewed as inferior and transient.

The novel's mystery is the question of the major's awareness. Does he know who this stranger is? Is he perhaps more cognizant of his wife's history than she has supposed? For whose benefit have the novel's deceptions been maintained? Marion has succeeded in presenting herself, "for the Major," as thirteen years younger than her age. When this secret is revealed to Sara, she agrees to help preserve it, reaffirming her acceptance of southern custom. The novel's depiction of a wife's self-serving deception of her husband, of a daughter's complicity in it, and of the husband's willingness to be deceived reveals the post–Civil War South as a place of stasis, collectively sustained. To live there is to accept the power of myth knowingly and to sever one's ties to a modern world considered inimical to it. Woolson's novel memorialized a stereotype of the late nineteenth-century South as trapped in a past that persisted well into the next century, in part because, like most stereotypes, it was based in fact.

It took an insider to acknowledge the precariousness of Edgerley's illusions. A Virginian who expressed her region, she often said, in body and soul, Ellen Glasgow wanted to write novels of national significance. Glasgow's family typified the tension between old South (her mother descended from the earliest English settlers in Virginia) and new (her father was a wealthy businessman, whose ironworks factory in Richmond prophesied the economic future). Her first novel, appropriately titled *The Battle-Ground* (1902), stages a contest between them. On the one hand, it offers a romantic, even glorified portrait of an antebellum aristocracy. Brimming with admiration for the "Lost Cause," the novel features aristocrats who address one another as "sir," and are as self-satisfied and authoritative as the complete domination of others allows. They inhabit a slave utopia: generational continuity is affirmed, all are happy, and nature expresses approval of the sovereign in the bounty of his fields. In keeping with this, the master is expert at dispensing just rewards to underlings (whether black or white). The sign of a patriarch in the making is the ability to pick a promising horse or slave. Blacks are unwavering in their devotion, and lower-class whites belittle differences between their own circumstances and those of landowning slaveholders, disputing Grant's claim that poor white southerners "too needed emancipation."[54] Indeed, they are eager to spill their blood for the Confederacy, as attested to by the illiterate recruit Pinetop, who says of Union soldiers, "They've set thar feet on ole Virginny, and they've got to take 'em off damn quick!"[55]

Land is land (whether or not you own vast tracts of it), and blood is blood. In Glasgow's depiction, the Confederate army includes the wealthiest aristocrats. Such claims epitomize fictional selective memory. The universal conscription decreed in February 1862 by Jefferson Davis, president of the Confederacy, exempted slaveholders who owned twenty or more slaves. As the war continued, however, southern aristocrats like the Lightfoots and the Amblers were more likely to enlist than their northern counterparts. Dan Montjoy, the novel's hero, is a southern hybrid descended from Jane Lightfoot, a proud aristocrat, and Jack Montjoy, a working-class Scot who beat his wife. Dan responds to war as a racial inheritance from both sides. Thus Glasgow harmonizes the traditional aristocracy of her mother with the new mercantile South of her Scotch businessman father.

The Civil War is transformative, affording a series of recognitions for Glasgow's aristocrats. When Dan sees Pinetop struggling over a child's primer, he recognizes the gulf that has divided the privileged and the poor—veritable serfs in a slave society. Betty, Dan's wife-to-be, gains perspective on the experiences of another casualty of slavery: free blacks. Searching for food during the final stage of the war, she comes upon Levi engaged in a similar foraging expedition and suddenly grasps the isolation of the free black, scorned by slaves (who feared and coveted his freedom) and by whites (who abhorred it). The most life-altering recognition concerns a common humanity, captured in the image of Union soldiers gently feeding starved Rebel troops in the wake of Lee's surrender. Such images excluded blacks, former slave and free alike, for unity was usually achieved at their expense.

Throughout this period, the restriction of black rights and opportunities was the price paid for harmony between North and South. This circum-stance was terribly familiar to Paul Laurence Dunbar, and he made it the subject of his Civil War novel, *The Fanatics* (1901), which depicted the suffering catalyzed by the migration of emancipated slaves into a stable society of blacks who had long been free. The setting for *The Fanatics*, Dunbar's most autobiographical work, is a fictionalized Dayton, Ohio ("Dorbury"), where he was born in 1872 to former slaves.[56] Dunbar's father, a plasterer who taught himself to read, served in the 55th Massachusetts Infantry and the 5th Massachusetts Colored Calvary Regiment during the war, and his mother, a washerwoman who loved poetry, worked for the family of Orville and Wilbur Wright. Raised by his mother, Dunbar was a precocious child who shared her aesthetic passions. The only black in his high school graduating class, he was editor of the school paper, president of the literary society, and renowned as a poet. Dunbar subsequently wrote for community newspapers and started an African American newsletter sponsored by the Wright brothers. He also worked as an elevator operator while waiting for a breakthrough, which occurred when his poetry was praised in a syndicated newspaper and caught the attention of the famous dialect poet James Whitcomb Riley. This enabled Dunbar to publish his first book of poems, *Oak and Ivy* (1892), which he hawked to elevator riders. The book made Dunbar's reputation, and in 1893, he was invited to recite at the world's fair in Chicago, where Frederick Douglass pronounced him "the most promising young colored man in America."

Dunbar's next book, *Majors and Minors* (1896), brought more national recognition. In his *Harper's Weekly* editorial column, William Dean Howells welcomed "the first instance of an American negro who had evinced innate distinction in literature. . . . God had made of one blood all nations of men," "and the prejudices which had so long constrained his race were destined to vanish in the arts."[57] With help from Howells, Dunbar published *Lyrics of a Lowly Life* (1898) and toured England as a poet of international repute. Tuberculosis, financial difficulties, a failed marriage (to fellow writer Alice Dunbar-Nelson), and alcoholism led to his death in 1907, but before then he managed to produce twelve books of poetry, four books of short stories, a play, and five novels.

The Fanatics depicts southerners sympathetic to the North, and north-erners sympathetic to the South, fathers who disown sons for joining the wrong side and daughters for loving the wrong soldiers. Fanaticism has no regional affiliation, and the novel's black community is ill-used by white northerners and southerners alike. The narrative embodies this evenhandedness; there is nothing in Dunbar's portrait that is inconsistent with the racialist assumptions of a good liberal like Howells. The novel's only black character, "Nigger Ed" (always in quotes), goes to war as the servant of a Union captain and is revered for his indiscriminate care of the wounded and dead. The only hint of the author's background is the steady focus on the wartime circumstances of Ohio's blacks, native and migrant. The established black society, free for over a century, includes a distinctive upper class as well as members of a peculiar "aristocracy of shame." Close to the South but free, Ohio was a preferred locale for slave mistresses of southern masters who sent them there to live with their mulatto offspring. During and after the war, former slaves, defined as "contraband," haunted the rear guard of Union troops and poured into border states like Ohio. Sometimes finding work with the army as cooks or valets, more often remaining destitute and homeless, these vulnerable migrants carried everything they owned.

The Fanatics emphasizes what most Civil War novels overlook: that neither the North nor the South could have successfully recruited troops to fight for black freedom. Once the war began, and long afterward, slave migrants were repudiated by whites as well as by settled blacks, whose security they threatened. White mobs seeking to reduce Dorbury's newly enlarged black population care little for class distinctions in the black community. Dunbar understood the role played by blacks of all classes as the social cement—scapegoats—essential to the reunification of North and South. By confronting with relentless honesty features of the conflict ignored by other literary historians, he also illuminated much that came after it.

In contrast to Dunbar's Ohio fiction poised on the border between slave state and free, Frances E. W. Harper's Iola Leroy; or, Shadows Uplifted (1892) takes readers deep into the South, detailing the experiences of blacks who stayed on plantations during the war and blacks who migrated south afterward to help the former slaves build new lives. Twice reprinted and respectfully reviewed in contemporary periodicals, Iola Leroy, like The Red Badge of Courage and The Fanatics, was part of a novelistic reimagining of the Civil War. Harper sought in her novel to redirect contemporary policies on race, while reminding black youth of the sacrifices of previous generations. Frances Ellen Watkins was born free in Maryland in 1825 and raised by an aunt and uncle who ran the William Watkins Academy for Negro Young, where she was educated. Watkins's early literary ambitions were inspired by abolitionism, and she became a regular contributor to William Lloyd Garrison's *Liberator*. Prior to her 1860 marriage to Fenton Harper, Watkins was active in both literary and political circles, publishing her poetry and prose and lecturing on the Anti-Slavery Society circuit. Her brief marriage ended with her husband's death in 1864 but produced three children. Harper resumed her lecturing as a single mother and became especially well known in the South. Though she was active in the women's movement, she denounced the 1869 decision by major feminists (Elizabeth Cady Stanton and Susan B. Anthony) to withdraw their support for black suffrage in order to attract southern women to their cause. In all of her lectures from this period, Harper emphasized continuities between patriarchy, capitalism, imperialism, and racism. She presented the culture and aspirations of black Americans as clear alternatives to prevailing American values. American blacks might well be martyred by the dominant culture; if so, she argued, nations are far more indebted to martyrs than to millionaires.

Harper's only novel, *Iola Leroy*, was infused with her political commitments. The main characters were based on famous black leaders—Ida B. Wells, known by her pen name, Iola ("Iola Leroy"); Lewis Latimer, poet and scientist who worked with Thomas Edison and Alexander Graham Bell ("Dr. Frank Latimer"); and Lucy Delaney, writer and activist ("Lucille Delaney"). The plot of *Iola Leroy* concerns a wealthy white woman growing up in the antebellum South who discovers, when her father dies of yellow fever at the start of the Civil War, that she is mulatto, and she is promptly sold into slavery. Iola is rescued by the Union army, works as a nurse, and is pursued by a white northerner, Dr. Gresham, who is willing to overlook her black ancestry. Iola resists passing, however, as does her brother Harry. Indeed, Iola and Harry are presented repeatedly with this option, a kind of Edenic temptation they resist because they believe their highest potential (and that of their race) will be realized with black partners. At the war's end, Harry and Iola are reunited with their lost family and married, respectively, to Lucille Delaney and Dr. Frank Latimer. The determined couples then head south, a reverse migration that enables their redemptive work among the most needy of their group.

The novel opens during the Civil War with an account of the secret language used by slaves on southern plantations to monitor the respective fortunes of Union and Confederate troops. The quality of produce—the relative freshness of butter or eggs—supplies the means of transmitting news of victory and defeat. Indeed, there is an abundance of codes by which to read war reports. One slave needs nothing more than his mistress's face to grasp the fate of the Confederacy. Another keeps nearby Union troops informed of enemy intentions by hanging her sheets in prearranged patterns. Such instances highlight Harper's interest in types of communication, particularly those used by the illiterate. In *Iola Leroy*, language is both a method of liberation and a means of oppression, which black folk, literate and not, learn to exploit because their lives depend on it. One slave recalls how previous generations of slaves spoke different dialects, a variety that was paralleled by their range of complexions—from near white to dark black. The heterogeneity of the oppressed slaves on plantations, separated from those with similar language and heritage, made resistance especially difficult. *Iola Leroy* reveals America's slavery system as uniquely virulent and secure: with diverse groups of Africans estranged from kin and confined to plantations where even limited information was difficult to obtain. But it also depicts the striking aptitude of these varied slave populations, how despite a regime of ignorance brutally imposed they managed to educate themselves and devise intricate modes of expression. A striking scene in Iola's classroom gives rise to what may be Harper's most radical claim: that the imposed ignorance of slaves conferred immunity from oppressive knowledge. Denied literacy, Iola's pupils have absorbed alternative, sometimes subversive ideas that protect them from postwar dogmas rationalizing their subordination. This is confirmed when a white gentleman lecturing the pupils on the achievements of his race makes the mistake of inviting response, which reveals their understanding of such "progress" as having been achieved at their expense.

Harper insists that American whites were dependent on their black brethren and points to the war itself, where black soldiers contributed decisively to northern victory, as proof. But she concludes her novel on a note of uncertainty. Whether black Americans would be accepted as members of a collective citizenry or be held to a subordinate position that drove their progress inward, toward more individualized, material gains remained in question well past the middle of the twentieth century. It was an issue that would be debated famously throughout the period by Booker T. Washington (on the side of intraracial uplift) and W. E. B. Du Bois (on the side of full equality between races).

The Civil War represented an irreparable break for all Americans—politically, economically, and socially. Despite the treacheries and brutalities suffered by black people after the war, and despite efforts of southern whites to institute a peonage system comparable to slavery, the fact remained that they were free and the slavery system would never be reinstituted. Civil War fiction by Paul Laurence Dunbar, Frances Harper, Constance Fenimore Woolson, and Ellen Glasgow dramatized the compromises and injustices that marked the transformation of "a thing into a man," during a time when the beliefs that supported that objectification remained strong.[58] However sober these accounts, they left no doubt that black people were destined to their rightful status as human beings. Civil War novels by Stephen Crane, Henry James, Maria Ruiz de Burton, Elizabeth Stuart Phelps, and Louisa May Alcott highlighted the material and economic revolution symbolized and accelerated by the Civil War. Whether they dwelled on the losses entailed, like Phelps and Ruiz de Burton, or anticipated, with ambivalence, the cultural possibilities of the modern order, like James, Alcott, and Crane, these novels attested that there was no turning back.

RACISM AS OPPORTUNITY IN
THE RECONSTRUCTION ERA

In 1861, at the beginning of the Civil War, Harriet Jacobs published an autobiography, *Incidents in the Life of a Slave Girl*. The book recounted her unusual experience of slavery; in particular, her ability, as a literate, light-skinned slave with free relatives in town, to resist the sexual advances of her master, Dr. James Norcom, and to seek protection from a local white lawyer (with whom she had two children) before escaping. Sheltered by white as well as black neighbors, Jacobs ended up in a tiny attic crawl space in her grandmother's house, where she hid for seven years. Born a slave in 1813 in Edenton, North Carolina, Jacobs was well treated until the Norcoms inherited her in 1824. In hiding, Jacobs suffered most from immobility and exposure to the elements through the thin roof. Her health permanently damaged, she fled to the North in 1842 but remained threatened by the prospect of recapture by Norcom, who pursued her (especially after the Fugitive Slave Law passed in 1850). Jacobs settled in Rochester, New York, where she lived with the Quaker feminist Amy Post and wrote in the antislavery reading room just above the newspaper offices of Frederick Douglass. When her book appeared, with an endorsement from Lydia Maria Child, its abolitionist audience was distracted by war.[1] Jacobs became a relief worker among contraband slaves and remained politically active until her death in 1897.

Jacobs's narrative provides a valuable introduction to race relations in the Reconstruction era, offering an acute sociological portrait of the American slavery system and its long-term effects on whites and blacks, North and South. Namelessness, invisibility, and constant degradation were means of conferring upon slaves a condition of "social death."[2] The master-slave bond, as Jacobs describes it, is parasitical as well as perversely intimate: the slave institutionalized as marginal is essential to the social structure that denies her humanity. The disturbing violence of *Incidents* helps to explain the barriers to real emancipation in the post–Civil War era.[3] As the national horror "hidden in plain sight," slavery was equally the province of the southerners who controlled it and the northerners who tolerated it. What united them was a virulent belief in black inferiority.

Yet Jacobs's narrative conveys another profound truth: that despite its design, American slavery could not extinguish the humanity of black people. Female slaves strove to mother their offspring, though masters treated them as commodities or as impediments to the nurture of their own white children. The flagrant abuse of slaves convinced witnesses like Jacobs of the institution's self-destructiveness. Against such uneconomical barbarism, she portrayed the black pursuit of freedom as a fulfillment of progressive Enlightenment ideals. Jacobs's own live burial in her "loophole of retreat" is a deliberate embrace of death that issues in her rebirth. While Jacobs ends her narrative free, she remains, like the nation as a whole, haunted by the institution that defined her existence well beyond its official end. In an essay on Reconstruction for a British audience, "The Economics of Negro Emancipation in the United States," W. E. B. Du Bois details the measures designed to exploit and extend some of slavery's most pernicious effects. Black subordination at work was systematized to ensure "a backward step in the organization of labor such as no modern nation would dare to take in the broad daylight of present economic thought." Disenfranchisement, imprisonment for debt and for breaking a contract, the neglect of black education, Jim Crow laws stipulating segregation in public, and the most vicious practice of all, lynching, supported the contradiction of a medieval caste system in a capitalist state.[4]

The following pages explore a range of writings—fiction, social treatises, political pamphlets—on the status of black Americans during and after Reconstruction. Popular pseudoscience (by analysts like Frederick Hoffman and William Benjamin Smith) rationalizing blacks' subordination and anticipating their imminent demise represented one extreme. This was countered by the writings of black leaders and northerners sympathetic to the cause (e.g., Ida B. Wells and Albion Tourgée) who appealed to the liberal-minded with graphic depictions of the suffering and injustice that threatened to make slavery universal in the postslavery era. Had blacks been emancipated, asked Frederick Douglass, only to exchange their enslavement "to individuals" for enslavement to "the community at large?"[5] Wells took her antilynching campaign to England after concluding (with Du Bois and others) that American abuses required international exposure. These activists confirmed the significant gains made by every class of blacks, while emphasizing that such advancement occurred in spite of prevailing customs and laws. The era's most prophetic observers (e.g., W. E. B. Du Bois, Mark Twain, and Pauline Hopkins) understood that the nation's destiny in this time of cultural and economic expansion was inseparable from the destiny of black Americans. Convinced that this would become widely accepted over time, they predicted with characteristic eloquence a painful future that was not without hope. For it was impossible, they recognized, in a country with so much opportunity, that an entire people, no matter how oppressed, could be long kept down. Nor would entrepreneurs (inside or outside the black community) overlook the potential labor and spending power of such a significant social group.

A curious feature of American capitalist development was the rich economic prospects sometimes concealed in debilitating realities. Racism itself, in certain circumstances, might be a means to achieving opportunity and progress, however compromised and limited. In keeping with this, some of the most common forms of black professionalism and enterprise in the Reconstruction era were economic niches or exclusives. Du Bois described one of them in his 1899 study of black businesses: the profession of undertaking. Given the taboo that persisted through the twentieth century that only blacks could bury blacks but members of either race might bury whites, black undertakers found they had a special niche in the national economy and thrived accordingly. Some of the greatest fortunes made by blacks in the twentieth century were in the funeral industry.[6] Pullman porters occupied another profitable niche that originated in racist assumptions. When he set out to expand his sleeper car business on a national scale, George Pullman decided that the ideal attendant for his luxurious mobile homes would be a black from the old slave states, "the blacker the better." Because they "embodied servility more than humanity," inhabiting a completely different social world, former slaves could be trusted to preside over the intimate affairs of Pullman passengers without violating their privacy.[7] Both examples show how blacks in the Reconstruction era attained expertise, social authority, and income by exploiting the consequences of prejudice. And they further demonstrate the remarkable resilience that made the eventual integration and social progress of the group as a whole inevitable.

Americans from the end of the Civil War through the first decades of the twentieth century seriously debated the possible extinction of black people in discussions carried out mainly in social scientific journals and books but extending as well to other aesthetic, juridical, and religious arenas. These debates were striking for the variety of participants and occasions: at conferences and in published forums, leading black academics confronted amateurs, and prominent social scientists echoed comparative dilettantes. The breadth of these discussions had something to do with the openness of social scientific research at this early stage of development. But it may have had more to do with the specifics of race questions. For the urge to draw tighter boundaries *between* blacks and whites gave rise, in an oddly equilibrating manner, to an utter disregard for boundaries in efforts to rationalize them. These debates bespoke a new "competitive" stage of race relations.[8] People crunched numbers and wrote tracts in defense of a race mythology that cast black Americans as the casualty of national advance. While some predicted their disappearance through a process of assimilation that would eliminate the weaker race, others agonized over the dangers of "passing," concerned that declining black population rates reflected the imperceptible infiltration of the white gene pool by mulatto elements. Still others expressed assurance and anxiety at once: certainty about black extinction, but worry about the group's deleterious impact while it remained. The racial numbers game was hardly self-consistent; the same writer might use the same data in support of opposite claims. But this was not because there was any ambiguity in the sentiments behind these claims. The notion of black morbidity was both the means to the containment of a black labor force and a critical psychic measure designed to feed the expanding sacrificial appetites of an American capitalist culture.[9]

These debates were specific to an era. Yet their echoes can be traced to recent literary, social scientific, and popular media. One reason for this persistence was the extent of their institutionalization at the turn of the twentieth century in standard businesses like life insurance and real estate.[10] It is also because national thinking on race, in particular, has been narrow and circular. This was what Du Bois seems to have had in mind when he declared it "a serious disgrace to American science . . . [that] with the tremendous opportunity that it has before it for the study of race difference and race development, race intermingling and contact among the most diverse of human kinds right here at its doors, almost nothing has been done."[11] Race problems seemed to elude scientific treatment because of the emotional investments on all sides (North and South; black and white). And this helps to explain the preference for foreigners as lead investigators on major projects: from the German Frederick L. Hoffman, whose *Race Traits and Tendencies of the American Negro* (1896) was commissioned by the Prudential Insurance Company, to the Swede Gunnar Myrdal, author of *The American Dilemma: The Negro Problem and Modern Democracy* (1944), commissioned by the Carnegie Foundation.

Du Bois's reference to "science" pointedly distinguishes serious empirical research from a specific group of pseudoscientific writings that set the tone of the era's race debates. The blatant racism of books such as George Stetson's *The Southern Negro as He Is* (1877) and Philip Bruce's *The Plantation Negro as a Freeman: Observations on His Character, Condition, and Prospects in Virginia* (1889) could have relegated them to idiosyncratic period pieces.[12] As Du Bois suspected, however, these works expressed the hopes of many contemporaries who either lacked the brutality to state it outright or the intellectual innocence to believe it wholeheartedly. This combination of brutality and innocence is what gives them historical value, because they provide detailed maps of the besieged white mentality, evoking assumptions that were widespread. When a southern amateur like George Stetson predicted in 1877 that the black race was "probably a diminishing factor" in American life, he was articulating a common hope of both North and South. That he was echoed years later by the northern sociologist Charles Ellwood, who wrote regularly on race topics for the *American Journal of Sociology*, should not be surprising. "Progress everywhere," he proclaimed, "waits on death—the death of the inferior individual—and nowhere more so than in racial problems." While Ellwood included blacks as beneficiaries of this natural winnowing, his liberalism didn't preclude a favorable review of one of the era's most blatantly racist tracts, William Benjamin Smith's *The Color Line: A Brief on Behalf of the Unborn* (1905).[13]

Among examples of racist pseudoscience, few were as bleak as Smith's. A mathematician who labeled his work "an ethnological inquiry," Smith's sources show how these race debates functioned as heated exchanges among an identifiable group of intellectuals whose positions were irreconcilable. In Smith's book science provides the script (race struggle) and religion gives it moral color (sacrifice for the common good), while social engineering and charity are equated and dismissed. Science and Christianity are thus monumentalized as twin towers with one awesome theme. And the sacrifice of the black race is a necessity both organic and divine. Smith regionalizes the color line at the start of his analysis in order to take credit for what is, in his view, an ultimate, national solution. In reviewing

The Color Line for the *Dial Magazine* in May 1905, Du Bois remarked that the book might "easily be passed over in silence," did it not reflect "the active belief of millions of our fellow countrymen. . . . This is the new barbarism of the twentieth century, against which all the forces of civilization must contend." The new barbarism, as confirmed by the most widely cited of contemporary studies on race, Frederick Hoffman's *Race Traits and Tendencies of the American Negro*, seemed to be everywhere.

Race Traits and Tendencies originated as research on the relative "insurability" of black lives and developed into a study of inherited characteristics versus social conditions. That it became an authoritative source for sociologists was a sign of the field's own steeping in Darwinism. A Prudential statistician without social scientific training, who also wrote a *History of the Prudential Life Insurance Company* (1900) and a book on pauper burials in large cities (1917), Hoffman was primarily interested in survival—from the competing claims of nations, to the social relations issuing from the natural inequality of different human "kinds." *Race Traits and Tendencies* is an eccentric blend of social psychology, liberal philosophy, reformism, statistical analysis, ethnographic description, and racist dogma. The book defines black culture as moribund and goes on to recommend that the group be isolated—socially, politically, psychologically—in every possible context, from the rural Black Belt to urban ghetto. Hoffman disputes arguments that attribute high black mortality to environmental factors, citing statistics from army and prison records showing it to be disproportionate among white and black recruits given identical food, clothing, and shelter. He finds black mortality to be highest among the younger generation—those at greatest remove from the sustaining framework of slavery. Yet Hoffman is convinced of the double determination of black doom, as reflected in his book's split title. "Race traits" describes the inherent basis of inferiority; "tendencies," the stylistic and cultural practices that nourish these genetic predispositions. Taken as a whole, *Race Traits and Tendencies* more than fulfilled its actuarial ambitions, with pages of tables on black deaths from diseases (consumption, yellow fever, malaria, small-pox) that many believed they were immune to.

Nathaniel Shaler's popular works on race also represented a departure from his field of expertise (geology), but this seemed to inspire his ambitious enlargement of the scope of race dogma to social psychology. A social Darwinist who believed that emotions were inherent, not learned, Shaler suggested that sympathy evolved and adapted like any other body part. In *The Neighbor: A Natural History of Social Contacts* (1904), he elaborated this Darwinian approach to the emotions into a theory of social relations. Born in Kentucky, Shaler retained his southern sympathies while fighting for the Union, just as he remained a disaffected southerner while studying and teaching at Harvard (where Du Bois was one of his students). Like most social Darwinists, Shaler saw progress as costly and requisite sacrifices as inequitable. While he regarded humanitarianism as the highest evolutionary form, he suggested it could only be achieved through a dramatic reduction of social strangers. According to Shaler, a sympathetic humanitarianism would not realize its potential until the disappearance of those who failed to arouse it. His recommendations therefore included immigration restrictions, the rapid assimilation of "valuable aliens" (Irish, German, Jew), prohibitions on interracial marriage, limitations on black suffrage, and the radical circumscription of black labor. Shaler believed the tragedy of modernity was its capacity to bring strangeness ever closer, while not having the means of keeping it within bounds. The result was the revival of an intratribal sympathy that was intensified by modern social variety. Positing the complexity of the sympathetic impulse, Shaler proceeded to recognize prejudice as one of its forms: a sympathetic hatred aimed at preservation of one's kind.

While Shaler himself regularly condemned lynching, his arguments provided a rationale for "the contagion of motive" underlying such mob behavior. W. E. B. Du Bois was in the minority when he commented, presumably after learning the fate of Sam Hose, an Atlanta victim, that lynching was beyond scientific treatment. His conviction was contradicted almost immediately by the appearance and positive reception of *Lynch-Law: An Investigation into the History of Lynching in the United States* (1905), by James Elbert Cutler, a disciple of the sociologist William Graham Sumner.[14] As a stage for the problems of social integration, intolerance, and mob violence, it is easy to see why lynching caught the attention of someone with Cutler's training. But his effort to explain lynching scientifically amounts to a defense of its perpetrators. In arguing that white settlers were the first to implement lynch law in the United States, initially against Indians, Cutler presents lynching as a frenzied unification of Anglo-Saxon sentiment. Lynch law prevails, he suggests, at pressure points when society requires reordering under new conditions. Lynch law could not have escalated were the majority of citizens antagonistic to the mob. Nor would lynching subside until the American legal system was forced to reconcile its abstract ideals with the social and ethnic factors driving race conflict. Political principles were one thing, social facts another. Like other authors of racist pseudoscience, Cutler believed that America was unique. The national crucible of race, with its particular history of slavery, was an experiment whose exceptionality made it unpredictable. According to Smith, Hoffman, Shaler, Cutler, and many others who shared their convictions, it was fruitless to draw comparisons between race dilemmas in the United States and those of other times and places.

By taking a global approach and framing discussion in terms that were explicitly international, the era's most farsighted parted ways with pseudoscience, though this did not prevent their conclusions from being bleak. In a 1908 forum published in the *American Journal of Sociology*, "Is Race Friction in the United States Growing and Inevitable?," the situation of American blacks was presented as inseparable from the problem of race contact everywhere. Alfred Stone Holt opened his title essay with an account of the 1855 "Nell Meeting" in Boston, which anticipated the imminent demise of race prejudice. Holt is as candid about the attractiveness of this proposition as he is about the democratic pressures he sees militating against it. Natural tendencies to divide along lines of racial difference are aggravated in a liberal meritocracy that offers little competition from more traditional distinctions. At the same time, Holt emphasizes the interdependence of all nations and the potential this affords for worldwide ethnic strife. The increased proximity of different peoples, a growing uniformity of aspirations stimulating competition for limited resources, and fears over disparities in population have actually enlarged the sphere of racism. Americans may have managed to subdue fears about black population statistics at home; they have yet to consider developments abroad. Holt pictures a parade of dark triumphs, linking the gains of black farmers across the South and competition from black workers in northern cities, to the then-recent victory of Japan over Russia.

As part of an international struggle, American race friction begins to look like a territorial dispute, whose resolution lies in the division of lands and securing of boundaries. Thus Smith's color line is revitalized: from an antiquated instrument of regional terror, to a rational method in an international age. If extinction has turned out to be a white fantasy of sorts, the disappearance of blacks can be ensured by other means. Walter Willcox, Holt's first respondent, seems relatively optimistic about the chances of keeping "race friction" within bounds, judging from decreased opposition to a caste system of black subordination.[15] U. G. Weatherly lends support to this view by highlighting the effects of black migration north. While the promise of a northern outlet intensifies unrest among southern blacks, the increase of race conflict in the North promises a more unified national policy.[16] Participants in the forum on "Race Friction" are in agreement that America's blacks are in motion: whether down (decline), or up (social mobility), in (migration), or out (emigration). And the consensus is that they must somehow be kept within bounds.

A single voice counsels the futility of this aim. As the final respondent and lone black participant in the forum, W. E. B. Du Bois's task is to confirm the inevitability of the changes acknowledged by his white colleagues, while minimizing their revolutionary implications. He stresses the appropriateness of black self-realization, recalling the Nell Meeting to highlight their political evolution from enslaved beneficiaries of white abolitionists in 1855 to citizens acting on their own behalf in 1908. The democratic ideals common to a wide spectrum of black Americans are continuous with global struggles. "The world is shrinking together," he proclaims, "it is finding itself neighbor to itself in strange, almost magic degree." Far from disappearing or receding as a decorative element in some future composite of world races, "the darker two thirds" of the globe will be prime contenders in the creation of a "new commerce" and "new humanity." Du Bois conveys a strategic commitment to economics, challenging Americans to solve the race problem and thereby "gain an advantage over the rest of the earth." This optimism, however, is implicitly qualified by Du Bois's aggressive echoing of his Harvard professor's best-selling book (*The Neighbor*). The magical extension of neighborliness in the modern era brings new obligations—to "be neighborly to the rest of the world"—and new ways of violating them—"lynching . . . helpless neighbors." Du Bois's conclusion, "God save us from such social philosophy," is seconded eerily by one southerner's explanation for why lynching crimes couldn't be prosecuted: "We're all neighbors, and neighbors' neighbors!"[17] Yet despite his pessimistic conclusion Du Bois manages to redefine survival as a biracial term. The hard logic of bodies and numbers, he insists, is bound in the coming century to favor the world's darker peoples.

Du Bois's very presence in this forum signals an awakening among its other participants, however stubbornly they resisted his claims. The country had come a significant distance on race relations, in part because the impressive gains of blacks themselves could not be denied. Indeed, the most extreme forms of racism registered enraged recognition of these gains. The battles waged by intellectuals like Du Bois in academic journals, at conferences both domestic and international, in newspapers and magazines for general audiences were fought by others on the streets and in the courts, through demonstrations and boycotts and legal suits. Protest was the classic American reform, destined to appeal to liberal interests on all sides of the race question. As such, it was perhaps the most immediately influential of any social action on behalf of black opportunity and progress. Though they have faded into obscurity over time, its chief exemplars both black and white were major figures in their own right.

PROTEST

"All the great reforms of the age have been accomplished through the efforts of men who were partisans. Passiveness never accomplished anything."[18] This observation in an interview near the end of his life conveys the spirit that guided Albion Winegar Tourgée's career of social protest. Tourgée's contemporary reputation as an uncompromising champion of black equality ("justice to all men, no matter what their color or previous condition") helps to explain the muted response to his death in the national press. By 1905, the country had taken a step back from the ambitious plans of the Reconstruction era, and members of the newly founded NAACP, who declared Tourgée, along with Frederick Douglass and William Lloyd Garrison, a true "Friend of Freedom," offered the only significant memorial.[19] Tourgée is best remembered today for his role as lead attorney for the plaintiff, Homer Plessy, in the famous *Plessy v. Ferguson* Supreme Court decision allowing "separate but equal" accommodations on railroad cars. But his accomplishments include fearless prosecution of the Ku Klux Klan as a North Carolina judge, the founding of a newspaper, the *Union Register*, and a major role in shaping the state's new constitution. Resettled in upstate New York in the 1880s and 1890s, Tourgée edited a magazine, the *Continent*, which featured sociology and history as well as literature under the umbrella of his ongoing radical Republicanism and budding Progressivism. In one editorial, for example, he condemned corporate greed and the perilous gap between rich and poor, commenting, "The South surrendered at Appomattox, the North has been surrendering ever since."[20] Tourgée, characteristically, put his rhetoric into practice in 1891 by launching the National Citizens Rights Association (NCRA), a biracial pressure group devoted to attacking segregation and other injustices throughout the nation's court system. But in a terrific irony that this dedicated social activist could fully appreciate, it was a novel, *A Fool's Errand* (1879), that ultimately brought him fame and fortune.

Published anonymously, the book's extraordinarily positive reception led Tourgée to embrace authorship of what remains the foremost fictionalization of southern Reconstruction and the rise of the Ku Klux Klan. Many reviewers recalled *Uncle Tom's Cabin*, declaring *A Fool's Errand* as strong a case for Reconstruction as Harriet Beecher Stowe's had been for abolition. The novel's commercial success (one hundred thousand copies sold within a year) inspired a signed second edition with an appendix, "The Invisible

Empire," documenting the activities of the Klan, in recollection of Stowe's *Key to Uncle Tom's Cabin*.[21] Written from the perspective of a Union officer come to the South after the war to heal his injured body and pursue legal as well as entrepreneurial opportunities, *A Fool's Errand* is by someone who experienced much of what he portrayed. Born in Ohio in 1838, Tourgée later moved to Massachusetts and published his first book of poems and essays, *Sense and Nonsense*, at age nineteen. A student at the University of Rochester, he was awarded a B.A. upon his 1862 enlistment, in keeping with the collegiate practice of awarding degrees to men who joined the Union army before graduating. Tourgée fought with both New York and Ohio regiments, but his tour was interrupted when he was arrested for insubordination after refusing to surrender a black fugitive who had aided his company. He returned to participate in a number of major battles toward the war's end. In 1864, Tourgée was admitted to the Ohio bar and discovered the beauties of North Carolina, one of the least devastated of southern states, while serving as legal counsel in a court-martial case. Tourgée moved his family there in 1865 and soon became a pariah among the local inhabitants for his outspoken support of black suffrage and equality.

Tourgée's turn to fiction following the great success of *A Fool's Errand* was an apparent expression of the limits of politics, a retreat somewhat qualified when his novel *Figs and Thistles* (1879) became an inadvertent campaign biography for Republican presidential candidate James Garfield. The very attributes that ensured the failure of Reconstruction, Tourgée argued in "The South as a Field for Fiction," made the region unparalleled as a setting for romance.[22] Though Tourgée sought to exploit some of that possibility, his own deeper tendencies were reflected in the realism of *A Fool's Errand*, whose disheartening predictions included a permanent rift between North and South, the transmission of a distorted master-slave psychology to succeeding generations, and the utter failure of Reconstruction to safeguard black freedom. The novel engages readers not only through vivid descriptions of a critical era in American history but also through the compelling idiosyncrasies of its carefully drawn protagonist, Colonel Comfort Servosse. To local inhabitants, Servosse's insistence that blacks be allowed to testify in court, serve on juries, and vote seems benign beside his revolutionary plan of selling them land in exchange for crops. But Servosse's greatest offense is smugness: his assurance that the freed slaves' legal advance is a foregone conclusion, which southerners would do well to meet half way. An astute reader of postwar southern society, his wife Metta delivers some of the narrative's keenest insights in letters home, describing the trials of northern women hired by the Missionary Association to educate blacks, the aspiration and suffering of blacks themselves, and the fear-some prejudice of poor whites, who were also degraded by the plantation system.

Tourgée's book is rare in its attempt to be evenhanded about Recon-struction. He reproduces an outline, for instance, of opposing southern and northern views on a range of issues. Exposing the tyranny that ruled the antebellum and Confederate South, he also reveals persistent nationalist resistance. Some of Tourgée's ire is directed at the northern officials whom he believes fatally underestimated the Klan when it first appeared during the winter of 1868–69. Misconceived as a relatively controlled effort to regulate blacks by exploiting what was prejudicially believed to be their collective fear of ghosts, it quickly evolved into a reign of terror against anyone who dared to espouse racial equality or even interracial respect. Tourgée emphasizes the operational zeal of this soldierly enterprise, which made it so difficult to oppose. The masks—on horses as well as men—helped them to elude prosecution; their success in recruiting from every class of whites ensured the shared incrimination of the powerful. Indeed, the Klan was adept at identifying itself with the best elements in any community.

The difficulty of countering the Klan makes for the most appealing section of Tourgée's fiction: the climactic chapters on Servosse's daughter thwarting a Klan plot to lynch him. The episode is rich in romantic cliché: the love between this daughter of Reconstruction and a prince of southern aristocracy, the parental opposition to the romance that is Shakespearean in intensity, a night ride to prevent murder. The drama culminates in the repudiation of the Klan by its members, an implausible resolution given their former self-righteous violence. It is also difficult to reconcile with Tourgée's largest claim—that Servosse's efforts represent a "fool's errand." By appropriating southern principles in order to understand them, Tour-gée's fool enacts the North's comparatively tenuous commitment to alter-native values. The novel demonstrates that northern enlightenment on race was not nearly a match for the ferocious ideological conviction of the southern side. Moreover, during this postwar era, the claims of economic development and opportunity served to further weaken northern ideals.

By contrast, it seemed nothing could compete among bona fide south-erners with that "jewel of the southern soul," the color line. In light of this deeper message, Tourgée's subsequent work in the 1890s on the *Plessy v. Ferguson* case testing the constitutionality of the separate car law on rail-roads seems another "fool's errand." This was despite the fact that the railroads themselves were receptive to the plaintiff's case because of the cost and inefficiency of segregated cars. But the majority on the Supreme Court (only John Marshall Harlan, a former Kentucky slaveholder, dissented) concurred with Massachusetts native Henry Billings Brown, who noted that it was a "fallacy of the plaintiff's argument" to assume "that the enforced separation of the two races stamps the colored race with a badge of inferiority."[23] Though he lost the case, Tourgée succeeded in introducing an extraordinary argument into legal debates on race: the notion of whiteness as "the most valuable sort of property . . . the master-key that unlocks the golden door of opportunity." In this sense, "separate but equal" effectively reconstituted slavery by imposing a permanent subordinate status that locked anyone defined as black out of the American kingdom of opportunity.[24] While the *Plessy v. Ferguson* decision was largely ignored when it came down in 1896, according to Supreme Court Justice Robert H. Jackson, who played a pivotal role in the 1954 triumph of Brown over the Topeka Board of Education, the 1896 judgment laid the crucial groundwork for school desegregation. "What was a defeat for him in '96" became, in the words of Judge Jackson, "a post-mortem victory" in 1954. This would have meant a great deal to Tourgée, who recognized himself as a man born too early, but who believed that behaving foolishly in the name of valuable causes made life worth living.

As mutual crusaders against the "Invisible Empire," Albion Tourgée and Ida Wells-Barnett were well known to each other. Wells-Barnett was one of the first black leaders to respond positively to Tourgée's NCRA, and she, along with Frederick Douglass, credited Judge Tourgée with having inspired their cowritten booklet *Why the Colored American Is Not in the World's Columbian Exposition.*[25] Wells-Barnett was among the most prominent of "Tourgée's old militant allies" to attend his funeral on November 14, 1905.[26] No other black leader of the post-Emancipation era demonstrated more courage than Ida Wells-Barnett, who achieved international fame for her vigorous campaign against lynching. During the 1880s, the number of blacks lynched averaged 100 per year; by the 1890s this had risen to 162. When three black businessmen were lynched in 1892 in Memphis, Tennessee, Wells published a rousing denunciation in her local newspaper, *Free Speech*. Whites destroyed the paper's office, and Wells's friend, T. Thomas Fortune, editor of the *New York Age*, offered a forum for her antilynching articles on his paper's front page. Thus began her career as one of the most important political crusaders of her time.

Wells was born in Mississippi in 1862, the eldest of eight children of former slaves. Her devout mother and educated father (he was a member of Rust College's first board of trustees) endowed their daughter with a passion for learning and justice. When both parents died from yellow fever in 1878, Wells managed to preserve the family, working as a schoolteacher while attending Rust College nearby. Wells's first act of resistance came in 1884, after whites forcibly carried her from a nonsmoking to a smoking car—the only one open to blacks—and she promptly sued the Memphis railroad. A lower court awarded her $500 in damages, but a higher court reversed the decision. Following the Memphis lynching, Wells rallied a black exodus from the city, which cast such a pall on its economy that white leaders appealed to her to stop it. In 1893 she was invited to England by feminists there to lecture about lynching, and upon her return Wells joined Susan B. Anthony for a similar American tour. Her reputation was broadened by her protest against race discrimination at the 1893 World's Columbian Exposition in Chicago. Now living in Chicago, Wells married the lawyer and activist Ferdinand L. Barnett, who shared her interests, having started the first newspaper for Chicago's black community, the *Conservator*, following his graduation from Northwestern University Law School. They had four children, the first born in 1895, and from then on Wells balanced child rearing with her continuing activism. Often these labors were synonymous: in 1901, for example, the Wells-Barnetts became the first black family to move east of State Street in Chicago. The family sons were regularly attacked, and Wells kept a gun in the house, teaching her children what she had learned from her southern campaigns: if you must die by violence, try to take your persecutors with you.

Like all successful social reformers, Wells was motivated by a powerful intellectual conviction: that economic interest furthered political justice. She noted, for instance, that white Americans were moved to action on lynching when British financiers (inspired by Wells) said the practice was an impediment to their investments. Likewise, the mob violence designed to punish black social mobility was best resisted by the organized removal (boycotts and emigration) of black workers and consumers. Above all, Wells insisted that social reform required collective action, as she argued in her case for the pivotal role of black voting, "How Enfranchisement Stops Lynching."[27] For this reason, she lamented the comparative tightness of Chicago's wealthy blacks, whose contributions to her own Negro Fellowship League fell far short of white contributions to Jane Addams's Hull House. Wells documented her experiences and beliefs as a lifelong activist in two books on lynching, *Southern Horrors: Lynch Law in All Its Phases* (1892) and *A Red Record: Lynchings in the United States, 1892–1893–1894* (1895), and an autobiography, *Crusade for Justice*, published after her death in 1931. Her children recalled their mother as perpetually moved by injustice to "do something" (one of her favorite phrases). Indeed, Wells's life provides a contrast to those of fellow blacks who struggled within the constraints of racism. Her achievements demonstrate the need for a multifaceted approach when vast social changes are in order. Without those prepared to name outrages for what they were, the era's more limited advances would have been impossible.

Among the "old militant allies" with Ida Wells-Barnett at the funeral of Albion Tourgée was Charles Chesnutt, who offered a moving testimonial celebrating Tourgée's support of black people and their civil rights. A lawyer as well as the first major black realist author, Chesnutt had been deeply engaged with the *Plessy v. Ferguson* case, writing journalistic critiques of the decision and a fictional response in *The Marrow of Tradition* (1901). The principal subject of Chesnutt's writing was the color line: its personal, political, and philosophical implications, particularly for the mulattoes who could evade it. In a 1928 acceptance speech for the NAACP's Spingarn Literature Medal, Chesnutt observed that the unique psychology and complex circumstances of people with mixed blood proved an especially rich field for fiction. Chesnutt, who was light enough to pass, was the son of mulattoes who had inherited property from their white fathers, which ensured a relatively comfortable upbringing in Fayetteville, North Carolina. He was well-educated and drawn to literature because he believed that it could transform the public conscience on matters of race. "The Negro's part is to prepare himself for recognition and equality," Chesnutt wrote, "and it is the province of literature to open the way for him to get it—to accustom the public mind to the idea; to lead people out, imperceptibly, unconsciously, step by step, to the desired state of feeling."[28] Chesnutt's long life spanned turbulent times in race relations, from the Civil War and Reconstruction to the "Great Migration" of blacks to the North in the 1930s and 1940s. A resident of the South and the North, a lawyer and businessman as well as a man of letters, Chesnutt grew accustomed to what Du Bois termed "double-consciousness." Admitted to the Ohio state bar in 1884, Chesnutt built a successful business in legal stenography and documentation during the same period in which he became a regular contributor to major periodicals (publishing his first story, "The Goophered Grapevine," in the *Atlantic Monthly* in 1887). Despite dividing his time between writing and business, Chesnutt was able to produce over the course of two decades several essays, three novels, two story collections, and a biography of Frederick Douglass (in the prestigious Beacon Biography series).

Chesnutt's first novel, *The House behind the Cedars* (1900), exploits the dramatic possibilities of the color line. The narrative opens upon a common ritual invested with an uncommon twist: the North Carolina home-coming of John Walden, a young mulatto lawyer, recently widowed, who has built a successful career by passing in South Carolina. John's conceal-ment is enabled by the racial particulars of South Carolina: the sizable population of free blacks, Indians, mulattoes, and mestizos mediating the divide between slaveholders and slaves before the war and blurring the color line after it. Avoiding army service, John marries the daughter of a white plantation owner who has preserved his wealth and finds legal clients among southerners eager to avoid carpetbagging lawyers. Fixing on his sister Rena, who can also pass easily, as a maternal replacement for his newly orphaned son, John talks her into returning with him to South Carolina. While Rena is guilt-ridden about leaving their black mother, Molly Walden, Charleston is full of opportunities, educational and roman-tic. After finishing school, Rena falls in love with a wealthy young aristocrat, George Tryon, but their lives are subsequently destroyed by their mutual attraction. Reluctant to inform George of her mixed race, Rena's secret is exposed when George visits the Walden's hometown on business. Tryon struggles against his prejudicial revulsion, but by the time love triumphs over culture, Rena has died of brain fever.

Chesnutt had loftier ambitions for his second novel, *The Marrow of Tradi-tion*, which he envisioned as "the legitimate successor of Harriet Beecher Stowe's *Uncle Tom's Cabin* and Albion Tourgée's *A Fool's Errand*."[29] The hope was apt, given the book's basis in a historical incident: the Wilmington, North Carolina, riots of 1898, initiated by white Democrats whose munici-pal power had been in eclipse since the 1870s. Because Wilmington's blacks voted regularly through the 1890s, representation in government and in official agencies reflected their demographic dominance. But whites ob-jected increasingly to being arrested by black police or tried before black judges. The riots were triggered by Alexander Manly's August 1898 editorial in the *Wilmington Record* condemning lynching and the white journalists who inspired it. Manly, a mulatto, went to the heart of white hypocrisy, denouncing the predation of white men (like his father), while highlighting the gender myths that made black men attractive to white women. White newspaper editors expressed outrage, and South Carolina's Senator Ben-jamin Tillman added fuel to the flames at a white supremacist rally in October 1898. In addition to those killed, thousands of blacks were driven from their homes, and a grandfather clause effectively nullifying black enfranchisement was ratified by the North Carolina legislature. In a letter to his editor, Walter Hines Page, Chesnutt described the riots as a disgrace-ful display of race hatred.

In *The Marrow of Tradition* blackness is a stigma. Without a degraded and constantly menaced black community, white southerners could not bear their own sense of failure. The myth of black doom mirrors southern decline; black morbidity is an expression of southern degeneracy. This is dramatized in the plot of reverse passing, where the dissolute aristocrat Tom Delamere, who specializes in "coon" impersonations, assumes blackface in order to rob and murder his aged aunt. As suggested in so many other works of the period, crime is colored black. The question of punishment raises inevitably the prospect of lynching. From the white perspective, the object is to lynch a black regardless of guilt, a principle recalled from ancient Rome, where slaves were held collectively responsible for the crimes of any one of them. The Roman allusion confirms what is already clear: lynch law is designed to perpetuate slavery. Moreover, white civilization depends on it. Equally essential (to white and black communities) are the peculiar atavisms representing a common subculture of belief. In the first chapter, an old black woman performs a mysterious rite of burying a bottle under a full moon on behalf of a white editor's ailing infant. Assimilation rituals, by contrast, are divisive and mutually diminishing. The hair straightening and skin bleaching of the black servant Sandy reinforce white supremacist doctrine.

But in *The Marrow of Tradition*, both blacks and whites are steeped in the logic of sacrifice, which culminates at the novel's end in the prospect of a double offering—of two firstborn sons. While the black Dr. Miller's son is sacrificed (killed in a riot incited by the white Colonel Cateret's inflammatory editorial), the novel closes on Dr. Miller's successful treatment of Cateret's son. Sacrifice here is not universalized but particularized as the black man's burden. White supremacy is rewritten as sacrificial doctrine: blacks provide the offering, whites reap the bounty. Soon after the completion of this novel, Chesnutt abandoned writing to give full attention to his lucrative stenography business, apparently disheartened by the limited impact of his literary productions. W. E. B. Du Bois, a significant author in his own right, had less faith in the influence of cultural artifacts. And his greatest success as a writer was achieved with a work that was most notable for its interdisciplinary content. While this didn't prevent *The Souls of Black Folk* (1903) from becoming an eventual classic in the American literary canon, it does suggest that the color line of his time extended to the cultural marketplace. It was therefore appropriate that literature afforded Du Bois, as it did Mark Twain, Pauline Hopkins, and James Weldon Johnson, a forum for his deepest fears about American racism.

Sociologist, historian, editor, writer, and reviewer William Edward Burghardt Du Bois (1868–1963) was truly a Renaissance man of the modern era, contributing significantly to the fields of social science, journalism, and literature. A major leader as well as public intellectual, Du Bois was the first African American to earn a Ph.D. at Harvard University. He spent his career confronting institutionalized racism, that he believed was aimed at the social extinction of American blacks. Du Bois embodied the split between reformist faith and critical despair. On the one hand, he expressed optimism about capitalism's expansive tendencies, citing, as he did in "The Negroes of Farmville," flattering statistics on the gains of black landholders and businessmen. Elsewhere, however, he presented such advances as improbabilities achieved against tremendous odds. Black failure was likely not only because whites expected it, but because its likelihood was deliberately institutionalized. Throughout writings of this period, Du Bois outlined what he called "the economic core" of black subordination.[30] Economic relations, according to Du Bois, were *productive* of other differences. Racial distinctions were *less natural* than the class distinctions they so often overshadowed, a point made in his description of the color line dividing most American cities.

> The winding and intricacy of the geographical color line varies, of course, in different communities. I know some towns where a straight line drawn through the middle of the main street separates nine-tenths of the whites from nine-tenths of the blacks. In other towns the older settlement of whites has been encircled by a broad band of blacks; in still other cases little settlements or nuclei of blacks have sprung up amid surrounding whites. Usually in cities each street has its distinctive color, and only now and then do the colors meet in close proximity. Even in the country something of this segregation is manifest in the smaller areas, and of course in the larger phenomena of the Black Belt.
>
> All this segregation by color is largely independent of that natural clustering of social grades common to all communities.[31]

Du Bois's description dramatizes the making of a race mythology. Someone, presumably white, has "drawn" the initial "line," which, in final form ("sprung up") appears like an act of nature. This explains how colloquial practice can assign "each street . . . its distinctive color." The social policy's effectiveness is confirmed by the fact that the different people inhabiting these distinctly colored streets seldom meet. But Du Bois's shifting geometry of race ("line," "circle," "nuclei") pictures an unexpected and threatening process of expansion that culminates in the "Black Belt." Signaling the potential of any "policy" to subvert its design, segregation helps to create a resistant black constituency, while failing to eradicate black social prospects. Du Bois's claim is one that will sound over the course of his career, that no matter how comprehensive and malevolent a social policy or institution, its impact is always qualified. It can never fully limit the human imagination and spirit, which finds opportunities in the most unlikely places. *The Souls of Black Folk* is a testament to that imagination and spirit, a powerful group biography of those struggling against, beyond, and within the borders of the color line.

When the book first appeared, William James sent a copy to his brother Henry with a note characterizing its author as "that mulatto ex-student of mine." Henry was impressed and pronounced the book among the best he had read in years. A popular as well as critical success, *Souls* was widely admired by intellectuals, including the German sociologist Max Weber. Du Bois's multiple vocations are variously reflected in the narrative, which was published as separate articles prior to its publication as a book. These different parts cohere through a shared thematic interest in that most privileged of literary subjects—death—and a view of black culture in America as one intimately associated with its rituals.

Du Bois's elegiac reflections in "Of the Passing of the First-Born," the chapter on the death of his son, provide the book's symbolic center. Here, personal loss is deflected and sustained by an apprehension of its collective ramifications. Grief assumes a monumental aspect because individual death among certain groups can never be separated from the dilemma of group survival. In this sense, Du Bois's treatise on mourning offers a significant contrast to its Emersonian analog, "Experience." For Du Bois, it is not the elusiveness of death that appalls, but the ease with which it envelops black life, destroying an already provisional domesticity. The son's airborne illness, devastator of parental dreams, recalls passages from Du Bois's sociological works describing the perilous exposure of black homes. He struggles to reconcile private grief and collective identity, to join black elite and black masses. But he can't help bemoaning the disproportionately low reproductive rates of a black elite (in contrast to other blacks), nor distinguishing the relative values of different black lives.

Souls opens with Du Bois's declaration of affinity with his people; the chapter on his son dramatizes his ambivalence toward such identification. The most poignant sign of this is his refusal to bury the child in the mass grave of the South. The body of this small black hope is shipped north, separated from the doomed collectivity, just as his life is memorialized. In contrast to those of the anonymous multitudes, his soul ascends like a star. Du Bois elevates death and grief, symbolically, to the level of sacrifice. The chapter recalls two biblical moments of sacrificial substitution. In one, blood drops are substituted for human bodies; in the other, God's body is sacrificed for the sins of humanity. The chapter's title, "Of the Passing of the First-Born," recalls the plot of Passover, where the Hebrews are commanded to mark their doorposts with blood, a sacrificial sign that ensures the angel of death will "pass over" their homes and spare their firstborn sons. At the same time, the son is characterized in terms that associate his birth and death with the story of Christ.

The echoing lines near the chapter's beginning—"I saw, as it fell *across* my baby, the shadow of the Veil. . . . I saw the shadow of the Veil as it *passed over* my baby" (my italics)—seem to equalize the sacrificial symbols of crucifixion and Passover.[32] But, of course, they are not equivalent. In the first sentence, the boy's body, enclosed in commas, appears caught by the shadowy Veil (though perhaps also draped, as in royal robes). It recalls a New Testament sacrifice that was enacted. The second sentence is a single breath, suggesting immunity through unimpeded movement. It highlights an Old Testament sacrifice that was averted. These two biblical alternatives provide insight into Du Bois's view of black American experience at this time: as a sacrificial possibility realized or avoided. The death of Burghardt Du Bois is both the work of an uncommon fate and an all-too-common agency. His uncommon fate is that of a Christian God whose suffering provides eternal justification for the torture of innocents. The common agency is the economic and social exclusion whose brutal extension is lynch law.

The link between his son's death and Christ's sacrifice evidently resonated for Du Bois with lynching. Surveying the Atlanta lands of the Cherokees earlier in *Souls*, Du Bois draws our attention to the place of Sam Hose's "crucifixion." According to Du Bois's biographer, the display of Hose's charred knuckles in an Atlanta storefront a month before his son's death turned Atlanta into "a poisoned well, polluted with the remains of Sam Hose and reflecting the drawn image of Burghardt." The proximity of these events highlights Du Bois's burden throughout this chapter to accommodate his analytical distance from a black America stigmatized by high mortality with a firsthand experience that tragically confirms his own implication in it. Such a split defines the social scientific perspective and might be regarded as its classic plight: being part (and product) of the society one seeks to study objectively. Yet in research on race, investigative objectivity was more often impaired by distance or outright hostility.

When the *New York Evening Post* announced in 1903 that the Atlanta

University Studies were the "only scientific studies of the Negro question being made today," it was acknowledging the tide of pseudoscience that had preceded their publication. The Atlanta volumes were composed with a view of the social scientific frontier on race as open, with vast territories of knowledge still to be charted, and as closed, saturated with theories and statistics, many of them inaccurate or incendiary. Du Bois began his editorship of the Atlanta University Studies with the third volume, *The Negro in Business* (1899), and the next sixteen volumes represent a subtle shift in emphasis: from losses to gains, from mortality to segregation. One consequence of segregation, for instance, is the development of undertaking into an exceptionally lucrative black profession. Undertaking is profitable because it's an *exclusive* concern (blacks alone can bury their dead), not because there are higher percentages of black deaths. A major insight of *The Negro in Business*, then, is the real compensations afforded by segregation. *The Negro in Business*'s portrait of black enterprises formed as morbid offshoots of the larger economy represents what Du Bois terms "the advantage of the disadvantage."

Inaugurating the second cycle of the Atlanta University Studies, *The Health and Physique of the Negro American* (1906) was the most significant statement of the time on the relationship between black population figures and the rise of the color line. The book opens with a stunning photographic procession of "typical Negro-Americans," ranging from the darkest black to white, a wordless narrative, articulating in the strongest possible terms the doom of racial separation. The paradoxical foundation of this display is familiar to students of race theory: the attempt to catalog racial difference, the very rise of ethnology as a field of interest, accompanied the discovery of the hopelessly mixed character of all races. Over the course of the nineteenth century, ever more sophisticated techniques for measuring and classifying human kinds were set against the realities of assimilation. The fact was that America was absorbing its different populations whose own internal variety mirrored the racial variety of "native" Americans themselves. The same historical events—immigration, colonization, capitalist-industrial expansion—that had given rise to ethnology were rapidly eroding its analytical base. Racial ambiguity, as these developments imply, ran in all directions. The only pure blacks were those of stereotypes, as the Scottish explorer David Livingstone recognized when he declared that "the hideous Negro type, which the fancy of observers once saw all over Africa" existed only on "signs in front of tobacco-shops."[33] Du Bois goes on to cite the data from prominent social scientists that confirm the high percentage of black blood in white. Even more alarming is Du Bois's insinuation that black population statistics are somehow dependent on this indeterminacy. In the commentary that follows his silent parade of "Negro" types, Du Bois points out that passing is so easily accomplished by large numbers of mulattoes that the size of the black population may be impossible to estimate. *Health and Physique* thus makes short work of three dominant theories: that black and white races have become increasingly distinct; that African culture is limited to its American and African variants; and that black culture is regressive. With Africa redefined as the first productive culture of the ancient world, black mortality statistics in modern America become an obvious outcome of social conditions. Place any other group in similar circumstances, and the results will be similar. Du Bois's comparisons range from Russia, England, and Sweden, to the Chicago stockyards, where white death rates surpass black.

The Atlanta University Studies were designed to expose black existence to the light of empirical method. This explains their magnitude: endless tables on black businesses, hospitals, and medical schools, extended photographic series (on the evolution of the Negro body and home), protracted "correspondence" to close each volume. Only detail could fill the vacuum of hearsay and grim mythology, could transform black Americans from phantoms of sociological analysis to the "bone and flesh" collectivity ushered in by Du Bois at the start of *Souls*. Literary classics, as Du Bois was well aware, provided a different kind of challenge to the racial stereotypes that pervaded dominant media and cultural works through the first half of the twentieth century. The prospect that readers might find in these pernicious emblems what they most and least expected made their roles in contemporary race debates unpredictable, as confirmed by a renowned race drama of the era, Mark Twain's *Adventures of Huckleberry Finn*. Whether a book about friendship and love, a study of freedom, or an exploration of how scapegoat rituals help to preserve the color line, *Huckleberry Finn* locates the black slave Jim at the center of moral value.

Twain sold 50,000 copies of the novel within three months of publication in 1885, sales assisted by its controversial content as well as by tantalizing excerpts in *Century Magazine* in 1884–85. Banned in the nineteenth century by the Concord Public Library for coarse language and antisocial role models, *Huckleberry Finn* was condemned in the twentieth century for racial stereotyping. The novel confronts a host of national demons—from slavery and racism to the subordination and repudiation of women. Like other works by Twain, *Huckleberry Finn* with its forgetful hero confirms the importance of collective memory. It highlights cultural pressure points—instances of conflict and contradiction that resist the coherence of mythic paradigms. In so doing, it fulfills Kenneth Burke's notion of literary narratives as answers to specific historical situations, answers that highlight the basic structure and contents of the situation in a way that conveys an attitude toward them.[34]

The question that has preoccupied critics of *Huckleberry Finn* has to do with Twain's perspective on the racist stereotypes he portrays. Is Twain himself faithful to such norms, as his hero Huck seems to be? Or is he subtly undermining them through a "thick description" of his culture? The novel does in some sense defy racist norms by representing them so complexly through Huck's struggle against them. Huck progresses and then falls back time and again. This is because the book is as much about the enslavement to prejudice as it is about the institution of slavery. Twain's adolescent narrator continually confirms that children harbor the prospect of change, just as they are acutely susceptible to acculturation. Through their absorption of a culture's norms, they pinpoint what that culture stands for. And when they resist those norms, in response to experience, the resistance is always passionate. Slowly, against his will, but surely, Huck comes to recognize Jim's humanity. Huck gradually grasps ideas of racial equality that we now take for granted and then pulls back from those ideas. It's like watching a whole nation awaken and then recede back into darkness. Or like watching dawn at the beginning of chapter 19, which is among the most lyrical passages in the novel. Huck is on a roll: piling image upon image in a breathless heap, his voice gaining momentum as the sun rises. Yet daylight is as imperiling as it is inspiring, for Huck and Jim must hide when the sun comes up, traveling at night to avoid Jim's recapture.

Huckleberry Finn shares the principal concern of all Twain's works in the mechanics of belief. How do people come to believe what they believe? How do they ever come to change those beliefs? The most prominent of the novel's beliefs is the belief in slavery and black inferiority. To the extent that slavery is a stigma inscribed on black culture, it remains an enduring legacy, a view of the black condition handed down from generation to generation. This is the meaning of the excruciating ending, which Ernest Hemingway instructed readers to skip, where Jim's imprisonment is mercilessly protracted for Tom's amusement. Twain's description of how slavery is perpetuated in the era of Reconstruction suggests that blacks can be freed by legal fiat but remain enslaved in racist minds, both white and black. For Twain, son of southern slaveholders (his family owned *one*), married to a daughter of northern abolitionists, understood slavery and freedom as an American dialectic. Only a culture that knew slavery intimately could grasp the deepest meanings of freedom. *Huckleberry Finn* shows how the persisting identification of black people with enslavement gets rationalized, via stereotypes and labels, such as the word "nigger," which punctuates the narrative like a lash.

This is consistent with the introductory "Notice" and "Explanatory," which present language as a weapon and talk as a means of trickery and aggression. Signed by "G. G. Chief of Ordnance," "ordinance" (decree) minus the "i" becomes "ordnance" (artillery). This is the drama of the West itself: the rule of law is replaced by the rule of force, power trumps knowledge, and humor undermines moral absolutes. The Explanatory Note foregrounds the importance of dialect and the diversity of tongues spoken in the book, reinforcing the notice's insistence on straight talk. In *Huckleberry Finn* speech, lyricism does not transcend social context but expresses it. Language is not liberating but revelatory, of who we are, and of what we can't escape—our class, ethnicity, region, and culture. Indeed, the novel's primary narrative forms—storytelling, dialect, and dialogue—foreground the fact that language is a product of social interaction. Such a view of language is at odds with criticism that views Huckleberry Finn as a transcendent hero, or the book as a celebration of the freedom from culture. Indeed, Huck, like Henry Thoreau, is culturally common in his rebellion against civilization; a conformist in his pursuit of his own unique relationship to the wild, and to the cultural "other," Jim. Huck is also typically American in talking of freedom while capitulating to forces that threaten it—for example, Tom Sawyer, the King, and Duke. Huck's Americanness extends to his naiveté. He's an innocent foil for Twain's own jokes, which makes him vulnerable in a novel where jokes are weapons. Perhaps most important, Huck shares a national penchant for amnesia, which gets him into scrapes, when he forgets who he's supposed to be impersonating.[35] Some memory lapses are strategic; we know little of Huck's previous life because it's too painful to contemplate.

Similarly, Huck's resistance to formal religion represents a classic form of Protestant inwardness. Institutional Christianity simply doesn't make sense to Huck, in keeping with Twain's own response elsewhere to hierarchical Christianity and the Christian Science Church of Mary Baker Eddy. Like other works by Twain, *Huckleberry Finn* values spiritual practices that are spontaneous and common. The book is preoccupied with the cultural rites imbibed by poor children like Huck in antebellum southern communities. Huck is devoted to the spirits that haunt the world, especially at night, demanding propitiation—the burning of a spider in a candle requires a compensatory turning in one's tracks, breast-crossing, and tying of hair. Huck's superstition is a bond with Jim, whose representativeness as a slave is confirmed by his fear of such spirits. According to Huck, "Niggers is always talking about witches in the dark by the kitchen fire."[36] Huck overlooks what the novel as a whole emphasizes: the universality of superstition as the faith of the powerless. For folk belief in *Huckleberry Finn* is also recognized as another means of enslavement. In presenting these ordinary pieties as reaction formations, opiates for the most oppressed of the masses, Twain anticipates the hard-nosed prophecy of the grandmother in Toni Morrison's *Beloved*: "There is no bad luck in the world but whitefolks."[37] Still, there are critical distinctions in the applications of this ecumenical faith, which is sometimes a method of comfort, sometimes of cruelty. The band formed by Tom Sawyer, with its imaginary blood oaths, ravaging of disloyal members' kin, and marking of victims with crosses, recalls an all too real secret brotherhood in Twain's South: the Ku Klux Klan.

Indeed, lynching is a perpetual threat in *Huckleberry Finn*: a savagery that expresses a general state of moral disrepair. The novel abounds in sacrificial scenes: scapegoat rituals, the victimization of animal substitutes, and melodramas of self-sacrifice. This propensity for sacrificial theater is a key component of the novel's burlesque. There may be no scene that more powerfully evokes this theater than the depiction of a sow suckling her young in contented squalor until vicious dogs are set upon her. With characteristic generosity fueled by need, Huck manages to convey the despair of the human "loafers" who initiate this small tragedy, while making us feel the terror of the pig.

> She'd stretch out, and shut her eyes, and wave her ears, whilst the pigs was milking her, and look as happy as if she was on salary. And pretty soon you'd hear a loafer sing out, "Hi! *So* boy! Sick him, Tige!" and away the sow would go, squealing most horrible, with a dog or two swinging to each ear, and three or four dozen more a-coming; and then you would see all the loafers get up and watch the thing out of sight, and laugh at the fun and look grateful for the noise . . . There couldn't anything wake them up all over, and make them happy all over, like a dog-fight—unless it might be putting turpentine on a stray dog and setting fire to him.[38]

The flaming dog has an obvious reference point for Twain's post-Reconstruction South: the lynching of blacks. In the hazy world of *Huckleberry Finn*, where moral discriminations are as obscure as the "dull line" of the sky at sunrise, ritual murder is possibly the only thing that makes people feel alive. The desire of readers to believe Huck superior to these people is not always satisfied by Twain. Though Huck's urgent mobility is the opposite of being stuck in the mud (like the townspeople), it is morally indistinguishable. Good-hearted, full of empathy, with a powerful gift-of-the-gab, Huck is nevertheless culturally common.

Huckleberry Finn is a deeply pessimistic, antisocial novel whose rhythm consists of continual flights from society justified by periodic sojourns into rotten-to-the core communities. Yet the power of the book is its ability to invest a plot of this kind with so much humor and compassion. Jim is far more than an object of mockery. He substantiates the moral relativism that is a moral of the book, by resisting the wisdom of King Solomon, and by recognizing that both Pap and the Widow Douglas are partly right in their antithetical notions of stealing. And for all his associations with the deadly forces of slavery, Jim is the novel's most daring speculator. He is drawn to questions about property, fascinated by money and the money that money can bring. Jim's early speculations might pass as burlesque, but they register his awareness that only by mastering finance will the black man make a place for himself in American society.[39] Jim's biggest economic gamble is running away (to prevent himself from being sold down the river), and he recognizes that in doing so he is now his own capital investment. "I wisht I had de money, I wouldn' want no mo," he says.[40] At the novel's end, Jim owns himself in the eyes of the law as well, but has little to show for it. He feels rich with his $40, which is linked symbolically to both the forty shekels Judas receives for turning in Christ and the forty acres promised but never granted American slaves following their emancipation.[41] The passage confirms the rapid decline in value of black people from slavery to freedom, a devaluation made terribly vivid by lynching.

It is telling that the best prospects for black Americans are captured in the figure of a mulatto, who appears only through a drunken harangue of Pap's. "Most as white as a white man," this freeman from Ohio sports the finest clothes, including a gold watch and a silver-headed cane, "was a p'fessor in a college, and could talk all kinds of languages, and knowed everything." Worst of all, he has the temerity to vote. Pap fumes his way into a "tub of salt pork," to confirm that racists mostly get what they deserve. Yet it is small comfort at the end to see Huck and Tom heading off "for howling adventures amongst the Injuns, over in the Territory." The irrevocable link between one of the great American literary heroes and Indian genocide casts a pall on the narrative. Because it is routinely overlooked in commentary on the novel, the ending also qualifies assurances about national progress on race.[42]

Major avenues for ambitious black Americans in a consumer-capitalist society that remained largely racist can be summarized accordingly. Those who could might "pass," renouncing their black origins to blend imperceptibly into the dominant culture. Whether a bad memory, or a simple "inconvenience," as James Weldon Johnson's ironic alter ego from *The Diary of an Ex-Colored Man* (1912) termed it, the past for those who chose this route was dispensable. Another possibility exemplified by the lives of Wells and Du Bois was tireless political advocacy on behalf of one's people, which required tremendous reserves of strength in the face of continuous setbacks and ongoing evidence of the vitality of American racism. Indeed, both Wells and Du Bois demonstrated in their own lives how exceptional talent and determination could bring a family in one generation from poverty and illiteracy to worldwide fame. Yet a third possibility was personal and family-centered, struggling against the indignities of life as a black American and exploiting opportunities where they could be found, while taking consolation in religion. In her novel *Contending Forces: A Romance Illustrative of Life North and South*, Pauline Hopkins, a New England author educated in the Boston public schools during the 1860s and 1870s, tests these different prospects through the lives of her black middle-class characters. Traumatized by a history of slavery and plagued by humiliations and injustices, Hopkins's cast nevertheless manages to succeed in their Boston environment. Along with contemporaries such as Frances Harper, Emma Dunham Kelley, Anna Julia Cooper, and A. E. Johnson, Hopkins helped to launch a tradition of novels about black upward mobility.

Contending Forces features a melodramatic plot and a range of settings, from Bermuda to North Carolina and Boston. Hopkins begins in the Americas, with the brutal slavery of the British Bermudas at the turn of the nineteenth century. The opening "Tragedy" section recounts the story of the Monforts and their sons, Charles and Jesse, who discover their mother's slave status at their father's death and are immediately sold into slavery. The shift to late nineteenth-century Boston is equally abrupt, and here more characters are introduced; most important, Sappho Clark, a beautiful mulatto who will in turn reveal another major setting—mid-nineteenth-century New Orleans, with its custom of slave concubinages. Hopkins's Boston plot concerns the achievements wrested from a largely hostile turn-of-the century society. While excluded from every viable business and profession, black families still manage to live decently and to cultivate the talents of their children. She compares the plights of blacks with Jews, who also suffer prejudice, and highlights the patient but persistent striving on the part of both peoples. She cites economic inequities, the role of trusts and combinations, and the need for tariff reform as major social problems but insists that none of these is more critical than the problem of racism.

Nor are blacks themselves immune to this pathology. Hopkins seems determined to provide her own form of consciousness-raising in the novel, by introducing an insider's hierarchy of color. Will Smith, the hero and eventual suitor of Sappho, has an almond complexion and curly black hair, unmistakably "Negro," his racial identity is a disappointment to the wealthy, white, female patrons who adore him. Loosely modeled on W. E. B. Du Bois, Smith is an intellectual, aggressive in his attacks on lynching and demands for equal rights. The novel's villain, the weak and hypocritical John Langley, is fair and unidentifiable as a black. Sappho, who lodges at the Smith house and works as a stenographer, is like Will, gorgeously light but definitively "black." The light-skinned Negro, who draws on the best traits of both races, is Hopkins's ideal. His opposite is John Langley, sprung from inferior specimens of white and black. Hopkins specializes in historical figures, and in addition to Du Bois, Booker T. Washington appears in the guise of Dr. Arthur Lewis, a businessman, doctor, and educator with a large industrial school in the South. Then there is Luke Sawyer, a New Orleans mulatto who endures the ruin of his successful father, a store owner, and then the destruction of his family, which includes Sappho herself. Hopkins controls these improbabilities through the usual means—the promise that these characters are all kin and will eventually realize the tangled lines of relation that form the legacy of American blacks. This is the past; as for the future, there is Will Smith, who renounces both subordination and miscegenation. Blacks must advance as a people on their own terms, through education, political activism, and exercising the right to vote.

By insisting that any account of the black American future be informed by its enslaved past, *Contending Forces* satisfied W. E. B. Du Bois's plea for critical engagement with history over preoccupation with one's victimization by it. Du Bois and Hopkins focused on self-improvement—building up the black community from within—as well as self-respect—demanding equal opportunities and legal rights from society at large. Only high ambitions and radical political positions, they believed, would give their people realistic hope of full citizenship in the modern era. James Weldon Johnson, in his *Autobiography of an Ex-Colored Man*, a novel about passing, charts a different course through the prospects and perils of modernism. "It's no disgrace to be black, but it's often very inconvenient" might be taken as the ex-colored man's simple rationale for passing, until the terrible moment when he witnesses a lynching firsthand. Down South to research spirituals, he happens upon the burning alive of a black man for some indeterminate crime. The scene is rendered with all the vividness one might expect from an author who dedicated his political life to the ill-fated Dyer Anti-Lynching

Bill and was almost lynched himself (for sitting in a park with a very light-skinned black woman). The victim writhes, cries, and groans while the crowd cheers, until his body is reduced to scorched bones and skin. The ex-colored man is convinced that the smell of charred human flesh will remain forever with him, as he reacts not with the rage he might have expected but with something more vulnerable and human—shame that he belonged to a nation (America) where something so unimaginable could occur, and shame that he belonged to a people (blacks) who could be so treated.

Johnson understood that lynching was sanctioned in part because it distracted from more civil forms of oppression. But it also helped to rationalize these forms as the inevitable lot of a wretched group. The paradox, as Johnson saw it, was that it took such an effort on the part of whites to keep blacks in the place where inferiors naturally fall. At the same time, Johnson's visceral portrait of lynching confirms how this practice dehumanized everyone. The ex-colored man eventually marries a white woman to whom he reveals his black ancestry. They have children who appear white and who are never told of their father's past. The narrative ends at a Carnegie Hall benefit where the ex-colored man hears Hampton students singing spirituals, and he feels a powerful longing for his mother and her people. The speakers include Mark Twain, but it is Booker T. Washington who arouses the ex-colored man's admiration; he concludes that passing has exiled him not only from his people but also from history.

That history has been the subject of this chapter, and as I have shown throughout, it was a highly contested one. To illustrate, in conclusion, just how ambivalent American cultural attitudes toward black people remained, let me offer an advertisement from the period. If there was any venue where purposes and relationships might be expected to be clear, it was advertising. According to one cultural analyst, American advertising was "happy talk," and it was capable of draining even "from the subject of race nearly all upsetting connotations, making it part of a stylized social backdrop."[43] The analyst refers to a specific advertisement for "Nodark Camera" from *Harper's Magazine*, May 1900, which undeniably promotes the camera's luminous, democratic appeal (Fig. 2). The Nodark camera, named for what it can do—develop photographs without a darkroom—is also universally accessible. "With this camera," reads the small type, "the entire tedious and difficult science of photography is reduced to such simplicity that any child can use it." But the ad also exposes a grim subtext: the persistence of barbarism in a time of technological innovation. For the African American in this ad, arrayed in a costume of alternating black and white, is also, and more resonantly, associated with the images of lynching

Three Minutes

Only required to take, develop, and
finish the above picture with the

NODARK
CAMERA

Size of camera, 3½ in. wide, 4½ in. high, 12 in. long.
Size of pictures, 2½ in. x 3½ in.

With this camera the entire tedious and difficult science of photography is reduced to such
simplicity that any child can use it.

NO DARK ROOM.
No Costly Chemicals.
No Printing Frames.
No Blurs or Hazy Results.

The process is so perfect that every plate comes out
right. There is no secret about the Nodark Camera—
simply a new dry-plate tintype is used instead of glass
plates or films. Every Nodark Camera is complete and
perfect. Also includes 26 plates, 1 developing
chamber, 2 bottles of solution, and instructions
how to operate and make the pictures.

Price $6.00.

Express prepaid.
Buy from your dealer. If he won't supply you, write us.
Free booklet sent on request.

POPULAR PHOTOGRAPH COMPANY,
112 Bleecker Street, New York.

FIGURE 2 ::

Advertisement for Nodark
Camera. From *Harper's
Magazine*, May 1900.

often reproduced in postcards and trade cards of the time that would have been fresh in the minds of *Harper's* readers.

Note how the stark contrasts set in play by the man's clothes—white hat / black brim, black face / white collar; black jacket / white shirt and scarf; white pants / black belt; black left sleeve / white left cuff / black left hand—transform his body and clothes into an ascending series of racial oppositions that are realized in the tree, which appears in the ad as an extension of his body. The tree is drawn into the antipodal play of shades, providing yet another black contrast for the white top of the man's hat, a contrast that is continued in the dark leaves that are set against the light ground and sky. The ad captures the attention of consumers by building subliminally on one of the most vivid and gruesome associations they would have had of black men near trees. *Because* the white scarf, arrayed jauntily on his right shoulder and set in relief by its black-jacket background, *is* a scarf and not the noose that it implies, the man in the Nodark camera ad can smile directly at the camera. His lynched counterpart dangling from a tree in this next image cannot (Fig. 3). Though its conclusion is definitive, the race drama completed by a lynch rope remains essentially ambiguous, from the haphazard clothing, torn partly away from the victim's light-skinned body, to the stick at his ankle that forms an inadvertent cross. The man in the camera ad offers his body in testimony of the "perfect" images produced by Nodark cameras—"No Blurs or Hazy Results." But in race terms the implication of this narrative is less clear. While the man's body is useful for the sake of contrast, there is no suggestion of a role for him in the consumer exchange beckoned by his image. There seems little expectation that *he* will buy a camera.

Instead the man assumes the place, in W. E. B. Du Bois's phrase, of "the swarthy spectre" in "its accustomed seat at the Nation's feast." Almost forty years of extraordinary economic development since the Emancipation Proclamation had bypassed the majority of blacks.[44] And well past the turn of the century, black Americans remained primarily *objects in* advertisements, rather than *subjects to* whom they were addressed. Indeed, the ad for Nodark camera suggests that it was considered better business to exploit prejudice against blacks than to pursue them as a potential growth market. Unintentionally, the camera rationalizes and extends the containment of commercial ends by social customs. The survival of the barbaric practice of lynching in the modern era of mechanical reproduction seems ensured by firsthand reports like the following from the lynching of Thomas Brooks in Fayette County, Tennessee. "Hundreds of kodaks clicked all morning at the scene of the lynching. People in automobiles and carriages came from miles

FIGURE 3 ::

"The lynching of William Brooks. July 22, 1901, Elkins, West Virginia." Courtesy of the Allen-Littlefield Collection, Plate #71. From *Without Sanctuary: Lynching Photography in America*, edited by James Allen, with essays by Leon F. Litwack and Hilton Als, foreword by John Lewis (Santa Fe: Twin Palms, 1999).

around to view the corpse dangling from the end of a rope. . . . Picture card photographers installed a portable printing plant at the bridge and reaped a harvest in selling postcards showing a photograph of the lynched Negro."[45] The link between lynching and what was, by the turn of the twentieth century, a pervasive new technology of photography reminds us that, despite the promises of advertisers who insisted that buying could change being, human behavior, and the beliefs that inspired it, were far more intractable than modern Americans were prepared to admit.

COSMOPOLITANISM

The borders of the American nation were flexible in the late nineteenth century both for those who sought entry and for those who sought exile.[1] This was due in part to the expansion of the American economy and workforce and the growth of tourism among the middle and upper classes. At the same time, migration and resettlement became increasingly common within the country. Some of the most prominent American literature of the period was inspired by these human displacements. The writings examined in this chapter represent a variety of encounters among different types of people in the national and international crucibles where mixing, antagonism, and Darwinian struggle took place. American social life demanded a disposition of cosmopolitanism, which might be characterized as openness to other cultures and to cultural others, as well as to the global interconnectedness that such others implied. As William Dean Howells put it, "The world was once very little, and it is now very large." Moreover, there was growing awareness that the most profound interdependencies of the emerging modern world were undetectable. Such recognitions incited trepidation as well as wonder, and I will be as much concerned in the following pages with anticosmopolitanism as with its embrace. One sign of resistance is the Jewish characters that arouse such vitriol in the fictional worlds of Frank Norris and Edith Wharton, among others, recalling the "rootless cosmopolitans" derided in capital cities across Europe in the post-Enlightenment era. The most consistent form of cosmopolitanism is that conceptualized through the global consumer goods that give, in the words of Karl Marx, "a cosmopolitan character to production and consumption" everywhere, drawing "from under the feet of industry the national ground on which it stood." And the ideal type of cosmopolitanism is exemplified by the heaven of Mark Twain's Captain Stormfield, where earthlings confront their insignificance and begin to appreciate the radical differences afforded by a galactic humanity.[2]

Cities were especially conducive to cosmopolitan consciousness, and major novelists immortalized the ways in which urban environments expanded thought: Frank Norris, San Francisco; Henry James, London, Venice, Paris; Kate Chopin, New Orleans; Abraham Cahan and Edith Wharton, New York. Yet they also revealed regions more remote (the infinite whiteness of Helen Keller; the hyperconsciousness of Henry James's "life after death"; the heaven of Elizabeth Stuart Phelps) as productive of their own kind of worldliness. The human characters introduced in these works are memorable, usually for their peculiarity or excessiveness. These are people incapable of simply "adjusting"—often distinguished by their adventurousness or marginality. Some are suicides (Lily Bart, Edna Pontellier); some murder victims (Trina McTeague); some die of disease (Milly Theale, Alice James); many endure as fragments of their original selves (Yekl, Merton Densher, Vandover). The works discussed in this chapter include classic novellas, immigrant novels and letters, social scientific studies of immigration and religious extremism, autobiographies, biographies, and classic American novels.

These writings offer intimate explorations of a central American theme of mobility and self-transformation during a time when the country was triumphing over competitors like Argentina, Brazil, and industrializing western Europe in the international competition for cheap immigrant labor and averaging more than 5 million newcomers each decade between 1880 and 1920. Due in part to extensive industrialization and technological innovation (and the jobs, housing, and modern transportation systems they produced), the nation's total urban population during the 1880s increased by 56.4 percent. Twenty farmers moved to the city for every urbanite who moved to the land (where recurrent depressions and mechanized farming reduced job opportunities), while ten farming offspring became urbanites for every one who remained a farmer. In 1860, immigrants comprised 40 percent of the populations of major American cities, including New York, Chicago, and San Francisco; by 1910, the population of immigrants and their American-born children had risen to 70 percent in major cities like New York, Chicago, Boston, and Detroit. The result of this rapid expansion and diversification was the fragmentation of urban social life, which however charged with opportunity, could seem vast and unsettling to native, migrant, and immigrant alike.

These urban landscapes proved a critical testing ground for the new science of sociology, which specialized in studies of immigration and urbanization. The German sociologist Georg Simmel, whose writings were translated and published in the *American Journal of Sociology* during the 1890s, and University of Chicago sociologists W. I. Thomas and Robert Park described the new forms of social alienation issuing from international industrial capitalism. In his pioneering study, *The Philosophy of Money*, and in highly original essays on such subjects as fashion, miserliness, and marginality, Simmel described the cosmopolitanism and rationalization of modern global societies, which afforded greater individual freedoms at the same time that they intensified demands for conformity and typecasting. The social deviance issuing from this uprooting of humanity, together with increased racial and ethnic heterogeneity, were of central concern to Thomas and Park. Thomas gained renown for work on the psychology of race prejudice and on delinquency among female adolescents and also for his major account of the Polish peasantry in Europe and America. Park, a close associate of Booker T. Washington, studied the impact of popular media, journalism in particular, as well as the process of assimilation, focusing on how a common culture might be created from the diverse populations of the modern American city and the geographic mobility that helped to produce them.

Cosmopolitanism aroused dis-ease: depression and disaffection were prevalent in a society whose pace and variety seemed relentless. Yet the same circumstances also instilled hope. For it was widely recognized that the burgeoning heterogeneity of a newly global America would be a source of enduring vitality.

COSMOPOLITAN CASUALTIES

Frank Norris, one of the great American novelists of the turn of the twentieth century, was a product of urban life and specialized in its representation. Like so many other realists, Norris began his writing career as a reporter for a city paper. His assignments at the *San Francisco Wave* focused on local sketches: a carnival; a group of Italians making claret; a fresh oyster meal on the wharf at Belmont camp. In an 1897 *Wave* article, Norris celebrated the aesthetic potential of a city whose inhabitants seemed made for fiction. He attributed this to San Francisco's unique isolation; the city was a cauldron for nourishing idiosyncrasies both psychological and cultural. The extreme art of Zola, with its predilection for human weakness, for passionate, sometimes criminal characters who were likened to animals, proved an invaluable model for Norris's representations of this western capital.

Norris's first novel, *Vandover and the Brute* (1897), is a bildungsroman in reverse, its title suggesting an essential divide between the protagonist's civil self, ambitious and well-mannered, and his animal self, overpowered by sensual appetites. Vandover is a San Francisco painter whose ultimate dissipation is confirmed by his inability, late in the novel, to reproduce the great allegorical work "The Last Enemy," a moral commentary on Vandover's own bestial state and that of humanity in general. Featuring a dying British cavalryman, his loyal horse beside him, beset by a menacing lion, the painting mirrors the struggle between the good Vandover (cavalryman), whose refinement is supported by his domesticated dog (horse), and Vandover the Brute (lion), suffering from *Lycanthropy-Mathesis*, Norris's term for the wolfman that Vandover becomes.

The plot elaborates an inevitable Darwinian regression, drawing consistent parallels between individual and social decline. The shipwreck of the *Mazatlan*, during Vandover's passage home after a rest cure, reveals the destructive impact of the survival instinct, as the cruel barring from the lifeboat of a Jewish traveling salesman makes every other life less worthy of salvation. The scene covers all of one chapter and part of another, culminating in a fierce struggle: the scrappy "diamond expert" tries to battle his way aboard (with some passengers defending his inclusion) but loses, the water reddening as his battered body sinks. The narrative's neutrality on the Jew's fate suggests a potential nativist allegory consistent with Norris's other fictions: to rescue the Jew is to doom the Anglo-Saxon collectivity. Though Vandover vomits in response, the event has no lasting impact. Neither does the death of his father, which deals the final blow to Vandover's humanity. These deaths—of the ultimate stranger and ultimate kin—register a failure of affect. Soon after his father's funeral, Vandover marvels at the ease with which he has adjusted to his new circumstances. Espying his father's effects, Vandover slips the pen and knife into his pocket, reserving cigars, gum, and used handkerchiefs for a special collection. Like the "flawed and yellow diamonds" offered Vandover by the Jew, these cosmopolitan commodities stand metonymically for the people who own or seek to transact them. Whether reminders of male potency (pen, knife) or symbols of international trade (cigars, diamonds), these objects suggest a foiled transmission while arousing strong emotion. The power of things, which absorb both the affect and sense of obligation that has been drained from human relations, is a constant in Norris's work. Materialism bordering on fetishism is the key to social degeneration, and it is invariably presided over by a Jew (*McTeague*'s Zerkow, *The Octopus*'s S. Behrman). Jewish characters assume a similar role in Edith Wharton's most successful novel, *The House of Mirth* (1905), which features its own striking continuum between the human and the material.

Indeed, Wharton's decadent New Yorkers, ever on the point of reversion to savagery, share a common destiny with Norris's San Franciscans. Vandover, a janitor at the San Francisco workers' cottages he formerly owned, who is subject to recurrent bouts of lycanthropy, and Lily Bart (the protagonist of *The House of Mirth*), a suicide in a shabby New York boardinghouse, present shocking mirrors of downward mobility. "To think I was a Harvard man once!" Vandover mourns, just as Lily recalls how she socialized with women whose hats she now decorates in an "underworld of toilers." A flood of immigrants, a newly radicalized working class, a vibrant commerce and fluctuating economy that empowers innumerable parvenus—all this is matched in elite minds by their own diminishing work ethic, by moral and spiritual turpitude, and by shrinking birth rates. The somber fates of Vandover and Lily register convictions of class crisis that were widespread.

As the "poet of interior decoration," thoroughly dependent on beautiful houses and furnishings, Wharton could hardly have imagined a more trying end for her heroine.[3] Wharton's first published book, *The Decoration of Houses* (1897), coauthored with Ogden Codman, a celebrated architect, argued that homes should reflect the tastes of their female inhabitants while conforming to classical principles of design. This is consistent with the extent to which things in Wharton's novels, like dresses, hats, books, and rugs, speak worlds about those who use them. Wharton appreciates material splendor (she is in sympathy with her heroine Lily Bart's rapture over her dresses) but recognizes the cost of that appreciation. In *The House of Mirth*, her first major novel, which was serialized in *Scribner's Magazine* (January–November 1905) prior to its publication as a Scribner book, Wharton treated the New York leisure class from the perspective of an intelligent observer, spawned by it but never wholly committed to its norms. When the novel first appeared, some critics complained that Wharton had preyed on her own circle and exposed it to the scrutiny of society at large. The best-selling novel's success was due in part to the voyeurism of ordinary Americans whose infatuation with the rich is integral to its plot.

Wharton seems to have been aware that the novel betrayed class secrets. She was familiar with Thorstein Veblen's 1899 *Theory of the Leisure Class*, and the correspondence between his searing analysis of elite economic habits and Wharton's fictional critique is noteworthy. According to Veblen, those of the upper class maintained their status through aggressive spectacles of consumption supervised by wives. Capitalism, Veblen theorized, encouraged compulsive imitation, cycles of competitive desire fueled by the need to surpass one's neighbors. In *The House of Mirth*, this cycle is sustained by publicity.[4] Newspapers and magazines mediate a growing sense of distance among people by making different social classes seem accessible to one another. The novel's class system is regulated by the advantages and disadvantages of different kinds of exposure: where an unmarried woman is profitably seen (alighting from a train) versus where she is not (entering a bachelor's apartment). It is ruled by an equally ruthless ethos of exchange. In the novel's climactic *tableau vivant* scene, Lily and other marriageable women literalize their commodity status by impersonating the subjects of famous paintings. Lily's transformation into Sir Joshua Reynolds's *Mrs. Lloyd* liberates the passion of the withholding male hero, Selden, whose love requires this confirmation of her value as an artistic masterwork. Selden's ultimate inability to "invest" in Lily, to risk his emotional capital, seconds the miserliness that seals her doom: Lily's disinheritance by an aunt who considers her profligate.

Wharton sets an ideal of inherent nobility against the punishing randomness of market forces. The deepest impoverishment results from the betrayal of long-standing loyalties and beliefs. The Darwinian rapaciousness of her novel's social set signals how far it has fallen from a dignified traditionalism. Yet it is not so far gone that it fails to repudiate the mildly sympathetic Jewish character Rosedale. While marriage to the wealthy Rosedale would offset the financial and moral collapse brought on by Lily's stock market speculations, such a marriage is for her indistinguishable from it. For Wharton, as well as for her characters, aliens represent an insuperable boundary as well as a threat to social stability. In contrast, a genteel working class, exemplified by the virtuous maternity of Nettie Strether, confirms the perpetuation of the class system. Nettie, whose dismal home is likened to a bird's nest on the edge of a cliff, typifies the industrious and sympathetic poor who, Wharton suggests, will always succor the rich. Meanwhile, those who are made for each other, the Seldens and the Barts, must realize their prospects together. This is Selden's tragic recognition at the novel's end. If the white, Anglo-Saxon, aristocratic tribe can grasp this renewed sense of obligation, then Lily Bart will not have died in vain.

Lily Bart's dilemma arises from dispossession and displacement. Her father's lost fortune, Lily's subsequent dependence on self-serving relatives and friends, and her own resentment of this dependence that leads to self-destructive behavior all contribute to her demise. Yet the roots of Lily's doom lie in the particular plight of leisure-class women, who were taught to cultivate their irrelevance. To lack a sense of purpose in a society where success across classes was increasingly defined by the possession of marketable skills or professional status was a predicament unique to female members of a paradoxical American aristocracy. No figure in the late nineteenth century was more sadly representative of this situation than Alice James, who was unable to exploit her own talents or the material and intellectual opportunities afforded by her distinguished family. As with other (mostly female) members of Anglo-American and European elites in the era before Freud's "talking cure" became widely available, the fruitless search for a life's purpose *became* James's vocation. She eventually achieved some fame of her own posthumously, through the 1934 publication of her diary, which provided an original perspective on the transatlantic lives of gifted but unfulfilled women.

In 1894, shortly after James's death, her friend and apparent lover, Katharine Peabody Loring, edited the manuscript of Alice's diary and sent copies to the surviving James brothers. William never acknowledged receiving it, and Henry destroyed his copy, advising Loring not to publish it because it compromised the privacy of so many. These responses epitomized the indifference Alice's brothers had always shown toward her ambitions. Though she belittled them herself, these ambitions were appropriate to a family of cosmopolitan intellectuals. Born in New York City in 1848, Alice was the youngest child and only daughter of Mary and Henry James Sr. Her education, like that of her four brothers, was often disrupted by their father's urge to relocate. Alice suffered from this peripatetic childhood; by adolescence, which coincided with the Civil War, she was a semi-invalid. While brothers Bob and Wilky fought for the Union and William and Henry tested vocations, Alice bemoaned the national spectacle of death while suffering mental and physical trials of her own.

It's unclear exactly what was wrong with Alice, but it appears to have been, at least in part, the notorious neuroses that plagued the whole family and ranged from anxiety and addiction to overwhelming encounters with phantoms. That the most vulnerable members of the James family were the most impaired by such afflictions suggests they suffered from feelings of deprivation and inadequacy. Hence Henry's rather insidious characterization of his sister Alice: "Tragic health was, in a manner, the only solution for her of the practical problem of life." Prevailing antidotes for undiagnosed ills were tried: ice and electric therapy, blistering baths, the notorious S. Weir Mitchell "cure"—force-feeding and compulsory inactivity. When Alice met Katharine Loring in 1873—she was twenty-six and Loring twenty-five—there was an immediate attraction. Alice saw in Katharine an ideal blend of masculine strength and feminine sensitivity. Observing the pair in Europe in 1884, Henry James noted the benefits of the relationship and recommended that his family simply accept it. Alice lived as an invalid without a specified disease until 1891, when doctors discovered breast cancer. Alice faced what she called "the great mortuary moment" with her usual blend of irony and awe. She died in March 1892, with Katharine and Henry by her side, and was cremated, her ashes buried in the family plot in Mt. Auburn Cemetery, Cambridge, Massachusetts.

Alice's diary began as a commonplace book where she stored quotations and ideas from her voluminous reading. But she came to take the book more seriously as she recognized how it allowed her to convert lifelong limitations of mind and body into imaginative art. "The paralytic on the couch can have if he wants them wider experiences than [African explorer Henry M.] Stanley slaughtering savages," she proclaimed. Despite Alice's apparent belief in her intellect's subjection to her body, there's much in the James family history to suggest that Alice's body was a casualty of her devalued mind. Alice's biographer notes how her father underrated female intellect and highlights a familial economy in which one member's rise required another's fall. William's and Henry's professional triumphs, as philosopher and as literary author, respectively, were measured against the failures of the younger brothers and the irrelevance of Alice.[5] This explains the abjection of the diary's speaker, who characterizes herself as a "little rubbish heap," or "mildewed toadstool." Strong-willed yet overlooked, Alice exercised her unfulfilled ambitions through identification with the powerful, claiming, for instance, "the potency of a Bismarck." In keeping with this, the diary is full of aggression—toward servants, acquaintances, her family most of all. But this resentment disappears in the pages devoted to her impending death, which are striking for their lack of self-pity or fear. While this may signal the emptiness of her life, it also confirms the singularity of this lone James sister. Alice confronts death without religious comfort, dismissing requests to deliver messages in heaven and repudiating brother William's latest spiritual adviser. She is a full participant in the ritual plans for her body and speaks openly of cremation, anticipating Katharine's transport of her remains across the ocean.

Alice James, who never felt at home anywhere, might have fancied herself an immigrant, forced to abandon her country in search of the material security that provided her little consolation. Among these immigrants, none knew better than Abraham Cahan the stresses of transplantation and the limitations of affluence in offsetting its effects. Editor of the *Jewish Daily Forward* from its founding in 1897 until his death in 1951 and author of one of the first significant Jewish American novels, *The Rise of David Levinsky* (1917), Cahan was the leading proponent of Jewish socialist culture during the great wave of eastern European immigration. Born in Padberberezer, Lithuania, in 1860, to an orthodox family of rabbis and teachers, Cahan chose a secular over a religious education and taught in government schools until his revolutionary activity forced him to immigrate to America in 1882. Finding work in a New York sweatshop, he joined the labor movement and was soon the main Yiddish speaker for the Propaganda Verein, a socialist-anarchist group whose rallying cry was "In the mother tongue we must agitate among the Jews." A Renaissance man whose professions included teaching, labor organizing, oratory, editing, authorship, and journalism, Cahan was equal to the challenge of a life as an ethnic outsider determined to reform his new country.

Though his early writing appeared in Yiddish American periodicals, Cahan aspired to an English readership and cited Hawthorne, James, and Howells as primary influences. Howells praised Cahan's first story in English, and Cahan returned the favor by translating Howells's *A Traveller from Altruria* into Yiddish and publishing it in the *Jewish Daily Forward*. Howells admired Cahan's fresh depictions of Jewish immigrants and declared Cahan "a new star of realism" in a *New York World* review of *Yekl: A Tale of the Ghetto* (1896). Howells later commended Cahan's *Imported Bridegroom and Other Stories of Yiddish New York* (1898) and *The Rise of David Levinsky*, whose title paid homage to Howells's *The Rise of Silas Lapham* (1885). But Howells's ignorance of Yiddish prevented his firsthand engagement with what many consider Cahan's greatest triumph, his fifty-four-year editorship of the *Daily Forward*. When Cahan took over, the paper's circulation was less than 6,000, attributable largely to its overintellectualized Yiddish and penchant for abstract theory, which alienated even the East Side Jews who sustained a local pushcart trade in works by Tolstoy, Spencer, and Darwin. Cahan introduced colloquial language and expanded the human-interest features. "Within a few months" of Cahan's stewardship, the *Forward*'s circulation "had tripled"; by 1912, it exceeded 130,000.[6] Cahan's democratizing efforts included the "Gallery of Missing Husbands," which printed pictures of men who had deserted families, and an advice column called the "Bintel Brief," or "bundle of letters," where readers expressed the sorrows as well as the miracles of immigration. Begun in 1906, the column grew so popular that writing letters to the Bintel Brief on behalf of others became a profession in its own right. Early on, Cahan answered every letter himself, a veritable

"Miss Lonelyhearts," assuming the roles in turn of confidant, spiritual adviser, job counselor, and therapist.[7] A wife whose husband had survived a Russian pogrom and emigrated, only to become obsessed with the ritual-murder trial in Kiev of a Jew named Mendel Beilis, was advised to find him a good psychiatrist; others were directed to relief agencies, unions, and back to the Old Country.

Whether they wrote to offer wisdom or to obtain it, Bintel Brief correspondents confirmed the losses of assimilation, as do the characters in Cahan's fiction. The gradual replacement of "Yekl" by "Jake" reflects Cahan's ambivalence toward the dominant American values that dazzle his protagonist. Still, powerful impulses persist: Jewish spirituality, which sometimes expands with the avoidance of religious obligations, enlivens the world, investing material things with awesome power. Jake's guilt feelings over his father's death lead to dread of his ghost. The helplessness of Jake's transplanted wife, Gitl, is reflected in her fear of American novelties—stoves, washtubs, painted broomsticks. Bedclothes become burial shrouds as Jake prepares to abandon his wife and child. These images draw on Jewish as well as American legacies, revealing in the process unexpected affinities between the tortured souls of midrashic tales and Hawthorne's stories. Cahan's multicultural realism is as complex psychologically as it is morally. The spurned wife is far from a victim as she establishes herself in a new marriage and grocery business. Yekl is miserable and made all the more so by the culminating recognition that his misery is justified. Cahan's immigrant world administers harsh justice: those who suffer deserve to; those who don't are lucky. Yet they all serve to confirm Cahan's unique contributions to an American literary tradition.

The continuous prospect of revitalization represented by immigration at its best is acknowledged by American social scientists who were professionally preoccupied with its effects. Yet these experts—among them MIT economist Francis A. Walker and University of Wisconsin sociologist Edward A. Ross—could also be formidable gatekeepers. Social scientists appraised immigration from the standpoint of "native" Americans, as Ross did in his influential book *The Old World in the New: The Significance of Past and Present Immigration to the American People* (1914). Ross emphasized the vigor and piety of the English, Dutch, Germans, and Scots, who settled a wilderness for the sake of principle, surviving hardships that would have been intolerable to more recent arrivals. The challenges of immigration in the seventeenth and eighteenth centuries ensured that only the strong would transmit their traits. The greater ease of immigration since the mid-nineteenth century, Ross declared, had enabled the incorporation of weaker foreign strains. Citing Francis Walker's well-known statistics on the causal relationship between high rates of immigration and falling native birth rates, Ross argued that American elites were in danger of extinction. By claiming that Americans were more imperiled by immigration than immigrants themselves were, these analyses provided a curious counterpart to immigrant narratives that lamented the overpowering effects of Americanization.

Increased reproduction rates for the middle and upper classes were one solution to immigration problems proposed by Anglo-American social scientists and echoed by many at the turn of the century.[8] This is why novels like Kate Chopin's *The Awakening* (1899), which portrayed a leisure-class Protestant woman devoid of maternal instinct, disturbed readers. The book was removed from the public library in Chopin's hometown of St. Louis and prompted her expulsion from the city's Fine Arts Club. Most reviewers condemned the wife and mother who neglected her children, committed adultery, drank, gambled, and then drowned herself in an apparent fit of ennui. Chopin was forty-eight and well established when *The Awakening* was published, having authored more than a hundred stories, essays, and sketches. A widowed mother of six with a plantation to run, Chopin wrote in her spare time. While the novel's protagonist, Edna Pontellier, seemed self-indulgent and inarticulate to a degree that appealed to some and maddened others, no one denied that a new sensuality and precision had been introduced in American writing.

Chopin's portrait of Edna Pontellier anticipates Freud on the troubled lives of upper-class women and corroborates the conclusions of feminists as well as more conservative social scientists. For feminists (e.g., Charlotte Perkins Gilman and Willa Cather), women are burdens to themselves and others because they are denied educational and professional opportunities. For social scientists (e.g., S. Weir Mitchell, G. Stanley Hall, and Herbert Spencer), women are dissatisfied because they resist what comes naturally— mothering, housekeeping, modeling virtue. Chopin's narrative begs the question of "what's wrong with Edna" by having so many characters pose it. Edna may be a classic "hysteric," or a "normal" woman driven to rebellion by the limitations of her social role. Yet Edna's discontent is also rooted in her family and culture. Born in Kentucky, raised as a Presbyterian, Edna's lifelong struggle with affect and attachment make her marriage to a Creole Catholic partly therapeutic. In contrast to the warmth and cohesiveness of her husband's world, Edna's background suggests isolation: her mother's early death, her father's narcissism and alcoholism, the mutual hostility between Edna and her sister. Protestant individualism is directly invoked by way of Emerson, whose work puts Edna to sleep but also supports her increasing tendency to see others as threatening to self-development.

The novel's significance lies in its candid presentation of dilemmas generated by modern democratic society: the status of women, the limitations of materialism, the value of life itself. By picturing a discontented wife and mother who chooses suicide over her comfortable existence, Chopin raises questions about the liberal individual's relationship to death and women's potential to *be* liberal individuals. *The Awakening* can be read as defending suicide against the claim that one is socially obligated to choose life. Chopin's is the first American novel to confront death without the qualification of religious faith. Death is a return for Edna to the womb of same-sex desire implied in her attraction to the voluptuous "mother-woman" Madame Ratignolle. Standard feminist interpretations see Edna Pontellier awakened to the limits on her aspirations, whether they deem it disappointing (she might have chosen feminist activism) or inspiring (for yielding a feminist martyr). Yet the novel also supports a more radical feminist alternative: the story of a "consciousness raised" beyond the norms of her society. Nature, represented by the sea, prevails at the novel's end, affirming women's basic affinity with its rhythms. By picturing the allure of nature over the dissatisfactions of modern urban life, Chopin was joining a cross-gender dialogue that included, among others, Frank Norris.

Like Chopin, Norris was drawn to the forces that resisted civilization. To grasp and re-create this primitivism, Norris implied, was to gain insight into the most intractable social problems and the social designs that were simply unworkable. Norris's convictions drew on a turn-of-the-century social scientific perspective that feared the savagery of human nature, at the same time that it lamented a modern order's alienation from it. Contemporary efforts to institutionalize the wild, such as the creation of urban parks, zoos, and conservation areas and the popularity of the Rough Riders and the Boy Scouts, were means of communing with nature while identifying its imperilment. The future of American fiction, according to Norris, lay in the repudiation of an artificial modernity and the realistic recognition of life as a Darwinian struggle. The urban settings of his fiction—typically miniaturized, claustrophobic—appear incommensurate with the simple power of his protagonists, who struggle against a punishing social order until they are merged with the wilderness.

McTeague, the novel that earned Norris respect and even celebrity as a writer, according to William Dean Howells, ignored the "provincial proprieties" in favor of "the savage world which underlies as well as environs civilization." Norris took heart in such reviews, as he did in the book's strong sales. The novel's immediate inspiration was the 1893 San Francisco murder of a washerwoman at a local kindergarten, killed by her husband, a brute made more terrible by alcohol, who had become enraged because she would not give him money. These facts, together with the Lombroso-inspired descriptions of the murderer from the *San Francisco Examiner*, were incorporated into the novel.[9] Set in San Francisco, *McTeague* opens on a bachelor dentist's typical Sunday: dining at a saloon, resting in his dental parlors, drinking steam beer from a pail, and playing his concertina, his lone companion a canary. The final scene depicts McTeague in Death Valley, chained to a lifeless body, the same canary half dead. Between these bookends, Norris weaves a grim plot, with occasional moments of relief. A love story at base, *McTeague* emphasizes the gender polarities that drive love and make brutality so often its issue. *McTeague* features miserliness, wife battery, sterility, senility, individual degeneracy, and social decline. Stripped of his professional title, McTeague becomes a toolmaker, a piano mover, a miner; his wife, Trina, descends accordingly: homemaker, toy maker, washerwoman. Characters struggle up the social ladder to be dashed down: from the mediation and control of sensual appetites (reconceived as "tastes" and "pleasures") by bourgeois rites of passage (professionalism, courtship, marriage), to the rule of animal instinct.[10]

Social bonds have worn thin in the novel's profane-sacred world: kinship counts little; friendship counts less. Bloodlines transmit debility rather than aptitude. One four-block radius features German, Scotch, Irish, Mexican, black, and Jew: a society of hoarders and misfits, consumed with losses and assets, devoted to the miserly prospect of self-containment. Yet Norris also specifies miserliness and reduction as female traits, exemplified by the withdrawal of the most precious social commodity. Women in *McTeague* are reproducers who don't reproduce, their shriveled bodies likened to empty money bags. Thus, the novel nullifies the means to the immigrant poor's notorious advantage over Anglo-American ruling classes in this era. The community's lone offspring, the frail "hybrid" of the Jewish Zerkow and Mexican Maria Macapa, dies shortly after birth. The novel's close, a fight to the death between McTeague and the German Marcus Schouler, provides a multiple offering in the desert. No less than three victims are laid before the desert gods—two humans and a canary. But like everything else in this novel of stylized excess, the scene ends without spiritual edification, weighed down (rather than lifted) by its sacrificial freight.

Violence results from the discrepancy between human need and social forms. To some extent this discrepancy is gendered—males are wild; women are urban. Yet what makes *McTeague* so complex and moving is the instability of these gender polarities. The agent of civility, Trina, is as a miser the most socially resistant of characters. Meanwhile, the wilderness that eradicates all humanizing prospects is plainly feminized. The drive toward extinction in *McTeague* is thus independent of gender. It is both feminine and masculine: evident in Trina's refusal to hand over her gold, though she knows McTeague will kill her, and in McTeague's desert battle with Marcus. Both are forms of suicide: flights from civilization and its trappings, toward the death that is as "interminable" and "measureless" as the desert itself. In this way the plot of *McTeague* recalls Norris's characterization of San Francisco for the *Wave*, as a "pinpoint" in the wilderness "circle of solitude." Civilization out West is provisional, aching to be submerged in the surrounding terrain.

The preceding section of this chapter explored the experiences of those crippled by cosmopolitanism, by being at home nowhere, neither in their country of origin nor in their adopted one. The following section features individuals who managed to find creative license in their displacement. It includes some of the most distinctive voices of the period—Helen Keller, William and Henry James, Mark Twain, Elizabeth Stuart Phelps, Mary Baker Eddy—all of whom deliberately violated the borders between the familiar and the alien; the scientifically legitimate and the unexplained; the normative and the estranged. They pursued these borders involuntarily: Helen Keller was deaf and blind; the James brothers were subjected to nervous illness; Eddy was psychologically fragile; Twain and Phelps were continually plunged into mourning for dead family and lovers. Yet all of them understood their explorations into the unknown in collective terms and took their roles as spiritual guides seriously.

In so doing, these individuals fulfilled trends that were widespread among intellectuals in this turn-of-the-century era. Despite their extensive knowledge of advances in social science as well as in "hard" science and their repudiation of conventional religious practices, they each resisted thoroughly secular explanations of human experience. While all of these thinkers struggled variously, in public, to accommodate the challenge to religion represented by the advent of Darwinism and the establishment of the social sciences, they also provided, in private, living testimonies to the limits of such paradigms. In this way, they personify the qualification of the secularization thesis—the idea that religion was being replaced by scientific understanding in this era. Figures like the James brothers and Elizabeth Stuart Phelps, Mark Twain and Helen Keller thus serve to exemplify the persisting power of spirituality in the age of science. As a leading American sociologist of the time put it, "From first to last, religions have been men's more or less conscious attempts to give finite life its infinite rating. Science can never be an enemy of religion . . . the more science we have the more are we awed and lured by the mystery beyond our ken."[11]

Mark Twain once observed that the two most interesting people of the nineteenth century were Napoleon and Helen Keller. He only met one of them, however, and Keller herself describes in *The Story of My Life* how she "listens" to his stories by holding her hands to his lips. Keller, who became blind and deaf from scarlet fever at the age of nineteen months, was a major figure of her time in part because the account of how her darkness was relieved touches upon so many significant cultural developments. An Alabama native whose father was a Confederate officer, Keller was adopted by an eastern educational establishment—the Perkins Institute for the Blind, the prestigious Cambridge School, and Radcliffe University—eager to make amends with the South in this post–Civil War era. She was discovered by Alexander Graham Bell, who introduced her to Michael Anagnos, director of the Perkins Institute, and was later befriended by such prominent figures as William Dean Howells, Oliver Wendell Holmes, William James, and Henry H. Rogers, the Standard Oil trustee who supported Twain.[12] Keller's intellectual ability and the unique sensitivities she developed as a result of her physical condition and her experience of different regions and environments made her a "cosmopolitan" in body and soul.

Keller's southern background heightened her awareness of the racial caste system that became even more entrenched in the years following Emancipation. Her teacher, Anne Sullivan, noted the seven-year-old Keller's fascination with racial distinctions, expressed in a view of how minds might replicate the nation's notorious color line, with her servant's thoughts "black" and hers "white." The most dramatic event in Keller's childhood was her recognition of language: the moment when she connected the sensation of running water on one hand with her teacher's spelling out "w-a-t-e-r" on her other. Language, she later recalled, delivered her from an alien existence to "kinship with the rest of the world." Keller excelled in particular, according to Sullivan, in the "unconscious language of the emotions," divining the dispositions of others from the slightest movement, in confirmation of the fact that every thought and emotion has a corresponding physical expression.[13]

Keller's appreciation for her limited but intensified faculties is evident throughout *The Story of My Life*, which was partly serialized in the *Ladies Home Journal* (1901) before its publication as a best-selling book (1902). She absorbed the world through every sensible pore, registering daybreak at a campout by inhaling the rich aroma of coffee and by feeling the stamping feet of horses and the warm breath of awakened dogs. She thrills to the experience of tobogganing down steep slopes across a frozen lake. At Niagara Falls in 1893, she responds to the vibrating air and trembling earth. She tours the Chicago world's fair with a special presidential pass that allows her to touch the exhibits so that "wonders from the uttermost parts of the earth—marvels of invention, treasuries of industry and skill and all the activities of human life actually passed under my finger tips."[14] Keller in all her writing and lectures distinguished between deep, intuitive learning and education, which demands coverage without time for the careful synthesis of material. Because readers failed to grasp Keller's ironic wit, and also because her views on her elite Ivy League education *were* genuinely subversive, Keller's assessment of her college years incensed readers. In Anne Sullivan, the daughter of poor Irish immigrants who was partially blind herself, Keller had an innovative educator whose style suited her own. Sullivan believed that education was a natural process and emphasized freedom and play over rote instruction. A pragmatist at heart, Sullivan saw no reason why the acquisition of sign language should be any different from more conventional modes of language acquisition. Months of listening and responding to others provided a critical pathway to speech, instilling an intricate grammar well before average children could speak. Sullivan performed the same operations manually with Keller, "talking into her hand" in complete sentences, modeling the speech forms she sought to instill. Sullivan's success was ensured by her empathic pedagogy, which was marked by a willingness to admit defeat while remaining optimistic and an abiding respect for her pupil.

Keller excelled in literary critical pursuits. Reading for her involved the creation of an inner sanctum where thought was wholly internal and intensified. In this way, reading provided a means of luxuriating in her separateness, of locating some advantages in her plight. Here, for instance, Keller reacts to Omar Khayyám: "I feel as if I had spent the last half-hour in a magnificent sepulcher. Yes, it is a tomb in which hope, joy, and the power of acting nobly lie buried."[15] Reading entombed provides an alternative to the other kind of death toward which Keller demonstrated a primed sensitivity. As she observed of plant growth in one of her essays for Radcliffe English professor Charles T. Copeland, "Now I understand that the darkness everywhere may hold possibilities better even than my hopes."[16] Keller's life exemplified the prospects of this darkness, astonishing her compatriots with the bounty of the unknown and invisible. This bounty was always apparent to Keller's friend and contemporary, the great American philosopher William James, another "cosmopolitan mind" who shared her boundless curiosity, as well as her resistance to artificial boundaries of all kinds.

Among the divisions that James challenged were those between professional and amateur science. Once described as having "a pathological repugnance to the processes of exact thought," James was in his element in the series of essays he wrote on mysticism and the occult for a large general audience.[17] "The Hidden Self" appeared in *Scribner's Magazine* in 1890, a popular forum that welcomed James's claim for the interdependence between the emerging science of psychology and the work of mediums and mystics. In occasional debates between scientists and mystics, James notes, the scientists prevail in theory, but the mystics command the facts. James praises French scientists for their receptivity to commonplace practices, which he attributes to the culture's appreciation of human variety. In the Havre study of hysteria conducted by Monsieur Janet, the discovery of different levels of consciousness as well as alternative consciousnesses within individuals radicalized the therapeutic prospects for a range of ailments. James believed that psychic research and Christian Science held the same potential. He especially admired the research of Frederic Myers, founder of the British Society for Psychical Research, whose liberal explorations—of unconscious cerebration, hypnotism, hysteria, hallucinatory voices, mediumtrances, demoniacal possession, clairvoyance, thought-transference, and ghosts—led James to conclude that nature is "gothic, not classic."[18]

James's democratic intellect was realized in the pragmatic insistence that ideas be rooted in experience, a view whose magnum opus was *The Varieties of Religious Experience* (1902).[19] Religion, James suggests, involves "the feelings, acts, and experiences of individual men in their solitude, so far as they apprehend themselves to stand in relation to whatever they may consider the divine."[20] James's science of particulars requires concrete examples from all times and places: Tolstoy, John Bunyan, St. Francis, Rousseau, Mohammed, Martin Luther, George Fox, Jonathan Edwards, Ignatius Loyola, the Spanish Jesuit Molina, the Persian philosopher and theologian Al-Ghazzali, Walt Whitman, Joseph Smith, Nietzsche, Tennyson. The spiritualities of these "representative men" encompass extrasensory perception, optimism, Lutheran theology, mind-cure, pessimism, self-division, conversion, saintliness, mysticism, asceticism, automatism, and anthropomorphism. The religious temperament as he presents it is marked by painful extremity. In keeping with this, James's lone firsthand experience concerns a profoundly "Sick Soul": a black-haired, green-skinned asylum patient with whom the visitor feels a terrifying kinship. James avoids identifying the visitor and remains a nervous wreck long after the encounter, but the persona was widely believed to be James himself. Indeed, the incident resembles the disabling "vastation" experienced by Henry James Sr. when his sons were boys. Such delusional instances, James observes, explain the persistence of revivalism and other orgiastic religions: powerful anxieties require powerful solutions. Hence, the most successful religions—Christianity, Buddhism, and Judaism—have the most highly developed pessimistic elements.

In a postscript to the book version of the lectures, James describes his own beliefs. He conceives that for every individual there is a "godlike self, of which the present self would then be but the mutilated expression."[21] With as many types of divinity as there are human beings, James's theology amounts to a rejuvenated polytheism in modern American dress. *The Varieties of Religious Experience* revealed James's respect for the authority of individual experience as well as the humility of one of the era's great minds. What some dismissed as hallucinations, James treated with scientific care. He saw credibility in the continuity of religious faith across time and place. Worshippers in widely varying settings advanced the same evidence for their belief in God. James's tolerance for experiences both remote and diverse exemplifies his lifelong commitment to human idiosyncrasies and his enduring attraction to the unknown.

John Dewey noted of William and Henry James that "the former is concerned with human nature in its broad and common features . . . while the latter is concerned with the special and peculiar coloring that the mental life takes on in different individualities."[22] Mental differences, however, should not obscure the cosmopolitan mind-sets they shared as both a familial legacy and acquired intellectual dispositions. The cosmopolitanism that William cultivated as a disciplinary method in the fields of psychology and philosophy Henry transformed into a formal literary art. The volumes Henry James produced over a long literary career provide a wealth of views on morality, religion, and psychology. But one distinctive essay, "Is There a Life after Death?" (1910), reveals Henry engaged in the type of inquiry professionalized by his brother. Both Henry and William confronted the mortality question against a paternal backdrop of optimistic Christianity and Transcendentalism to which neither subscribed. Their own conceptualizations originated in their experiences of consciousness: having inhabited such fertile minds and interacted with so many others, neither accepted that these vital organs could simply expire at death. As William wrote in a 1908 letter to Charles Eliot Norton, "I am as convinced as I can be of anything that this experience of ours is only a part of the experience that is, and with which it has something to do; but *what* or *where* the other parts are, I cannot guess."[23] Henry shares William's confidence, suggesting that preparation for an imaginatively heightened afterlife is made through life-long devotion to the intellect. Far from a loss, then, death is a release for the most cultivated minds into an elite republic of consciousness.

Henry's novels, where the thoughtfulness of characters often over-whelmed the plots, reflected his fascination with intellection. William com-plained that his brother had "reversed every traditional canon of story-telling, especially the fundamental one of *telling* the story." William was referring to *The Wings of the Dove* (1902), which, Henry conceded, had a head "too big . . . for its body." He had sought, he continued, "to write one with the opposite disproportion—the body too big for its head. So I shall perhaps do if I live to 150."[24] The dramatic action of *The Wings of the Dove* consists of a series of minds grappling with the meaning of death. By setting a beautiful American heroine, Milly Theale, rich, generous, ill, and entirely alone, against a pair of British lovers, Kate Croy and Merton Densher, handsome in their own right, intelligent, and penniless, the novel asks whether death can ever be beautiful and whether the dead care about anything, including what happens to their money.

The Wings of the Dove is notorious for what it fails to represent: the late sexual encounter between Densher and Kate; the devastating interview in which Lord Mark reveals to Milly Kate and Densher's scheme to inherit her money; Milly's final meeting with Densher; and Milly's letter accompany-ing her bequest to the lovers. The novel's closing account of Milly's trium-phant afterlife might be understood as James's ultimate fantasy of immor-tality. In death, she embraces her designation as the dove of the title, offering her gift on Christmas Eve, enfolding all in a winged mantle that divides as well as protects. Milly's design is inescapable, especially after Kate burns Milly's letter, ensuring that her bequest will remain open to inter-pretation. Densher's subsequent devotion to the dead Milly recalls his mas-turbatory reenactment of his sexual consummation with Kate. While this parallel possibly suggests an erasure of the first scene (sex) by the second (death), it also highlights a prevailing novelistic economy. Kate forsakes her virginity and Densher for a fortune; Densher exchanges a live woman for a dead one he will never lose. Death itself is incommensurable, a nullification of the very idea of commensurability. Yet it is in death, according to James, where we exist solely in consciousness and are known only in the hearts and minds of others, that we have the most power to arouse love and to control loved ones.

Like *The Wings of the Dove*, *The Turn of the Screw* is centrally concerned with the control of the living by the dead. As the narrator, the governess transfixes her audience with her story from the beyond, and the divide between the dead and the living remains permeable throughout. The narrative highlights boundaries of all kinds—architectural (doors, windows, corridors, stairways), natural (dawn, twilight), class (uncle / governess, servants / children, governess / housekeeper)—and their regular violation. Indeed, James often characterized art as a region to be entered, frequented, and haunted. Writing is ghostly, a means of communing with and reanimating the dead. Thus, the governess apprehends the ghost of Quint while writing—"I saw him as I see the letters I form on this page." James anticipates Walter Benjamin in suggesting that novels provide an essential access to death. We need the novel, according to Benjamin, "because this stranger's fate by virtue of the flame which consumes it yields us the warmth which we never draw from our own fate. What draws the reader to the novel is the hope of warming his shivering life with a death he reads about."[25] Defined as spectacles of extinction, novels provide the continuous satisfaction of substituting our own death with that of others.

Elizabeth Stuart Phelps and Mark Twain used the novel form to slightly different ends in this era: to comfort reading audiences by picturing, with seriousness and humor, what the afterlife might really be like. Phelps's great success with the *Gates* trilogy was attributable in part to the ordinariness of their assumptions: that the spirits of the dead were accessible; that heaven was an ideal place, recognizable to all Christians, including the least devout; and that popular visions of the afterlife were reconcilable with orthodox Christianity. The books were inspired by the ideas of a thriving spiritualist movement, which, according to Harriet Beecher Stowe, counted four to five million adherents after the Civil War. Phelps's receptivity to alternative spiritual practices expressed her intellectual commitment to making Christianity amenable to new psychic, religious, and scientific developments. The vitality of Christianity in the next century, according to Elizabeth Stuart Phelps, required its redefinition as cosmopolitan.

Beyond the Gates (1883) and *The Gates Between* (1887) surpass their predecessor, *The Gates Ajar*, by providing protagonists who actually experience the afterlife firsthand. *Beyond the Gates* is the story of forty-year-old Mary, the unmarried daughter of a clergyman, who has worked tirelessly on behalf of others: as a teacher, Civil War nurse, and member of the Sanitary Commission, the Freedmen's Bureau, and the State Bureau of Labor. Despite this, she is neither pious nor ecstatic, having struggled to believe in God, immortality, and the history of Jesus Christ. Ill from scarlet fever, she falls into a deep sleep and finds her long dead father in her sickroom, prepared to escort her to heaven. Throughout her celestial odyssey, Mary emphasizes that her accounts only approximate what she has witnessed, for there is no language to express the perfection of heaven. The place where every individual is fully realized through the patient, loving counsel of Christ embraces even Mary, who has always been wracked by doubt. A site of unlimited potential, heaven incorporates all times and cultures. Here one meets great minds and leaders—Loyola, Joan of Arc, Luther, Newton, Columbus, Darwin—beholds cavemen, tours the solar system, encounters literary characters in the flesh—Hester Prynne, Uncle Tom, Jean Valjean—and is compensated for life's disappointments. Mary is just on the point of uniting with a lost beau, when she awakens to a bitterly cold New England winter morning to discover her visit to heaven was a dream.

When *he* dies, the protagonist of *The Gates Between*, the final work of Phelps's trilogy, actually gets to stay. The year is 187—, and the protagonist, forty-nine-year-old Esmerald Thorne, has been married four years, having met his wife after building a medical career and a fortune. While fully apprised of Helen's goodness and beauty, he remains a self-involved work-aholic, preoccupied with power, pleasure, and money. His first challenge is letting go: he hovers about the living, absorbing reactions to his death, poring over stock returns. In heaven, he wanders aimlessly, until his young son appears. Thorne learns to care for him, meets Christ, gains faith, and is rewarded by the heavenly reunion of his family through the ascension of his wife. The book closes with a taunting epigraph. "Perceiving that inquiry will be raised touching the means by which I have been enabled to give this record to the living earth, I have this reply to make: That is my secret. Let it remain such."[26]

Phelps's treatments of the afterlife were profoundly appealing to readers who made best sellers of all three *Gates* books. Mark Twain's *Extract from Captain Stormfield's Visit to Heaven* was conceived as a satire of Phelps's series that centered on its exclusiveness: Phelps's heaven is designed on behalf of white, middle-class readers who can expect to find only people like them-selves there. Despite this disdain, however, Twain's conceptions of the afterlife, like Phelps's, grew out of deeply held beliefs. As all his writings attest, Twain was well versed in a complex religious legacy, featuring his father's free thought, his mother's Presbyterianism, and his indoctrination into a Hannibal, Missouri, culture of Campbellite revivalists. *Captain Storm-field* was revealing of Twain's thinking on death at the same time that it cashed in on the popular accounts of heaven that it critiqued.[27] Profits from the magazine publication of the novella went into a wing of a new house in Redding, Connecticut, appropriately called "Stormfield." The novella origi-nated, Twain claimed, in the dream of a friend, Captain Ned Wakeman, who loved the Bible and knew it through and through. Yet Twain's mark is everywhere, and it's clear that what irked him especially about Christian heavens he had encountered was their exclusivity and parochialism. The act of imagining heaven was typically an exercise of control. In Twain's hands it became the opposite: an assertion of humility, the recognition of the meager position of human beings in an infinite universe. Methods of measurement devised on earth are inadequate to the cosmos. Captain Stormfield arrives in heaven after spinning through space for countless light years and finds himself in line behind a sky-blue man with seven heads and one leg. The captain's heavenly indoctrination will involve an ongoing recognition of human insignificance. Officials at heaven's gate have never heard of San Francisco, California, the United States, or even earth. When they finally manage to locate earth's solar system on a map, after days of searching, Stormfield learns that it is referred to as "the Wart."

Twain's cosmopolitan heaven offers a further repudiation of nationalism by highlighting the "mongrel" character of all peoples. In keeping with its multicultural composition, heaven's luminaries come from all times and places, some of them recognizable, some of them obscure. Shakespeare, Homer, Confucius, Buddha, and Mahomet walk behind a common tailor from Tennessee and a horse doctor named Sakka from Afghanistan. The Christian precept "the last shall be first" prevails: the Tennessee horse doctor was a scapegoat in his village, so humble that he never imagined getting to heaven, let alone being exalted there. Twain's mass-society heaven reveals life forms everywhere: when Captain Stormfield perches happily on a cloud, he finds a million others perching nearby. Stormfield wonders late in the narrative about the dearth of blond angels and is given a quick demography lesson: white people are a blip in a human history dominated by copper-colored peoples. Other traditional doctrines are likewise dispensed with. Suffering and pain exist in heaven just as on earth, for "happiness ain't a *thing in itself*—it's only a *contrast* with something that ain't pleasant . . . there's plenty of pain and suffering in heaven—consequently there's plenty of contrast, and just no end of happiness."[28]

Twain's receptivity to an alternative afterlife paralleled his receptivity to Christian Science, which dated back to his childhood. As a boy, he watched a farmer's wife, a renowned healer, relieve his mother's suffering from toothache. A similar practitioner miraculously cured his wife Olivia's paralysis. His daughter Clara, diagnosed with hysteria, became a Christian Scientist, and his other two daughters, Susy and Jean, sought help from its novel practices. Twain's conversance with Christian Science complicated his writings about it. Though he despised its institutionalization under Mary Baker

Eddy, he knew that it had helped people. Thus the *Philadelphia Medical Journal* expressed dismay at what they took to be Twain's sincere respect for Christian Science, while Harper and Brothers understood Twain's message to be the opposite when they withdrew the book from publication in 1903 for fear that it would offend the Eddy establishment. It's easy to see how Twain's *Christian Science* (1902) could have aroused such different responses.[29] For Twain demonstrates his usual capacity to authenticate belief, even when he is at odds with or ridiculing it. He describes how "loving mercifulness and compassion . . . heals fleshly ills and pains and griefs—*all*—with a word, with a touch of the hand" that "any Christian who was in earnest" might "cure with it *any disease or any hurt or damage possible to human flesh and bone.*"[30] Thus Christ's touch is revived through the ages by the simple miracle of faith. Given the wonder Twain displays in all of his writings toward the tenacity of belief and its dramatic possibilities, his fascination with a religion based on the positive powers of mind is understandable. Twain admired Christian Science's granting of such awesome authority to the mental faculties, especially in matters of health.

Yet Twain was contemptuous of Eddy's exploitation of human vulnerability. "I do not think her money-passion has ever diminished in ferocity, I do not think that she has ever allowed a dollar that had no friends to get by her alive."[31] A consummate businesswoman, Eddy's astonishing success as the prophet of Christian Science raised disturbing questions about the roots of great spiritual leadership. Twain's central claim in *Christian Science*, which opens with a burlesque about a man who falls off a mountain, breaks every bone in his body, and discovers that the only doctor for miles is a Christian Scientist, is that alternative medicines are reasonable responses to a medical establishment that is often helpless toward the most basic afflictions. Problems arise, however, when alternatives themselves become doctrinaire. Twain tended to welcome any method, spiritual or physical, that lightened the load of human beings, relieving a burden of suffering that grew in Twain's mind the older he got and the more loved ones he lost. But like his yearning for miracles, Twain's resentment toward frauds grew as he aged.

Twain was not the only major American writer to appreciate the possibilities in Christian Science. Theodore Dreiser sent his ailing "Genius" to a Christian Science practitioner in the final chapters of his 1915 novel, and Harold Frederic, author of *The Damnation of Theron Ware* (1896), was subjected, controversially, to a Christian Science treatment after suffering two strokes in 1898 because his lover, Kate Lyon, a devotee, refused conventional medicine. But the writer who was most profoundly conversant with the history and doctrines of Christian Science was Willa Cather, who ghost-wrote a major biography of its founder as her first assignment at the New York editorial offices of *McClure's Magazine*, advertised in its time as "the marketplace of the world." Cather began work at *McClure's* in 1906 at the age of thirty-two, after having published thirty stories of her own. The materials on Eddy's life and Christian Science had been collected by Georgine Milmine, a newspaperwoman, who was given credit for both the Eddy articles serialized in *McClure's* in 1907–8 and the book, *The Life of Mary Baker G. Eddy and the History of Christian Science*, published by Doubleday in 1909. According to editors close to the project and Cather's companion, Edith Lewis, however, Cather was the principal author. Cather scholars have recently recognized the biography as her first long work, to which she devoted eighteen months of sustained attention.

Although Cather sought to minimize her ties to the book because of its controversial nature, and although she disdained journalism, her biography of Mary Baker Eddy addressed concerns that run throughout her career. The book emphasizes the significance of a religion headed by a woman, while questioning the effects of Eddy's charismatic authority. Cather appears both fascinated and disturbed by the spiritual craving that drew converts from the isolated, snowbound villages of Vermont and Massachusetts and the remote settlements of Nebraska and Colorado to the patent deceptions of Mary Baker Eddy. But what most impressed Cather was all that Eddy lacked, personally, intellectually, and morally. According to Cather, Eddy was a failed daughter, wife, mother, and writer, as well as a failed religious leader, to the extent that such a vocation required a gift for fostering spiritual community. The fact that Eddy succeeded on the scale that she did is evidence for Cather of what counted in her time: commercial skills. The ability to capitalize on opportunities and to synthesize the innovations of others, combined with overweening ambition and greed—these characteristics enabled Eddy to launch a religious empire.

Cather proves an adept biographer, combining critical toughness and understanding. She is at once comprehensive and precise, filling her narrative with memorable images: Eddy's father, Mark Baker, haranguing neighbors for violating the Sabbath when he had mistaken Monday for Sunday; Mary's childhood hysterics, which undermine her widower father's domination; the adult-sized cradle hauled through the streets by Mary's second husband, so she can be rocked to sleep every night; Mary abandoned by her family and forced to be a guest in a series of homes, where she is waited on like royalty. Eddy, it appears, was a hypochondriac and at the same time genuinely fragile; she absorbed fads like a sponge. Her various enthusiasms, for mesmerism, spiritualism, and homeopathic healing, cover a range of her era's popular spiritual movements. But the crucial event was her visit to Phineas Parkhurst Quimby, who had devised a method of healing through the simple, benevolent power of mind. A clock-maker by trade, inventor of the famous Quimby clock, he had a natural aptitude for mechanics. In Cather's words, he was "a mild-mannered New England Socrates, constantly looking into his own mind, and subjecting to proof all the commonplace beliefs of his friends."[32] Drawing on Christ's mission of healing, Quimby argued that the very concept of disease indicated false reasoning, derived not from God but from man. When Eddy came to him in 1863, she was impoverished and emaciated. Quimby's treatment for her spinal trouble left her miraculously pain-free. She became a disciple, poring over his manuscripts and writing letters to local newspapers to champion the cure. Quimby died in 1866 from a stomach tumor that stubbornly resisted his own methods; nine years later Eddy published *Science and Health*, a book largely based on his ideas, which failed to identify him as their originator.

The 1875 version of *Science and Health* was riddled with errors and poor writing, and it was largely ignored. Eddy began with the basic principle that mind is the only causation and the body is the mere instrument of spirit. Building on Quimby's association of the imperfection of matter with human beings and the perfection of mind with God, Eddy identified Adam in the book of Genesis as "the man of error," the source of all sickness.[33] The expulsion of Adam from Eden resulted in the separation of matter from mind, a breach that persisted for centuries, until the appearance of Christ, "the most scientific man of whom we have any record" and "the Great Teacher of Christian Science."[34] Eddy joined numerous theologians in positing a New Testament notion of divine sentience favorably against an Old Testament notion of divine omnipotence. Christ succeeded in blending "the idea of God with the belief of Life in matter" and triumphing ultimately over matter.[35] Two problems remained, however. First, the problem of matter's source: if God is all, and yet there is no God in matter, where does matter come from? Second, Christian Science offered the healing powers of time, but it could not prevent death. Eddy's response was that Christian Science healers must transcend matter and death in their thoughts. Her system, in Cather's words, amounted to "the revolt of a species against its own physical structure; against its relations to its natural physical environment; against the needs of its own physical organism, and against the perpetuation of its kind."[36] Christian Science was the expression of an individual steeped in paranoia. Most dangerous of all was Eddy's faith in "malicious mesmerism," her belief that malevolent people, especially vengeful former disciples, could possess and dominate her from within.

Yet Eddy was a woman of her time: exceedingly ambitious, antiprovincial, and cosmopolitan. Cather records with grudging admiration how Eddy came to preside over the remarkable expansion of Christian Science across America. "Never, since religions were propagated by the sword," Cather writes, "was a new faith advertised and spread in such a systematic and effective manner."[37] Eddy's genius was to recognize the spiritual potential of certain ideas and to adapt them to her culture. She had an instinct for all the ways in which the body had become a site of subjection—partly through images of the suffering, wounded, and dead during and after the Civil War, and partly through the trying spectacle of difference that confronted Americans in a time of mass immigration. Eddy's radical renunciation of the body, her insistence that it was a mere instrument of spirit, seemed comforting to leisure-class members in urban areas who comprised the majority of church followers. But Eddy was always less concerned with the ideas themselves than with their institutionalization as a personal monopoly. Mark Twain confirmed Eddy's success in characterizing her venture as "the Boston Christian-Science Trust," "the Standard Oil of the Future."[38]

Like other growth industries of the period, Christian Science nourished both progressive impulses and backward ones. As a religion originated by a woman, investing modestly trained, usually female healers with divinely infused powers that rivaled those of an emerging male medical establishment, Christian Science was consistent with a movement for women's rights that grew in a variety of cultural, legal, and political ways between the mid-nineteenth century and the early decades of the twentieth. In harking back to an era when the link between an individual's spiritual and physical state was assumed and health care was an integral part of pastoral practice, Christian Science represented a reaction against a new industrial capitalist order where occupational specialization and institutional expansion were the rule. Above all, it expressed a yearning among modern urbanites for something beyond the material; it expressed needs that could not be answered by accumulation, aspirations that resisted the marketplace. This is all despite the paradox that the religion's founder managed to build a substantial fortune upon these aspirations, a paradox that confirms how deeply American the movement was.

4

INDIAN SACRIFICE IN AN
AGE OF PROGRESS

"The love of possessions is a disease among them," observed Sitting Bull, seeking to distinguish the dominant from the indigenous culture and to explain America's increasingly predacious behavior toward Indians over the course of the nineteenth century. The pillaging and slaughter that was sanctioned by an Indian removal policy before the Civil War intensified after it, as Reconstruction treaties commandeered Indian lands for railroads and white settlement. Lincoln's promise to redress these injustices, which was echoed in the 1867 Doolittle report, confirmed the ongoing gap between rhetoric and reality in governmental dealings with Indians. The Doolittle report criticized military brutalities and the greed of reservation officials but predicted the gradual displacement of the weaker race by the stronger, a theory that ignored Indian survival through centuries of warfare, epidemics, and forced migration. The passing of the Dawes Act during the Grant administration resulted in the expansion of reservations, the establishment of reservation schools, and most important, the allotment of land to individual Indian families. According to the 1886 commissioner of Indian Affairs, these measures were designed to instill "the exalting egoism of American civilization so that he will say 'I' instead of 'We' and 'This is mine' instead of 'This is ours.'" But the Dawes Act directly contradicted *U.S. v. Kagema*, an 1886 Supreme Court decision that declared Indians wards of the nation (which remained in effect until the Indian Citizenship Act was passed in 1924). And the division of lands among individual families invariably resulted in tribal losses, in part because American taxation and leasing codes were so opaque, and neighboring cattlemen and farmers were prepared to exploit Indian missteps. Every tribe lost land this way, and for some—the Chippewa in the Great Lakes and the Shawnee of Indian Territory—the outcome was landlessness and destitution. As one Oklahoma Creek Indian complained, "Egypt had its locusts, Asiatic countries their cholera, France had its Jacobins, England its black plague, Memphis had the yellow fever . . . But it was left for unfortunate Indian territory to be afflicted with the worst scourge of the nineteenth century, the Dawes Commission."[1]

The diversity of Indian tribes was reflected in their different responses to the daunting transformation of their circumstances; for instance, by the turn of the twentieth century, a population estimated at 1.5 million in the seventeenth century had dwindled to 237,000. Some sought spiritual solace in messianic religious movements such as the Sioux Ghost Dances, which anticipated the return of dead relatives and a lost way of life, and the sacred peyote rituals, which combined consumption of hallucinogenic cacti with a Pan-Indian politics that united adherents from various tribes. Others like the Cherokees and the Creeks chose military resistance.[2] Still another option was represented by a considerable Indian leadership, which formed the Society of American Indians in Columbus, Ohio, in 1911. Comprised of self-proclaimed full-bloods and half-bloods, mostly graduated from industrial or boarding schools, the group appealed to "the race to strike out into the duties of modern life and in performing them find every right that had escaped them before."[3]

White and Indian authors writing about cultural conflict and the annihilation of Indian tribes in this period faced the difficult task of explaining, whether in political, philosophical, or religious terms, the sacrifice of a people in an age of progress.[4] Some writers, such as Sarah Winnemucca Hopkins and Charles Alexander Eastman, wrote from inside the culture in a tone of suppressed anger, detailing the lost rituals of a civilization, while bearing witness to a nation's crimes. Eastman's stance recalled Frederick Douglass's ambivalent autobiography: at once appreciative of dominant cultural ideals and profoundly critical of the consistent hypocrisy that authorized their violation in the name of principle. Others, for instance, Lewis Henry Morgan and Zane Grey, wrote appreciatively from the outside, convinced that Indians offered an admirable social model but prepared to consign it to a heroic past. Still others, like Helen Hunt Jackson and Zitkala-Ša, vigorously opposed government and military policies and pled for reform in their fiction and nonfiction.

This chapter offers biographies of major figures in American Indian affairs between the Civil War and World War I, focusing in turn on Ely

Samuel Parker, Lewis Henry Morgan, Charles Alexander Eastman, and Helen Hunt Jackson, who together cover territory from the East Coast to the West and professions ranging from law, engineering, the military, and early anthropology to government, literature, and medicine. What this group of public servants, intellectuals, and literary authors shared was a state of enlightenment that was exceptional in a time of pervasive misunderstanding, bad faith, and violence. They accepted the inevitable—that American culture would prevail—while declaring the superiority of Indian culture in key respects. They protested the overriding of Indian land claims at the same time that they insisted on the challenge posed by Indian values to the debilitating effects of modernization. While their lives intersected in various ways, the ties between Parker and Morgan were the most direct. Parker, a Seneca, who served as secretary to General Ulysses S. Grant during the Civil War, assisted Morgan in the Indian researches that provided the basis for his theories of kinship. The experiences and achievements of Parker and Morgan afford a bridge to those of Charles Alexander Eastman, a prominent public intellectual who followed Parker in showing what an Indian could accomplish in the white world and also echoed Morgan's Iroquois studies in his inside ethnographies of Sioux education and spirituality. Helen Hunt Jackson offers a striking case in combining elements of all the lives discussed below. Like Parker and Eastman, she was a government official (serving as co-commissioner of Mission Indian Affairs in California), while she shared Morgan's reasoning—partly Christian, partly naturalistic—on the fate of the Indian tribes. She aspired, like Eastman, to a literary career with political efficacy, even as her most famous novel, *Ramona* (1884), helped to launch the more insular western romance genre developed by Owen Wister and Zane Grey in the first two decades of the twentieth century.

The life histories highlighted here will be amplified through other contemporaneous accounts, which reveal both the uniqueness and the ordinariness of the individuals at the center of this narrative. Thus, for example, the stories of two Indian women, Sarah Winnemucca Hopkins and Zitkala-Ša, who ended up exiles from dominant *and* native cultures, will contrast with the comparatively secure marginality of Parker and Eastman. In the final section, I explore the life and work of three novelists, Maria Ruiz de Burton, Owen Wister, and Zane Grey, who together establish the conventions of Indian representation for future generations. Throughout this period, the American identification of acquisitiveness as an "instinct" that Indians lacked, making them resistant to "civilization," served as a persistent rationale for their dispossession and displacement.[5] Ely Parker, Lewis Morgan, Charles Eastman, and Helen Jackson together confirmed the sacrifice of the Indian nations on the altar of American property relations. The elegists of conquest, whose writings complete the chapter, reveal how Indian losses were submerged in authoritative accounts of settlement that emphasized, respectively, the exile of the Mexican, the closing of the frontier, and the supplanting of an ethic of survival by the pastime of sports.

GENERAL ELY SAMUEL PARKER, LAST GRAND SACHEM OF THE IROQUOIS

The presidential administration of Ulysses S. Grant featured instances of generosity and justice toward the nation's Indian wards.[6] But there was perhaps no greater testimonial on Grant's behalf than his choice of a personal secretary during the Civil War, Ely S. Parker, who had the honor of drafting Lee's surrender at Appomattox. Refused admission to the New York state bar despite years of legal training (because Indians were not citizens),[7] Parker became a civil engineer instead, and this expertise also proved invaluable to Grant throughout his successful military campaign.[8] Parker's term as the first Indian commissioner of Indian Affairs was cut short by a fraud charge, which was subsequently rescinded. In this incident and in others, his life betrayed the trials endured by Indians who sought to navigate the white world as equals. But he remained throughout "a high type of the Iroquois in transition."[9] In a fascinating biography authorized by the Buffalo Historical Society, his nephew, Arthur C. Parker, writes that he was "the only American Indian who rose to national distinction . . . who could trace his lineage back for generations to the Stone Age and to the days of Hiawatha" (7). In keeping with the characteristic and also cultivated modesty of his subject, Arthur Parker's biography is as much a story of the Iroquois people as it is the record of one of its most important nineteenth-century descendants. Devoted equally to intellectual enlightenment and to physical prowess, the five Iroquois nations (Mohawk, Oneida, Onondaga, Cayuga, and Seneca) that occupied much of upstate New York were known for their skill as hunters and craftspeople. During the seventeenth and eighteenth centuries, the Iroquois sided with the British against the French, helping to ensure that the East Coast would be English-speaking. The indecisiveness of the Five Nations during the American Revolution had little impact on the treaties that followed the American victory, which overlooked Indian rights to territory. While some Iroquois migrated to

Canada, to occupy lands circumscribed by the British, those who remained in New York were forced to sell most of their land to white settlers and were increasingly restricted to reservations.

Ely Parker's father, William, fought on the American side in the War of 1812 and five years later had developed one of the best farms in the Genesee Valley. His mother, Elizabeth, granddaughter of tribal chief Jemmy Johnson, the successor to "the peace prophet" Handsome Lake, was a beautiful and accomplished woman with prophetic abilities. Just before Parker's birth in 1828, Elizabeth dreamt that her new son would be "a peace-maker . . . a white man as well as an Indian" (48). Parker's childhood home was legendary for its hospitality, because his parents lived their religious teachings: "food like air was the gift of the Creator and should be as free to the visitor as the spring water." His parents worked hard and shared their bounty, but traditional morals such as these were under challenge even as Parker imbibed them. Missionaries converted some Iroquois to Christianity, a creed that was not always reconcilable with indigenous Indian beliefs, in part because Christian settlers so often betrayed its precepts.[10] The commercialization of Indian crafts to appeal to white markets further weakened the Iroquois social order (52–54). All five of the Parker children were sent to white schools and encouraged to be ambitious; Parker took his parents' directives to heart and was appropriately named "The Reader" (58).[11]

Yet Parker was a mournful spectator of transition: Indian bark houses replaced by log cabins, buckskin replaced by cloth, his people's land wrested away by false treaties that resulted in their forced migration westward. Parker's first response was flight: at ten, he convinced his father that he should join the Indian settlement on the Grand River in Ontario, where a league of nations—now six in number—had been reinstated. There he perfected Indian skills of hunting, woodcraft, and dialect speech, while the knowledge acquired from his mission schooling declined. But even at this age, Parker recognized that the future lay with the mastery of English and the ways of the white world. Upon his return, he entered the Yates Academy as the lone Indian student and later the Cayuga Academy, where he studied alongside whites from elite families. Parker's school years were tumultuous ones for his people, and the educated, eloquent youth was a frequent messenger to Albany and Washington. By the age of eighteen, Parker had met many New York officials and had dined at the White House as a guest of President Polk (77). In recognition of this service and of his distinguished ancestry, Parker was proclaimed Grand Sachem of the Six Nations at an Indian council in 1852, a title that confirmed Parker's role as a leading spokesman for his people in a volatile political context.[12] Parker was the last

Seneca-Iroquois to exercise the position of sachem in the manner his fore-fathers intended.

It was on a trip to Albany in 1844, where Parker served as interpreter for a delegation of Tonawanda Seneca elders seeking restoration of reservation land, that he met Lewis Henry Morgan. Morgan was a lawyer from Aurora, New York, with an abiding interest in the Cayuga Iroquois, Aurora's original inhabitants. An alumnus of Cayuga Academy and Union College, Morgan was the founder of a Masonic chapter at the academy called the Gordian Knot, which he subsequently modeled on the Iroquois Confederacy. Morgan had recently moved to Rochester and organized another chapter of the Freemasons there, presiding over an anniversary meeting in Aurora where both Henry Schoolcraft and Alfred B. Street delivered addresses. But it was Parker who sparked the researches that resulted in *The League of the Ho-dé-no-sau-nee, or Iroquois* (1851), coauthored by Morgan and Parker, "the first methodological treatise along scientific lines ever written of an ethnic group of mankind" (88).[13] Morgan later accompanied Parker to Washington to protest unjust land treaties involving the Tonawanda Senecas. Morgan's support of the Senecas led in 1847 to his honorary adoption (into the Hawk clan) and renaming—"Ta-ya-da-o-wuh-kuh," meaning "One lying across," or "Bridging the gap" (81–82).

Perhaps the most significant aspect of the Parker-Morgan researches was their recuperation of material cultural remains, which was part of a larger nineteenth-century American preoccupation with local and national history. In 1845, the regents of the State of New York created a "Cabinet of Natural History" to which Parker and Morgan became regular contributors. In a letter to the Board of Regents outlining his plan to supply "Indian antiquities and relics," Morgan noted that a vast collection of such items would provide "a memento of the Red Race who preceded us," enabling it "to speak for itself through these silent memorials."[14] Morgan's pursuit of materials was systematic and tireless, and he relied on the Parker family as a whole to provide artifacts of various kinds, descriptions of tribal customs (such as dances), recollections of ancient longhouse designs, even boyhood essays on Indian life (by Nicholson and Ely Parker). No ornament or utensil was too small or trivial to escape Morgan's attention; he considered every item a key to a culture, its social conditions and highest skills, its powers of invention.[15] Thus, he pressed Ely Parker for original Indian names and functions of mortars and corn mills, earthen vessels and kettles, stone chisels and deer bone. He gathered traditional clothing from the Parker family and had daguerreotypes made of Caroline, Newton, and Levi Parker arrayed in them. And he questioned Elizabeth Parker on the domestic economy of her upbringing in one of the grandest longhouses of the Iroquois. Ely Parker's own cradleboard from infancy was displayed in the New York State Museum until the March 1911 fire that destroyed much of the Morgan collection and, in addition, ten thousand Iroquois specimens.

Ely Parker and Lewis Henry Morgan shared a passion for another means of preserving and memorializing Indian ways of life, American Freemasonry, which seemed to them more durable than people and their possessions. As Parker observed in his oration at an 1859 Masonic banquet in Chicago, "Where shall I find home and sympathy when our last council fire is extinguished? . . . I will knock at the door of Masonry. . . . If my race shall disappear from this continent, I shall have the consoling hope that our memory will not perish" (97). During the years when Parker was building a career as an engineer, supervising improvements on the western section of the Erie Canal and then working as chief engineer on the Chesapeake and Albemarle Canal, Masonry provided a source of fellowship and community. Raised in the Batavia (New York) Lodge in 1847, he later joined lodges in Rochester, New York, and in Galena, Illinois, where in 1857 he oversaw construction of a customhouse and marine hospital. In Galena, Parker met the other individual whose patronage changed his place in history, Ulysses S. Grant. Grant at that time was a clerk in his father's harness store, and he and Parker became friends after Parker rescued Grant from a mishap caused by the "overflowing bowl," the Indian euphemism for drunkenness (96).

When the Civil War began, Grant recruited a regiment, but Parker remained at work on the levees of the Mississippi, assured that the war would be short-lived. In 1862, he returned to Tonawanda, prepared to apply in Albany for a commission in the Union army. Parker was rebuffed, but his devotion to the country that refused him citizenship, and his considerable self-confidence, spurred an immediate trip to Washington to meet with the secretary of war. Parker recorded William Seward's reply: " *'The fight must be settled by the white men alone . . . Go home, cultivate your farm and we will settle our own troubles without any Indian aid'* " (102–3, italics in original). Hence Parker went to work on his father's farm, having resigned a major engineering post in the expectation of an army commission. Parker's nephew speculates about his feelings, noting that when "called a failure by his people," the proud and ambitious man sowed his fields. "Iroquois philosophy is [a] strange philosophy to modern Americans in our day and it may be safe to say that his spirit was at peace with itself" (103–4). On June 4, 1863, these fortunes were reversed when Parker accepted a commission (signed by Secretary Seward) in the Union army at the rank of captain. Within a few months, he was on the staff of Major General Grant, where he spent the rest of the war, participating in all the major battles from Vicksburg and Lookout Mountain to Richmond and Cold Harbor.

During this period Parker came to know Mathew Brady, the Civil War photographer, and also dined with President Lincoln, to whom he conveyed distress over the condition of his people and his plans for their improvement.[16] Known as "the Indian" astride his black horse, Parker was often engaged in engineering operations, but due to his superior penmanship and writing, he also worked on Grant's correspondence (110–16). General Horace Porter tells of an incident where a civilian visiting the army asked to see Grant and found Parker at work in Grant's chair. "That's him," the man was overheard remarking, "but he's got all-fired sun-burnt."[17] In August 1864 Parker was appointed military secretary to Grant, which made him intimate with the final stages of the war and instrumental in its representation. The most dramatic moment in Parker's military career was his drafting of Robert E. Lee's surrender at Appomattox. Parker, along with other officers, accompanied Grant to the McLean farmhouse where Lee was waiting with his own military secretary. Lee was introduced to each of Grant's officers and seemed surprised by Parker's presence, perhaps because "he first mistook Parker for a negro."[18] After staring at Parker, Lee extended his hand and, according to Parker, said, "I am glad to see one real American here." To which Parker replied, "We are all Americans" (133). Once the terms were agreed upon, Grant asked Bowers, his senior adjutant, to record them in a final copy, but Bowers was too nervous to write. In the words of Arthur C. Parker, "The nerves of the Anglo-Saxon tingled with suppressed emotion, but Parker, the red man, whose life's discipline had steeled him for composure during times of crisis, was as calm inwardly as outwardly." Thus, Parker assumed the task (131), remaining behind to detail the special directives for each side.[19] There is bitterness beneath the pride in Arthur Parker's conclusion to the section on his uncle's war years: "Thus, after all, it must be said that it was in the handwriting of an Iroquois sachem, and an *Indian* that the two warring factions of the white race were finally united" (141).

That bitterness extends to the account of Parker's final contributions to the country that had only awarded him citizenship following his sacrifices in the war (141). Parker stayed with the War Department until April 1869. During this period he managed to secure the Seneca's Tonawanda landholdings with an 1867 act that ensured the territory for generations to come. With the 1869 presidential inauguration of Grant, Parker was appointed commissioner of Indian Affairs. Calling for a redefinition of Indians' legal status and rights and for the codifying of Indian laws themselves, Parker also emphasized the anarchy that prevailed on reservations, dominated by rogue elements from both white and Indian groups. Contractors who had made fortunes by defrauding both Indians and the government were held accountable for the first time. But such challenges to the status quo in Indian affairs resulted in Parker's own indictment by a member of the commission board, who bemoaned Grant's appointment of an individual "but a remove from barbarism" (155). In 1871, Parker was tried before a committee of the House of Representatives and was cleared of all charges. But six months later, he resigned his post, finding it "easier to build a fortune in Wall Street" (157–59). Despite fortunes gained and lost (in the Freedmen's Bureau Bank, an insurance company, and a publishing venture), Parker retained the stately home he built in Fairfield, Connecticut, until his death in 1895. In his final years, he took a position in the police department in New York City, where he befriended, among others, Jacob Riis, who featured Parker in his *Making of an American*. Parker was buried in the Forest Lawn Cemetery in Buffalo, New York, in grand ceremonial fashion.

Four years before his death, Parker delivered an address at Gettysburg, Pennsylvania, an occasion he used to outline a brief national history. Drawing out the significance of Tammany, the Delaware Indian chief, as the figurehead of the Gettysburg monument, he told his military comrades of the constant hostilities that had prevailed among the Indian tribes before the arrival of whites and of how the Delawares were ultimately conquered by the Iroquois (182). He noted how the Indians saw the first white men as gods but soon reacted against their violence and avarice. The remainder of the address dwelt on the high points of American culture: its ideals of equality and liberty, the war fought to end slavery, the freedom of speech, the principle of universal education. Parker's history was distinctive in two ways: its identification of the antagonistic prehistory of the Indian nations and its embrace of major American values. All this was directed toward his ultimate aim: the recognition of Indians as historical agents who were prepared, no matter how diminished in numbers, to participate fully in the future of an expanding nation.

LEWIS HENRY MORGAN: FATHER OF AMERICAN ANTHROPOLOGY

What made the Parker-Morgan relationship mutually beneficial was the fact that each man approached the other's culture with a sense of necessity. Parker's sense of necessity was perhaps the greater, as he beheld the destruction of his civilization and worried about the prospects for its preservation. Morgan's was fused by a conviction of the powerful authenticity and pristine classicism of Iroquois culture. He believed that here in still vital form was a model civilization for America, a model that was integral to the young nation, rather than imported, like the Greek and Roman models emphasized by American educators.[20] The central purposes of the re-searches undertaken by Morgan and Parker were to repudiate the claim that Europeans had encountered a vacant wilderness in North America and to establish the social organizations of the Iroquois as archetypes for the whites who had usurped their New York lands.[21] Geography, according to both men, shaped human consciousness and national destiny: Indians and whites were bonded through the land they inhabited. As they put it in *League of the Ho-dé-no-sau-nee*, "The Iroquois were our predecessors in the sovereignty. Our country they once called their country, our rivers and lakes their rivers and lakes, our hills and intervales were also theirs."[22] Moreover, in the minds of both, the Iroquois represented a higher order of civilization, without private property, and relatively immune to the materialism and inequities that motivated whites' aggression toward Indians.[23] Perhaps most intriguing of all was their shared interest in Iroquois religion and the relationship between indigenous Indian faiths and Christianity. On this issue, they were not in agreement. Morgan was a Christian who saw the truest form of his religion as key to Indian survival. This didn't preclude his fascination with indigenous spiritualities, in particular the early nineteenth-century revivals associated with Handsome Lake, a relative of Ely Parker. Parker followed Handsome Lake's teachings in his lifelong distance from Christianity. Unable to reconcile the vast discrepancies between Christian principles and the acts of Christians, Parker declared in a late letter that he hoped his people would never forsake "their tribal organizations and re-ligious traditions . . . for a mess of Christian pottage."[24]

Morgan's investigations of Indian culture were made in the years before the Civil War, beginning in earnest around 1844, and their direct fruits were *The League of the Ho-dé-no-sau-nee, or Iroquois* (1851), a two-part article on American Indian ethnology published in the *North American Review* (1869–70), and his final book, *Houses and House-Life of the American Aborigines* (1881). Morgan's early engagement with the Indians of upstate New York were also formative for the books that provided the foundations of the new American science of anthropology: *Systems of Consanguinity and Affinity* (1871) and *Ancient Society* (1877). Both became standard works of early an-thropology, and the study of social evolution undertaken in *Ancient Society* had a significant impact on the theories of Karl Marx and Friedrich Engels.[25] But it was his establishment of the category of kinship in *Systems* that proved an enduring contribution to his emerging field.[26] In the words of one anthropological historian, "Kinship had to be discovered, and it was discovered through the discordant, non-commonsensical kinship of the cultural other."[27] The conceptualization of blood relationships and inter-generational transmission, grasping the social effects of the most intimate ties, required the distance afforded by the contemplation of alien peoples.

Morgan was born on a sheep farm near Aurora, New York, in 1818, the fourth of eight children of Jedidiah Morgan and his second wife, Harriet Steele. When Morgan was four, his family moved to town because his ailing father (who died in 1826) could no longer farm. Morgan received a classical education in Greek and Latin languages and literature, as well as a solid grounding in math and science, but he was equally influenced by the remnants of the Cayuga Indian culture that haunted the white village of Aurora. The Sullivan-Clinton campaign of 1779, authorized by General George Washington and designed to punish the Five Iroquois Nations for aiding the British, had succeeded in destroying Indian settlements through-out central New York. Among these was Chonodote, or "Peach Town," the Cayuga name for Aurora that commemorated its wealth in peach trees. By 1807, the Cayugas had sold the last of their reservation lands and migrated. But they remained a preoccupation for many townspeople who believed that the former Indian inhabitants provided a key to the meaning of the fledgling American nation. The Masonic chapter Morgan renamed "the Order of the Iroquois" in 1844 reflected similar assumptions. This fraternity sought to protect, in Morgan's words, "so far as it lay in our power, the remainder of the Iroquois living in this state; and particularly, the band of Senecas at Tonawanda who then and since the year 1838 had been beset and hunted by the Ogden Land Company, to despoil them of the remaining lands." Visiting these Iroquois tribes, attending their councils, listening to their grievances, and above all studying "the structure and principle of the ancient League, by which they had been united for so many centuries," Morgan's practical schooling in Indian culture past and present had begun.[28]

Ely S. Parker and his family played an indispensable role in that process, and Morgan recognized early on what a remarkable "find" the Parkers were: truly bicultural, with unparalleled knowledge of native traditions and an eagerness to master dominant cultural methods.[29] William Parker, Ely's father, had built one of the most productive farms in the area, substituting plow agriculture for the subsistence brand of Indian horticulture managed by women. The Parker children were encouraged to compete with whites, an ambitiousness reflected in the observations of William's great grandson Arthur C. Parker: "Every Indian who has achieved a high position in business or commercial life has been educated away from his people and amid surroundings that compelled him to keep on his mettle. It is competition with keen intellect that awakens and develops great intellect."[30] This assimilationist resolve to show whites what Indians were capable of was balanced by the Parkers' devotion to the separatist religious values of their distant relative Handsome Lake, who preached from 1799 until his death in 1815. Handsome Lake's teachings were a response to the demoralization of the Iroquois in the years after the Sullivan-Clinton campaign and the white settlement that followed it. Stressing temperance and spiritual devotion, while prohibiting birth control, abortion, divorce, and all contact with whites, the prophetic religion sought to restore Iroquois self-discipline and self-respect. Handsome Lake's effort to establish a new code of ethics in the name of a general cultural revitalization has been compared to the religious revivals of surrounding whites, whose spiritual fervor earned the region the label of "the burned over district."[31] Though the religious views of Morgan and Parker diverged, as each might be said to have imbibed his own culture's form of nationalism (imperialist in Morgan's case, imperiled in Parker's), their intellectual agendas cohered in their concern for how best to protect the remaining New York Iroquois and how best to memorialize those who were gone.

One form they settled on was *The League of the Ho-dé-no-sau-nee, or Iroquois*, the scholarly product of their joint research into Iroquois material culture remains, including burial mounds, much of it plowed up by local farmers. The book's purpose was both social scientific and spiritual: the effort to catalog for posterity the attributes of a culture was inseparable from the need to come to terms with the culture's destruction.[32] The two most important aspects of Iroquois society in Morgan's view were the foundation of its entire organizational structure in family relationships and the transmission of all titles, rights, and property through the maternal line. Family ties defined the civil and social system, from individuals, to tribes, to nations, to the Iroquois League as a whole. Iroquois consanguinity involved a merging of the collateral in the lineal line: the maternal grandmother and her sister were equally grandmothers; the mother and her sisters were equally mothers; the grandfather and his brothers equally grandfathers; the father and his brother equally fathers. While Morgan acknowledged the reasonableness of matrilineal rule, which ensured purity of descent against the perpetual uncertainty of paternity, he also noted its departure from "the canons of descent adopted by civilized nations."[33] Morgan's experience devising a constitution for his Masonic group modeled on the Six Nations and his conversance with Roman law informed significantly what he considered his final word on the Iroquois before devoting himself exclusively to his legal career.[34]

So too did his sense of the injustices endured by the Iroquois at the hands of Americans, which he struggled to explain, partly in religious terms. How could God allow so much suffering and death? How could the misery of some be necessary to general progress? Morgan remained ambivalent toward such notions throughout his life, disturbed by a universal order that seemed to ask more of the most vulnerable.[35] This recognition was elaborated in the research he undertook in the decade after "The League," which culminated in *The American Beaver and His Works* (1868). Married in 1851 to his first cousin, Mary Elizabeth Steele, Morgan moved to Rochester and focused on earning a living as a lawyer for his growing family (Lemuel, born in 1853, Mary, in 1855, Helen, in 1860). But his intellectual curiosity never abated, and while he was building a fortune through investments in Michigan railroad and iron ventures he advised, he spent free time studying the engineering feats of local beaver. The extent and variety of American beaver projects revealed the mental acuity of what Morgan called the "Mutes." The different structures built by beaver in different environments (canals, dams, mudslides) demonstrated their ability to respond rationally to nature. Insisting that the thinking principle was common to all animated nature, Morgan speculated that animals had powers beyond those of humans, appropriate to their needs. He ends on a cautionary note, condemning the wanton domestication or extermination of whole species: "the annual sacrifice of animal life to maintain human life is frightful."[36] Morgan's ending also draws an implicit parallel between the beaver and the Iroquois, enablers and victims alike of "colonization and settlement."[37]

The books that followed the beaver study in the next decade paid homage to Morgan's ideal of interdependence by claiming "primitive" peoples as brethren. The first step was the identification of the Iroquois system of consanguinity as common to all the Indian tribes of North America. Morgan's investigations convinced him that a classificatory system of relationship was generally shared by diverse American Indian peoples and could be traced to Asia. Morgan pursued this theory in *Systems of Consanguinity and Affinity of the Human Family*, a six-hundred-page analysis with nearly two hundred tables listing the categories of relationship within tribes and nations of North America, Europe, Asia, Oceania, and Africa. Though the book's theory on Indian origins was unsupportable, Morgan had helped to invent "a new instrument for ethnology," the category of kinship.[38] Morgan advanced a key distinction between primitive and modern societies: while primitive social relations were based on family relations, modern ones were based on property. His subsequent exploration into the nature of these property relations in his polemical *Ancient Society* (1877) revealed his admiration of Indian culture. A combination of moral fervor and scholarly substance made *Ancient Society* the most celebrated and popular of Morgan's works. He described the advent of property as a kind of Frankenstein's monster, which had grown to such proportions and become so diversified, its effects radiating into all aspects of society—economic, political, spiritual, and psychological—that these effects had become impossible to limit. "The human mind," he observed, "stands bewildered in the presence of its own creation. The time will come, nevertheless, when human intelligence will rise to the mastery over property, and define the relations of the state to the property it protects. . . . A mere property career is not the final destiny of mankind, if progress is to be the law of the future as it has been of the past."[39]

What made Morgan distinctive as a thinker in his time and deserving of the title "father of anthropology" was his interest in the concrete habitats of his subjects. Unlike comparable scholars (Bachofen, Maine, McLennan), Morgan's writings were based in "original fieldwork" among, in turn, the Iroquois, the Indian tribes of the Midwest and West, and the Michigan beaver.[40] In keeping with this, his conceptualization of evolutionary progress tied every stage to a tool that transformed the prospects of the human beings who invented it: Middle Savagery—fire; Upper Savagery—the bow and arrow; Lower Barbarism—pottery; Middle Barbarism—domesticated animals and irrigation; Upper Barbarism—iron smelting; Civilization—writing.[41] Delving deeply into the materials of the past made him, paradoxically, more of a modern than most of his contemporaries, and in so doing, allowed him to see more clearly what modern society, for all its ingenuity and privilege, stood to lose.[42] Morgan lamented the recklessness of nineteenth-century Americans who seemed indifferent to the natural, animal, and human resources wasted in the name of progress.

From the fragments of pottery and bone collected in youth, to the customs cataloged and people befriended in adulthood, Henry Lewis Morgan's access to the Indians he made the basis of his incipient science was admittedly partial. However deeply he probed their social organization and familial connections as he transformed them into categorical guides to evolutionary advance and kinship, he could never overcome his status as an outsider. The authors discussed in the next section were products of Indian culture, proficient in its skills, devoted to its values, and aware of its likely transience. Because they had also mastered English and writing, they were able to leave permanent records of the destruction of their home communities by American settlers. For Indian writers living between cultures and alert to the challenges issuing from such cross-cultural contact, the question of how to formulate a language that could accommodate their splintered loyalties was paramount.[43]

Sarah Winnemucca Hopkins's *Life among the Piutes: Their Wrongs and Claims* (1883) exemplifies a relatively early moment in nineteenth-century Indian writings. Hopkins recalls the rhetorical strategies of slave narrators like Harriet Jacobs (*Incidents in the Life of a Slave Girl*), who combines clinical accounts of offenses against her people with sentimental appeals to her reader's sense of justice. Because Winnemucca inhabits a still-vibrant indigenous culture, her form is advocacy rather than elegy. The implicit contrast between the oral culture of Indians and the literate culture of whites in her book's opening yields unexpected results. "I was born somewhere near 1844, but am not sure of the precise time. I was a very small child when the first white people came into our country. They came like a lion, yes, like a roaring lion, and have continued so ever since, and I have never forgotten their first coming. My people were scattered at that time over nearly all the territory now known as Nevada."[44] The narrator's uncertainty of origin (when she was born, the name of the territory) expresses her resentment of the invaders whose penchant for documentation belies their bestiality. Winnemucca eloquently overturns Darwinian theory on the transition from savage to civilized: to a small Indian girl out West, the coming of whites is a violent predation. While his ultimate aims were closer to those of Parker and Morgan, Charles Eastman's writings on Indian life in late nineteenth-century America share Winnemucca's tone of ironic condemnation. Like her, he recognized literacy as a barbed tool, whose very deployment confirmed the devastation it protested.

CHARLES ALEXANDER EASTMAN: INDIAN CITIZEN

Born thirty years after Parker, Charles Alexander Eastman (or "Ohiyesa," his Indian name) had a traditional Santee Sioux upbringing in Canada before his abrupt introduction at the age of fourteen to the customs of Christian Indians on his father's South Dakota farm. Perhaps because his initial encounter with whites was more dramatic than Parker's and was mediated by a father who was also a stranger, Eastman remained to the end of his life ambivalent toward the dominant culture that aroused his filial respect and intellectual curiosity. Eastman's decision to spend his final years in a cabin in the Canadian woods suggests that he was more disenchanted with American society than Parker was, who expected less from it. Eastman had been thoroughly schooled in Indian ways and heard much about whites before he encountered them. The experience of his (presumably dead) father reappearing after a decade, clothed as a white man, to spirit him away to another world was undoubtedly formative. His ability to overcome this crisis to graduate from college (Dartmouth) and medical school (Boston University, where he was the first Indian graduate), en route to becoming a public leader and popular author, indicated his exceptional gifts of mind and character. Eastman accomplished all this while distanced from the Santee Sioux culture that was disintegrating before his eyes and from the white Christian culture he had yet to fully accept. That this allowed him to produce some of the most important books on Indian-white relations in the modern era is a sign of the personal sacrifices often required by the most powerful and enduring political testimony.

Eastman, whose forebears included Chief Cloudman of the Mdewakanton Sioux and the western artist Captain Seth Eastman, was a trained physician, government agent, secretary of the YMCA, and founder of the Boy Scouts. He was president of the Society of American Indians, Indian representative to the first Universal Races Congress, and a principal agitator for Indian citizenship. Eastman's mother, half-Sioux Mary Nancy Eastman, married a Wahpeton Sioux, Chief Many Lightnings, and died in 1858 giving birth to Eastman, who was raised by his paternal grandmother and uncle before being reunited with his father in 1873. Eastman's first medical appointment was at the Pine Ridge Agency reservation near Wounded Knee, where he tended the casualties of the 1890 massacre. While working for the government, he found time for literary pursuits, which resulted in the commercial as well as critical successes *Indian Boyhood* (1902), *The Soul of the Indian* (1911), and *From the Deep Woods to Civilization* (1916). These books emphasized the prospects for Indian attainment in modern America and the importance of an indigenous literature that preserved for posterity the distinctive qualities of separate tribes. Advocating restitution and equality for all Indians, Eastman was also pragmatic: he believed that Indians must moderate their loyalty to tradition and exploit the opportunities provided by the dominant culture. He saw the possibilities in a liberal Christianity that might unite diverse peoples under the canopy of one faith. Though he condemned whites for failing to practice what they preached, he criticized Indians for denying the value of the ideals themselves.

Such evenhandedness made Eastman a reliable historian of cultural conflict. His account of the events at Wounded Knee, where two hundred Sioux, mostly women and children, were killed by American cavalry, is a case in point. Eastman had high hopes for his appointment as a reservation doctor. If the doctor spoke the language and sympathized with the customs of his patients, Eastman had written to Thomas Jefferson Morgan, commissioner of Indian Affairs, he could be "the most useful civilizer" on "any Indian Reservation."[45] Eastman's charge on the Pine Ridge Indian reservation where he arrived in November 1890 was daunting: one doctor served six thousand in an environment beset by disease and poor sanitation. Still he made significant headway, alleviating the distrust of modern medicine and encouraging better health conditions and treatment for Indians at local mission schools. Other events, however, long in the making, diverted these efforts.

The messianic Ghost Dance religion of 1890, led by the Piute holy man Wovoka, prophesied the imminent resurrection of Indian dead and the annihilation of whites in a selective catastrophe that would restore the West to its presettlement state of peace and prosperity. Newly literate Indians played a significant role in disseminating the prophetic religion through their "messiah letters." According to contemporary chronicler James Mooney, Wovoka's message would not have spread without the "efficient aid it received from the returned pupils of various eastern government schools, who conducted the sacred correspondence." Of a total reservation Indian population of 146,000 in 1890, 60,000 were estimated to be followers of the Ghost Dance religion. To the rhythm of drums and song, dancers moved in a slow circular sidestep, full of awe at the thought of their dead "close at hand." Though the Ghost Dances were peaceful, white reservation officials, alarmed by the crowds and the passion they aroused, prohibited them. Indeed their power was palpable: Wovoka, who termed his followers a "Chosen People," succeeded where centuries of missionary Christianity had failed, uniting disparate Indian tribes into a Pan-Indian collectivity.

The religion thrived among the South Dakota Sioux, a nation beleaguered by crop failures, epidemics, fraudulent treaties, and, in the fall of 1890, hunger. Eastman's Pine Ridge reservation had the added misfortune of an inexperienced agent, Daniel F. Royer, referred to as "Lakota Kokipa-Koshkala," or "Young-man-afraid-of-Indians." Few details of the Wounded Knee massacre, reconstructed from military records and survivors' testimony, are undisputed. By November 1890, on the order of President Benjamin Harrison, a cavalry regiment 3,000 strong had assembled in Rapid City, South Dakota. On December 29, a group of Sioux Ghost Dancers, about 120 men armed in response to the troops, and 250 women and children had gathered near Wounded Knee Creek, prepared to surrender to the cavalry. As the Indians relinquished their guns, one Indian fired at the soldiers, a single shot that ignited a relentless volley of "2-pound explosive shells at the rate of nearly fifty per minute, mowing down everything alive." The result was 153 Indians killed and 44 wounded, 25 cavalry killed and 39 wounded.[46]

From the start of tensions, Eastman had opposed the military buildup, convinced that the Ghost Dance religion would recede on its own with the improvement of the Sioux's material circumstances. He argued to other officials that there was no "widespread plot, or deliberate intention to make war upon the whites," and that the arrival of troops would make confrontation inevitable. Overruled, Eastman's only choice was to deal with the tragic consequences of an official policy gone awry, when he was asked to supervise the treatment of Indian survivors. "Frightfully torn by pieces of shell," he recalled, the traumatized victims, few of whom survived, refused to allow any whites "in uniform to touch them." Eastman's testimony on his experience as doctor and witness at Wounded Knee, the final battle between Indians and the United States Army, provided an important corrective to mainstream journalistic coverage. Noting how reservation officials "first robbed the Indians, then bullied them, and finally in a panic called for troops to suppress them," Eastman pronounced the events "a severe ordeal . . . for one who had so lately put all his faith in the Christian love and lofty ideals of the white man."[47] He was struck by the concurrence of the massacre and Christmas, describing how he tended wounds in a mission chapel beneath a glowing tree. He derived what little solace he could from his Yuletide engagement to Elaine Goodale, a New Englander, who was the first supervisor of Indian education in the Dakotas.[48]

Eastman never recovered his optimism about the potential good works of the reservation doctor. Two years later, following a conflict with the principal agent at Pine Ridge, Eastman resigned his position and in 1894 became Indian secretary of the YMCA, finding a job in the private sector more congenial. But he later returned to government service, as clerk of the Sioux Renaming Project from 1903 to 1909 under Hamlin Garland, the noted fiction writer and Indian reformer. Like Eastman, Garland distrusted the allotment system while advocating Indian assimilation, and he emphasized the necessity of preserving valued Indian customs. Most important, Garland believed that Indians would never gain legal and civil rights without proper English names. Called "the Name Giver" by his Indian clients, Eastman was credited with renaming "the entire Sioux nation." His success in this endeavor was ensured by his certainty of the benefits to Indians (a significant reduction in property title disputes) combined with his respect for their traditions (if original names could not be preserved, meanings would be).[49] Throughout this period, Eastman's reputation as a writer and lecturer was growing. Despite the eloquence and charisma that made him to the end of his life a coveted spokesman for Indian causes, he reached his largest audiences through his writings.

Eastman's dedication of his first book, *Indian Boyhood* (1902), to his namesake, Ohiyesa II, "who came too late to behold for himself the drama of savage existence," registers loss as well as purpose: "Ohiyesa" is as adaptable to an Indian boyhood (I) as he is to an American (II) one.[50] The book's opening presents Indian life as a choice and sets it within an American literary tradition of rugged scouts, whale hunters, and runaways who survive in the wild: "What boy would not be an Indian for a while when he thinks of the freest life in the world?" Natty Bumpo, Ishmael, Huckleberry Finn, and Ohiyesa I comprise a heroic lineage of skills that Eastman was helping the Boy Scouts to institutionalize.[51] There are differences: women are admirable and critical to survival (on his mother's deathbed the infant is given to his grandmother, a vigorous woman of sixty); and *Indian Boyhood* is less about individual triumph than about collective labor and communal celebration. Survival depends on a decade-long process of cultural transmission presided over by Eastman's grandmother and uncle. Trained to distinguish tree barks, bird calls, and hunting methods for deer and bear, Indian boys are tested in fasting, running for days, finding water in the night forest, and mastering their emotions. Eastman demonstrates this final skill in his first significant offering to the "Great Mystery": the sacrifice of his beloved companion, "the jet-black dog" Ohitika, "with a silver tip on the end of his tail and on his nose."[52] Heartbroken by the sacrifice, he is fortified by the gravity of the occasion.

Eastman approaches Indian ways of life in *Indian Boyhood* as an ethnological insider. He is sufficiently distanced to present comparatively the means by which Indians are *made*, not *born*. But his knowledge of the events is such that he can invest them with feeling. He *is* the eight-year-old boy encouraged to sacrifice his dog, and he is also the adult mediator who knows to omit the rite's essential component—his consumption of the dog's body—because it would offend American readers.[53] The book ends with Eastman's shocking realization that his father and brothers are alive, having been imprisoned by the "Big Knives," converted to Christianity, and set to farming. Curious about whites and their technologies, Eastman confesses nevertheless to feeling "as if I were dead and traveling to the Spirit Land."[54] *From the Deep Woods to Civilization: Chapters in the Autobiography of an Indian* (1916) counters the gloomy ending to *Indian Boyhood* by offering a balanced ledger of loss and gain. Literacy and Christianity are celebrated; the abandonment of Indian culture's superior aspects is lamented, as are the injustices rationalized by the self-serving notion that suffering and progress are inseparable.

In this "pro-civilization" book, Eastman assumes the role of representative Indian, emphasizing his distinguished Sioux ancestry and his connections through blood and marriage to a New England elite. Introduced to Ralph Waldo Emerson, Henry Wadsworth Longfellow, and Matthew Arnold, he is also aided in his search for a vocation. At Knox College, he befriends future notables such as Samuel S. McClure, Edgar A. Bancroft (lawyer for the International Harvester Company), and John S. Phillips of *American Magazine*, and at Dartmouth he is inspired by Indian precursors Occum and Daniel Webster. An admirer of invention and enterprise, Eastman is a man of his age, though he is alienated by the preoccupation with money and property. Throughout college, he identifies with poor students who are also working their way through (the government offered no support for Indian education), and he reflects on the extremes of poverty and wealth in American cities, noting that no Indian nation would tolerate such disparity. How much more civilized civilization would be, Eastman suggests, if it only practiced what its best preacher preached: "Jesus was an Indian. He was opposed to material acquirement and . . . inclined to peace."[55]

Eastman's aim in all of these writings, and in his life as a whole, was to recall Christianity to its true potential as a harmonizing force in modernization and to convince Indians of the fundamental affinity between their values and a theoretical Christianity. Christianity was the last hope of a spiritually bankrupt nation, where "the dollar is the measure of value, and *might* still spells *right*." A society without a strong sacred dimension could not survive. Eastman's faith in Christianity was based in his admiration for its most idealistic forms, including Asceticism and Shaker doctrine, and his sense of their consistency with Indian first principles, such as the divinity of nature. An ideal Christianity, or liberal universalism, involved a commitment to "the broad brotherhood of mankind; the blending of all languages and the gathering of all races under one religious faith."[56] Eastman's liberal universalism was strengthened by his 1911 experience as the Indian representative to the First Universal Races Congress in London. He was pleased to discover his commitment to racial equality affirmed by his colleagues there and distinguished himself by his demand that religious diversity also be respected, a demand seconded by Jewish and Buddhist representatives. While joint partnership with Indians, Jews, and Buddhists was not what most Christians of the time had in mind, Eastman can be forgiven for believing in 1911 that racial and religious ecumenicalism stood a good chance of flourishing in the new century. When Eastman declared, "I have never lost my Indian sense of right and justice," calling modern capitalism a type of "primitive savagery," he did so as an American, whose criticism expressed commitment to his adopted country.[57] He would always be Indian, but this heritage was part of, indeed enhanced, an American identity.

For tribeswoman Zitkala-Ša, such syncretism was impossible; she felt permanently destabilized by her attempted assimilation into American society, as confirmed by her self-characterization as "neither a wild Indian nor a tame one."[58] Though her stories of growing up Sioux in America were published in major magazines (*Atlantic Monthly* and *Harper's*), Zitkala-Ša was troubled throughout her education—at mission schools, Earlham College, and the Boston Conservatory of Music for solo violin—by the recognition that her people were less than immigrants in their own land.[59] In contrast to Eastman, who highlighted similarities between Indian and Christian religions, Zitkala-Ša saw only differences: the idea that earth, animals, and humans were kin was unlike any Christian precept, and she repudiated Eastman's merciful divide between Christian creed and deed. A pluralist at heart, she identified a "Great Spirit," known only to Indians, that connected all vital things.[60] The alternative, conversion, was tragic, as confirmed by her most poignant story, "The Soft-Hearted Sioux," about a youth who becomes Christian during nine years at a mission school and returns home to preach. Near starvation, the Sioux ignore his message, and he steals from neighboring cattle-rich settlers in order to save his ailing father. Pursued by a settler, the gentle Sioux kills in self-defense, and closing images of white snow bathed in blood frame his trip to the gallows. His error was to misconstrue the role of Indians in American Christianity as defined by three hundred years of colonial encounter: rather than messengers of sacrificial principles, the story reveals them to be objects of sacrificial practice. In fiction filled with images of tombs and live burial, Zitkala-Ša portrayed an Indian experience at the end of the nineteenth century haunted by death. She conveyed the existential and social despair of peoples whose cultures were viewed by the dominant society as the "price" of progress.

HELEN HUNT JACKSON: NEW ENGLAND REFORMER

Her own terrible intimacy with death helped to make Helen Hunt Jackson a valuable and empathic advocate of western Indians. Her parents, because they were chronically ill and died young, were absent through much of her childhood, and she later endured in rapid succession the deaths of her first husband and their young sons. As witness to the Civil War, as well as to the ruin of her beloved rural countryside in western Massachusetts during postwar industrial expansion, Jackson was acutely attuned to loss. It was, in her case, therapeutic to challenge a contemporary form of loss so blatantly due to injustice. Jackson was constitutionally passionate, even fierce, tendencies that were muted by suffering she was trained to face stoically. But Jackson's energies were fully mobilized by a mass death that she recognized as political and for which there could be no possible moral defense. Thus fired by a fervor that was personal as well as intellectual, rooted in a Calvinist sense of moral obligation, Jackson's commitment to redressing the ravages of American Indian policy was unsurpassed in her time.

What made Jackson's advocacy on behalf of Indians significant was the variety of forms it took, each one exploiting a different aptitude. Writing was her vocation, and she seemed to excel at every major genre from poetry, domestic essays, and short stories to literary novels and travel writing. She was frustrated, however, by the limited efficacy of art before "the huge sin and wrong."[61] As this dissatisfaction grew, Jackson turned to direct political agitation, through government petitions, journalism, and social organizing (helping to launch the Boston Indian Citizenship Committee and joining the Women's National Indian Association). Inspired by Standing Bear's 1879 Boston presentation in which he described his Ponca tribe's forced migration from Dakota to Indian Territory, she took up their cause along with that of Colorado's White River Utes, whose misery was also brought to her attention. Aware of how wrongs against Indians transcended specific tribes, Jackson settled on a chronological account of America's broken treaties as a focus for her reform energies. The result was *A Century of Dishonor* (1881), which sought "to show our causes for national shame in the matter of our treatment of the Indians."[62] While the book was positively reviewed, it sold a mere 2,000 copies, and Jackson was greatly disappointed. A year later Jackson was appointed commissioner of Mission Indian Affairs in California, an official status that provided a unique perspective on western colonial struggle, the subject of her late travel pieces for eastern magazines (e.g., *Century*, *Christian Union*, and *Independent*). Jackson also produced an 1884 report on the condition of mission Indians, resulting in the 1891 Act for the Relief of the Mission Indians in the State of California. The act preserved thousands of acres for California tribes, but it did not pass, sadly, until six years after her death. Jackson did live to experience the triumph of her best-selling novel, *Ramona* (1884), though she couldn't have anticipated the extent of its future popularity.[63] It was appropriate that the most renowned contribution to Indian reform made by this wandering New Englander was a work of literature.

Like Elizabeth Stuart Phelps, Jackson was born to the literary life in a college town, her father an author-minister and her mother a writer of children's fiction. Amherst, Massachusetts, in 1830 was defined by the academic institution that employed so many of its residents, including Jackson's father, Nathan Welby Fiske, a professor of Latin and Greek at Amherst. Fiske and his wife, Deborah, were orthodox Calvinists who brought up Helen and her sister Ann in their stringent faith, which stipulated, above all, cheerful submission to God's will. Yet they also instilled a deep sense of justice: Nathan Fiske was among a group of Amherst College faculty protesting the forced removal of the Georgia Cherokees by the administration of Andrew Jackson.[64] Calvinist notions of innate depravity and duty dominated Jackson's childhood home, as did illness: her mother had tuberculosis and died when Helen was thirteen, her father had bronchitis and died when she was sixteen, and Helen herself had perpetual sore throats that she feared were signs of tuberculosis and bronchitis. Despite this, she felt loved and supported by her family and was encouraged by her parents' example, as well as by their confidence in her, to be intellectually ambitious. But illness and death continued to plague Jackson's early life. In 1852, she married civil engineer and Union army lieutenant Edward Hunt and later that year gave birth to a son, Murray, who died of a brain tumor before he was a year old. Her husband, Edward, was killed in a weaponry accident in 1853, and her surviving son, Rennie, died at age nine of diphtheria. Jackson never recovered emotionally from these losses, but her conversance with grief and its mastery gave her the means to function outwardly. Within two months of Rennie's 1865 death, she had published her first poem in the *New York Evening Post*, to mark the beginnings of her career as a writer. While Jackson conceded to a friend, "I keep a brave face. . . . But the heart of me is sorely tired out," she was able to channel her sorrows into expressive forms that touched others profoundly.[65]

Jackson's health problems provided an empathic window onto the suffering of others and also prompted a remarkably peripatetic life. Jackson was always on the move, seeking climates or air she believed conducive to good health. Evidently, constant travel was also necessary to her emotional well-being: making any home permanent, she feared, might result in the demise of its inhabitants.[66] Jackson was suited creatively to this lifestyle, which also proved professionally and personally advantageous. In 1866 at a Newport, Rhode Island, boardinghouse she met Thomas Wentworth Higginson, who was there with his ailing wife, and he became her literary mentor. A trip to Colorado (considered a "sanctuary for people with respiratory infections") resulted in a second marriage—to William Sharpless Jackson, a Quaker businessman, banker, and railroad administrator. Though William Jackson was relatively uneducated, Helen Hunt was drawn to his solidity and warmth: "He rests me," she wrote to a friend. "I trust him to the *core*."[67] Moreover, he was supportive of her writing, encouraging in particular its liberalism and tolerance. The son of antislavery activists, who recalled driving fugitive slaves north at night, Jackson wrote to his fiancée, "I despise and utterly condemn any and every thing that borders on cast [sic] or exclusiveness."[68] He helped to ease the racialism she had imbibed along with her New England Calvinism, just as he softened her hostility to business and development.[69] Jackson's economic success had little impact on the habits of his new wife; she had long been a shrewd literary businesswoman herself. As she explained to the patrician editor James T. Fields, who protested her fee for an *Atlantic Monthly* contribution, and especially the temerity of her mentioning it, "cash *is* a vile article, but there is one thing viler . . . a purse without any cash in it."[70] Jackson deliberately preserved her financial independence in her second marriage, in part because she conveyed her devotion to her sister's six children and her many friends through monetary gifts, and also because she had rather expensive tastes, in house servants and fine clothes, that she felt might disturb her frugal, though wealthy husband.

When she took up the cause of Indians in America, Helen Hunt Jackson was professionally and financially secure, her poetry admired by Ralph Waldo Emerson, her writings solicited by major periodicals. Though she continued producing the type of literature (largely domestic essays, fiction, and above all poetry) that characterized her first decade as a professional author, following her remarriage and relocation out West, Jackson was increasingly drawn to regionalism and realism, the novel in particular. These genres allowed her to articulate her passion for the countryside and small towns: "If I were God," she once said, "I would not let such a thing as a city exist."[71] It was the writing on Indians, published in the last decade of her life, that captured her lifelong rural longings, which is one reason she favored them. Shortly before her death, she remarked that they were "the only things I have done for which I am glad now. They will live on and they will bear fruit."[72] For Jackson, Indian reform was inseparable from regionalism: loyalty to a particular territory and respecting the rights of its original inhabitants were complementary goals. As a woman of her time, Jackson reproduced prevailing prejudices in her portraits of California Indians and Mexicans. Yet she also took conscious steps to challenge such prejudices, for example, by inverting the conventions of regionalist dialect in which whites spoke formal English, and ethnic others spoke the local vernacular. Instead, *Ramona* represents Indian and Spanish characters as normative by rendering their speech in formal English, while white settlers alone speak in dialect.[73]

Ramona garnered the immediate attention Jackson sought, but it was her treatise, *A Century of Dishonor: A Sketch of the United States Government's Dealings with Some of the Indian Tribes* (1881), that proved the more lasting in terms of what it set out to do.[74] Still respected in the twenty-first century as a historical record of America's betrayal of the Indian nations, the book's aims were foreshadowed in a series of open letters to newspapers (e.g., *New York Evening Post*, *New York Times*, *Springfield (Mass.) Republican*, and *Boston Daily Advertiser*). Focusing on seven tribes—the Ponca, Cherokee, Delaware, Cheyenne, Nez Percé, Sioux, and Winnebago—*Century of Dishonor* proceeds to show that the Europeans who encountered the Indians of North America from the early 1600s recognized "the Indians' right of occupancy." Not only were these land rights documented by the "discovering Powers" (England, Spain, France, and Portugal), but they were also ratified in turn by the American Constitution, by several Supreme Court rulings, and by every state that ever drew up a treaty with the Indians who lived there. To underline her point, she cites, among others, President John Quincy Adams's Message of 1828 ("At the establishment of the Federal Government the principle was adopted of considering [the Indians] foreign and independent powers, and also as proprietors of land"); Justice James Kent's ruling in *Clark v. Smith* ("the natives were admitted to be the rightful occupants of the soil, with a *legal* as well as just claim to retain possession of it"); and Dr. Walker's *American Law* (the Indian right of occupancy "can only be *extinguished by treaty, and upon fair compensation*; until which they are entitled to be protected in their possession"). Nations, she insists, must be as obedient to written laws as individuals. Indeed, the violation by the United States of the principles of international justice leaves it open "to all punishments that follow upon such sins—to arbitrary punishment at the hands of any civilized nation that might see fit to call us to account, and to that more certain natural punishment, which, sooner or later, as surely comes from evil-doing, as harvests come from sown seed."[75] Jackson's narrative continues in this vein, as fierce rhetorically as it is irrefutable factually. The history of Indian and colonial encounters from the seventeenth through the nineteenth centuries is uniformly reprehensible: "Colorado is as greedy and unjust in 1880 as was Georgia in 1830, and Ohio in 1795." Were the "right-thinking, right-feeling men and women of this land," she writes in conclusion, made aware of the injustices done to Indians by their government, the result would be no less than "revolution."[76] The purpose of Jackson's book was precisely to raise such awareness: but the righteous men and women, apparently, were nowhere to be found. What was clear was the preference of readers for sugarcoating on their bitter pills: Jackson's intent to inform Americans of the national record on Indian affairs needed a better story.

Harriet Beecher Stowe's *Uncle Tom's Cabin* was Jackson's model for *Ramona*. "If I could write a story that would do for the Indian a thousandth part [of] what *Uncle Tom's Cabin* did for the Negro," she wrote in 1883, "I would be thankful the rest of my life."[77] Jackson recalled Stowe in feeling guided by higher powers in writing about Indians. Albion Tourgée confirmed Jackson's triumphant appropriation of New England's literary-divine pathway by naming *Ramona* and *Uncle Tom's Cabin* the century's two great ethical novels.[78] For *Ramona*, Jackson drew on the extensive reading in western history she had done after being commissioned by *Century Magazine* to write four pieces on southern California.[79] She also explored the origins of California's missions and ranchos at the Bancroft Library. She was drawn to the state's multiculturalism, which she tended to romanticize, from the tragic Mission Indians to the "gay, idle southern peoples. Their rich brown skins, their shining dark eyes . . . their attitude, and their rags, all are picturesque." As was typical of "romantic racialism," Jackson highlighted what she took to be the languor and simplicity of Mexicans: lacking the drive and culture of the Anglo-Saxons who pressed upon them, they were certain to be superseded.[80] Linked with tendencies that could not survive, they were ideally suited to a novelistic treatment that preserved them as aesthetic objects. Yet despite the condescension that emerges at times in Jackson's travel narratives and sketches, there is in *Ramona* another dimension, a political identification and outrage that drives the novel toward different ends.

Jackson's experience of writing *Ramona* was legendary, as was the site of composition. In four months at New York's Berkeley Hotel, in a room decorated with a shrine of Indian baskets and busts resembling the novel's hero and heroine, she produced a manuscript requiring minimal revision. Colonial conflict among Americans, Mexicans, and Indians in nineteenth-century California proved an ideal subject for Jackson's skills as a New England regionalist, known for moral directness. The novel's plot and characters were appealingly colorful and predictable: an idealized heroine (Ramona), daughter of a Scottish father and Indian mother, is raised by a forbidding Mexican stepmother (Señora Moreno), marries a noble, aristocratic Indian (Alessandro), is widowed, marries the stepmother's son (Felipe) who has always loved Ramona, and becomes queen of the manor. What was powerfully original about the novel was its recasting of leading Anglo-American mythologies in multicultural terms. *Ramona* is a story of romantic exile, a latter-day Exodus narrative, that depicts the hapless hero and heroine wandering from one ravaged Indian village to another, tracking as they go the destruction of Indian lands and culture. Americans are the villains: crude, uneducated, avaricious, they feed on the victimization of ethnic others. Their chief antagonist is the singularly empowered Señora Moreno, whose anti-Americanism signals the author's sympathy for her: "It gave her unspeakable satisfaction, when the Commissioners, laying out a road down the valley, ran it at the back of her house instead of past the front. . . . Whenever she saw, passing the place, wagons or carriages belonging to the hated Americans, it gave her a distinct thrill of pleasure to think that the house turned its back on them . . . a pleasure in which religious devotion and race antagonism were so closely blended that it would have puzzled the subtlest of priests to decide whether her act were a sin or a virtue."[81] The novel ends with the expatriation to Mexico of Felipe, who abandons his flourishing ranch, and Ramona, who is content to spare her half-Indian daughter the oppression she herself faced. Felipe's decision expresses aristocratic disdain for California's nouveau riche; his return to Mexico is an embrace of his own class and kind. Jackson thus values controlled intermixing among the highest racial types, while preserving the class system.

Meanwhile, America is repudiated for barbarism against the gentle Indians, as well as for its violation of a sacred (by the lights of New England and Mexico) upper-class code. While championing the lost cause of California's Indians, whose only means of endurance is mixing their blood with stronger peoples, the novel succeeded in sanctioning many high-culture ideals. The most striking outcome of *Ramona* was the passion it instilled in readers, which was exploited by entrepreneurs in the years following the novel's publication. Independent pilgrims, whose visits to Jackson's Colorado grave resulted in so many tributes and so much debris that Jackson's husband had her body moved to a private cemetery, worshipped *Ramona*. Then there were restaurants, tourist sites, souvenirs, and even museums that over time generated millions of dollars for those able to attach themselves to the novel's magic.[82] Nothing, however, equaled the Ramona pageant, an elaborate theatrical adaptation begun in 1923 and performed annually ever since in Hemet, California, one hundred miles east of Los Angeles. Displaying, like the novel, a multicultural harmony of Indian and

Mexican, struggling to protect their land from Americans, the pageant, like the novel, fanned the flames of the forces it critiqued so decisively.[83] For its attraction was its portrait of Indians as romantic commodities (Ramona was played by Raquel Welch in 1959 and Anne Archer in 1969) that could be readily assimilated by audiences without much concern for the violent history at its source.

As these examples show, despite *Ramona's* anticapitalist themes, it played a critical role in the marketing of the latest national commodity: Indian authenticity. It also provided the ultimate example of the Indian reform novel. For all its contradictions, *Ramona* was the height of reason on Indian affairs among popular novels set in the West. The novels about western expansion that followed Jackson's were elegies that took the demise of the Indian nations for granted and sought to put the best face on this fact in representing colonizers and colonized alike. These works by Maria Ruiz de Burton, Owen Wister, and Zane Grey depicted Indians on the margins of society, interlopers on land that had until recently been recognized as theirs by right of occupancy.

ELEGISTS OF CONQUEST: MARIA RUIZ DE BURTON, OWEN WISTER, ZANE GREY

Where a cultural insider like Helen Hunt Jackson was poised to protest the nineteenth-century sacrifice of the Indian nations, Mexican American author Maria Ruiz de Burton was preoccupied with the wrongs against her own people. In *The Squatter and the Don* (1885), one of the first English-language novels by a Mexican American, she described the gradual displacement of the Mexican population by white settlers in the Southwest. While the 1848 Treaty of Guadalupe-Hidalgo granted citizenship to Mexicans, subsequent local and national measures resulted in the transfer of their land to the open market, making the "Californios," victims of the U.S. Congress, the State of California, and the agents of capitalist development. Land disputes in Ruiz de Burton's novel are between Americans and Mexicans, because Indian dispossession is assumed. Indians in *The Squatter and the Don* are but shadows of their formidable historical selves: lazy and dishonest, they work as servants or day laborers.

Maria Amparo Ruiz de Burton was born in Loreto, Baja California, in 1832, to a family of wealthy landowners who had distinguished themselves in the military. The property owned by Ruiz de Burton's grandfather, governor of Lower California, included territory in Baja, which his grand-daughter would spend her life contesting. Ruiz de Burton met her husband,

American army captain Henry S. Burton, in 1847 when he accompanied General Winfield Scott's expedition to Mexico. Burton presided over the surrender of La Paz and the signing of articles of capitulation by the Mexicans. Their 1849 marriage, which produced a son and a daughter, was celebrated as a romantic union of "natural enemies." Ruiz de Burton's career as an author seems to have begun after her husband's death in 1869.[84] Her novels and correspondence show her to be widely read in Anglo-American literature, and she was also a shrewd businesswoman, with varied cultivation and building enterprises. But her main energies were devoted to gaining legal title to her land. In this undertaking, she fought foreign investors backed by American entrepreneurs, wrote letters to the newspaper, and initiated legal proceedings in New Mexico.

The sense of justice that motivated Ruiz de Burton's losing battle for her land informs *The Squatter and the Don*, whose characters often deliver speeches airing their grievances. These exchanges are commonly between Clarence Darrell, the novel's hero and son of the American "squatter," and the Mexican aristocrat, Don Mariano. Significantly, the don barely acknowledges the seizure of Indian lands by Mexican developers, echoing when he does American social Darwinism: the rightful displacement of primitive by more civilized peoples. While Clarence Darrell insists that Americans would renounce their government's treatment of California's Mexicans, were it publicized, both peoples bear responsibility for the Indian experience of colonization—land-theft and extermination. Still *The Squatter and the Don* provides a stirring exposé of the corrupt means by which land was made available to western settlers, illegalities consistently detrimental to Indians and Mexicans. Focusing on the Central Pacific Railroad Company run by Leland Stanford, Collis P. Huntington, Charles Crocker, and Mark Hopkins, the novel recapitulates a chapter of California history in notably confrontational terms.

Granted 9 million acres of free land and millions of dollars for construction by the U.S. government in 1869 to build a transcontinental railway, the Central Pacific used these assets to assert control over all western freight and passengers. From 1870 to 1910, the company appropriated a major share of the profits from virtually every industry in the state. Stanford, Huntington, Crocker, and Hopkins amassed unparalleled fortunes and fought tenaciously to preclude all competition; most importantly, a plan that would have made San Diego the western terminus of the transcontinental railway. Ruiz de Burton was heavily invested in the San Diego extension, so that some of her animus against the Central Pacific was personal. But the collective distress caused by these machinations was covered in the press. In contrast to Frank Norris, who limits his indictment of the railroad trust in *The Octopus* to a Jewish scapegoat, S. Behrman, Ruiz de Burton lays the guilt of empire building at the feet of California's leading Anglo-Saxons.

The Squatter and the Don is a powerful example of the historical romance, with an intriguing cast composed of three principal families, two American (the Darrells and the Mechlins) and one Mexican (the Alamars). Women characters reject the misjudgments and racial prejudices of their husbands, particularly Mary Darrell, whose husband, William, has a history of squatting on Mexican lands. While much is open to prospective settlers, Mexicans own the most fertile territory, so Americans "squat" to initiate litigation. The struggle between William Darrell, the squatter, and Don Mariano Alamar, the Mexican owner, is thus a struggle between an American settler's "right," sanctioned by his government, to secure the best land and the "right" of the conquered Mexican to keep it. Clarence Darrell, who surpasses his father in every way (as a businessman, a lover, and a moral being), becomes independently wealthy, which allows him to pay the Alamars secretly for their land and win the love of Don Alamar's favorite daughter, Mercedes.

The novel concludes with a series of tragedies and a prospect of hope. Don Alamar dies after being ruined by the thwarting of the San Diego railroad. His family moves to San Francisco to pursue banking and finance, supported by Clarence Darrell and his new wife, Mercedes. The American nouveau riche is ascendant, as confirmed by Don Alamar's wife, who draws a mournful contrast between their spendthrift habits and the culture at the former rancho. American and Mexican bloodlines fuse beneficially, and there are hints that a healthy competitive capitalism prevails, but the supplanting of Mexican gentry by an American commercial class is an unqualified loss. Ruiz de Burton's version of western expansion bears few traces of the indigenous inhabitants. And the very late recuperation of *The Squatter and the Don* shows literary history to be as Darwinian as the colonial struggles the novel represents.[85]

Of all the novels written in the period between the end of the Civil War and the beginning of World War I, no other combined the popular and critical appeal of Owen Wister's *The Virginian* (1902). An immediate best seller, the novel was reprinted thirteen times and much discussed by the author's powerful friends, among them President Theodore Roosevelt, its dedicatee. Wister's feat was to capture in novelistic form a dominant mythology of the West as virgin land. As he confided in a journal of his 1885 trip, "It's like the scenery on the moon must be. Then suddenly you come around a turn and down into a green cut where there are horsemen and wagons and hundreds of cattle, and then it's like Genesis."[86] Wister's journey by Pullman train was in fact a rest cure for a jaded youth prescribed by Dr. S. Weir Mitchell, a family friend who was famous for treating nervous illness. Wister's western trip helped to reconcile him to the practical career favored by his father, and he entered Harvard Law School soon after it. In 1889, Wister launched a legal practice in Philadelphia, where he had grown up, the son of Dr. Owen Jones Wister and Sarah Butler, whose mother was the actress Fanny Kemble. The family's social status afforded connections to notable artists such as Frederic Remington and Henry James, who encouraged Wister in his ongoing literary endeavors. It was the enthusiastic acceptance of two of these stories by *Harper's Magazine* in 1891 that emboldened Wister to embark on a full-time writing career at the age of thirty-one.

In keeping with generic conventions, *The Virginian* portrays the West as a territory of sensory deprivation, hostile to all forms of domesticity. Though its tendencies are ascetic, it is anti-Christian, replacing God with ideals of masculine skill and fraternity. The novel's heroes are silent and impenetrable, courting death and belying its violence through stylized methods of killing and dying.[87] In contrast to the nineteenth-century examples of James Fenimore Cooper and Lewis Henry Morgan, Wister's Indians are excluded from this male solidarity, presented instead as ignorant leaders and mass aggressors. The Indian chiefs who listen to the tall tale about frog legs are objects of derision whose uncomprehending attention confirms the Virginian's power as a storyteller. The chiefs are either objects of tourism, arrayed conspicuously in traditional garb, or salesmen themselves, plugging their baubles. Overall, the novel's Indians are stereotypes; consigned to reservations, they leave sometimes with permission and sometimes without, to commit atrocities upon undeserving whites.

Wister's embrace of these classic features of the western reflects his alienation from a modern consumer culture of increasing class conflict and social heterogeneity. His correspondence is marked by anti-immigrant vitriol, as when he describes "the encroaching alien vermin, that turn our cities to Babels and our citizenship to a hybrid farce." To "survive in the clean cattle country," he continues, "requires a spirit of adventure, courage, and self-sufficiency; you will not find many Poles or Huns or Russian Jews in that district."[88] Like *The Squatter and the Don* and *Ramona*, *The Virginian* confirms an antidemocratic principle of natural aristocracy. Where Helen Hunt Jackson retains the genetic inheritance of the aristocratic Indian Alessandro, Maria Ruiz de Burton unites the inherently noble Clarence Darrell with the elite Mexican Mercedes Alamar. Similarly, Wister provides a biosocial rationale for class privilege, justifying the ascent of his hero through his exceptional attributes. Thus a poor Virginian, with all the Anglo-Saxon virtues, earns the respect of the rich and powerful, becomes a captain of industry, and marries a New England blue blood.

Before the closing of the blessed West that Wister identified with everything that was admirable, the nation's purest specimens would unite there to forge "the true America."[89] The Indians, from whom his brave future wife rescues the Virginian, like the immigrants Wister maligned, have no place in this Edenic landscape. Neither, it seems, do Americans themselves. For the forces of progress highlighted in the novel's ending signal the fall of Wister's idyll: "But the railroad came, and built a branch to that land of the Virginian's where the coal was."[90] Neither a casualty of the railroad, like the Indians, nor of its failed extension, like Don Alamar, the Virginian finishes triumphantly. The development that promises to enrich him, however, spells the doom of Wister's ever-expanding frontier.

The writings of Zane Grey surpassed Wister's in popularity and confirmed that western Indians were no longer agents in regional history. But they did so in terms that conveyed respect for Indian traditions, a profound sense of kinship (Grey claimed his own Indian ancestry), and recognition of the outrages committed against them by Americans whether through dispossession, extermination, or assimilation. In contrast to Wister, Zane Grey was a wilderness devotee who schooled himself in the novels of James Fenimore Cooper, echoing Cooper's commitment to Indian forms of ingenuity and providing central Indian characters. *Riders of the Purple Sage* (1912) was the first Grey novel to find a vast readership, whose appetite for his fiction never waned.[91] Though literary critics spurned Grey, his audience was assured; in 1924, it was noted that "of all living novelists," he had "the greatest reading public."[92] By the time Grey was fifty-five, he had sold 17 million novels and had an international readership estimated at 56 million, his books translated into twenty different languages. In the United States, Grey drew readers from both genders, all classes, and every imaginable walk of life. Significantly, his sales were higher in New York and Boston than anywhere else in the country. This suggests how Grey's fiction served to articulate mythologies of the West for those unlikely to know it firsthand. A lifelong fisherman (his record-setting 1,040-pound marlin was exhibited at the Museum of Natural History), hunter, and semiprofessional baseball player, Grey's passion for sports took him around the world and enhanced his admiration for those with more authentic proficiencies at home.[93]

Zane Grey was born in 1872 in Zanesville, Ohio, a town founded in 1796 by his great grandfather. The son of a dentist, Grey was talented enough to win a baseball scholarship to the University of Pennsylvania, where he studied dentistry. He set up a dental practice in New York City but was drawn to writing, specifically sporting and adventure fiction with western settings. Though it took time for Grey to develop his signature style, he managed to support his young family through juvenile fiction and essays about his wilderness expeditions.[94] *The Heritage of the Desert* (1910) sold moderately well, but his 1912 novel about religious conflict in Utah, *Riders of the Purple Sage*, became a best seller and launched him into the mainstream of popular American literature. Grey's narratives were detailed apprecia- tions of natural splendor, that of the places where he traveled before settling in California in 1918—Arizona, New Mexico, Cuba—and the more exotic locales he could afford to visit after he became famous—Tahiti, New Zea- land, Newfoundland. Grey's California home proved opportune for his connections to the movie industry: in 1918 film adaptations of three of his novels, *The Border Legion*, *Riders of the Purple Sage*, and *The Rainbow Trail*, appeared. While Grey complained that his profits were inadequate, the films increased his fame and boosted the novels' sales.[95] Grey's annual income in 1929 topped $340,000; but the Great Depression leveled the cul- ture industry, and he was forced to rely on endorsements for income. His fortunes had only slightly recovered when he died in 1939. During all the years of success, Grey was plagued by depression and restlessness, seeking to allay these demons through affairs with ever younger women, which tried the loyalty of his wife. Grey's intimacy with despair was chronicled in a 1920 essay, "Death Valley," where he detailed his attraction to "the awful, the appalling and terrible because they harked me back to a primitive day where my blood and bones were bequeathed their heritage of the ele- ments."[96] Grey expressed this compulsion for a generation of Americans and did so partly through vivid engagement with what remained of Indian ways of life.

Grey's early novels recalled those of Cooper most directly, and none more so than *The Spirit of the Border* (1905), which was set in a particular region, featured characters drawn from history, and centered on a well- known historical event: the 1872 massacre of Christian Indians and Mora- vian missionaries in the Ohio Valley. In *Spirit of the Border* two lovely white sisters are sent to aid their missionary uncle, thus providing pawns in the wars between the military, missionaries, white Indians, and Indians. The story defined heroism as the ability to navigate the wilderness with the sagacity of an Indian. And it sanctioned all but the most gratuitous forms of killing, thereby distinguishing a frontier morality from the morality of civilization. Grey diverged from Cooper in representing a series of harmonious intermarriages between white males and Indian women and in attributing most Indian-white conflict to the seizing of Indian land by white settlers.

Indians are no more than a memory in *Riders of the Purple Sage*, a means for celebrating survival skills, while Mormons assume the position of the threatening other—cultish, greedy, and malevolent. The gentle Gentile gunman, Jim Lassiter, deprograms the Mormon heroine, Jane Withersteen, and in the novel's climax saves her from the church elders. What made *Riders of the Purple Sage* something more than a formulaic western was Grey's understanding of the West and its conflicts through a thousand-year history of migration and displacement. Cliffs and valleys are silent reminders of a remote, yet continuous history whose different actors looked upon them with reverence as divine emblems. This is reinforced by the discovery of an entire world of stone, houses with fireplaces, the accoutrements of domesticity, intact within a cave. Cultural conflict, Grey suggests, is an interminable story of human vitality, survival, and extinction.

Grey's inspiration for the novel grew out of a journey to the Utah desert, where he viewed Navajo shrines and ruins with a group of traders and scholars assisted by a Piute guide named Nasjah Begay. They saw Nonnezoshe, or Rainbow Bridge, which was declared a national monument in 1909, as well as the cliff dwellings of Keet Seel. Significantly, *The Rainbow Trail* (1915), which Grey wrote as a sequel to *Riders of the Purple Sage*, was his first novel to feature an Indian protagonist, whose name, Nas Ta Bega, was a variant spelling of the Rainbow Bridge guide's name. Including in its cast Lassiter, Withersteen, and Fay Larkin from *Riders*, *The Rainbow Trail* forged new ground by portraying an Indian whose heritage reinvigorates the spirituality of an American minister, John Shefford. Shefford is disenchanted with American religion and culture as a whole and listens sympathetically to Nas Ta Bega's mournful experiences of forced assimilation in a mission school. In representing Nasjah Begay and the failure of an assimilation policy that overlooked the superior aspects of Indian culture, Grey drew on the experiences of the Indian football hero Jim Thorpe, who was declared "the greatest athlete in the world" at the 1912 World Olympics. At the novel's end, Shefford beholds Rainbow Bridge in the company of Begay and his lover, Fay: "There was a spirit in the canyon, and whether or not it was what the Navajo embodied in the great Nonnezoshe, or the life of the present, or the death of the ages, or the nature so magnificently manifested . . . the truth for Shefford was that this spirit was God."[97]

Grey was captivated by Indian traditions, and their exploration was integral to his travels: in Utah he studied the Navajo, in Arizona the Hopi, and in Mexico the Yaqui. These studies in turn became integral to his fiction and sometimes central. The Yaquis, for instance, who were attacked and subjugated in the Sierra Madre after gold was discovered on their land, were featured in one of his most poignant stories, "Yaqui," which described the brutal enslavement of an Indian by wealthy Mexican planters in the Yucatan. While the humble Indian slave exacts a bloody toll, as do oppressed Indians in other Grey fiction from the 1920s, he emphasizes that stray acts of revenge hardly compensate for what North American Indians endured at the hands of the Europeans. Grey's most famous Indian hero was Nophaie of *The Vanishing American* (1925), a novel serialized in the *Ladies Home Journal* in 1922 and made into a film the year it was published. Nophaie is the son of a chief, who was taken from his tribe to be educated but is forever dispossessed, because shortly after his removal his people are sent to a reservation controlled by hostile officials and missionaries. Alienated from his people, depleted spiritually, unmarried and childless, Nophaie enlists in World War I to fight Germans as a way of repaying the German missionaries for destroying his culture. Near the novel's end, Nophaie falls in love with a white missionary, who shares his resentment toward reservation officials and missionaries and welcomes his "red blood . . . as proof against white blood [their children] must inherit from me." *The Vanishing American* aroused a storm of protest during its serialization, from missionaries and the Bureau of Indian Affairs, among others, and the prospective film producer, Jesse Lasky, urged Grey to mute the controversial elements, as did the novel's publisher, Harper's. So the embittered author reduced the villainy of reservation officials and missionaries and killed off his Indian, along with any hints of interracial romance. Grey thus accommodated the mainstream culture industry's position on Indians in the post–World War I era: mixing with the white race was repudiated, and the Indian people were doomed. It was left to artists, writers, and intellectuals to catalog the attributes of this extinguishing civilization before it was completely gone. What was perhaps less expected was the role played by salesmen and advertisers in the preservation of Indian ways of life.

On one of his fishing trips in the early 1920s, Zane Grey chanced to meet John Wanamaker, the owner of the great Philadelphia department store, who told him: "I have given away thousands of your books and I have sold hundreds of thousands in my store. . . . *Never lay down your pen!*"[98] Wanamaker was a self-made man who recognized the power of the department store in American life and its ability to promote values, especially those pertaining to ethnic and national identity. His appreciation for the market appeal of Zane Grey was extended to his immediate grasp of what John K.

Dixon had to offer his store. Dixon was the author of *The Vanishing Indian* (1913), which argued that pure-blooded Indians were dying out, while dismissing "half-breeds" as representatives of authentic Indianness. Eager to record the tribal traditions that were fast disappearing, Dixon managed to sell his North American Indian project to Wanamaker after he became the store's "educational director." With the approval of the commissioner of Indian Affairs, Dixon traveled the country, studying and photographing Indians and assembling slides, lectures, and films for presentation at the Wanamaker stores, free to the public. Transformed into spectacles, with titles like "The Romance of a Vanishing Race," sometimes featuring Indian performers, these events were attended by thousands of schoolchildren in New York and Philadelphia, many of them immigrants.[99] Wanamaker's successful packaging of threatened Indian ways of life within the larger world of the department store reveals how ethnicity was used in the American marketplace to symbolize the universal, even transcendent aspirations of commerce. Because it was almost gone, Indianness was now a precious commodity, so dear in fact that Wanamaker considered it priceless, a part of the common heritage that could not be sold, only revered, by American citizens in the benevolent communal atmosphere of Wanamaker's department store. The sacrifice of the Indian nations in the age of progress had taken an alarmingly literal turn, a cultural mythology for distribution at the country's supreme mercantile establishments.

MARKETING CULTURE

During television coverage of the 1984 Winter Olympics, novelist John Updike found himself riveted not by the Games but by the high-stakes advertising that accompanied them. "I have no doubt that the aesthetic marvels of our age, for intensity and lavishness of effort and subtlety of both overt and subliminal effect, are television commercials," he commented, adding, "except within narrow professional circles, the artists involved, like Anglo-Saxon poets and Paleocene cave-painters, are unknown by name."[1] Updike's observation was anticipated almost a century earlier by editors at *Munsey's Magazine*, who noted in a July 1895 column that "some of the cleverest writing—the most painstaking, subtle work turned out by literary men today—can be found in the advertising pages of a first rate magazine." Advertising expenditures rose from $50 million just after the Civil war to over $500 million by the century's end, and magazine editors recognized how fully implicated they were in the business end of their enterprises.[2] Periodicals endorsed implicitly the commodities they advertised, even raising concerns about liability. The reciprocity between editors and advertisers was clear: magazines sought the highest bidders and advertisers sought the most illustrious forums. "Magazines like *McClure's*," a boy declared to his mother in a 1904 ad, "tell you what you want, and show you where you can get it. *McClure's Magazine* is the marketplace of the world." With the magazine defined as a marketplace, leisure-class women and children became its key consumers. Advertisements provided new conceptions of reading (as shopping), as well as new categories for classifying social experience, fresh areas of need (clean teeth, disposable tissues, carpet cleaners), and trademarked items to satisfy them (*Colgate* ribbon toothpaste, *Kleenex*, and *Scourene*). In some instances, literary works incorporated brandname items, foreshadowing "product placement" practices that were later standardized.[3] Protagonists previously characterized by their taste in reading (Catherine Morland's appetite for gothic fiction in *Northanger Abbey*) or by their appearance in other books (Huckleberry Finn from *Tom Sawyer*) are now typified by cereal preferences—the *Honeycomb* and *Cap'n Crunch* in Jerry Seinfeld's kitchen signal a familiar American longing for childhood.

In the late nineteenth century, for the first time, advertisements, literature, and images from photographic to painterly were packaged together as mutually enhancing products. In addition to greater profits for authors, advertisements gave the literature they appended the aura of modernity. To appear beside an intelligently conceived advertisement for Sapolio soap in a widely circulating magazine conferred upon a story by William Dean Howells a stamp of relevance. The increasingly common practice of serializing novels, biographies, memoirs, and so on in magazines also provided indispensable advertising for forthcoming books.[4] Excerpts or serials of works, such as Mark Twain's *Huckleberry Finn* and *Chapters from My Autobiography*, earned authors money while generating publicity and subsequent readership.[5] One publisher testifying in 1885 before a Senate Patents Committee considering international copyright stated: "It is impossible to make the books of most American authors pay unless they are first published and acquire recognition through the columns of the magazines. If it were not for that one saving opportunity of the great American magazines . . . American authorship would be at a still lower ebb than at present."[6]

What literature had to offer advertisers was at once more complex and contradictory. In selling their stories and novels to magazines for the sake of self-advertisement, literary authors were helping to enhance the authority and appeal of the magazines themselves and the goods that were advertised in them. The literature—high and low, popular and obscure—that was serialized in American magazines from the 1890s to the 1920s joined a continuum of promotion. It entered a cultural dialogue about capitalist development, participating with advertisers in a process of translating the terms of a new market culture to a motivated yet ambivalent populace. That was the case with Jack London's *Call of the Wild*, which was serialized in the *Saturday Evening Post* from June 20 to July 18, 1903. Consider the juxtaposition of a serialized section of the novel and the text of ads surrounding it (Fig. 4): "Inventions patented and sold," "Colorado isn't far away," "The 'Best' Light," "Keeping Cool." It's a notable instance of intertextuality. Many of the ads concern writing practices, whether the "Writing

Paper" sold "by Weight" courtesy of the Hoskins Store, or the Page-Davis Company offering classes on how "to Write Advertisements." The ad for "Talking Parrots" on sale from Geifler's Birdstore in Omaha, Nebraska, recalls the hyperintelligent dog-hero Buck, who provides the novel's dominant consciousness. The literary text can be seen as vitalized by this sea of advertising. Rather than drowning, these paragraphs float upon the entrepreneurial wave, emboldened in their nostalgic message by the support of these other "novel" commodities. The passage from *The Call of the Wild* depicts Buck becoming part of the wild fraternity of wolves after he has avenged the murder of his beloved owner, John Thornton, by Indians of the Yeehat tribe. Buck's massacre of the Yeehats leads to his commemoration as the "Ghost Dog" whose terrible feats ensure that one select valley of the Alaskan Klondike will be forever free of Indians. London's point seems to be that each species must stick to its own, however blissful certain cross-species alliances (such as that between Thornton and Buck) may be. Buck's nature is only realized among wolves. A return to one's essential condition is the ideal sought by the highest human and animal specimens, and London successfully cultivated the appetite for such transformations, as confirmed by the sales of his writings.

Advertisers of the time understood transformation (of the buyer) as the ultimate promise of commodity transactions. And restoration to the natural world is the ultimate kind of transformation, which is why they regularly exploited (and still exploit) nature in promoting their products. The car in the Haynes-Apperson ad, for instance, is posed on a country road, surrounded by trees, which is where it will take you if you can afford to buy it.[7] The Darwinian reversion of London's formerly domesticated pet dramatized in the serialized text is fully compatible with the accompanying ads on this page from the *Saturday Evening Post*. Indeed, the chunk of prose in one respect is hardly distinguishable from the other commodities advertised there. For the price of a book (or magazine), London promises urban readers a sojourn in the wild and identification with an animal that will ultimately be liberated from the overdeveloped modernity that has hemmed it in.

This *Saturday Evening Post* layout reveals an American literary realism actively engaged with the new rhetorical medium of advertising, whose proponents routinely championed the aesthetic power of their work. In fact, realist literature in America had to compete directly with advertising for the attention of readers. The idea of readers as consumers, together with heightened awareness of their own commercial prospects, preoccupied authors of the time in a way never before seen. That is the subject of this chapter, which explores key post–Civil War developments in advertising, editing, and au-

24 THE SATURDAY EVENING POST July 18, 1903

THE CALL OF THE WILD

(Concluded from Page 23)

bank which the men had made in the course of mining, and in this angle he came to bay, protected on three sides and with nothing to do but face the front.

And so well did he face it that at the end of half an hour the wolves drew back discomfited. The tongues of all were out and lolling, the white fangs showing cruelly white in the moonlight. Some were lying down with heads raised and ears pricked forward; others stood on their feet, watching him; and still others were lapping water from the pool. One wolf, long and lean and gray, advanced cautiously, in a friendly manner, and Buck recognized the wild brother with whom he had run for a night and a day. He was whining softly, and, as Buck whined, they touched noses.

Then an old wolf, gaunt and battle-scarred, came forward. Buck writhed his lips into the preliminary of a snarl, but sniffed noses with him. Whereupon the old wolf sat down, pointed nose at the moon, and broke out the long wolf-howl. The others sat down and howled. And now the call came to Buck in unmistakable accents. He, too, sat down and howled. This over, he came out of his angle and the pack crowded around him, sniffing in half-friendly, half-savage manner. The leaders lifted the yelp of the pack and sprang away into the woods. The wolves swung in behind, yelping in chorus. And Buck ran with them, side by side with the wild brother, yelping as he ran.

And here may well end the story of Buck. The years were not many when the Yeehats noted a change in the breed of timber-wolves; for some were seen with splashes of brown on head and muzzle and with a rift of white centring down the chest. But more remarkable than this, the Yeehats tell of a Ghost-Dog that runs at the head of the pack. They are afraid of this Ghost-Dog, for it has cunning greater than they, stealing from their camps in fierce winters, robbing their traps, slaying their dogs, and defying their bravest hunters.

Nay, the tale grows worse. Hunters there are who fail to return to the camp, and hunters there have been whom their tribesmen found with throats slashed cruelly open and with wolf-prints about them in the snow greater than the prints of any wolf. Each fall when the Yeehats follow the movement of the moose there is a certain valley which they never enter.

In the summers there is one visitor, however, to that valley, of which the Yeehats do not know. It is a great, gloriously-coated wolf, like, and yet unlike, all other wolves. He crosses alone from the smiling timberland and comes down into an open space among the trees. Here a yellow stream flows from rotted moose-hide sacks and sinks into the ground, with long grasses growing through it and vegetable mould overrunning it and hiding its yellow from the sun; and here he muses for a time, howling once, long and mournfully, ere he departs.

But he is not always alone. When the long winter nights come on and the wolves follow their meat into the lower valleys, he may be seen running at the head of the pack through the pale moonlight or glimmering borealis, leaping gigantic above his fellows, his great throat a-bellow as he sings a song of the Younger World which is the song of the pack.

(THE END)

A Safe Wager

AMONG the many annoyances to which men prominent in the nation's service are subjected is the constant effort of irrepressible strangers to affect an appearance of the greatest intimacy with them.

In Washington Admiral Dewey is, perhaps, the greatest sufferer in this respect. Courteous and genial as he is, the Admiral invariably greets every one saluting him; but he detests the species of strange individual who endeavors to approach him in the manner usually reserved for his intimate friends.

Not long since the head of the Navy was astonished suddenly to feel his hand grasped by a man whom he had never to his knowledge seen before. This person had the effrontery to exclaim:

"George, I'll wager you don't know me!"

The Admiral disengaged his hand and replied grimly:

"You win your wager!"

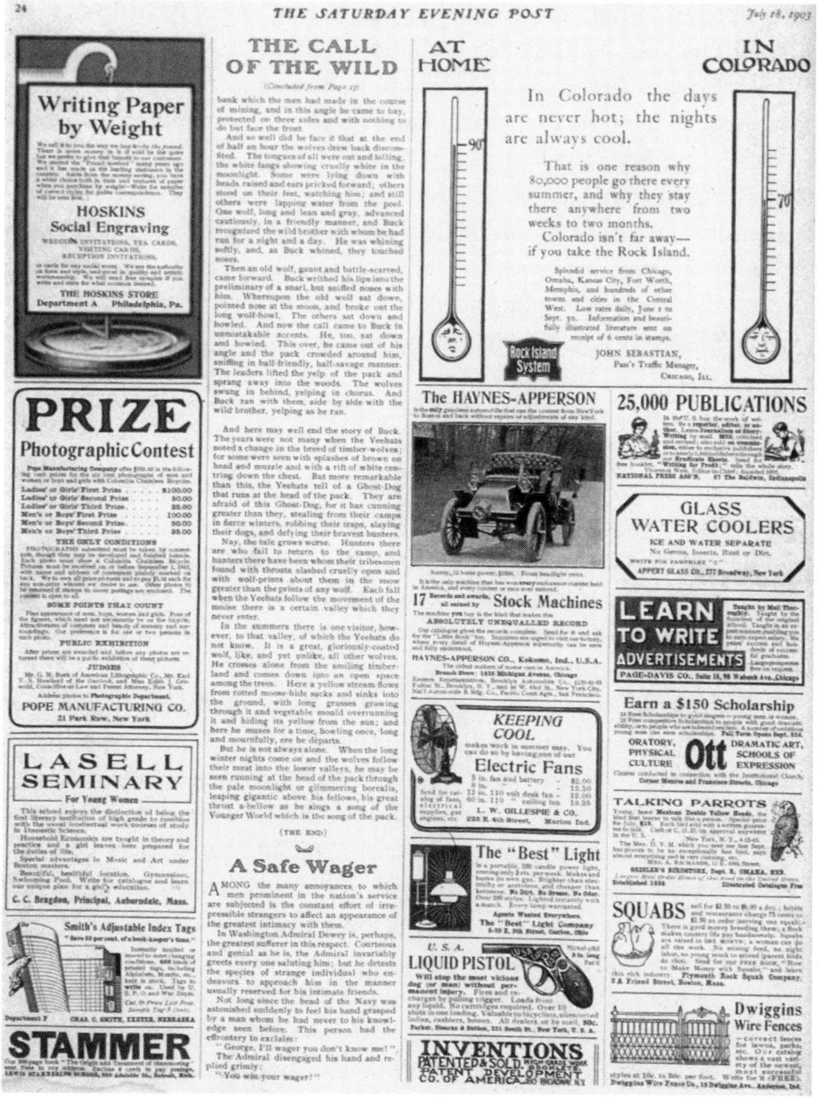

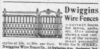

FIGURE 4 :: Serialized text of *The Call of the Wild* by Jack London, surrounded by advertisements. From *Saturday Evening Post*, July 18, 1903, back page.

thorship. The section on advertising charts the history of the field's expansion and analyzes theories by its leading practitioners as well as examples of influential advertisements. The section on editing focuses on two major magazines of the time that set the tone for their communities, Samuel S. McClure's *McClure's* and W. E. B. Du Bois's *Crisis*, and also discusses novelistic portraits of editors by Henry James and William Dean Howells, whose professional fortunes and misfortunes are profiled in the subsequent chapter on authorship. The chapter ends with an examination of the early careers of Willa Cather and Theodore Dreiser, two writers intimately engaged with advertising, editing, and authorship through World War I.

ADVERTISING

When the first transcontinental railroad was built in 1869, most businesspeople were writing their own ads; by 1910, the majority of them were commissioning it. At the same time, there was a shift in the emphasis of advertising rhetoric from production and manufacture to consumption and market diversification. Several circumstances resulting from the Civil War contributed to the rise of advertising as a profession. The selling of war bonds, which proved so advantageous to the Union, benefited from successful advertising campaigns. And the distribution of farm machinery (to replace workers at war) and standardized clothing (an outgrowth of factory-made uniforms) generated more need and revenue for advertising. Because women were diverted from the domestic production of necessities by greater demand for their labor outside the home, they relied on advertising for information about manufactured goods. The growth of the economy during the war and subsequent higher standards of living, which intensified after it, all worked to advance the new profession.[8] During the 1870s and 1880s, new technology and larger factories enabled faster and cheaper production, while inventions such as light bulbs, telephones, streetcars, and railroads ensured a mass supply of goods as well as the means of transporting them. In addition to the widespread substitution of coal fuel for wood, electricity was beginning to transform industry; it would eventually influence every occupation in American life while adding to the comfort of average people.[9]

Economic progress portended new markets and customers; advertisers zeroed in on a growing consumer population that was increasingly literate.[10] They not only encouraged the public to buy soap, bread, and clothes, instead of making their own, but to buy the same goods repeatedly. Facilitated by the invention of the paper bag and the folding box, factory-produced, brandname merchandise gradually replaced bulk goods. The brand name gave rise to what advertisers called "the soft sell," which emphasized the manufacturer's reliability, while investing relatively expensive trademarked items with desirable associations.[11] The fact that consumers no longer had direct, or only limited, contact with producers lent an element of uncertainty to purchasing and seemed to imperil the ethics of exchange. Advertisers stepped into the vacuum created by the anonymity of modern commerce, manipulating the fears of consumers and advancing their own authority as antidote.

No one did more in the late nineteenth century to bolster that authority than John E. Powers, who was dubbed "the father of modern advertising." Powers, who had studied advertising in England during the 1860s, introduced focus advertising—the targeting of ads to specific groups—as well as the practice of limiting each ad to one idea. "Powerisms" were exemplified by memorable trademarked phrases, such as Ivory Soap's "It Floats"; Kodak Camera's "You Press the Button, We Do the Rest"; and Prudential Insurance's "The Strength of Gibraltar," whose value reached millions of dollars.[12] The Bostonian Nathaniel C. Fowler helped to popularize the profession of advertising in a series of books he referred to as "advertising counsel." Comparing the advertiser to the physician, who, at best, could hope to succeed more often than he failed, Fowler also recognized that leisure-class women were the primary household consumers, supervising the purchase of everything from oatmeal to shingles.[13]

By the 1890s, advertising had largely overcome the moral blemish of its uses in patent medicine sales, while views of its potential grew increasingly ambitious.[14] One industry analyst called advertising "the medium of communication between the world's greatest forces—demand and supply. It is a more powerful element in human progress than steam or electricity . . . Men may look forward to the day when advertising will be what it has long deserved to be, one of the world's greatest sciences."[15] This prospect awaited the dramatic changes of the 1890s for realization: mass production and distribution, increased exports and purchasing power, and, most important, a vast domestic audience. From 1880 to 1910 the U.S. population nearly doubled (from 50 million to 91 million, with 18 million new immigrants). What was needed were techniques of persuasion that would get all these people to buy.[16]

The field of advertising thus extended its artistic ambitions far beyond the scope of what had previously been imagined, while joining other fields in promoting its scientific attributes. An important aspect of this scientific expertise was the conceptualization of society in the nuanced terms of class identity and aspirations. Magazines provided an ideal venue for advertisers by offering segmented, self-selected audiences, communities constituted by status-defined tastes and interests.[17] From 1865 to 1880 the number of magazines rose from 700 to 2,400, en route to higher figures by the next decade. In 1879, the periodical business received a terrific boost from the federal government with the introduction of bulk mailing rates. Given the extreme competition, survival for these periodicals hinged on their ability to attract advertising. The introduction in the 1880s of electrotype plates and halftones for advertisements made them less expensive and more attractive, especially in color. Initially advertisements were confined to the magazines' end pages, and their perusal was encouraged by the convention of precutting these pages before distribution. When magazines, motivated by higher revenue and visually splendid advertisements, began to place them throughout, advertisers and editors sought increasingly to orchestrate their commercial, literary, and visual components.[18]

The growth of advertising's commercial stakes coincided with greater self-consciousness about its methods and purposes. In books such as *The Psychology of Advertising* (1908) and *Effective Magazine Advertising* (1907), leading practitioners (sometimes with the help of ordinary consumers whose comments they incorporated into their analyses) addressed the power of suggestion, differential consumption patterns (by region, gender, class), and the relation between marketing and ethnicity. Walter Dill Scott and Francis Bellamy argued that commodities not only denote but also confer lifestyle. They proposed, too, that magazines should always aim above the actual class position of their presumed readership, since flattery is the highest inducement to purchase.[19] American advertising methods and the values it promoted provided a critical means of mediating the growing cultural diversity and class stratification of American society.

What is perhaps most striking about the following set of advertisements is the portrayal of ethnicity. Take the advertisement for Racine Canoes that was run in *Harper's Weekly* in 1908 (Fig. 5). "Racine Canoes are as beautiful of line," the ad announces, "and as thoroughly comfortable and durable as the ideal 'Cheemaun' of Hiawatha." The fine print lists locations on West 34th Street, New York; Milk Street, Boston; and Michigan Avenue, Chicago, pinpointing the market for this antiquated enterprise—stressed-out urbanites. The brushed edges of the image provide a reflection of the ideal family of five, enclosing it in a utopian halo of tranquility. To own a Racine Canoe is to embrace the simplicity and peace of "primitive" existence; it promises liberation from the punishing pace of the modern city and the already dim memory of Indian-white conflict. This advertisement contrasts

FIGURE 5 :: Advertisement for Racine's Canoes. From *Harper's Weekly*, April 18, 1908.

with the mid-nineteenth-century scenes painted by Charles Deas (*The Voyageurs*) and Alfred Jacob Miller (*The Trapper's Bride*), which emphasize the active fusion of white and Indian cultures.[20] The stillness of the whites in the Racine ad conveys solemn respect for the artifact and for the original designers whose demise is a foregone conclusion. Advertising fosters the illusion that the power to buy is the only limit to what one can be: owning a Racine canoe affords membership in a community with the wealth and leisure to enjoy it.

Consider next the advertisement for Waterman Pens, which draws on ethnic and evolutionary themes to promote a new technology, the modern fountain pen (Fig. 6). To purchase a Waterman pen is to identify with progress, the ad suggested as it focused the attention of *Atlantic Monthly* readers on the 1907 Jamestown Exposition in Norfolk, Virginia, which was sponsored by manufacturers, government agencies, railroads, even cooking schools and featured displays, demonstrations, and samples (like the book-mark souvenirs "free" at "Booth No. 1"). In the spirit of these expositions, cultural variety and product innovation appear in the ad as twin ideals of a global marketplace. An avuncular John Smith gazes fondly upon his diligent student Pocahontas as the facts of dispossession and genocide are transferred from ethnic bodies (Pocahontas, Smith) to writing instruments (quill, fountain pen). Pocahontas and Smith are arrayed in the seventeenth-century costumes appropriate to their cultures and stations (hers in an Indian hierarchy and his in a military one), but the image is dominated by a tension between feathers and steel that distinguishes them irrevocably. The feather framing the left side of the ad is echoed in the headdress of the obsolete Indian, while the steel dagger protruding jauntily from the colonizer's left hip recalls the violent history latent in that emblem of civilized "genius": the steel fountain pen framing the image on the right.

The familiar ethnic characters and belongings in these ads (Pocahontas, ca-

FIGURE 6 :: Advertisement for Waterman's Ideal Fountain Pen.
From *Atlantic Monthly*, June 1907.

noes) serve as symbols of authenticity that reinforce the subliminal connection between buying and being. Ethnicity stands for the prospect of self-transformation through purchase that is a central message of turn-of-the-twentieth-century advertising. Ethnicity, converted into stereotype, functions both to erase history and to validate the potential of the product. Owning a Waterman fountain pen is tantamount to possessing the power of origins signified by the authentic person of Pocahontas, whose imaging here as a benign recipient of literacy encompasses a contemporary Indian role.

One of the most notorious and versatile advertising runs of this era, extending from 1884 through 1910, was for Hand Sapolio soap and Sapolio all-purpose cleansers in cake form. Its uses ranged from bathing and skin care, to washing dishes, floors, and even tombstones, to sharpening knives and polishing false teeth. From the outset, the mass marketing of soap was synonymous with the quest for moral perfection. This is no doubt why the Reverend Henry Ward Beecher took such pride in the effects of his own 1884 advertising for Pears.[21] Under the direction of its chief advertising manager, Artemus Ward, Sapolio—which was omnipresent in periodicals, such as *Century*, *Atlantic Monthly*, *Putnam's*, and *McClure's*, where major novels were serialized—was responsible for many inaugural feats in marketing. Enoch Morgan's Sons selected Sapolio for widespread advertising in the 1860s, primarily in *Harper's Weekly* and *Leslie's Illustrated Weekly Newspaper*, and its expenditures grew at a rate previously unimaginable. In 1871, $15,000 was spent on advertising Sapolio; in 1885, $70,000; and by 1896, Sapolio's advertising expenses reached $400,000. For creativity, Sapolio advertising had no equal in its time. In 1884, the manufacturer became the first to exploit the boredom of public transit audiences in New York's horse-drawn streetcars. In 1892, Ward engineered a reverse voyage to Columbus's Spain on a fourteen-foot dory named the *Sapolio*, which was covered widely in the popular press; and in 1900, he launched the notorious "Spotless Town" campaign with its own regular production of jingles. The campaign was so successful that "Spotless Town" became commonplace (in theaters, newspapers, political speeches) as a synonym for cleanliness and order. In the amount of free publicity it generated, Sapolio was second only to the Ford automobile.[22]

What makes the Sapolio ads noteworthy is their appeal to different social strata and their use of various historical events. Full-page ads prominently placed in *Putnam's* and *Century* between 1904 and 1907 reveal the ambitions of its promoters. They identified their product in turn with aggressive expansionism in Panama (Fig. 7); the superstitious wisdom of

FIGURE 7 ::

Advertisement for
Sapolio, "Making
the Dirt Fly." From
Putnam's Monthly,
June 1907.

the Gypsy fortune-teller (Fig. 8); the middle-class housekeeper awake at
dawn to clean (Fig. 9); the Turkish bath where men congregate to admire
and perhaps partake of the "sparkling eye and . . . limb" achieved by Hand
Sapolio (Fig. 10); and the "very peculiar, very strict . . . ceremonial law" of
the "Hebrew race" (Fig. 11). While this last image links doctrines of purification and consumption pertaining "for more than 6,000 years" to Jews exclusively, with the "strictly Kosher" "vegetable oils" of Sapolio, an ad for "The
House of Sapolio," the mansion that soap built, takes the product's spiritual
purpose even further (Fig. 12). For every class and kind, the caption holds,
Sapolio provides a "solid foundation on which to build a reputation or to
keep a home clean." The ad pictures an ecumenical estate open to all who
are clean, or perhaps even cleansing to all who enter. The view is prospective: the reader stands poised at the threshold. To enter is to *ascend into* this

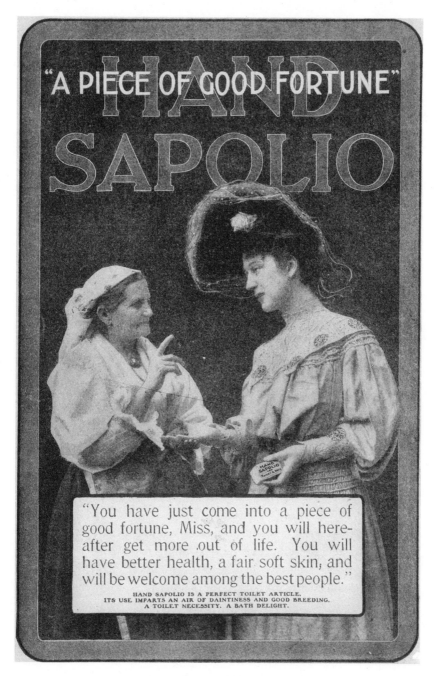

FIGURE 8 :: Advertisement for Hand Sapolio, "A Piece of Good Fortune."
From *Century Magazine*, September 1905.

FIGURE 9 ::

Advertisement for
Sapolio, "Has It
Dawned on Your
Home?" From
Putnam's Monthly,
May 1907.

soap palace, which is itself produced by the wizardry of E. Morgan's Sons. Through Sapolio, the modern marketplace claims the ritual power to eradicate the dirt and pollution that divides Americans. In this era of multicultural becoming, the daily rite of soap consumption holds the promise of harmonizing inequality and difference. The awesome power of Sapolio, "the safest soap for Toilet and Bath," reveals the anxiety aroused by mass production and commodity relations, as well as the role of advertising in mediating it.[23]

As the example of Sapolio shows, soap manufacturers, among all producers, took the greatest advantage of advertising, helping to make it a large-scale enterprise.[24] Like all the new "sciences" institutionalized at this time, advertising claimed exclusive mastery over a corpus of practical and theoretical knowledge. Agencies like J. Walter Thompson established rela-

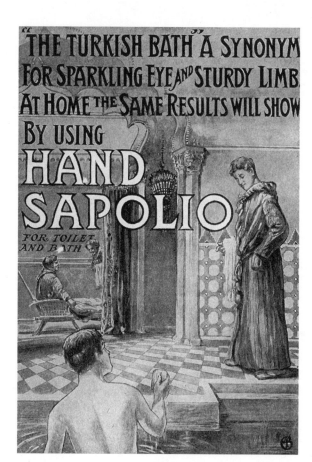

FIGURE 10 ::

Advertisement for Hand
Sapolio, "The Turkish
Bath." From *Putnam's
Monthly*, September 1907.

tionships with clients, compiling databases (population and distribution statistics by category and state; "split-run" evaluations of ad campaigns) that proved valuable to researchers throughout the twentieth century. Drawing on the new theories of Freud and Jung, as well as the work of Northwestern University psychologist Walter Dill Scott, advertisers addressed appeals directly to the mind and emotions.

Scott, a pioneer in the academic study of advertising, set out in his first book, *The Theory and Practice of Advertising*, to demonstrate what the psychologist had to offer the ad writer. Emphasizing the interdependence of academic and commercial endeavors, he suggested that the manufacturer recognized the uses of theory, just as scientists craved worldly application of their principles. "Ubiquitous" ads achieve a synonymous relationship between product and purpose (e.g., *Pears* and soap), while "fusion" ads, attentive to advertising medium and details of composition and placement,

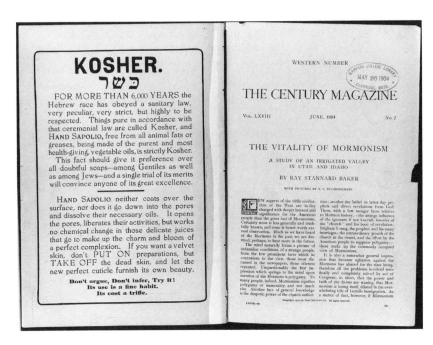

FIGURE II :: Advertisement for Hand Sapolio, "Kosher," opposite the opening
article, "The Vitality of Mormonism" by Ray Stannard Baker.
From *Century Magazine*, June 1904.

harmonized product and aura with targeted consumers. As a social con-
structionist, like many fellow psychologists and sociologists, Scott stressed
training and environment over inborn traits, acknowledging the inherence
of visual abilities alone. His subsequent book, *The Psychology of Advertising*
(1908), is the work of an academic who has thoroughly assimilated the
perspective of corporate America. Scott's commendation of advertising as
the engine of capitalism was designed to teach practitioners how to manage
their audience's class aspirations.[25] Scott theorized that most Americans
would respond sympathetically to a commodity identified with the upper
class and negatively to one that was identified with those they considered
beneath them. To exemplify an unsuccessful ad, he reproduced one for
Regal Shoes picturing a stereotyped Irishman, pipe in mouth, shamrock
hat, who quips, "Begorra—I'd Be Happy If I Could Only 'Get a Regal On'"
(Fig. 13).

Happiness seems remote, given the enormity of the Irishman's boot-clad
feet in comparison to the delicate Regal pumps. According to Scott, the
Regal Shoe ad misses the mark, by spotlighting a stereotyped figure that
cannot inspire identification. But Scott himself overlooks the ad's expecta-

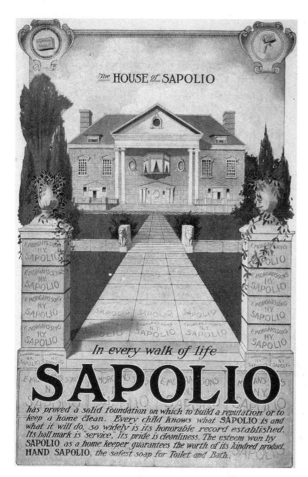

FIGURE 12 ::

Advertisement for
Sapolio, "The House of
Sapolio." From *Putnam's
Monthly*, July 1907.

tion that the consumer will identify with the message (social mobility), not the medium (degraded Irishman). The advertiser hopes that the middle-class consumer will *empathize* with this humble Irishman, who believes that squeezing himself into a pair of Regals would be his route to social mobility. What the ad offers the consumer is a satisfying condescension: a Regal life may be wishful thinking for the Irishman, but not for *me*. Indeed, one could argue that the ad succeeds precisely by driving a wedge through an American democracy of aspirations: everyone may *want* to be regal, but only some *can* be. The fact that many who want it never get it makes it only sweeter for those who do. Scott considers habit uniquely relevant to advertisements, which he believes are most powerful when they seep imperceptibly into the minds of consumers. Habit is what humans do unconsciously: how we dress—which coat sleeve invariably goes on first; how we read the

FIGURE 13 :: Advertisement for Regal Shoes. From Walter Dill Scott, *The Psychology of Advertising* (1908).

newspaper—last page first, section by section, or skimming all. Such behaviors, predictable and quantifiable, have various applications to advertising. As Scott explains in a penultimate chapter, "The Unconscious Influence
in Street Railway Advertising," streetcar advertising is effective because it
reaches people in states of relative repose, making it the *most* subliminal
form of advertising.

Elaborate tactics were required to induce these subliminal effects, as
illustrated by Francis Bellamy's *Effective Magazine Advertising: 508 Essays
about 111 Advertisements.*[26] Bellamy's book was based on a 1907 contest in
Everybody's Magazine, which asked readers to judge the best advertisement
in their November issue. A practical extension of Scott's theories, the contest revealed advertisers reading consumers as they read ads. While the
participants might well have been self-selected individuals, attracted to
commerce, their savvy about all aspects of marketing and exchange was
nevertheless remarkable.[27] Bellamy's introduction demonstrates that the
more money a company spends on a product, the better it is assumed to be,
hence the higher the sales, generating greater profits and more money for
advertising it. He goes on to show that the public grasps the circularity of
this process but participates willingly. A more obscure product might be a
better one, but consumers are prepared to capitulate to publicity and collective approval as values in their own right. Likewise, the success of an
advertisement is measured by the attention it receives, which depends on
directness and ingenuity. The best ads build on commonplaces, which they
present in unexpected ways.[28] The consumer reviews of the ads reproduced
by Bellamy are extravagant in their praise, confirming how an atmosphere
of advertising can be endlessly self-replicating, in this case inspiring consumers to hawk their own extraordinary powers of appreciation. The circle
of advertising ultimately envelops the audience, not simply as buyers, but as
participants in an adulatory climate of self- and object-love.

EDITING

Contests of this kind helped to enhance advertising's appeal to Americans
by representing it as a participatory democratic activity. By the 1880s, advertising was considered integral to magazines, and people even found it
engaging and useful.[29] The literary periodicals that had refused to sell
advertising space in the 1860s, or had limited its content in the 1870s, were
now accepting paid advertisements of all kinds.[30] They courted advertising
to defray the costs of competing with new magazines and to pay the fees of
contributors that rose with the profusion of publishing venues. By the turn

of the century, advertising had developed an aesthetic sophistication that reinforced its compatibility with the art and literature it increasingly bordered in magazines. Artemus Ward, for instance, who coined the most popular Sapolio slogan ("A clean nation is a strong nation"), combed foreign languages, drawing on proverbs from across the world. Ad agencies hired writers and artists just starting out on their careers or seeking to supplement inconsistent earnings. These included Bret Harte, who wrote for Sapolio; Theodore Dreiser, for the Butterfield Agency; and Sherwood Anderson, for the *Women's Home Companion*; as well as Maxfield Parrish, who painted for Fisk Tire; N. C. Wyeth, for Cream of Wheat; and Norman Rockwell, for Heinz Beans and Grape Nuts.[31] A major campaign for the Lackawanna Railroad's passenger service between New York and Buffalo that appeared in leading magazines began with a tip from Mark Twain. "Left New York on Lackawanna Railroad this A.M. in white duck suit, and it's white yet," Twain wired the company in 1899, thus initiating "The Road of Anthracite," a series of ads that ran until World War I. Featuring a young woman called "Phoebe Snow" dressed in white, the sparkling ads replete with rhymes ("Phoebe says / And Phoebe knows / That smoke and cinders / Spoil good Clothes") highlighted the soot-free hard-coal anthracite fueling Lackawanna locomotives.[32]

Arts and Crafts principles inspired classic typeface and realist images in advertising, while Art Nouveau gave rise to exaggerated lines, bold colors, and natural forms. Startlingly effective Art Nouveau covers for *Harper's*, *Atlantic*, and *Century* helped to harmonize their commercial, artistic, and literary parts.[33] These designs were thought to speak directly to women, the object of advertisers at the turn of the century who believed that they were responsible for 85 percent of purchases. Despite the perceived omnipresence of women as consumers, as advertising professionals they shared the fate of their counterparts in other developing fields—marginalization.[34]

Magazines attracted advertisers because their dramatically expanded circulation facilitated market segmentation. The magazines' editorially orchestrated focus was a great claim on advertising patronage. In keeping with larger business patterns of expansion and consolidation in the 1890s, as magazines benefited increasingly from advertising, their numbers declined dramatically. Of the thousands of magazines that appeared after the Civil War, by 1900 less than a third had significant audiences and advertising volume.[35] Successful magazine owners recognized that advertising revenue took priority over subscriptions and content. As Cyrus K. Curtis of the *Saturday Evening Post* observed in 1906, "I can hire men to conduct the editorial affairs of my magazines and to look after the circulation. . . . But the *promotion* of the business is a matter I feel it is my duty to attend to myself."[36]

William Dean Howells and the syndicate entrepreneur behind the magazine he created in *A Hazard of New Fortunes* (1890) would have understood this sentiment. Howells's novel confirms how magazines transformed American belles lettres into a big business. He was aware that already in the 1870s editors were paying $1,000 for a Fanny Fern tale and $30,000 for the serialization of Henry Ward Beecher's *Norwood*.[37] Starting out as an editorial assistant at the *Nation* and the *Atlantic Monthly*, which published his early poems, Howells was editor-in-chief at the *Atlantic* for a decade (1871–81) before his success as a novelist enabled him to write full time. The publishing house of James R. Osgood provided a comfortable income in exchange for exclusive rights to everything he produced; he signed an even more lucrative contract with Harper and Brothers in 1884. But Howells was a natural editor, and in 1886 he launched "The Editor's Study" (later "The Editor's Easy Chair") for *Harper's Monthly*, to which he contributed regularly until his death in 1920.[38]

American society in *A Hazard of New Fortunes*, like that envisioned by advertisers of the era, is sharply divided along class lines. The novel's ambitious managing editor Fulkerson, a southerner whose methods suggest the publisher and the adman in one, understands that his magazine's future depends on its ability to identify the biggest exclusive readership. Basil March is a New England editor of the *Atlantic* stripe; a contemplative moralist, preoccupied with art and craft and eschewing business, he circulates easily among urban elites, but his salary is decidedly middle-class. While the successful general-interest magazine aims at America's white Protestant majority, rural and urban, in Fulkerson's view it must also reflect the nation's growing social diversity, through generic variety and a cultural range of authors, artists, and subjects. The arrangement of these miscellaneous elements into an attractive whole, it is hoped, will be rewarded by widespread purchase.

Yet the very heterogeneity in background, politics, and taste of *Every Other Week*'s staff ensures its collapse. When the socialist translator Lindau insults the capitalist owner Dryfoos at a magazine dinner, and March is subsequently ordered to fire Lindau, he is thrown into a Howellsian moral quandary. Though he disagrees with Lindau's radical ideas, March cannot in good conscience work for a man who denies contributors free speech. These fundamental disagreements remain unresolved, but the novel ends happily with an ideal partnership of March and Fulkerson, who represent the reconciliation of North and South and the promise of ever-larger audiences for *Every Other Week*.

Henry James was also preoccupied with the business and culture of magazines, and one of his most memorable novels, *The Ambassadors*, featured an editor-protagonist. James not only made Lambert Strether an editor but also structured the novel according to the demands of serialization.[39] That the novel was also typically Jamesian in its deep rendition of consciousness, in its penchant for psychological abstraction, and in its plotting only confirmed how conducive his compositional strategies had always been to magazine adaptation. James's first full-length novel, *Roderick Hudson*, originated in a suggestion from an editor at *Scribner's Monthly* that James give them a serial novel. James took the offer to William Dean Howells at the more prestigious *Atlantic*, who drew up a $1,200 contract for *Roderick Hudson*, in twelve parts, running from November 1874 to November 1875.[40]

In *The Ambassadors*, James characteristically laments the commercialization of culture in America, while managing to profit by way of it. *The Ambassadors* is the aesthetic monument to James's dissatisfaction with his country—the poverty of social life, the preference for utilitarian over intrinsic value—conveying powerfully, through its deprived American hero, the allure of Paris. Strether's mission as the "ambassador" of his patron, the wealthy widow Mrs. Newsome, is to retrieve her son, Chad, from a prolonged Parisian sojourn. Upon meeting the mysterious French adulteress Madame Vionnet, responsible for Chad's delay, Strether recognizes that she is everything a prospective marriage and career awaiting Chad in Woollett, Massachusetts, is not. Strether also soon realizes that his own *Woollett Review* is a pathetic nod to culture, in the Newsome's vast "mercantile mandate." The novel's sympathy with Strether and Chad is expressed through its resistance to the material facts pulling them home. In an early scene, Strether manages to detail the life cycle of the Newsome enterprise without ever naming its purpose: "a big brave bouncing business . . . a roaring trade . . . a workshop . . . a great production . . . a great industry . . . a manufacture that, if it's only properly looked after, may well be on the way to become a monopoly." The ambassador succeeds in shipping his charge home but ruins his own prospect of return, while Chad's closing enthusiasm for "the art of advertisement," which "scientifically worked" and was "a great new force," seems false piety.[41] Profit may have motivated Strether's mission, with its success portending marriage to Mrs. Newsome and her fortune. But the novel's close implies that abandoning the mission is greater profit still. Loss in an economic sense is gain in a life sense. James's penchant for imagining reverse migration was distinctive in an era when so many were immigrating to America in pursuit of the golden opportunities forsaken by his characters. Yet the visions of James's novels were often at odds with his own commercial ambitions. Critics expecting consistency from an author's work to his life have overlooked the extent of James's interest in the rewards of an American literary marketplace. For James knew better than anyone how an American cultural establishment was vitalized by the capitalist ethos that overshadowed it.

These tensions were critical to the career of Samuel S. McClure, an Irish immigrant whose "real capital" when he started *McClure's Magazine* in 1893 was a large acquaintance with talented writers.[42] It took him less than a decade to build one of the leading magazines in the world. McClure's achievement followed from his conviction that the middle-class periodical so central to literary culture in England would appeal to Americans. With the shrewdness of the outsider, he satisfied the American appetite for heroes through Ida Tarbell's profiles of great men, which proved critical to the magazine's early success. A popular series on scientific innovations anticipated a general fascination with inventions. The magazine responded to growing populism and distrust of corporate greed by perfecting a type of investigative journalism that Theodore Roosevelt called "muckraking." Exemplified by Lincoln Steffens's essays on urban political corruption and Ida Tarbell's series on the cartel violations of Standard Oil, these pieces encouraged reform rather than radical change. In *McClure's*, identification of a broad democratic consensus was confirmed by the fact that at the height of its muckraking the magazine carried a greater volume of advertising than any other magazine in the world.[43] What made a series like Tarbell's acceptable to readers of different political persuasions was its vivid prose, comprehensiveness, and scientific rigor. The magazine's signature essays struck a balance between journalistic superficiality and professional impenetrability. McClure's journalists were able to master their subjects, because he paid them well and gave them adequate time for research and writing. Circulating stories across the country in urban and rural newspapers, McClure sought to enhance culture everywhere and to create new markets for writers he admired.

McClure's own storied life was itself worthy of his magazine.[44] Cowritten with Willa Cather, the biographical serial described his birth in 1858 and early years in Ireland and the immigration of his poor farm family to the American Midwest. McClure traced his passionate commitment to newspaper syndication to his own intellectually barren youth in rural America.

His self-education, however, was sufficient to gain him entrance to Knox College in Illinois, where he put himself through school by working as a peddler, further expanding his grasp of rural needs and tastes. "I had stayed all night at the homes of many of these people, and I had heard all about their business affairs. . . . I had found out that, for the most part, all these people were interested in exactly the same things, or the same kind of thing, that interested me. Years later, when I came to edit a popular magazine, I could never believe in that distinction made by some editors that 'this or that was very good, but it wouldn't interest the people of the Middle West, or the people in the little towns.' My experience had taught me that the people in the little towns were interested in whatever was interesting."[45] At Knox, McClure met people who would figure prominently in his magazine enterprise. These included John Phillips, a cofounder of *McClure's*; Albert Brady, the future business manager; and Robert Mather, later chairman of Westinghouse Electric and an investor.

McClure's experiences in Boston showed how much an individual could benefit from exposure to culture. At the home of John Phillips, McClure had read an issue of *Century Magazine* that included a serial installment of Howells's *A Modern Instance*, another piece about cycling, and advertisements for Pope bicycles. Drawing inspiration from Howells's portrait of a young man "making it" in Boston, McClure visited the Pope Company upon arrival and managed to talk its owner into sponsoring a magazine called *Wheelman*. As always, McClure had a keen eye for a prospect: bicycling was a popular new sport, and *Wheelman* thrived.[46] McClure moved to New York after *Wheelman* was sold, which was where he began to think seriously about the idea of syndication. Syndication was in its early phase, having been tested by newspapers like the *New York Sun*, which purchased stories by Howells, Harte, and James and published them simultaneously in New York, St. Louis, and New Orleans.[47] It had never been tried, however, on the scale imagined by McClure. In 1884, McClure and Phillips became partners in a syndicate business that eventually included such reputable literary clients as Sarah Orne Jewett, Elizabeth Stuart Phelps, Joel Chandler Harris, and Arthur Conan Doyle. By 1893, they were prepared to launch a new periodical, which they conceived of as a relatively cheap, general-interest magazine with as many illustrations as articles.

The first issue of *McClure's* coincided with the financial panic of 1893, but McClure and Phillips were bailed out by wealthy supporters, among them, Arthur Conan Doyle, A. A. Pope, and Henry Drummond. By 1894, Ida Tarbell's hugely popular biography of Napoleon had helped to double circulation, and it doubled again in 1895 with her even more successful "Life of Lincoln." The combination of staff writers like Tarbell, Willa Cather, Lincoln Steffens, and Ray Stannard Baker, literary authors like Robert Louis Stevenson, Rudyard Kipling, Joel Chandler Harris, and Israel Zangwill and series like "Real Conversations" with great Americans (Thomas Edison, William Dean Howells, Oliver Wendell Holmes) yielded a magazine that, according to one reviewer, "throbs with actuality from beginning to end."[48] Among the features that throbbed were stunning exposés of American corporations, political corruption, and union organizing. McClure denied that these investigations were orchestrated deliberately; an introduction to the January 1903 issue featuring articles by Tarbell, Baker, and Steffens highlights the "coincidence that this number contains three arraignments of American character as should make every one of us stop and think."[49] In his effort to locate a mass audience for his magazine, McClure aimed to educate as well as captivate. En route to this goal, he discovered muckraking and transformed American journalism permanently.

In the first decade of the twentieth century, when *McClure's* was at the height of its popularity, the influence of its editor was "hardly less . . . than that of Roosevelt himself."[50] McClure's journey from impoverished immigrant to leading citizen was a classic American success story. His idealism, which survived the disturbing reports of graft and greed uncovered by his staff, typified the reformist spirit that spurred American expansion in various fields at the turn of the century. Had McClure been looking for an individual to profile in his Great Individuals or Innovators in Science series, had he been interested in discussing the prospect of a vibrant magazine to address a particular community's problems and express its hopes, he need have looked no further than W. E. B. Du Bois. Indeed, McClure once bought an article by Du Bois but didn't publish it, deeming it too inflammatory for his liberal-minded readership. Experiences like this no doubt strengthened Du Bois's conviction that the black community needed its own journalistic forum.

From early in his long career as a public intellectual, author, and social scientist, W. E. B. Du Bois dreamed "that a critical periodical for the American Negro might be founded." The magazine *Crisis* originated in 1906 in a small Memphis, Tennessee, printing office as a weekly paper Du Bois called the *Moon*. Renamed the *Horizon* (1907–10) after he moved to Washington, D.C., it became the *Crisis* in 1910 when Du Bois assumed an executive position in the newly incorporated National Association for the Advancement of Colored People (NAACP). *Crisis* (a name inspired by the James Russell Lowell poem, "The Present Crisis") soon became a major vehicle for the black intelligentsia. From a starting circulation in 1910 of 1,000, the magazine reached 100,000 by 1918, with an annual revenue of $75,000. Providing graphic accounts of the injustices endured by black Americans, the *Crisis* also offered a constant reminder of the means at the nation's disposal for alleviating them.[51]

Du Bois's *Crisis* was inspired by the first national monthlies targeted at African American audiences: Frederick Douglass's *North Star*, William Garrison's *Liberator*, and Thomas Fortune's *Globe*. Most NAACP leaders shared the skepticism of Albert Pillsbury, who wrote Du Bois that "periodicals are as numerous and pestilential nowadays as flies were in Egypt, and most of them meet with the very same reception."[52] But Du Bois believed there was room for a magazine dedicated to exposing the virulence of race prejudice. Oswald Villard, of the *New York Evening Post*, provided office space, and fellow educator and journalist Kelly Miller joined the staff, along with magazine veterans Max Barber (*Voice of the Negro*), William Stanley Braithwaite (*Boston Transcript*), and Mary Dunlop Maclean (*New York Times*). Du Bois insisted on low subscription prices and varied content, mixing information and analysis with entertainment.[53] Regular features included "Along the Color Line," with sections on politics, education, science and art, "Talks about Women" (which urged black women to join the suffrage movement), "Men of the Month" (profiling distinguished individuals), and "The Burden" (detailing the latest racist atrocities).

Over the course of his twenty-three years as editor of *Crisis*, Du Bois was its dominant voice. Indeed, some readers complained that Du Bois's politics amounted to a gospel, but few denied the magazine's achievement in claiming the constitutional rights of black Americans. Du Bois described how federal agents investigating "foreign nationals" before World War I burst into the *Crisis* offices to inquire about "our objects and activities." Du Bois took great satisfaction in responding, "We are seeking to have the Constitution of the United States thoroughly and completely enforced."[54] Du Bois was equally relentless in upbraiding reform movements—woman suffrage, organized labor—for excluding blacks. But there was no subject confronted more aggressively in the *Crisis* than lynching. In an editorial on the lynching of a deranged black man in Coatesville, Pennsylvania, Du Bois described how thousands of whites poured out of churches on this September Sunday to see the smoking pyre, and he concluded, "The point is, he was black. Blackness must be punished. Blackness is the crime of crimes."[55]

When Du Bois left the *Crisis* in 1934, due to disagreement with key NAACP positions (he favored Pan-African solidarity and opposed segregation), he was credited with establishing "without a cent of capital," a fully self-supporting magazine responsible for widespread enlightenment on American race problems.[56] By recognizing the power of the mass circulation magazine to expand the national conversation on race both within and beyond the African American community, Du Bois proved himself once again uniquely capable of exploiting multiple disciplinary and media forms, while preserving a uniquely critical perspective on all of them.

AUTHORSHIP

No American writer in the post–Civil War era was more alert than Henry James to the commercial prospects of literature and the role played by magazines in developing them. Although (or perhaps because) his work through much of the twentieth century was synonymous with elitism and obscurity, the story of James's interest in the literary marketplace, his deep regard for readerships, and the significant contemporary reputation he enjoyed has sometimes been overlooked. But the details of James's shrewd efforts to establish himself as an American author of international significance help to illuminate the situation of authorship during the post–Civil War period. The tremendous expansion of reading audiences (so aptly exploited by Samuel S. McClure), the proliferation of periodicals, the rise of publishing firms, and the professionalizing of advertising—all of these changes paralleled James's career. According to an 1881 English census, 3,400 respondents identified themselves as authors, editors, or journalists; by 1901 the number had risen to 11,000. Figures in the United States were even higher. In the 1870s American publishers put out 3,000 new books a year; by the turn of the century the number had doubled. The absence until 1891 of an international copyright agreement between the United States and Great Britain subjected both British and American authors to pirating overseas. Because he remained an American citizen while residing in England, James enjoyed the copyright protections of both nations. Indeed, he effectively doubled his income by copyrighting his books in both countries and selling them for serialization beforehand in American and English periodicals. James's success in exploiting a transatlantic book industry that usually worked to the disadvantage of authors made him an especially informed advocate in this period for the professional author.[57]

Howells had long urged James to hire a literary agent to help him navigate the increasingly adversarial relations between authors and publishers, and by the 1880s James was eager for help in securing serialization agreements in particular. Following a rather disappointing engagement with A. P. Watt, James hired James B. Pinker, who remained his agent until his death. He wrote Pinker that if he were "able to arrange for the serialization of *The Golden Bowl* it would be a dream of bliss & I should bless your name forever!"[58] James's ability to live for the most part on his literary earnings was due to serialization as well as his success in securing British republication under secure copyright. Encouraging a fellow American author to seek British publication, James commented, "It is a patriotic fallacy that we read more than they. *We don't.*"[59] The English literary marketplace owed its comparative stability to the publication of novels in multiple volumes, the targeting of middle- and upper-class readerships, and high pricing (quadrupling American charges). Established book clubs and libraries ensured that novels would sell enough to keep them profitable for English publishers. In contrast, American publishers depended on significant earnings up front and continually sought best sellers. With the exception of *Daisy Miller* (1878), which sold 20,000 copies within weeks of its release, James's books commanded relatively modest sales.[60] In depending on serialization and in supplementing his professional income with other funds through most of his career, James was typical.[61]

While he enjoyed more acclaim than is usually acknowledged, James failed to achieve the celebrity to which he aspired. This was partly attributable to the uniqueness of his writing, which made him a target of ridicule for contemporary and subsequent critics.[62] His writings, especially as his style matured, displayed a keen theoretical interest in observation. A distinct point of view was a strict principle in his fiction; the reader was limited to a single narrative perceiver, who may roam the minds of different characters, but was indebted, for any particular insight, to a single consciousness. It was precisely by confining his narrative perspective to specific consciousnesses that James could dramatize the terrific power he accorded each one. Perceptions and thoughts were for him preeminent. The same went for emotions, which were privileged in James and provided the basis for his unique psychological realism. In his plots the principle actions consisted of seeing, thinking, and feeling, and violence was predominantly mental.

Born in 1843 in New York City, James descended from Irish immigrants who made a fortune in manufacturing and land investments. James's father, Henry James Sr., a philosopher and theologian, was independently wealthy and restless, and he raised his children (William, Henry Jr., Garth Wilkinson, Robertson, and Alice) in Europe and America and sent them to a variety of schools. After a year at Harvard Law School (1862–63), Henry Jr. began contributing stories to American magazines, and by 1865 he had made writing his vocation. His peripatetic childhood and his adult expatriation made him exceptionally alert to the defining rites of different cultures. One of the main concerns of his fiction was the complex process by which people adopted a country and assumed a set of traditions. Despite his lifelong "poet's quarrel" with his native land, he waited until 1915, the year before he died, to renounce his American citizenship.[63]

James pursued the craft of writing with an incomparable passion and industry, producing more novels, stories, and criticism than any other major American author. Among available models from an American literary tradition, none had a more profound impact than the work of Nathaniel Hawthorne, the subject of a biography James published in 1879 for Macmillan's English Men of Letters series. *Hawthorne* aroused a storm of protest in America for condescension toward its subject, but it revealed above all James's desire for distance—from his culture and from his overbearing family. The life of an American in Europe provided the detachment necessary to his art of social observation. Yet the rhetorical case for expatriation set out in *Hawthorne* could not disguise James's envy of Hawthorne's rootedness. In contrast to James, Hawthorne *belongs*—"the spell of the continuity of his life with that of his predecessors has never been broken."[64] While James's pigeonholing of Hawthorne—as democrat, as provincial, as primitive—supplies the route to his own emergence as the nation's even greater (because more sophisticated and cosmopolitan) novelist, it is also a ghostly revelation of James's feared aesthetic deficiencies. Is it possible to write as a man between countries?

James's ambivalence toward the American traditions that he absorbed along with more revered British and European literary legacies may well have motivated his incomparable exercise in memory-making: the eighteen prefaces he wrote beginning in 1907 for the Collected New York Edition of his works.[65] Part autobiography (the author writing), part biography (the novel developing), the prefaces provide an aesthetic past for author and work. Yet James's choice of photographs to use as frontispieces to each volume confirms his desire to locate his fictions in identifiable historical worlds. Writing to Scribner's in 1906, James emphasized his preference for a "scene, object, or locality . . . consummately photographed and consummately reproduced." James enlisted Alvin Langdon Coburn, a twenty-two-year-old photographer he had met in New York in 1905 when Coburn took his picture for *Century Magazine* to shoot twenty-four locales (St. John's Wood, St. Paul's Cathedral, Portland Place, the Luxembourg Gardens, the Arc de Triomphe) from London and Paris to Venice and Rome. James's choice of a "young American expert" and of photography itself as the medium for introducing the various parts of his opus identified his New York Edition with America's expansive modernity. The dramatic commercial failure of the New York Edition sent James into a depression. Four years of revisions on major novels and stories to make them representative of his authorial principles were met by indifference. Moreover, the project he had hoped to see him financially through old age left him "in bankruptcy," as he complained to Howells.[66] Concern for his pride more than his pocketbook prompted James's friend Edith Wharton to arrange the secret diversion by Scribner's of $8,000 from her own bountiful royalties to James in the form of an advance for *The Ivory Tower*, a novel left unfinished at his death.[67]

In March 1912 on the occasion of his seventy-fifth birthday, William Dean Howells was honored at Sherry's restaurant in New York, a banquet attended by President Howard Taft and four hundred other luminaries and aspirants from the worlds of literature, journalism, and politics, including Ida Tarbell, Zane Grey, and Willa Cather. Of all the tributes he received, there was none he liked more than Henry James's, which highlighted Howells's "exquisite notation of our whole democratic light and shade and give and take." Indeed, of all the great realist writers, Howells, whom Mark Twain liked to call "the Boss," was perhaps the most conventionally American in his grasp of authorship as "an affair of business." A self-made man, familiar with all facets of the writing life, from the most practical to the theoretical, Howells once remarked that he doubted "if there was anyone in the world who had his being more wholly in literature than I."[68] Howells from the start was the consummate author-expert with firsthand knowledge of the institutions—magazines, publishing houses, newspapers, and advertising agencies—that adjudicated literary reception in this period. Howells's prestige made him the clear first choice of major universities (Harvard, Yale, Johns Hopkins) when they began to establish literature departments in the 1870s and 1880s.[69] A key broker of reputations, he supported the diverse careers of Mark Twain, Henry James, Bret Harte, Stephen Crane, Charles Chesnutt, Frank Norris, Paul Laurence Dunbar, Sarah Orne Jewett, and Abraham Cahan. And he wrote one of the great American literary realist treatments of marriage and divorce set against the backdrop of the rise of professional journalism. Howells always considered that novel, *A Modern Instance* (1882), his best.[70]

Howells's conversance with so many facets of the culture industry resulted from his need to make money while pursuing his ambition of becoming a major American author. Born in Martins Ferry, Ohio, he was the son of Mary Dean and William Cooper Howells, a printer whose abolitionism and Swedenborgianism alienated people in the various small towns where the family lived during William's impoverished childhood. Set to work as a printer at an age when wealthier counterparts (like Cather, James, and Twain) were attending school, Howells educated himself. Printers had "living contact with literature," Howells wrote in retrospect, "and they must have got some touch of it whether they would or not." Howells was drawn to poetry in particular and modeled his own on that of Heinrich Heine, while he worked as a reporter for the *Cincinnati Gazette* and later the abolitionist *Ohio State Journal*. Many young men of the time were building major careers in journalism, and Howells worked alongside Whitelaw Reid and George William Curtis, but he never warmed to what he viewed as the sordid voyeurism of the news beat.[71] A subsequent job in the publishing house of Follett and Foster resulted in his enlistment as a campaign biographer for Abraham Lincoln. In the astonishing span of a week, Howells produced a biography responsible for many renowned Lincoln myths: the boy who could clear a field in hours, the tall-tale teller who mesmerized listeners, the voracious reader without books or candles who borrowed and read by firelight.[72]

By 1860, Howells had published five poems in the esteemed *Atlantic Monthly* and headed east to visit the New England literati, including Hawthorne, Emerson, Thoreau, Holmes, and Longfellow. His well-received campaign biography, read by Lincoln more than once, was rewarded with a Venice consulate, where he recognized his love for Elinor Mead.[73] From a wealthy and respected Vermont family, with a trace of religious fanaticism (utopian perfectionist John Humphrey Noyes was Elinor's uncle), Elinor married Howells in 1862.[74] Settled in Boston after the war, Howells soon became head of a household whose tastes and habits required a sizable income.[75] Though he enjoyed the power and content of his editorial work at the *Nation* and later the *Atlantic*, he struggled to the end of his life to reconcile the different demands of editing and writing. Howells pushed Henry James's fiction, saved writers from bankruptcy with timely acceptances, and boosted the emerging field of literary criticism.[76] His choice to make a reporter the protagonist of *A Modern Instance*, his most ambitious novel, was inspired by his experiences at newspapers and his wonder that "no one had struck journalism before."[77]

Howells also drew on an 1875 Boston performance of *Medea*, which he absorbed through the lens of "an Indiana divorce case . . . and the novel was born."[78] Subsequent summers at a farm in Shirley, Massachusetts, where the landlord and landlady, both previously divorced, fought continuously, intensified Howells's feeling for his subject. He described the novel's central concern in a note to *Scribner's* prior to its serialization, saying that it deals with "the question of divorce. . . . We all know what an enormous fact it is in American life, and that it has never been treated seriously." Howells's subject was reinforced by *Century's* simultaneous publication (January 1882) of Washington Gladden's article "The Increase of Divorce." Howells knew little about the legalities of divorce, so he sought expert advice and traveled to Indiana (a state with distinctively liberal divorce laws) to attend a trial. The Indiana trip anticipated the midwestern–New England regional axis that would be traversed in his novel. Howells's lifelong attraction to northeastern village life in post–Civil War America reverberates in *A Modern Instance*.[79]

As is typical of Howells's fiction, the novel is deeply attentive to class distinctions. Representing late nineteenth-century Boston as sharply divided along class lines, Howells highlights the snobbery of a Boston elite that excludes his Jason figure, Bartley Hubbard. Hubbard was reputedly based on Bret Harte, the multitalented writer, who excelled in journalism and was known for drinking, debts, and philandering. Opportunistic and indifferent to truth, Hubbard discovers a calling in the morally ambiguous journalism enterprise. Defining a type that transcends region and class, Howells's "modern instance" highlights the turmoil of contemporary values and beliefs, suggesting that divorce is necessary while repudiating its social effects. The novel was highly controversial, which in this case hurt rather than helped sales, but Howells remained undeterred, always preferring disturbing subjects to tame ones and crude antiheros to objects of reverence. This was acknowledged by W. E. B. Du Bois, who published a tribute in the *Boston Transcript* when Howells turned seventy-five, praising his handling of race in *An Imperative Duty*, a novel about intermarriage that, in Du Bois's words, confronted "our national foolishness and shuffling and evasion." Howells promoted justice in life as well as in books; he was the only notable American author to speak out on behalf of the defendants in the notorious Haymarket Affair of 1886, which resulted in the executions of four innocent men.[80] Among the letters of support that Howells received was one from Scandinavia by the daughter of Karl Marx, commending his artistry and bravery. Though he believed socialism the only answer to the terrible inequities of American society, Howells remained a lifelong Democrat in sensibility, driving a Ford car in his old age and fascinated by the new medium of film, which he watched as much as possible.[81]

When Willa Cather began a full-time job at *McClure's Magazine* in 1906, she entered a periodicals industry that was fully commercialized and an enterprise identified with progressive social change that strove to be "as imaginatively various as could be made."[82] As an editor at *McClure's*, Cather learned the modern business of editing but also gained unexpected forms of expertise. She attributed the courage to assume a male narrative voice in *My Antonia* (1918) to her ghostwriting of Samuel S. McClure's autobiography. Researching and writing *The Life of Mary Baker G. Eddy and the History of Christian Science* took her to Boston, where she was encouraged by a circle of women that included Annie Adams Fields and Sarah Orne Jewett. Fields and Jewett urged Cather to leave *McClure's*, where she felt overworked.[83] But because she appreciated the salary as well as the professional authority, Cather remained at *McClure's* until 1911, overseeing contributions on subjects like unionism and dynamite, the waning of Jay Gould's railroad dynasty, and the condition of modern matrimony, which were sometimes interspersed with her own serialized fiction.[84] When she finally took Jewett's advice to write about home, the result was *O Pioneers!*, her first effort to make the region she knew amenable to art. "Every one knows Nebraska is distinctly *déclassé* as a literary background," she wrote. "Its very name throws the delicately attuned critic into a clammy shiver of embarrassment. Kansas is almost as unpromising."[85] The novel's appearance on the *New York Times Book Review* list of the one hundred best books of 1913 confirmed that Cather had managed to make Nebraska chic.[86]

Cather was born in Virginia in 1873 to a family of landowners with Revolutionary War roots. Her father, a lawyer by training, brought his family to live on his parents' successful Webster County, Nebraska, homestead when Cather was four. While Cather never forgot the shock of a country "as bare as sheet iron . . . so bleak and desolate," she eventually warmed to the landscape, befriending the Scandinavian, German, and Bohemian immigrants who populated the area. A frequent audience to the stories of farmwomen in particular, she borrowed from the large library of a German Jewish couple and studied Greek and Latin with a British store-clerk.[87] But the Cathers, who were well off, had their own extensive library, and they encouraged the ambitions of their male-identified eldest child, who signed herself "William Cather, M.D." After moving into Red Cloud, the town named after the Sioux chief whose people were displaced by settlers like the Cathers, the family frequented the newly opened Opera House, where Cather sometimes performed in amateur theatricals. Entering the University of Nebraska in 1891, planning to study premedicine, she distinguished herself in literature. Through her college years, Cather published fiction, poetry, and essays in newspapers and magazines, and she wrote a regular column for the *Nebraska State Journal*.[88]

In 1896 she became editor-in-chief of the *Home Monthly*, a Pittsburgh magazine designed to compete with the *Ladies Home Journal*; the fearless and unequivocal reviews of American literary competitors written by the twenty-two-year-old Cather proved her up to the task. Mark Twain was "a clever Yankee who has made a 'good thing' out of writing," though neither "a reader nor a thinker nor a man who loves art of any kind." Of Howells she noted that "passions,' literary or otherwise, were never [his] forte," but she considered Frank Norris's *McTeague* a "great book" and declared the "masterly prose" of Henry James "as correct, as classical, as calm and as subtle as the music of Mozart."[89] In Pittsburgh, Cather had her first serious relationship with a woman, Isabelle McClung, the daughter of a wealthy Pittsburgh judge. McClung was a patron of the arts, and her belief in Cather's abilities and ongoing emotional and intellectual support were crucial to Cather's early development as a writer. McClung found places where Cather could write, such as the Cherry Valley, New York, cottage where she wrote *Alexander's Bridge* and drafted *O Pioneers!* And McClung helped to satisfy Cather's keen appetite for travel, accompanying her on her first trip to Europe in 1902.[90]

Indeed travel was a defining feature of Cather's life and work, and according to Elizabeth Sheply Sargeant, "rapid motion was essential to her." Cather kept her suitcases under her bed, and all her friends recognized "when the need to travel was upon her." This "migratory consciousness" heightened Cather's empathy for immigrants, those she encountered in New York when she worked for *McClure's* and those she had known in Nebraska, and it enabled her to be "the first to give immigrants heroic stature in serious American literature."[91] Such empathy didn't prevent Cather from displaying nativist animosities toward blacks, Jews, Italians, Mexicans, and even Germans as World War I approached.[92] Moreover, her recognition in a 1913 interview that Red Cloud was named "after the old Indian chief who used to come hunting in that country" evades the reality of dispossession that ensured her family's prosperity. Cather's appreciation for immigrants had limits and reflected prevailing national preferences for Germanic and northwestern European groups, but she nevertheless immortalized "a greater variety of European peoples than many of her contemporaries." The significance of Cather's choice for her figure of the artist was not to be underestimated: a Swedish American diva, inspired by the painting of a French peasant girl, scythe in hand, arrested in the fields by "the song of the lark."[93]

In the preface that Cather added to *The Song of the Lark*, seventeen years after its initial publication in 1915, she emphasizes that her central interest in the book was to tell the story of an opera singer's rise to success through "the play of blind chance" that "fell together to liberate her from commonness."[94] Cather's fascination with opera singers was long-standing and culminated in the 1913 *McClure's* profile of three who rose to fame in America during the first decade of the twentieth century. Among them was Olive Fremsted.

Cather had first seen the Swedish-Norwegian star, who later became a friend and the model for Thea Kronborg in *The Song of the Lark*, when she performed as Wagner's Kundry in *Parsifal* at the Metropolitan Opera. Like Cather, Fremsted had grown up on the Midwestern frontier, and she corroborated Cather's romantic portrait of the artist as self-originating, self-taught, and self-perpetuating. It is through the operas of Wagner that Thea Kronborg finds confirmation of her innate idea of music, which is simultaneously eroticized and spiritualized, as "the sole justification for life." Wagner saw music as a religion and was responsible for conventions that persist to this day, including the stipulation that all but the stage be enclosed in darkness and silence during a performance. His notion of the artist as androgynous, "a social being subject to the sexual conditions of both *male* and *female*," appealed to a generation of aesthetes, a considerable portion of whom were bisexual or homosexual.[95] Cather's novel was greatly admired by artists and bohemians of all kinds, including the influential critic and social satirist H. L. Mencken, who pronounced Cather among "the small class of American novelists who are seriously to be reckoned with." Fellow Midwestern writer Theodore Dreiser was also strongly supported by Mencken, the self-appointed antagonist of philistinism, who called *Sister Carrie* one of the best novels "this fair land has ever produced."[96]

Dreiser was Cather's exact contemporary, and both were honored by the American Academy of Arts and Letters in 1944. Like Cather, Dreiser sought to infuse his fiction with the expansive spirit of the Midwest and West, while extending the boundaries of what was acceptable to the arbiters of American literary culture. Dreiser's efforts to represent sexuality in terms consistent with literary realism led to conflict with censors throughout his career. He experienced his own coming of age in Pittsburgh, though his involved the recognition, while working as a reporter for the *Dispatch*, of the shocking contrast between the "low small yellow shacks" inhabited by workers and the palatial homes of the industrialists. More than any other American writer of the time, Dreiser understood the fascination and repulsion wealth represented for Americans and how these contradictory impulses enabled the vast discrepancies between classes. Still, he marveled at how labor could be expected to endure such indignities so that "Mr. Carnegie might give the world one or two extra libraries with his name plastered on the front."[97] Dreiser too had an extended apprenticeship in journalism and in magazines, which he pursued from necessity with astonishing energy. Between 1897 and 1900, Dreiser published nearly a hundred articles in periodicals including *Pearson's, Cosmopolitan, McClure's, Munsey's,* and *Ainslee's.* Though Dreiser would always identify with the poor, he could also empathize with the rich, as illustrated by his admiring profiles for *Success Magazine* of meat, merchandise, and train magnates Philip Armour, Marshall Field, and Robert Lincoln, respectively.[98]

Born in Terre Haute, Indiana, in 1871, Dreiser was the twelfth child of John Paul Dreiser, a German immigrant weaver with ambition, who did well enough to buy a mill. When the mill burned down, he struggled to rebuild it, was injured, and never recuperated fully. By the time Dreiser was born, his father was fifty and channeling his disappointment into strict Catholicism. While he was more sympathetic to his father's predicament than were his siblings, the intellectually avid Dreiser resented the narrow parochialism of his early Catholic education. When Dreiser was thirteen the impoverished family split up, and Dreiser moved to Warsaw, Indiana, with his more indulgent mother and began to attend public schools, where his mind was nourished with the study of chemistry, physics, history, and American literature. Dreiser was only fifteen years old when he set out alone for Chicago to make his fortune, a scene he would re-create fourteen years later in his first novel, *Sister Carrie* (1900).. Like his subsequent protagonists, Dreiser drifted from one low-wage job to another (dishwasher, busboy, clerk), until he was again rescued by public education, an opportunity through a friend to attend Indiana University for a year as a special student. A series of jobs in journalism followed, at the *Daily Globe* and *Globe Democrat* in Chicago, the *St. Louis Post Dispatch* and the *Toledo Blade*, which are recalled in Dreiser's *Newspaper Days* (1931).[99] By 1899, Dreiser was sufficiently established as a journalist and editor to make the first *Who's Who in America*.[100]

Two magazine pieces frame the writing of *Sister Carrie*: an interview with William Dean Howells for *Ainslee's*; and an essay, "Curious Shifts of the Poor," for *Demorest's*. Invited to Howells's elegant apartment overlooking Central Park, Dreiser was impressed by the "Dean's" sense of social justice but produced a profile guaranteed to irk his subject, with such observations as "[Howells] is greater than his literary volumes make him out to be" and "has helped thousands . . . and is a sweet and wholesome presence in the world of art." "Curious Shifts of the Poor" offered the first version of "Captain," the savior at the end of *Sister Carrie* who solicits contributions from wealthy theatergoers to buy beds for the homeless, along with portraits of a Catholic mission and a breadline. "The Real Howells" and "Curious Shifts of the Poor" reveal the departure represented by Dreiser on the point of entering the field of American letters.[101] Rejecting Howells's genteel tradition, which could only conclude "that life is difficult and inexplicable" when confronted with economic inequity and the suffering it sanctioned, Dreiser appears poised to articulate an alternative. As the controversy over *Sister Carrie* soon confirmed, Dreiser's moral positions were less ambiguous than his political ones. *Sister Carrie* was first rejected by *Harper's*, which noted that the author's "touch is neither firm enough nor sufficiently delicate to depict without offense to the reader the continued illicit relations of the heroine." Dreiser turned to Doubleday, where Frank Norris's enthusiastic support swayed reluctant readers. But Frank Doubleday had serious misgivings after accepting the novel, and though the house was forced to honor its contract, limited print runs and advertising minimized sales and profits.[102]

Though reviews of *Sister Carrie* were strong, especially in England (where it was reissued by William Heinemann), Dreiser fell into a long depression, from which he emerged desperate for money. His solution, as usual, was editing, and by 1907 he had the offer of a job on three popular women's periodicals, the *Delineator*, *Designer*, and *New Idea for Women*, at a starting salary of $7,000. Perhaps to mitigate his lucrative pandering to well-off philistines, Dreiser later bought the *Bohemian Magazine*, where he published pieces such as H. L. Mencken's "In Defense of Profanity" and "Days of Discovery," a critique of inherited wealth. But Dreiser remained conflicted, eagerly exploiting the luxurious options of a major New York editor and writer, attending banquets with J. P. Morgan, Andrew Carnegie, and Admiral Dewey, frequenting expensive restaurants, and dancing at yacht clubs.[103] Dreiser's ambivalence toward the literary high life was immortalized in his most autobiographical novel, *The "Genius"* (1915), which he began in 1911 just after he was fired from the Butterick Agency for his adulterous affair with the eighteen-year-old daughter of an assistant editor. Reviews of *The "Genius"* were evenly split between favorable and condemnatory; literary historian Stuart Sherman's "The Barbaric Naturalism of Theodore Dreiser," published in the *Nation*, was Dreiser's first academic review.[104] Suggesting in the xenophobic terms of these prewar years that the "animal behavior" of the characters was attributable to Dreiser's German heritage, Sherman's review still hurt less than the response of the Western Society for the Prevention of Vice, which succeeded in shutting down publication entirely. H. L. Mencken drafted a petition against the censors, securing signatures from such luminaries as Edward Arlington Robinson, Amy Lowell, Robert Frost, Ezra Pound, Willa Cather, and Mary Wilkins Freeman. But publishers held the novel hostage, refusing to print more copies, and Dreiser grew increasingly bitter toward a cultural establishment that he believed precluded "original thought," rigorously excluding social outsiders like him. Dreiser's feelings of marginality disposed him toward the socialism and communism that drew the allegiance of many American writers in the 1920s and 1930s.[105]

The story of the artist Eugene Witla's rise, following *his* breakdown, through the advertising department of the *New York World* and on to a successful career in magazine advertising, provides a valuable window on this new corporate sphere. Among the powerful creations in *"The Genius"* is the southern executive, Daniel Summerfield, brimming with ingenuity about prospective consumers and the psychology of marketing. Eugene is initiated with an ad campaign for a sugar refining company introducing packaged sugar. "It's a question of how much novelty, simplicity and force we can put in the smallest possible space," Summerfield tells Eugene, who is instructed in both the aesthetics and the science of advertising.[106] Eventually Eugene gets an offer from the United Magazines Corporation to oversee the art, editorial content, and circulation of seven magazines, a job with more power, responsibility, and risk. Lacking the ruthlessness to survive at United Magazines, Eugene loses his job, as well as his lover, and his long-suffering wife, and turns in desperation to Christian Science. Dreiser, whose two sisters were devotees, seems as fascinated by the religion as his philosophically astute hero—the notion of God as principle, the denial of the reality of evil, and the idea of pain as human error. And perhaps it was the very plainness, the simplicity, even banality of the faith and its practitioners that made it an appropriate cure for the complex material predicament of modernity and those who reflected too intensely on it.

Dreiser's choice to conclude his "Portrait of the Artist" with an exploration of Christian Science in its ideal rather than institutional form reflected the contradictory feelings among major novelists of the era toward materialism and capitalism. None of them could ignore the extent to which writing itself had become a serious business in this era, and they all tried to maximize the personal benefits of commercialization. But all confronted these circumstances with grave misgivings. This dissatisfaction was expressed in some cases through alternative political agendas, in others through different kinds of aesthetic withdrawal. Howells and Dreiser were actively engaged in radical politics. Tolstoy's *What to Do?* influenced Howells, as did the utopian nationalism of Edward Bellamy. He gave his allegiance to Christian Socialism, repudiating a system in which "a few men win wealth and miserably waste it in idleness and luxury, and the vast mass of men are overworked and underfed."[107] Dreiser was drawn to the communism he observed during the 1928 trip that culminated in *Dreiser Looks at Russia*, recognizing the benefits of a system designed to eradicate the poverty that had plagued his childhood. Cather admired the rich multicultural traditions—Native American, Bohemian, German, Czech—so prevalent in the western territories immortalized by her fiction and exploited, like Henry James, the prerogative of her class, travel and self-exile. Their various divergences from the commercial ethos engaged so fully in their writings and professional experiences confirm how exemplary these authors were. And this is what made their literary works such invaluable repositories of their time.

VARIETIES OF WORK

The nature of work changed in the second half of the nineteenth century. Advanced capitalist countries experienced the rise of the factory system, intensified machine production, and the massing and subdivision of labor. Between 1850 and 1900 every industry expanded dramatically, from the manufacture of locomotives, reapers, and Winchester rifles to textiles, cigars, and glass. The post–Civil War era ushered in what labor historian David Montgomery has called a "cult of productivity," characterized by ever-increasing rates of output and scientific methods of management, imposed by a professional managerial class.[1] While late nineteenth-century workers became habituated to an industrial time sense (a larger transformation signaled by the mass production of pocket watches), they also became aware of their ability to control rates of production.[2] As one efficiency consultant observed, every factory has "a fashion, a habit of work, and the new worker follows that fashion, for it isn't respectable not to." Employers could be equally tenacious: in 1885 managers at the McCormick reaper plant responded to a conflict with unionized iron molders by firing them all.[3] Moreover, the harmony of working-class interests was subject to constraints peculiar to the American context. According to Ira Katznelson, "what needs to be explained is not the absence of class in American politics but its limitation to the arena of work." He argues that American laborers, as distinct from European or British, saw themselves as workers at work but ethnics at home. Class solidarity prevailed in the workplace but ethnic identifications ruled elsewhere, dictating political behavior.[4] The fragmentation of working-class consciousness helped to foreclose the ratification of welfare benefits—unemployment insurance, health coverage, old age pensions—that became integral to industrial societies elsewhere.

While America's common laborers were less protected from the hardships of industrialization than their counterparts, their circumstances also increasingly belied traditional assumptions that hard work entailed economic reward. Such negative assessments were reinforced by economic depressions in the 1870s, 1880s, and 1890s, as well as widespread poverty amid abundance and surplus wealth: for instance, a 1901 Bureau of Labor survey reported that between 20 and 30 percent of wage-earners had poverty-level incomes. Already in 1877, an economic analyst, noting the eclipse of western expansion and of the capital necessary for entrepreneurial success, predicted the demise of social mobility: "born a laborer, working for hire," he concluded, the typical American would probably die that way.[5] The increasing difficulties of working-class life gave rise to the labor cooperatives movement, which demanded that workers share in policy-making and profits. Movement membership included many from the middle and upper classes, confirming a general wariness toward capitalist-industrial growth. The question to be answered, given the notorious distress of laborers at the time and the overt distrust of industrialists across socioeconomic classes, was why steps weren't taken to alleviate this distress and curb the excessive profits of corporate ownership.

These developments and the problems they generated were the concern of a vast literature, which will be the focus of the following pages. Upton Sinclair's *The Jungle* (1906), Mary Wilkins Freeman's *The Portion of Labor* (1901), and Theodore Dreiser's *Jennie Gerhardt* (1911) depicted characters struggling to survive in, respectively, the meatpacking, shoe manufacturing, and glassmaking industries. W. E. B. Du Bois's *The Philadelphia Negro* (1899), John Spargo's *The Bitter Cry of the Children* (1906), and Charlotte Perkins Gilman's *Women and Economics* (1898) explored the specific fortunes of blacks, children, and women, respectively, as workers in the new industrial order. Booker T. Washington's *Up from Slavery* (1901) and Mary Antin's *The Promised Land* (1912) demonstrated the durability of the "work ethic" at a point when its decline was widely proclaimed. Because some of these writers came from the working classes or struggled financially while building their careers, while others were socially positioned (as women or members of minorities) to understand how access to justly compensated labor affected life chances, they provided varied perspectives on the experience of work. Together with treatises by labor reformers and social philosophers Samuel Gompers, Jacob Riis, and Henry George, their writings will be viewed as exemplary testimonies of how the American workplace and the social relations that shaped it were reconfigured between the Civil War and World War I.

These testimonies reveal how fully cognizant Americans were of the unique virulence of the industrial capitalism that was institutionalized in this period. The greed of corporate ownership set against the deprivation of labor and the general indifference of the managerial classes to these circumstances were widely understood. Books documenting the exploitation of workers and the excessive profiteering of industrialists, some offering radical agendas for economic redistribution, were best sellers. Drawing on the rich and complex record provided by literary authors, social scientists, and reformers from various walks of life, this chapter argues that a critical force in the persistence of these extreme inequities was American multiculturalism: the social presence of different foreign types. Among them were immigrants from China and Japan, as well as from southern and eastern Europe; Catholics and Jews, Irish and Germans, who were incompletely assimilated; Indians and Mexicans and blacks, who would remain representative aliens for decades to come. Widespread perceptions of the dramatic diversity of American society served to minimize an ethic of collective responsibility and strengthen general tolerance for the cruel extremes of American consumer capitalism. As portrayed in novels like *The Jungle* and in studies like *The Philadelphia Negro* and *How the Other Half Lives*, differences of culture and race functioned consistently in this era to obscure the affinities among classes and to preclude the economic restructuring necessary to a civil society.

FACTORY WORK / PIECEWORK / WOMEN'S WORK

An international best seller within weeks of its publication, the popularity of Upton Sinclair's novel *The Jungle* was due to prevailing appetites for exposés and the disturbing relevance of his subject: the health violations of the American meatpacking industry caught the attention of anyone who ate sausages.[6] Equally gripping were the ties the narrative established between forms of corruption, from municipal and corporate illegalities to real estate fraud. The principal victims of this graft are poor Lithuanian immigrants depicted at a wedding feast in the novel's opening scene. Eager to make his way in Chicago's stockyards, the groom, Jurgus Rudkus, buys a house under fraudulent terms and slaves from dawn until dusk in Packingtown to meet the payments. When he loses his job after an injury at work, a cycle of despair ensues; his wife and child die, Rudkus is briefly imprisoned, and he turns to socialism. Throughout, Sinclair details the struggle to unionize Packingtown and the revolting filth of the production processes.

The Jungle presents a totalizing capitalist system whose analogous parts include slaughterhouse hogs and immigrant laborers. The system is designed to exploit everything; thus the hogs' own energy is used to drive them up the chute, just as everything "except the squeal," is ground into pork.

It was pork-making by machinery, pork-making by applied mathematics. And yet somehow the most matter-of-fact person could not help thinking of the hogs; they were so innocent, they came so very trustingly; and they were so very human in their protests—and so perfectly within their rights! They had done nothing to deserve it; and it was adding insult to injury, as the thing was done here, swinging them up in this cold-blooded, impersonal way, without a pretence at apology, without the homage of a tear. . . . One could not stand and watch very long without becoming philosophical, without beginning to deal in symbols and similes, and to hear the hog-squeal of the universe. Was it permitted to believe that there was nowhere upon the earth, or above the earth, a heaven for hogs, where they were requited for all this suffering? Each one of these hogs was a separate creature. Some were white hogs, some were black; some were brown, some were spotted; and some were old, some were young; some were long and lean, some were monstrous. And each of them had an individuality of his own, a will of his own, a hope and a heart's desire; each was full of self confidence, of self importance, and a sense of dignity. . . . And now was one to believe that there was nowhere a god of hogs, to whom this hog-personality was precious, to whom these hog-squeals and agonies had a meaning? Who would take this hog into his arms and comfort him, reward him for his work well done, and show him the meaning of his sacrifice?[7]

Indicting mechanized techniques that enable mass numbers of humans to consume mass numbers of animals, the passage contrasts implicitly Rudkus's memory of hunting in the Lithuanian forest and assembly-line killing. Though rational and utilitarian in theory, the science of meatpacking looks barbaric in practice. There is no creature here more guileless than Rudkus, who will soon have his own leg injury to match that of the "swinging" hogs. The troubling proximity of man and beast in Sinclair's portrait explains the effort to distance the carnage with the reference to "symbols and similes." Humans are distinguished from animals precisely through their access to language; yet what of the illiterate immigrant? Is he closer to the philosophers or the hogs? Perhaps the most curious detail is the mention of "rights," which recalls Sinclair's debt to *Uncle Tom's Cabin*. A creature that suffers, according to Stowe and Sinclair, is a creature that can be accorded "rights."[8] The possibility that the rights of suffering animals, like those of suffering slaves, might someday be recognized was anticipated in 1789 by Jeremy Bentham. Responding to the French decision to emancipate black slaves in the colonies, Bentham imagined a growing humaneness toward animals, likewise based on their capacity to suffer.[9] On behalf of his suffering hog brethren, in the manner of Stowe, Sinclair forges a community of empathic response that emphasizes their individuality and homage to a higher hog order.[10] Sinclair's anthropomorphizing furthers the ongoing claim of the novel that no one is safe in a society that tolerates such cruelty toward defenseless creatures.

This was precisely what made *The Jungle* a literary sensation: Sinclair's extension of his characters' helplessness to the American consumer. The sign that the novel's consumer audience was aligned with his suffering immigrants was the depiction of the latter as meat-eaters. Their *suffering* may be *akin* to the suffering of hogs, but *they* are not the hogs' *kin*. Throughout the novel, Sinclair's characters feast on sausages, while his animals avenge themselves, in one instance, by consuming a child worker locked in the factory all night. Miraculously, only one character dies from tainted meat.[11] But the novel featured enough death, and mystery surrounding that death, to confirm the unlimited deadliness of Packingtown. *The Jungle*'s impact seemed equally so. Charlotte Perkins Gilman wrote Sinclair "that book of yours is unforgettable. I should think the Beef Trust would buy it up at any price." And Winston Churchill proclaimed that Sinclair had made "the great Beef Trust stink in the nostrils of the world."[12] Shortly after its publication, President Theodore Roosevelt promised Sinclair in a widely publicized letter that the novel's abuses would be investigated.[13] A Labor Commission report verifying all of Sinclair's charges resulted in the immediate passage of the Pure Food and Drug and the Meat Inspection acts, which had been stalled in Congress for years.

Yet *The Jungle* fell short of Sinclair's aims, sparking lasting reform rather than radical change. And one of the novel's most significant insights was one of its subtlest: the difficulty of forging solidarity among American workers even under the most intolerable conditions. Sinclair's own racial and cultural prejudices, which become pronounced in the narrative's later episodes, suggest why. Black workers recruited from the South by factory owners to break the union strikes are represented as subhuman. In the redirection of the characters' (and author's) antipathy from factory owners to fellow victims, the novel reveals how owners and managers divided workers by fomenting racial and cultural conflict. In the vast urban industrial settings of Chicago and New York, with large numbers of foreign immigrant and black migrant workers, fundamental class affinities among workers were readily submerged.

Novels centered on factory life in smaller towns and cities, featuring more homogeneous groups of workers, afforded a view of the preeminence of class identification in America during this time. Yet to see class foregrounded in specific novelistic societies is also to understand the ways in which it could be denied at a time in the history of American work when it was most undeniable. John Hay's *The Bread-Winners* (1884) and Mary Wilkins Freeman's *The Portion of Labor* (1901), both set in the late nineteenth century, portray class as critical to individual psychology and social organization. Hay's novel, set in Cleveland, fictionalizes the labor strikes of 1877, and ends with a violent clash between labor and capital. Freeman's novel, which is set in a New England industrial town, is ultimately a capitalist fairy tale, ending with the marriage of the poor factory worker's daughter to the factory owner's son.

In *The Portion of Labor*, the divide between rich and poor is mediated by a culture of consumption, while the stock market is depicted as a democratizing medium capable of enriching the deserving regardless of class.[14] Early in the story, Ellen Brewster, daughter of a shoe factory worker, runs away from home and is picked up by Cynthia Lennox, the lonely sister of the factory owner, who takes her home; meanwhile the disappearance becomes a media event. Happily reunited with her family, Ellen protects the privacy of her aristocratic savior by failing to mention their time together, which spells the start of her divided class loyalty. The incident cements a bond between this daughter of the proletariat and the town aristocracy, which begins, significantly, in a moment of prospective consumption, as Ellen and Cynthia meet near a display window.[15] When Ellen returns to the same window with Cynthia's nephew, Robert Lloyd, she has realized the capitalist myth of consumption as a means of social mobility. The *mere desire* for commodities, the narrative suggests, enables class ascension. Ellen's yearning before the window as an impoverished child is rewarded by the appearance of a fairy godmother and subsequent marriage to a prince. Yet her return as a young woman with her upper-class lover features her own complex resistance to the myth. Ellen repudiates Lloyd's notion that advertisers perform an essential public role, serving aesthetic as well as carnal appetites. She highlights the illusoriness of a "democratized" consumption that merely accentuates divisions between rich and poor, by making material abundance *appear* accessible. While the upper-class hero Robert Lloyd appreciates the display, the working-class heroine, Ellen Brewster, recognizes in the glossy merchandise the fruits of labor her hardworking family cannot afford.

Ellen's divided loyalties are mirrored in her mixed birth, as a descendant of the aristocratic Brewsters and the shiftless Louds. It is unclear at the novel's end how Robert Lloyd will manage the repulsion he feels toward the coarser members of Ellen's family. Nor is it clear how Ellen will preserve her familial bond while embracing the ideals of her new husband. It is implied that the marriage will work because cross-class marriages are the rule. Robert Lloyd's own parents are from "vastly different stock": his father comes from a distinguished old family, and his mother, who supplies the capital for the factory, is the granddaughter of a cobbler.[16] And the long feud between Ellen's genteel grandmother and mother is resolved by the fulfillment of their shared ambition that Ellen "marry up." Yet such assurances are undercut by another ongoing claim of the narrative, namely, that class is inherent. Cynthia Lennox's elite friend wonders about her plan of sending Ellen to Vassar College: "Why do you want to increase the poor child's horizon farther than her little feet can carry her? You might as well teach a Zulu lace-work, instead of the use of the assagai."[17]

According to *The Portion of Labor*, class is as fixed as any inborn trait and functions, paradoxically, to subdivide the working class. The difference between Freeman's representation of class and Sinclair's representation of race is the ingredient of marriage, which has the potential to collapse these divisions. Marriage in Freeman's novel is consistent with another magical arbiter of human fortunes—the stock market. For the novel's marriage plot is reinforced by the story of Andrew Brewster's speculations in mining stocks, an investment that violates his deepest values both as an aristocrat and as a laborer committed to honest work. The vagaries of the market impair the family's security, leading to Andrew's decline and sending Ellen into the factory as a laborer. At the novel's end, however, it is not work that saves and ennobles but the stock market, whose dividends are redeemed, restoring Andrew Brewster's money and manhood. Robert Lloyd benefits from the same economic upswing, applying his increased assets to higher wages for his workers, thus regaining his proletarian beloved. The closing harmony issuing from the growth of stock dividends suggests an alternative democratization of speculation to replace the democratized consumption the novel highlights but rejects. The mixing and mobility of Freeman's fictional society provides a striking contrast to that of *The Bread-Winners*.

The depth of class and ethnic division in America at this time was illustrated by the popularity and admiration generated by Hay's novel, a best seller that was serialized beforehand in a prominent magazine.[18] In the introduction to the first edition, Hay's son Clarence reports that 1877, the year of the novel's setting, was notable for strikes among railroad employees that led to widespread riots and looting. John Hay (U.S. secretary of state from 1898 to 1905) was alarmed by the disorder and criticized politicians whose "sympathies were all with the laboring man, and none with the man whose enterprise and capital give him a living."[19] Designed to rectify the imbalance, The Bread-Winners depicts nobility as genetically limited to the upper class and disparages everything associated with workers. It is a badge of honor that the hands of the novel's aristocrat, Arthur Farnham, "showed they had done no work."[20] In the opening dialogue between Farnham and Maud Matchin, the ill-mannered though beautiful daughter of a hardworking carpenter, whose sole ambition is to marry wealth, the pair's polarization foreshadows all subsequent relations: grasping laborers continually imposing on cultivated elites. A possible exception to this rigid typology is Maud's father, Saul Matchin; but he is undermined by his devotion to the undeserving Maud, who spurns him along with his apprentice, who loves her. Though Maud's resistance to the dumb but decent Sam Sleeny is portrayed as class self-hatred, the bleak prophecy of their closing marriage appears to justify her behavior. Meanwhile, every politician in The Bread-Winners is corrupt. The worst of them, a sagacious Jew, Jacob Metzger, applies the same principle to butchery and politics—getting "the most out of a carcass."[21] The mastermind behind the "Brotherhood of Breadwinners" that launches the strike is a Dickensian villain whose ineptitude suggests that most labor violence issues from the incompetent workers. Hay's attack on social mobility and on workers themselves was one of the most visceral accounts of the time, approaching Sinclair's *Jungle* in its pessimism but failing to prompt a similar definitive response. In *The Bread-Winners* class difference is as absolute as race is in *The Jungle*, but any prospect for class solidarity is denied, for Hay's workers dislike themselves even more, if possible, than his aristocrats dislike them.

Some upper-class observers writing about workers in this era took a romantic approach more common among contemporary European writers. In a series of novels published around the turn of the century, Isaac Kahn Friedman, who was born into a wealthy Jewish family in 1870, claimed the unacknowledged pleasures of working-class life and did this in part on the basis of its rich multicultural traditions.[22] A writer who appears to have written about what he didn't know rather than what he did, Friedman's novels contained no hint of his Jewishness, featured narrators from different cultures, and even invoked Jewish stereotypes. Though this might have indicated self-alienation, it also reflected a desire to capture the cultural wealth of working-class experience. *Poor People* depicts the world of the working immigrant at the turn of the century. Its narrator, Thomas Wilson, who clerks in a department store by day and writes opera scores by night, lives in a slum while retaining a sense of its aesthetic possibilities. His Chicago tenement includes a range of cultures: a German woodcarver, an Irish blacksmith, a Jewish tailor, a Polish shoemaker, a Dutch fortune-teller, a Swedish seamstress. Some work at nearby factories, some do piecework at home, but all submit to the pace of modern industry, their survival dependent on their ability to accommodate it. Still, a key claim of Friedman's novel is the place of art in the lives of the laboring poor. Vogel, a watchmaker who cares for his alcoholic father while working on a dramatic masterpiece entitled "Poor People," exemplifies this.

Friedman's portrait of tenement life corroborates many ideas of contemporary Chicagoan Jane Addams. They agreed, for instance, that the poor were their brothers' keepers. They also shared a faith that people of different cultures could live together harmoniously under the most trying conditions. Wilson speculates during a wedding feast that "the good Lord must have beamed with satisfaction to have seen the children of His various nations gathered about the tenement table in amity and friendship."[23] The novel concludes on a series of marriages—the German woodcarver marries the Dutch fortune-teller, and the Polish shoemaker marries the Swedish seamstress. Another character ascends to the nouveau riche, moving her parents with her, but they return to the tenement.[24] Vogel's "Poor People," is produced to critical acclaim. Friedman's novel and Vogel's play share two morals: "Once you've known the wonders of tenement life, you can't bear to leave it; to those who are sufficiently subtle, its aesthetic potential is unlimited."

Had she known Friedman's work, Jane Addams would have approved of its message. As a founder of Chicago's Hull-House, an institution devoted to reforming the lives of working immigrants, she too sought to liberate the artistic potential of the working-class poor, which she located in their labor. Indeed, she believed that all classes would benefit from recognition of the creativity that was inherent in labor and that was being stifled by its rationalization in modern times. Part of that rationalization was the severing of foreigners from the cultures where they learned to work. Thus, from Addams's perspective, integral to the tragedy of Rudkus in *The Jungle* was the terrible chasm between hog killing in Lithuania and systematic slaughter in Chicago.

According to Addams, factory workers suffered from feelings of disconnection, from their home cultures, from one another, and from a larger industrial effort: help them reconnect to their traditions of work and to see their current jobs as part of a larger enterprise, and their work would be vitalized. The labor museum that Addams opened at Hull-House, which featured Old World craft shops, exhibitions of primitive tools, and forms of artisan expertise, was a testament to these assumptions. Built in 1856 by Charles J. Hull, a leading citizen of Chicago, Hull-House, which was reputedly haunted, had been a home for the aged, a secondhand furniture shop, and a factory, before it became the centerpiece of Progressive Era reform. Among the early projects initiated by Addams were clubs for boys, men, and women, a kindergarten, sewing classes, temporary housing, job counseling, a coal association, a music school, a gymnasium, a playground, a coffeehouse with adjacent theater, an art gallery, and the Jane Club—a cooperative apartment for women. During this time Addams also served as sanitation inspector for her ward, which was typical of her lifelong commitment to the mundane as well as the intellectual.[25] In *Twenty Years at Hull-House*, Addams shared the revelations of her career in social reform.[26] Emphasizing the inadequacy of "private beneficence . . . to deal with the vast numbers of the city's disinherited," she highlighted the generosity of the poor to each other, thereby rebuking social Darwinist assumptions that competitive survival was the deepest human urge.[27] She argued, furthermore, that an additional cultural heritage of immigrants was a blessing and was of great benefit to American society. Describing the respectful attention paid W. E. B. Du Bois by Mediterranean immigrants during a lecture he delivered at Hull-House, Addams suggested that the alternative legacy of immigrants made them less susceptible to American racism.[28]

The life and writings of Jane Addams reveal the role played by women in improving the circumstances of the working class. The entrance of women, many of them charged with religious and domestic ideals, into the arena of municipal reform was critical to the assimilation of urban immigrants (from foreign countries and from other regions of the United States, particularly the South) and to the revision of the attitude of the general public toward them. Women also helped bring about crucial improvements for native workers, especially in the areas of housing and sanitation. These urban reformers and the institutions they ran (the YWCA and the Salvation Army were typical) mediated between the private and public realms, allowing neighbors who were familiar but unrelated to come together. In the "borderland between charitable effort and legislation," in Addams's words, they provided temporary relief for the problems of labor in anticipation of more long-term solutions.[29] Yet perhaps even more important than essential services was the way these reform activities channeled the energies of middle- and upper-class women at a point when other American social institutions were unprepared to exploit this resource.[30]

Americans' ambivalence toward the professional capacities of middle- and upper-class women was particularly intense at the turn of the twentieth century. This was partly fueled by a vigorous eugenics movement that condemned any undertaking that impeded reproduction in women of the middle and upper classes, arguing that reduction in maternity rates of Anglo-Saxon women of the better classes was leading to dangerous population imbalances between the elites and the lower classes, or "natives" and immigrants.[31] Advancing the simple but powerful message that women would never achieve their full potential as long as they were dependent on men economically, Charlotte Perkins Gilman's *Women and Economics* (1898) won immediate worldwide recognition. Translated into seven languages, the book put Gilman in the national spotlight, which she was accustomed to as the great niece of Harriet Beecher Stowe. Among the influences on *Women and Economics* were Charles Darwin, sociologists Herbert Spencer and Lester Ward, and utopian novelist Edward Bellamy. Gilman drew especially on Bellamy's *Looking Backward* (1888) for its socialist ideas and enlightened views on women. Gilman's own system of "social motherhood" consigned child rearing to trained professionals and further radicalized domestic life through its reform of conventional fashions for both genders.

Women and Economics begins with the observation that the human female is distinctive among all living beings in depending on the male for subsistence. The consequence for women, and for the human species as a whole, warned Gilman, was crippling. The work in which middle-class women specialized—child care, cooking, cleaning—was not only unsatisfying but unremunerated and unrecognized as well. As Gilman pointed out, housework did not qualify as "work" at all, since it was both unproductive and inefficient, consisting of tasks that could never be completed. But Gilman's objection to domestic labor had less to do with the work itself than with the workers' isolation. In a vision that complemented that of Jane Addams, Gilman imagined women liberated from their lonely domesticity, working together for the common good. She spent a lifetime developing her ideas about women and economics, many of which remain relevant over a century later. But Gilman had her share of critics too. In a 1909 debate in New York City with the feminist orator Anna Howard Shaw before an audience of working-class women, Gilman's claim that women were "parasitical" was heartily refuted by Shaw. Shaw's counterargument, that women's work, both domestic and public, was the salvation of family and society, won majority approval. Indeed, the problem, as one woman writing to *Harper's Bazaar* saw it, was that American women hadn't learned to be "parasitical enough."[32]

When major writers around the turn of the twentieth century wrote about women and work, they wrote about the lower classes. Significantly, some of the most perceptive portraits were by some of the nation's most esoteric authors. Two of them, Gertrude Stein and Henry James, spent most of their lives in Europe, a distance that may have afforded them some perspective on the American class system. Though Gertrude Stein has not always been recognized as a keen social observer, her account in *Three Lives* of the relationships among racial and ethnic groups and of class stratification in nineteenth-century Baltimore is noteworthy.[33] A series of case studies, featuring two German immigrant maids and a mulatto laundress, the book is remarkable for its relentless homogeneity: the characters are few and spare, the narrative repetitive and monotonous. It is no accident that Stein was writing about maids and that each example in a work about the struggle to domesticate social difference concerned a *domestic*. Stein's subject in *Three Lives* was the daily theater of heterogeneity become homogeneity: the ways in which different class, ethnic, and racial idiosyncrasies were transformed, through the impact of head servants, community pressure, even death itself, into normative behavior.

Stein emphasizes the process of internalization in her "servant girls" and "real Negroes"—the forms of self-hatred that permeate their relationships. "Melanctha" explores racism within Baltimore's black community, the collective morality that is shocked by the friendship between the light-skinned Melanctha and the black-skinned Rose. Among these blacks, beauty and intelligence are typed white, and their opposites, black. Similarly, Stein's immigrant maids despise themselves and each other. According to the subject of the first story, "The Good Anna," who considers herself a servant, not a maid, every maid's life is a battle against her own slovenly instincts. Servants, in contrast, identify with their mistresses in a symbiosis of master and slave. Though Richard Wright defended Stein's portrait of racism in the second story, "Melanctha," others found Stein's parody duplicitous, replicating what it professed to mock.[34]

A similar tension between condescension and sympathy marks Henry James's *In the Cage*, which depicts a telegraph operator and sticks close to the details of her working-class life. It is about the small intimacies that modern society affords through its distances, distances created by technology and also by increasingly pronounced class and racial divisions. In his notebook, James identified the novella as a product of his prowls about London, "the thick jungle of the great grey Babylon."[35] In his guise as explorer, he is struck especially by the proliferation of small grocers housing telegraph machines. In the 1890s, before the use of telephones became widespread, telegrams provided a quick, though expensive, means of communication in large cities such as London and New York. The telegraph office attached to a grocer's shop was one avenue for the intersection of classes across a chasm of anonymity; in this case, between working-class operators and wealthy customers.[36] James's novella centers on two aristocrats who send urgent messages from the telegraph office where James's unnamed operator works. The telegraph operator is barely visible behind her cage, and James makes clear that these exalted personages regard her as a mere appendage to her machine. She, however, comes to feed on their comings and goings, investing their every move with fantastic intrigue. All that James allows us to know is that the telegraph operator's voyeurism enables her to rescue them (by remembering the content of a telegram) from disaster. The novella ends with her realization that she means nothing to the pair, however much they have meant to her, and that her own life is barren.

The telegraph operator is an addict of sorts, a condition that comes naturally to her as the daughter of an alcoholic. She inhabits a dream world for a time but discovers that dreams are not shared across classes, which is reinforced by the novella's bleak ending. Hovering over a parapet on a canal, the telegraph operator is regarded uneasily by a strolling policeman. It is not clear whether she is contemplating suicide or merely reflecting on her own previous blindness. Nor is it clear which side of the parapet represents death. James may be suggesting that by resigning herself to a monotonous job and a dull marriage to a grocery clerk, the telegraph operator might as well be dead.

As a member of the laboring poor who had seen his sisters employed in factories and working as maids and prostitutes, Theodore Dreiser was familiar with the desperate dynamics of the American class system. At times, this familiarity seems to limit his exploration, especially where his subject demanded confronting it. *Jennie Gerhardt*, for instance, centers on the trials of a family much like Dreiser's own, whose patriarch, a German immigrant, is injured at a glass factory and loses his job, which proves to be the final blow to his impoverished kin. His daughter, Jennie, becomes a maid, making her vulnerable to the seductions of upper-class men. The novel is full of nostalgia for a precapitalist Eden and closes with a tribute to Jennie, now a poor single mother who by giving and loving, as Dreiser would have it, transcends both ruthless market capitalism and a genteel culture that devalues passion. In *Sister Carrie*, capitalist desire appears to nullify class divisions, though the novel's two irreconcilable endings leave much in doubt. What makes these novels more than exercises in the denial of class, however, is Dreiser's choice to keep both protagonists single. By repudiating the prospect of "marrying up" and keeping Jennie Gerhardt and Carrie Meeber as naïve at the close of their novels as they are at the start, Dreiser disarms the dream of social mobility that defuses the class-consciousness of comparable American novels. Indeed, his most mature work, *An American Tragedy*, featuring a male protagonist, would probe with great insight the contradictions of the success myth and the fixity of the American class system.

Sister Carrie's ending raises irresolvable questions by introducing an advocate for the homeless and a rich young inventor, to highlight the selfishness and triviality of Carrie's success. Why does one individual fall by the wayside and another achieve prosperity? Why does one individual sleepwalk to old age with the same dissatisfactions that drive another (Hurstwood, the middle-aged saloon manager who impulsively abandons his job, wife, and family for Carrie) to risk everything? How is it possible to tolerate a daily spectacle of poverty versus abundance without taking action? Dreiser's portrait of a society built on a rhythm of loss and gain, a perfect equivalence between social casualties (Hurstwood) and victors (Carrie), is consistent with classic works of Progressive Era protest, such as Henry George's *Progress and Poverty* (1879) and Jacob Riis's *How the Other Half Lives* (1890).

PROTEST WORK

Two lines of argument predominated in social protest writings from the post–Civil War period. The first, exemplified by the theories of Henry George and W. E. B. Du Bois, focused on prevailing ideologies. They targeted an "ethics of scarcity" that suggested one group must flounder for another to thrive and saw destitution for some and abundance for others as inevitable to a healthy economic system. George located his critique in the monopoly of land, which he argued should be recognized as a collective resource of material benefit to the whole community. Du Bois identified the manipulation of labor as a central problem, specifically the efforts by owners and managers to set different types of workers in competition with each other. The second line of argument was exemplified by the exposés of Jacob Riis, John Spargo, and Samuel Gompers. These writers argued that the exploitation of child laborers and immigrants, who worked often in dangerous conditions, without adequate air, light, or rest, was more compatible with medieval barbarism than with a modern American democracy.

The story of Henry George's meteoric rise to fame, after the tepid reception of *Progress and Poverty* by prospective publishers, was legendary.[37] The book was translated into twenty-five languages and celebrated worldwide, the 2 million copies sold by 1905 making it one of the most popular works of economics ever. Leo Tolstoy and George Bernard Shaw, among others, claimed their lives had been changed by George's study; when he died in 1897, more than 50,000 people lined the streets of New York to view his coffin. The first version of *Progress and Poverty* was published as a pamphlet entitled "Our Land and Land Policy" (1871). In forty-eight pages, George described how a single land tax could meet the costs of government, even providing surpluses and giving workers a share in the fruits of progress. By destroying land monopolies and shifting the burden of taxation from labor and capital to landowners, George's scheme promised to alleviate extremes of wealth and poverty. George understood that his ideas contradicted social Darwinism, which viewed suffering as the cost of progress in which weaker civilizations and individuals were naturally replaced by stronger ones. He countered that progress was susceptible to retrogression once widespread inequalities developed and that laissez-faire led ultimately to socialism, the reconciliation of social with moral law.

George's argument was revolutionary but popular, because it was consistent with Democratic ideals: a plea in a common tongue for the salvation of the ship of state. For all their groundbreaking force, George's arguments were marked by political restraint. He characterized Karl Marx as "the prince of muddle heads" (a judgment reciprocated) and expelled all socialists from his United Labor Party.[38] His views were also marked by a nativist passion, foreshadowed in his scurrilous news piece, "The Chinese on the Pacific Coast" (1869), where he characterized Chinese immigrants as "sensual, cowardly, and cruel . . . incapable of understanding our religion" and "our political institutions." George was still defending these sentiments twenty years later.[39]

Born into poverty in Philadelphia in 1839, George left school at fourteen to go to sea. Settling in San Francisco, he worked as a printer and then a journalist. In 1861, penniless but in love, he married, and by the time he moved to New York to launch a new branch for his small San Francisco paper, he was the father of two. George's eastern journalistic venture failed, due to the combination of powerful press and telegraph monopolies. But his confrontation with the raw vitality of New York and its spectacular extremes of poverty and wealth was decisive. The key to such a gap, he believed, was the monopolizing of natural resources, land in particular. Progress had increased the value of land, enriching landowners while leaving wages untouched. The remedy seemed obvious: eliminate all taxes save those on land, allowing producers their full wages, government its natural revenue, and the community its right to land value.

In addition to its sensational triumph as a book, *Progress and Poverty* had genuine political consequences. The argument that one tax could eliminate poverty and suffering spawned a political party based on the idea. George became a public figure and spent the rest of his life trying to implement his plan, through politicking, lecturing, and writing. In 1886, George ran for mayor of New York as a candidate of the reform party, losing the election to Abram S. Hewitt, but amassing more votes than the Republican candidate, Theodore Roosevelt. While George's agenda was far more influential in his own time than beyond it, it has continued to effect tax legislation throughout the world. The measure of a work of social protest is contemporary political effect; according to that standard, George's book was a triumph.

By the same measure, Du Bois's book *The Philadelphia Negro*, whose impact was felt years after its publication, was a failure. *The Philadelphia Negro* was not conceived as a work of social protest but as a guide to social reform. White leaders in the Quaker city commissioned the young black sociologist to study the morbid condition of the black community, which, they believed, was responsible for a more general municipal malaise. Their conviction reflected the organicism that dominated urban studies at the time: the presence of one diseased part inevitably infected the social whole. But Du Bois's conclusions challenged the hypothesis they were supposed to sustain. Drawing on statistics that revealed Philadelphia's black population to be the largest of any city in the country, he outlined the threat posed by blacks as a result of their progress, which included the rise of a substantial black middle class. The very commissioning of Du Bois's study exemplified the search for racist explanations of failure when in fact all evidence pointed to black success. Indeed, no contemporary study was more roundly critical of turn-of-the-century American society than Du Bois's, which argued that there was an interdependence of racism and capitalism.[40]

Emphasizing black poverty and criminality while denying black gains had become a critical means of controlling an increasingly volatile labor force. The degradation of black labor, Du Bois pointed out, was systematic: all it took for an occupation to be downgraded was its identification with blacks. He countered claims that blacks resisted technical training and were incapable of professional advancement with evidence of the deliberate undermining of black labor. "Most people were willing and many eager that

Negroes should be kept as menial servants rather than develop into industrial factors," he observed. "Special effort was made not to train Negroes for industry."[41] Owners and managers encouraged racial prejudice because it ensured a surplus population, desperate for jobs at any wage. This included scab work during union strikes, dramatized in the ending to *The Jungle*. At the same time, most trade unions had exclusion clauses admitting black workers only when their numbers demanded it. He went on to show how continuing high rates of black migration not only threatened whites but also impeded efforts by established blacks to locate occupational niches. Each new wave of black immigrants resulted in a "dark age" for the established black community.[42]

This led to the paradoxical privileging of invisibility among successful blacks such that inconspicuousness became an index of achievement within the black community. Moreover, the rush to demarcate black Philadelphia, Du Bois showed, signaled the increasing imprecision of racial boundaries. White demands for a delimited black population were satisfied by one type alone: the criminal-paupers, whose attributes justified their marginalization and censure. Meanwhile, interracial marriage and amalgamation proceeded apace. "The white and black races have mingled their blood in this country to a vast extent," Du Bois observed. Despite the special difficulty of such unions, after the Civil War, the incidence steadily increased. In a single ward of the city, he verified thirty-three intermarriages.[43] Du Bois closed his book with a plea and a warning addressed to each side of the class and color lines. The black elite had a responsibility to the hardworking black masses. But white America had a larger obligation—to recognize that its fate was tied to that of black Americans. The "avoidance of that which wounds and embitters," the "granting of opportunity," and the "desire to reward honest success," Du Bois concluded, would go far toward realizing "the City of Brotherly Love."[44]

John Spargo's *The Bitter Cry of the Children* (1906) was one of the most popular works of social reform produced in the first decade of the twentieth century.[45] A dedicated socialist over a long writing career, which lasted until his death in 1976, Spargo wrote books on subjects ranging from Karl Marx and John D. Rockefeller to histories of Vermont and early American pottery. Spargo left the Socialist Party in 1917 to protest its antiwar policy and together with Samuel Gompers formed the American Alliance for Labor and Democracy. Spargo's principal qualification for writing about child poverty was personal. "When I write of hunger I write of what I have experienced," he declared in the preface to *The Bitter Cry of the Children*. "So, too, when I write of child labor." He began by challenging American notions of "the democracy of birth," which he renamed "the democracy of death."[46] Before giving birth, poor women's hunger, malnutrition, and exhaustion from overwork imperiled their children, and immediately after it, the multiplied dangers included contaminated milk and inadequate supervision. Such conditions permanently compromised the children of the poor, impeding irrevocably their progress in an increasingly competitive industrial society.

Spargo argued that child labor in twentieth-century America was analogous to nineteenth-century British conditions, which were so wretched that members of Parliament were sickened by the graphic details. "Small children were being tortured to death in the industrial pit of capital" while British philanthropy focused on abolition. Often a century behind England in humanitarianism, America now confronted its own industrial crisis. The nationwide problem extended from the canning factories of New York State, which employed four-year-olds, to the cotton mills of the South, where six-year-olds labored long into the night.[47] Spargo rejected both parental responsibility and the role of custom as explanations. Child labor traditionally had involved domestic enterprises where children learned a trade. Now children and adults were consigned to ruthless factory oversight. Parents often had no choice in such decisions because employers coveted low-wage and docile child-workers, sometimes hiring adults with the provision that their children work too.[48]

The 1900 U.S. Census reported almost 2 million workers under sixteen, but Spargo insisted that actual figures approached 2.5 million.[49] In one Pennsylvania town, for example, Spargo discovered 150 illegally employed "breaker boys" in the anthracite mines, harvesting the miraculously clean coal prized by railroads like the Lackawanna. Hunched over coal chutes from dawn to dusk, they cut fingers, inhaled dust, and lost limbs, disposing them as adults to spinal deformities, asthma, and consumption. As an experiment, Spargo took the place of a twelve-year-old boy, working ten-hour days for sixty cents; by the end of the shift, his hands were terribly cut, and he coughed up particles of anthracite for hours afterward.[50]

A major problem was that even those most inclined to help were blind to the facts. Spargo derided the sentimental reformers more likely to offer flowers than legal advocacy. He described a New York women's guild that sought to "refine" and "spiritualize" 10,000 tenement-house children by supplying each with "a potted plant." Every child who could preserve a healthy plant for a year would earn a ribbon. A year later, many of the children given flowers were themselves gone, Spargo commented acidly, having "drooped during the summer and died like flowers in parched ground."[51]

Spargo's book appeared in a field that had been gaining momentum since the 1870s. Portraits of slums and articles about the stresses of the working class appeared regularly in magazines, newspapers, and best-selling books, such as Charles Loring Brace's *The Dangerous Classes of New York* (1872) and Josiah Strong's *Our Country: Its Possible Future and Its Present Decay* (1885). This literature and the establishment of the highly publicized New York City Tenement-House Commission in 1884 intensified middle-class desires to know more about the laborers congregating in urban centers. Among these works, none were more popular than photo-documentaries, and the ultimate example of the form was Jacob Riis's *How the Other Half Lives: Studies among the Tenements of New York* (1890). While Riis was less radical politically than Spargo, he too wrote about conditions he knew firsthand, on behalf of those excluded from affluence.

How the Other Half Lives reflects the immigrant status of its author perhaps most markedly in its respect for dominant American values and institutions. Trained as a carpenter in his native Denmark, Riis immigrated to America at twenty-one and spent three years working odd jobs, building houses, selling furniture, and drumming flatirons. Ending up in New York, Riis became a freelance journalist and then a police reporter for the *New York Tribune*, where he perfected the short vignette, the narrative foundation of his famous study. The skill of summarizing character, by describing individuals in their environment and their status and relations, led Riis to his book's thesis: people did not make slums, slums made people.

In the late 1880s, Riis began to gather photographs, which he believed was critical to appreciating the plight of "the other half." Riis's photographs were first presented as lantern slides, which produced images about ten-feet square with two projectors. The accompanying lectures featured stories about the subjects, personal anecdotes, and a moral. Delivered at churches in addition to other reform venues, the lectures were sometimes preceded by scripture reading, prayer, and gospel music. The lectures gained widespread notoriety when the *New York Sun* published a sample in 1888. *Scribner's* followed in 1889 with nineteen pages of text and illustrations entitled "How the Other Half Lives," which Riis expanded into his book. An immediate success, *How the Other Half Lives* launched Riis on a nationwide lecture tour. Though recent critics have questioned both Riis's sympathy for his subjects and his responsibility for all the photographs published under his name, the book was the most influential portrait of the working poor produced between the Civil War and World War I. Everyone interested in social reform read *How the Other Half Lives*—journalists, social scientists, policy makers, average citizens. Theodore Roosevelt considered the book invaluable to his tenure as the police commissioner of New York and praised it as "both an enlightenment and an inspiration for which I felt I could never be too grateful."[52]

As historians have pointed out, the Lower East Side of New York profiled in Riis's book was unique among urban slums for the density of its housing and the youth of its inhabitants. The crime rate was unusually high. Deviance thus became a central focus, which suited Riis, given his beginnings on the crime beat. Like most urban slums of the time, this one was, in Riis's words, a "queer conglomerate mass of heterogeneous elements, ever striving and working like whiskey and water in one glass."[53] Riis's cataloging of this diversity featured ethnic and racial stereotypes, sometimes as acerbic as those employed by nativists. But Riis directed his moral outrage against the greed of landlords, the indifference of the comfortable classes, and the lack of involvement by the city's religious community, which was drawn to more distant and exotic suffering. Riis's proposed solutions included increasing general civic responsibility, outlawing dilapidated tenements, and undertaking a new initiative for remodeling and building. Riis recommended the use of private enterprise backed by municipal law, and he included testimonials from Philadelphia businessmen that tenement construction pays. This combination of ethical concerns and practicality, the vividness of his empathic documentary archive, together with the conventionality of his perspective, ensured the book's wide appeal.

But it was the quality of the photographs, the profound engagement with their subjects, that gave *How the Other Half Lives* enduring significance. The first edition contained thirty-nine images: photograph after photograph capturing the intimate geography of slum life. Children rolling barrels stop to pose with wonder for the camera in a dark and narrow alley in the image "Gotham Court" (Fig. 14). The sun's rays filtering in stand for the camera and its reform aim: to illuminate and thereby alleviate poverty and suffering. The rigid angles of balconies and banisters and the billowing clothes and sheets seem to leave no room for human inhabitants like the three boys looking up at the camera from a ground-floor balcony in "Rear Tenement, Roosevelt Street" (Fig. 15). "Street Arabs in Sleeping Quarters" finds some boys huddled together, two of them barelegged and caught in an embrace, the third in profile hugging the wall (Fig. 16). The carefully arrayed populace of "Mullin's Alley" manages through sharp focus and casual poses to preserve independence within a deliberate arrangement (Fig. 17). A blond boy with superb features and wearing a cap occupies the foreground, his slim, molded hands lightly gripping his waist; a smiling, darker boy leans against the wall, one hand in a pocket, his gesture and

FIGURE 14 ::   "Gotham Court." From Jacob Riis, *How the Other Half Lives* (1890).
Photograph courtesy of the Museum of the City of New York,
The Jacob A. Riis Collection.

FIGURE 15 ::   "Rear Tenement, Roosevelt Street." From Jacob Riis, *How the
Other Half Lives* (1890). Photograph courtesy of the Museum
of the City of New York, The Jacob A. Riis Collection.

FIGURE 16 ::   "Street Arabs in Sleeping Quarters." From Jacob Riis, *How the Other Half Lives* (1890). Photograph courtesy of the Museum of the City of New York, The Jacob A. Riis Collection.

expression conveying both bravado and warmth; two girls, one in a white dress, another in stripes, are sequestered secretively in a corner, one facing the camera, the other at a perpendicular angle to it.

These images present a reform agenda of their own: an argument for variety. Ghetto dwellers come in all shapes and sizes, with varied personalities as well as ethnicities. By turns they are vibrant, curious, dull, observant, enthusiastic. They dress distinctively, despite their poverty, and they think diverse thoughts; their parents dream different dreams on their behalf. Riis's photographic object is to detail and thereby to humanize the inhabitants of New York's tenements. However high-pitched the tones of his narrative, however much it satisfies the prevailing initiatives of middle-

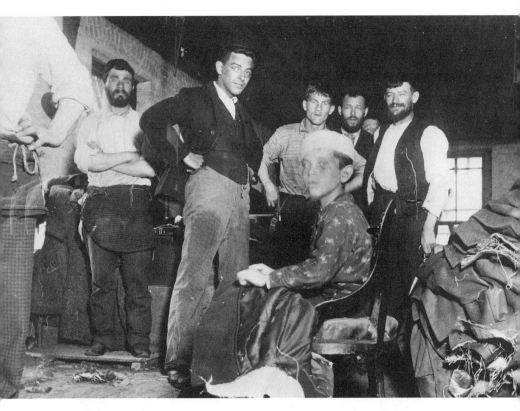

FIGURE 18 :: "In a Sweatshop." From Jacob Riis, *How the Other Half Lives* (1890). Photograph courtesy of the Museum of the City of New York, The Jacob A. Riis Collection.

class reform, the photographs themselves tell a deeper story. This story concerns the power to retain individuality in circumstances designed to render people uniform, to remain a self, able to stare questioningly for posterity at a camera lens, to cling to another for comfort in sleep, to have a friend with a different-colored dress. All of these aspects of being human persist in the ghetto and are captured in pictures.

This is not to deny the grounds for Riis's pessimism. The handsome boy pulling threads from silk upholstery in a photograph titled "In a Sweatshop" has a black eye that might have been caused by any of the strong men surrounding him (Fig. 18). The four laborers with the policeman burying coffins in the snow in "The Trench in the Potters Field" are putting some very small bodies to rest (Fig. 19). And the Madonna figure gazing heavenward in an image titled "In the Home of an Italian Rag-Picker, Jersey Street," her brown hands encircling the swaddled infant, her own body

FIGURE 19 :: "The Trench in the Potter's Field." From Jacob Riis, *How the Other Half Lives* (1890). Photograph courtesy of the Museum of the City of New York, The Jacob A. Riis Collection.

FIGURE 20 :: "The Home of an Italian Rag-Picker, Jersey Street." From Jacob Riis, *How the Other Half Lives* (1890). Photograph courtesy of the Museum of the City of New York, The Jacob A. Riis Collection.

stilled with exhaustion, can barely plead to a higher order (Fig. 20). Each picture, of conspiring men arrayed in black, the homeless in a rooming house, or sweatshop workers, is part of Riis's message. Through the formalizing scrutiny of the camera, these people become characters; thus transformed, their case for a human chance is made.

As a Danish immigrant who studied his adopted country well, Jacob Riis recognized how essential claims to individuality were to the fortunes of any social group. Samuel Gompers, the founder of the American Federation of Labor (AFL), born in England to Dutch Jewish immigrants, shared Riis's perspective. Throughout the twentieth century, Gompers was credited by labor leaders with identifying the requisite principle for an American labor organization—voluntarism. While Lenin called Gompers's method "a rope of sand," most considered it a practical realism that ensured his federation success in the United States.[54] From the beginning of his career as a labor organizer, Gompers displayed an eagerness to accommodate the American system, despite his awareness of its injustices. Convinced that compromise worked, he sought to build a labor movement based on the opportunities of America, rather than on the situation of labor abroad.

In *Seventy Years of Life and Labor* (1925), Gompers recounted his formative years in England. He recalled being greatly affected when French Huguenot neighbors, silk weavers, were ruined by machinery that replaced their skills. His education at a Jewish free school, where he studied the Talmud (in addition to basic subjects), gave him training in logic that he believed was critical to his later success as a champion of labor. As the oldest son, Gompers left school at the age of ten to learn his father's trade, cigar making. Three years later, his family emigrated to America with the assistance of the English cigar-makers' union through a program that relieved competition among English workers by financing the relocation of surplus workers. Gompers's introduction to America upon arriving in New York was a conflict over race: For shaking hands with a black boat employee who had helped the family on the difficult sea journey, his father was attacked by white bystanders. His father's refusal to back down provided Gompers a lifelong lesson in defending one's beliefs and a model for his own efforts to forge alliances between black and white laborers. In 1864 Gompers joined the cigar-makers' local union, and three years later, he married another cigar-maker, Sophia Julian.

Because one could think and talk while stripping tobacco leaves and rolling cigars, the work was conducive to intellectual debate and politicking. The cigar shop became a forum where books by leading economic theorists—Karl Marx, Ferdinand Lassalle, Henry George—were read aloud and discussed. Gompers recognized the potential of trade unions, but the financial crisis of 1873, which caused widespread unemployment, and the violence incited by union factions made him wary of radicalism. Though he participated in cigar-makers' strikes and in solidarity demonstrations with striking railroad workers, he never lost faith in free enterprise. Gompers became a U.S. citizen in 1872, and it was a point of pride with him that in a career of unionizing he was arrested only once. In the early years of the AFL, he specialized in organizing fellow Jews, specifically Russian immigrant tailors exploited by clothing manufacturers. But the reform with which he was most identified was the shortened workday. "Eight Hours for Work," went a contemporary slogan, "Eight Hours for Rest, Eight Hours for What We Will."[55] On May Day 1886, Gompers led an all-trades eight-hour demonstration, which was so successful that labor unions expanded across the country. Defending workers against scientific management expert Frederick W. Taylor's charge of declining productivity in the workplace, Gompers argued that the eight-hour day was not just a means of increasing wages and alleviating unemployment but also a human right.

Gompers was always judicious in his handling of potentially volatile political relationships, such as that between his AFL and the Socialist Party. While he refused an official affiliation, he publicly supported socialist principles, just as he backed the Haymarket anarchists, and Eugene Debs, when he was jailed during the Pullman strike. Like other principled and prominent immigrants, such as Jacob Riis and Abraham Cahan, Gompers tried to keep his adopted country faithful to its ideals. However challenging the task, through a long life of labor Gompers never wavered in its pursuit.

THE WORK ETHIC

As codified by Max Weber, "the Protestant Ethic," which used Benjamin Franklin as a model, involved the spiritualization of daily life, the conviction that everyone had a vocational calling, the obligation to be useful, and the tie between effort and reward.[56] While the qualification of Weber's "ethic" was underway by the mid-nineteenth century, the post–Civil War expansion of industrial capitalism accelerated the process.[57] Self-denial and productivity remained important values, but America was becoming "a culture of consumption," a transformation assisted by the rapid rise of advertising. Consumer culture encouraged alternative values, in particular those of abundance and leisure. In this period of changing industrial processes and changing productive and consumptive ideals, the work ethic persisted as a significant register of Americanization. Indeed, by the turn of the century, the work ethic was perhaps most in vogue among immigrants, as exemplified by three social outsiders who commemorated its principles in classic works of literature. Through their respective best sellers, *Up from Slavery*, *The Promised Land*, and the Ragged Dick series, Booker T. Washington, a former slave, Mary Antin, a Jewish immigrant, and Horatio Alger, a homosexual, revitalized an imperiled work ethic while using it as a guide to personal fame and fortune.

Booker T. Washington was the most powerful black American leader of his time and gained renown for his program of industrial education at Tuskegee, the institute he founded in Alabama. His policy of accommodating white prejudice and relinquishing black claims for civil and legal rights in exchange for economic opportunities made him a controversial figure. Indeed, materialism was a veritable religion for Washington, and his social philosophy was remarkably consistent with the Protestant ethic. But it was no idle embrace of a prevailing capitalist ethos. He internalized that ethos and made it amenable to the rural conditions of black southerners. Members of the Tuskegee faculty recall how they dreaded the sound of wagon wheels signaling the principal's return from his travels and the resumption of morning inspections. Touring the campus on horseback, Washington would note every piece of trash, every stray animal, every missing button on a coat. Each sign of waste or indifference would be recorded in his red notebook and later redressed in the name of the black Protestant kingdom on earth under construction at Tuskegee.[58] Tuskegee was Washington's brick-and-mortar version of this utopia; *Up from Slavery* was the rhetorical version. In both, he emphasized spiritual necessity, building from the ground up, and manual labor. In arguing that the highest office of southern blacks was doing "a common thing in an uncommon manner," Washington secured a permanent place for himself, for good or ill, as an architect of ordinariness.[59]

Washington's policies won him extensive political authority but also provoked attacks from fellow black leaders. Yet over the course of his highly publicized career as an accommodator, he secretly financed a range of court suits, challenging injustices against blacks, Jim Crow cars, peonage, and the denial of jury service. After the publicity generated by his 1895 Atlanta Exposition address—featuring the notorious aphorism, "In all things purely social we can be as separate as the fingers, yet one as the hand in all things essential to mutual progress"—Washington was urged to begin work on his memoirs.[60] His first effort was *The Story of My Life and Work* (1900), which was largely ghostwritten by the black journalist Edgar Webber. Dissatisfied with the result, Washington resolved to take more control and the outcome, *Up from Slavery* (1901), became a best-selling account of his rise from slavery to national and international prominence.[61] Washington undoubtedly appreciated the response of Kodak head George Eastman, a check in the amount of $5,000 for Tuskegee.

One of his sharpest critiques was by W. E. B. Du Bois in the *Dial*.[62] Washington's policies, according to Du Bois, overlooked three barriers to black progress in the South: the greed of capital that reduced black workers in country districts to "semi-slavery"; the competitive fears of southern workers that encouraged black disenfranchisement; and the passions of the ignorant and bereft, which perpetuated horrific abuses. Du Bois's criticisms did not prevent Washington from inviting him to Tuskegee for the summer, an indication of Washington's political skills, his ability to put aside differences for the sake of valuable alliances. As one contemporary observed, "Washington had no faith in white people, not the slightest, and he was most popular among them, because if he was talking with a white man he sat there and found out what the white man wanted him to say, and then as soon as possible, he said it."[63] Washington was nicknamed "the wizard," which suggested the enigmatic quality of his character and thought.

Up from Slavery was a story of making it in America. While Washington described his childhood as a slave, the book confirmed his belief that progress for African Americans required their redefinition as immigrants. Thus Washington characterized slavery as a "school," seeking to reduce it to a form of training and to acknowledge that, like any other experience, it had, as part of God's plan, inadvertent benefits.[64] Slavery had educated black people according to His will, their trials signaling divine favor and eventual reward. "Success," Washington held, was not measured by "the position that one has reached in life," but by "the obstacles which he has overcome while trying to succeed."[65] Like Benjamin Franklin, whose *Autobiography* was recalled in reviews of *Up from Slavery*, Washington distrusted desire. Where Franklin considered it disruptive to a balanced social system, Washington believed its end could be a lynch rope. Washington's emphasis on moderation and self-effacement was perfectly suited to the post-Emancipation South where black ambition was considered an incitement.

One of the book's most memorable vignettes was Washington's declaration of his preference for the weekly molasses treat of slave days over the fourteen-course dinners of the lecture circuit. The boy who shut his eyes "while the molasses was being poured" in the hope of being surprised by a big helping becomes the statesman who knows that control over whites demands he display no cravings. Washington's comforting message to whites is: no matter how big this particular black man gets, his appetite remains stuck like molasses in slavery days. He may enjoy his "share" but has "never believed in 'cornering'" the market on desirable things. The more threatening point is the transformation of the slave into a famous man who feasts on fourteen-course dinners while recalling the lean molasses days of youth. Like a titan modeling the road to wealth, Washington's childhood deprivations make the fruits of success all the more sweet.[66]

Blacks would develop healthy appetites for work and rewards, suggested Washington, when they were free to regulate themselves. Washington's devotion to the soil, his conviction that his people would progress through connection to the elements, was an attempt to eradicate the stain of slavery, to cleanse and purify in order to begin anew. The acquisition of skills and the identification of proper vocations were means to an end rather than ends in themselves. In fact he never opposed black higher education or professional training: "When a Negro girl learns to cook, to wash dishes, to sew, to write a book, or a Negro boy learns to groom horses, or to grow sweet potatoes, or to produce butter, or to build a house, or to be able to practice medicine as well or better than some one else, they will be rewarded regardless of race or color." Washington's offspring fulfilled his prescription, aspiring to professions while excelling in a variety of practical skills. His daughter was a dressmaker who dreamt of becoming a musician; his oldest son was a brick mason who wanted to pursue architecture; his youngest son was a manual worker who set his sights on medicine.[67] Though some argued that Washington overlooked the overwhelming barriers to the professional advancement of blacks in his time, he clearly recognized the necessity of that advancement.

Work, Washington argued, was the great casualty of American slavery; black and white laborers suffered equally under a system that undermined a value essential to human dignity. "The whole machinery of slavery was so constructed as to cause labor, as a rule, to be looked upon as a badge of degradation, of inferiority. Hence labor was something that both races on the slave plantation sought to escape. The slave system on our place in a large measure, took the spirit of self-reliance and self-help out of the white people."[68] Implicit here is the idea that southern whites might benefit from a Tuskegee of their own. Washington's adaptation of the work ethic for black Americans was consistent with other aspects of a black-centered social policy. What made Washington a singular spokesman for black Americans at the turn of the century was the intensity and narrowness of his vision. While convincing whites of his deference, he cared for fellow blacks alone.

Booker T. Washington claimed Protestant fundamentals as the means to the recovery of his people in the postslavery era. The problem for Jewish immigrants portrayed by Mary Antin was their tribal susceptibility to Americanization. The very adaptability of Jews as citizens of the Diaspora challenged their preservation of religious and cultural traditions. Antin did more than articulate the work ethic; she personified it. *The Promised Land* (1912) was a best seller, and the energetic Antin embarked on a lecture tour to publicize an open immigration policy, public education, and Zionism. Perhaps most revealing about the critical response to Antin's book were the reviews that were hostile to the eagerness of her assimilation. The Jewish philosopher Horace Kallen, for example, lamented Antin's tendency to be "excessively, self-consciously flatteringly American." Brahmin purist Randolph Bourne disdained "the Jew who has lost the Jewish fire and become a mere elementary, grasping animal."[69] Such criticism missed the struggle Antin dramatized between realizing the prospects of "the Promised Land"

and her sense of guilt and loss in doing so. For all its hubris and enthusiasm, her narrative was also an act of mourning, for the spiritual and familial ties forsaken in the effort "to win America."[70] These critics did convey, however, their own discomfort with a female Jewish immigrant so primed to adopt American Protestant values.

Antin, who immigrated to Boston in 1894, was the hope of her Russian Jewish family, encouraged especially by her father, a businessman sufficiently enlightened to seek a liberal education for his daughters. Precocious and hardworking, Antin attended the prestigious Boston Latin School for Girls, where her abilities were brought to the attention of Edward Everett Hale, a philanthropist who liked to assist "deserving" newcomers. A middle-class market for immigrant narratives facilitated Antin's literary debut, after caseworkers at the Hebrew Immigrant Aid Society showed Israel Zangwill a series of Mary's letters to Russia. Translated from Yiddish to English, the letters were published in 1899 with an introduction by Zangwill. Antin's rapid ascent in her literary vocation aroused inevitable conflicts between her poor family and the wealthy American patrons who discovered her, increasing the likelihood that she would make a rebellious marriage. At a Natural History Club outing sponsored by the immigrant agency Hale House, Antin met Amadeus Grabau, a German paleontologist at Columbia University. She was nineteen and he was thirty-one when they married in 1902; their daughter born in 1906 would be their only child. Antin's mentors were unhappy about her intermarriage, but Antin insisted on her devotion to Jews if not Judaism. Her second book, *They Who Knock at Our Gates: A Complete Gospel of Immigration* (1914), confirmed her ongoing identification with persecuted Jewry everywhere.

The Promised Land was structured by a series of conversions: from Russian outcast to American citizen; from traditional Judaism to liberal transcendentalism; from the communal ethnicity nurtured in the Pale to American individualism; from impoverished immigrant to famous author. Like other Protestant autobiographies to which it was compared, the book treated major life events as signs of election. But the book conveyed more admiration for religious feeling than evidence of it. Antin commends from a distance the Russian Jews who sacrifice chickens on the Eve of Atonement. Proper religious behavior in the Old Country becomes familial psychology in the New, as Mary Antin's sister Frieda is sacrificed to factory work while Mary attends school. As a product of the Pale, Antin knows that glory comes to those who sacrifice. As a product of America, she knows that sacrifice is the lot of inferiors; in a society that extols success, it is a deprivation experienced by some and not by others. The difference in individual apportionments must be rationalized, in this case by what Antin calls the "family tradition, that Mary was the quicker, the brighter of the two, and that hers could be no common lot."[71]

The most unqualified source of spiritual purpose in *The Promised Land* is food. "It takes history to make such a cake," Antin observes of Old Country cheesecakes.[72] The food nostalgia of Antin's Russian scenes is paralleled by food revulsion in the American scenes. America is associated with "food, ready to eat, without any cooking from little tin cans," and with the "pink piece of pig's flesh," which Antin eats more of "than anybody at the table" to demonstrate her susceptibility to assimilation.[73] Consumption in *The Promised Land* is a sacred mediator that allows the narrator to move back and forth between the Old World and the New.[74] But Antin's immigrant is most like the commodity, the cheesecake, rather than the consumer of it. Lost to Antin in America is the sense of completeness derived from the place of origin, even a place as narrow as the Russian Pale. Like the "advantage of the disadvantage" described by W. E. B. Du Bois, there were clear benefits in the Russian setting. The Old World Jew enjoyed a fierce sense of belonging, a religiosity so strong that it seemed "a fortress." The greater the suffering, the more intense the Diaspora vision, a tremendous longing that was its own reward: "in the dream of a restoration to Palestine [the Jew] forgot the world."[75] The paradox of the Jewish Diaspora is that Jews always lived most richly and cohesively as Jews in countries that were most intolerant. By allowing Russia to upstage America, Antin pinpoints the unique dilemma for the Jew in the land of material opportunity and religious acceptance. Can a Jew be so much in the world and remain a Jew? Is Jewishness to be preserved at the expense of self-development? These questions are submerged in the triumphant rhetoric of *The Promised Land* but fully present in the highs and lows that define its deepest vision.

Recalling the world of reading that was opened to her in America, Antin notes that after Louisa May Alcott, her favorites were "boys' books of adventure, many of them by Horatio Alger."[76] That a Jewish female immigrant was reading Alger suggests how omnipresent his works had become by the turn of the twentieth century. As the live-in tutor to the children of prominent Jews Joseph Seligmann, the banker, and Albert Cardozo, father of the future Supreme Court judge Benjamin Cardozo, Alger might well have encountered some of Antin's future benefactors.[77] Like Antin, Alger refashioned on behalf of a particular group—poor boys—the American drama of upward mobility through predestination and hard work. Alger published 110 novels during a three-decade-long writing career that ended with his death in 1899, each with a continuous moral code: poverty ennobles, inspiring thrift and ambition; virtue and diligence are always re-warded; and merit creates its own aristocracy. The only simpletons in Alger are spoiled rich boys, while good manners and taste are innate. Once the hero's superior qualities are established, the narratives invariably introduce a wealthy benefactor, who conceives a liking for the hero and provides means for his improvement, which begins with the purchase of a new suit. Alger's titles—*The Train Boy*; *Dan, the Newsboy*; *Young Bank Messenger*; *Frank Fowler, the Cash Boy*; *Tom, the Bootblack*; *The Errand Boy*—reflect a preoccupa-tion with work, but the books support a work ethic while repudiating contemporary forms of labor. Modern industry is ignored in favor of rela-tively timeless jobs in mercantilism, farming, and banking.[78] Yet Alger's books often featured the modern activity of speculation, whether as a distant enterprise that fascinates a character like Ragged Dick, who refers to his mythical shares in the Erie Railroad, or as a practice in which protago-nists themselves profit.[79] Too much investing is a bad thing, but approached with wisdom and modesty by humble people, it is always remunerative.

Alger, the son of a poor but respected Unitarian minister in Marlborough, Massachusetts, was an outstanding student with ambitions to write. Though it was not long after his graduation from Harvard that he began to publish stories in good magazines—*Harper's*, *Putnam's*, *North American Review*—he couldn't support himself on his earnings, so he turned to the ministry, graduat-ing from Harvard's Divinity School in 1860. Alger served a small congregation in Brewster on Cape Cod, where he managed to write on the side, but within two years, rumors of homosexuality and child molestation led to his firing. After moving to New York City, Alger devoted himself to writing full time. Whether he sublimated his passion for boys in writing about them or dis-covered a physical outlet in the anonymity of New York is unclear. A friend of the James family, Alger was candid about his desires, though he classified them as a form of "insanity." Years later, he could refer openly to his "natural liking for boys" and comment that he had "leased his pen" to them.[80]

Alger's first major success was the best-selling *Ragged Dick, or Street Life in New York* (1868), and one of its consequences was Alger's acquaintance with Charles Loring Brace, a philanthropist who ran the Children's Aid Society and a lodging house for homeless newsboys. Alger became a regular visitor to these institutions, drawing on their inhabitants as fictional subjects. *Ragged Dick*, which portrayed a highly competitive order of bootblacks in midtown Manhattan, provided in Dick a hero who smoked, swore, was extravagant when he had money, and indulged in pranks at the expense of country rubes and unsuspecting old gentlemen.[81] Dick was also prone to morbidity and sympathy toward the criminal poor, exhibiting a depth lacking in subsequent Alger heroes. Dick speaks a rough dialect, and the sign of his upward mobility at the novel's end is deliberate speech. Dick is also versed in the financial rhetoric of bulls and bears and jests about his "man-shun up on Fifth Avenoo."[82] The catalyst to his ascent is an impropriety: his eavesdropping on a wealthy boy and his uncle, who needs someone to show the nephew, Frank, around the city. Dick offers his expert knowledge of Manhattan (his ragged clothes and speech are no deterrent), and there begins a reciprocal education. Dick introduces Frank to street life, and Frank introduces Dick to the upper class. The twenty-two years separating *Ragged Dick* and *Struggling Upward* (1890) reveal the gradual abandonment of Ragged Dick's memorable qualities, such as his sense of humor, moodiness, and critical intelligence, as the Alger hero learns good manners and grammar. Set in a small town, *Struggling Upward* features Luke Larkin, who is the loving son of a poor widowed mother and a thorough conformist, incapable of a fresh thought or statement. *Ragged Dick*'s New York setting is integral to the novel's story, while abstraction is the rule in *Struggling Upward*; in the latter, Alger's talents seem compromised by success, the obligation to produce profitable, if formulaic works on a tight schedule.

Yet a remarkable scene in *Struggling Upward* suggests that Alger still found ways to complicate his narratives and make important points. On a stagecoach out West, Luke meets Mortimer Plantagenet Sprague, who is unmistakably homosexual and an unqualified hero. A New Yorker, introduced as "a genuine dude, as far as appearance went, a slender-waisted, soft-voiced young man, dressed in the latest style, who spoke with a slight lisp," Sprague elicits Luke's immediate approval. "In spite of his affected manners and somewhat feminine deportment, Luke got the idea that Mr. Sprague was not wholly destitute of manly traits, if occasion should call for their display." In the dialogue that follows, Sprague flaunts his lisp and his weakness, substituting "weally" for "really," ending each sentence with "don't you know," welcoming the sharp turns that send the novel's real coward, the brawny Colonel Braddon, into his lap. "If it's all the same to you," he quips, "I'd rather sit in *your* lap." Robbers predictably appear, barking orders at the terrified passengers. Sprague produces a pair of revolvers "and in a stern voice, wholly unlike the affected tones in which he had hitherto spoken said: 'Get out of here, you ruffians, or I'll fire!'" Minutes later, the "dude" is back, lavishly praising others while downplaying his own heroism. Exhibiting prized Alger traits—bravery, modesty, skill—in the guise of a homosexual, Sprague completely controls his erotic exhibitionism while demonstrating mastery in the Wild West.[83]

Mortimer Plantagenet Sprague is not a deceiver but rather a human being in Alger's deepest sense of the term: combining the impulses of weakness and courage, the aspiration to self-display and self-effacement, passivity and assertiveness, masculinity and femininity. As an allegory for Alger's authorship, it stands as both an appeal and a self-justification. Alger himself was the dude, and he looked the part, at five feet even, boyishly slender, with a slight stammer and an effusive manner, yet capable of producing strings of best sellers featuring manly little heroes. These manly little heroes were as needy as they were resourceful, fulfilling every task, however daunting, and then turning to their mothers, or to one another, for comfort. And it was precisely the reciprocity he highlighted between Protestant values and homosexual desire that make Alger's books worthy of literary study in their own right.

Booker T. Washington, Mary Antin, and Horatio Alger succeeded in extending the work ethic to experiences and types of people not ordinarily identified with Protestant norms. Washington accomplished this through the revaluation of manual labor, which he believed required a complete renovation in the postslavery era, for whites as well as blacks. Mary Antin demonstrated how a talented and motivated individual, even an immigrant girl, could exploit the opportunities of an American meritocracy. And Horatio Alger created fictional worlds comprised of gentle youths justly served by fate and fortune. It was a tribute to his legacy that two of the best and most ambivalent fictionalizations of the American work ethic, F. Scott's Fitzgerald's *The Great Gatsby* (1925) and Theodore Dreiser's *An American Tragedy* (1925), depicted their heroes as readers of Horatio Alger. At a time when the practical and theoretical legitimacy of the work ethic was uncertain, Washington, Antin, and Alger ensured its survival by translating it into the terms of myth.

CORPORATE AMERICA

In his widely influential *Business Cycles: A Theoretical, Historical, and Statistical Analysis of the Capitalist Process* (1939), Joseph Schumpeter observed, "It was not enough to produce satisfactory soap, it was also necessary to induce people to wash."[1] During the post–Civil War era, Americans were induced to wash. The rise of big business and the extraordinary expansion of the American economy between 1860 and 1920 were facilitated by several factors. Between 1860 and 1900, 676,000 patents were granted by the U.S. Patent Office, spurred in part by the development of steel production and the application of electricity to industry. The dramatic influx of new inventions supplied techniques for converting the nation's vast natural resources into manufactured products. Long before Standard Oil, there was the American railroad, organized in the 1830s and 1840s; by the 1890s there were over 200,000 miles of track throughout the country.[2] The national railroad system educated employees, Andrew Carnegie as well as unionized workers, in the methods of big business, while helping to transport people and products to growing domestic and foreign markets. America's economy could not have developed as it did in the nineteenth century without the continual renewal of the American labor supply by immigrants who came for economic opportunity and helped to perpetuate economic growth. From 1800 to 1900 America was transformed into a mass society (its population increasing from 5.3 million to 76 million) distinguished by an astonishing diversity unequalled by any other nation in the world. While multiculturalism was especially identified with urban areas like New York and Chicago where 80 percent and 87 percent of the population, respectively, were immigrants or children of immigrants, small industrial towns like Fall River, New York, and Scranton, Pennsylvania, were even more ethnically mixed. The same was true of the West, which absorbed more than 8 million immigrants who came to stake land claims in places like South Dakota, Kansas, and Nebraska. These settlers brought with them foreign agricultural strains that often proved more durable than the homegrown ones. The Kubanka and Kharkov wheat introduced by Russian Mennonites in Minnesota, for example, flourished so remarkably that by 1914 half of the winter wheat consumed in the United States was of the Kubanka and Kharkov varieties.[3]

In addition to these material and human resources, American investors and entrepreneurs benefited from a general economic commitment to diversification, toward manufacturing, banking, and services and away from agriculture. Above all, the American legal system was uniquely hospitable to business enterprise. Not only were there few inhibiting tariff barriers between states and regions but venture capitalists were protected against foreign competition by direct and indirect subsidies. Corporate and contractual laws, lenient bank and bankruptcy laws, and the relative freedom from the demands of organized labor and the claims of environmentalists, all made for a society unusually hospitable to business enterprise. With a government comparatively young and small, no aristocracy, no church, and no standing army, the nation had few impediments to the expansion of market forces. In 1861, the only big business in America was the railroad; by the time the Supreme Court dissolved Standard Oil, American Tobacco, and Du Pont in 1911, trusts were a fixture of the economy. Henry Adams and his brother Charles characterized the railroad as a modern form of piracy in their scathing and prophetic critique of big business, *Chapters of Erie* (1886). But critiques of this kind did little to prevent what one business historian called the great explosion of mergers between 1895 and 1905, when three hundred business firms were formed into trusts, many of them firms that became household names over the course of the twentieth century: Chiquita, Eastman Kodak, Coca-Cola, Reebok, General Electric. One hundred and eighty nine of the *Fortune* 500 firms of the 1990s were founded between 1880 and 1920. In the seven years between 1897 and 1904 alone, 4,227 American companies were reduced to 257 combinations, occasionally by force.[4]

The theoretical purpose of the trust was to consolidate smaller companies and centralize their management, thus making production processes cheaper and more efficient. Recurrent depressions or panics—in the 1870s, 1880s, and 1890s—also motivated a search for means of controlling prices and output in order to regularize profits. While their methods paralleled those of industrial giants, many of the companies that participated in combinations were mainly interested in keeping their manufactures running full bore to compensate for high capital investments and costs. But John D. Rockefeller's Standard Oil Company, which was worth almost a billion dollars by the turn of the century, epitomized the giant corporation with its conspiratorial monopolizing of production, ravaging of competition, and price-fixing. The term "robber baron"—coined in 1880 by Kansas farmers in an antimonopoly pamphlet—expressed widespread fears that an American individualist ethos of enterprise and innovation was imperiled by trusts.[5] Rockefeller himself was eventually prosecuted under the 1890 Sherman Antitrust law, designed to curb the worst abuses of combination and ensure healthy competition. Significantly, Standard Oil was readily revived as a conglomerate when its services were needed by the nation upon entering World War I.

Next to the American legal system, there was perhaps no other cultural domain more interested in the affairs of business than American literature. One of the most notable features of realist novels was their preoccupation with economic enterprise in all its facets. This was partly because writers like Howells and Phelps, Twain and Dreiser, were coming to terms with the commercialization of their own literary profession in an era when magazine serialization, advertising, larger reading audiences, and literary celebrity could yield profits previously unknown to authors. Another reason was the powerful intellectual and aesthetic claims exerted by a culture of business that was changing society in ways that were of direct concern to realist writers, transforming American senses of time, conceptions of material possessions, as well as the conditions of opportunity and value. Every writer discussed in the following pages was profoundly ambivalent about the changes wrought by rapid capitalist development in this period. They were all as enchanted as they were repelled by it. That fascination-repulsion constitutes the very texture of their novels: the economic rhetoric, particularly the language of sacrificial exchange, in Henry James, the absorption with class and conscience in William Dean Howells and Elizabeth Stuart Phelps, and the pervasive categories of speculation, consolidation, and credit in Mark Twain, Frank Norris, and Theodore Dreiser.

MANUFACTURERS

Poised between Christian disdain for materialism and dismay over the class conflict catalyzed by unrestrained capitalist development, Elizabeth Stuart

Phelps and William Dean Howells offered two of the most profound critiques of manufacturers in the post–Civil War period. In Phelps's novel *The Silent Partner* (1871) and in Howells's *The Rise of Silas Lapham* (1885), these authors invoked familiar settings and themes to voice their apprehensions about a new and dangerous economic-industrial order. Phelps wrote about the New England mill towns close to her home in Andover, prescribing bonds among different classes of women as one means of assuaging some of the worst abuses. Howells stressed the strict Protestant morality of his self-made businessman, repeatedly staging conflicts between Silas Lapham's economic interests and his conscience. It was a conflict that would intensify before it disappeared from the portraits of businessmen in Dreiser, Norris, and James, who lived according to an independent moral system of their own devising.

The stark opposition between moral values and business practices depicted by Phelps in *The Silent Partner* was inspired by an actual case where the negligence of manufacturers resulted in the deaths of employees. Phelps herself had vivid memories of the Pemberton Mill disaster of 1860, when a faulty construction (overlooked by "careless inspectors") collapsed on 750 workers, burying 88 of them alive. Phelps recalls in her autobiography "how the mill girls, caught in the ruins beyond hope of escape, began to sing . . . their young souls taking courage from the familiar sound of one another's voices."[6] Phelps's fictionalization of the tragedy was consistent with her view that "the province of the literary artist [was] to tell the truth about the world he lives in." A "fully-formed creative power" was ethical as well as aesthetically pleasing.[7] Phelps visited the rebuilt mills, consulted engineers, officials, physicians, journalists, and people who had survived the mill's collapse. The result of her investigations was "The Tenth of January," published in the *Atlantic Monthly* in 1868. While the story was faithful to fact, Phelps felt that it failed to confront the social problems behind the incident, raising more questions than it answered. What were the prospects for political alliances among women across classes? Was capital-labor conflict inevitable, and what was the role of Christianity in its mediation? How far did manufacturers' responsibility toward their employees extend? *The Silent Partner* represented Phelps's attempt to probe deeply the relationship between factory-owning capitalists and the laboring poor who worked for them in a New England mill town. The representatives of these groups are two women: a wealthy young socialite of twenty-three, Perley Kelso, whose father is an owner of the Hale and Kelso Mills; and Sip Garth, an uneducated factory worker of twenty-one, who is instinctively eloquent and preternaturally aware. Both women are orphans: motherless at the narrative's start, they are soon fatherless as well. Perley's father dies in a train accident, Sip's in a factory accident—a "kindred deprivation" that stirs immediate sympathy in Perley.[8]

The novel's opening scene involves a chance meeting of the pair on a rainy night that Perley experiences from the warmth of her coach while Sip goes uncovered on the street. "As Lazarus and Dives, face to face," this confrontation defines the remainder of the narrative.[9] Perley, since her father's death a "partner" in the town's leading manufactory, is guided by Sip on a Dantesque tour from the perspective of those who suffer its operations. She encounters a spirited eight-year-old boy, illegally employed, who is literally consumed by a grinding machine. She sees an old laborer fired for meager productivity, compelled to await death in the almshouse. And she meets Sip's younger sister Catty, the novel's Christ figure: deaf and dumb because her mother worked punishingly long hours up to the moment of her delivery; and now blind from a hand disease contracted at her wool-picking job and rubbed into her eyes. The round of misfortune that is Sip's life culminates in Catty's death by drowning when she gets lost in a flood and is crucified in a log avalanche. Thus, Sip and Perley watch "the world of the laboring poor as man has made it, and as Christ has died for it, a world deaf, dumb, blind, doomed, stepping confidently to its own destruction before our eyes."[10]

This is the rhetoric that initiates Sip's career as a Christian messenger of peace. Perley opts for a life of genteel reform, removed from both the manufactory's elite and Sip's working class. The lone continuity between Perley and Sip is their mutual (one could argue) feminist repudiation of men. Perley breaks her engagement with Maverick Hale, the callous son of her father's partner, and refuses the more sympathetic Stephen Garrick, the self-made man who has risen from poverty to part ownership of the factory. Perley's decisions have to do with her own self-realization: the need for independence that resists life as a "silent partner." Sip rejects marriage in recognition of her class status as inborn and inescapable. "I've heard tell of slaves before the war that wouldn't be fathers and mothers of children to be slaves like them. That's the way I feel," she tells the man with whom she has known her only happiness.[11]

Phelps has no sympathy for the mill owners, whom she characterizes as heartless, caring only for profits. Nor does she have a taste for the high society their livelihood supports. But Phelps's potentially radical Christianity amounts to a strategy of appeasement just as her model of feminine self-reliance is limited to mild social reform. Finally, her ethics seem a rather nostalgic means of redress against forces whose challenge required more systematic and sophisticated tactics.

Howells's novel *The Rise of Silas Lapham* features a similar moral quandary.[12] His most renowned work, it was also the first major American novel to feature a businessman as protagonist, a tradition that includes Henry Blake Fuller's *The Cliff Dwellers* (1893), Robert Herrick's *Memoirs of an American Citizen* (1905), Henry James's *The Golden Bowl* (1904), Frank Norris's *The Pit* (1903), Theodore Dreiser's *The Financier* (1912), and Abraham Cahan's *The Rise of David Levinsky* (1917). Whether these authors portray manufacturers or financiers, the question of their heroes' ethical sensibilities is always a central point of concern.

Howells's preoccupation with the impact of business on social morality affirmed his conviction of its cultural ascendancy, as did his designation of *The Rise of Silas Lapham* as "typically American." What he meant by this is clarified in the words of the novel's aristocrat, Bromfield Corey: "Money . . . is the romance, the poetry of our age. It's the thing that chiefly strikes the imagination. The Englishmen who come here are more curious about the great new millionaires than about any one else, and they respect them more."[13] The making of large fortunes, through manufacturing, developing land, creating commodities, and locating markets had become a distinctly American activity. Building material empires in this post–Civil War period was the nation's contribution to world civilization. Unlike Dreiser, who sought to establish the aesthetic possibilities of this materialism, Howells was interested in its moral impact. Thus his novel foregrounds costs, consequences, and compensations: the price paid by individuals and by society as a whole for the nation's unequivocal embrace of capitalism. Howells's purpose, like Phelps's, keeps his narrative at a remove from enterprise itself. His characters discuss their feelings about manufacturing and its products; they indulge in the pleasures afforded by their successful ventures, including house building and romance; and they torture themselves about their responsibilities to those who have been casualties of the new economy rather than beneficiaries like themselves. They question their own motives whether in charity or in money making and contemplate the larger social effects of business.

The center of all this deliberation is Silas Lapham, introduced in an interview with Bartley Hubbard, the cynical journalist from *A Modern Instance*, whom Howells resurrects as a reporter doing a feature on "Solid Men of Boston." The conceit provides distance on Lapham, a morally ambiguous figure throughout, and establishes him as worthy of respect and sympathy, since he appears at the mercy of Hubbard. The conceit also enables Howells to relate the details of Lapham's rise, beginning with the recognition of the commercial potential of the paint-mine discovered years ago on the family farm. Just before the Civil War, when the need for nonflammable paint has been highly publicized by a ship explosion in the West, Lapham decides to test the properties of his inheritance. An expert review pronounces the paint fireproof, waterproof, and resistant to decay. Like all new products, Lapham's paint seems like a miraculous gift to its manufacturer. Lapham's paint business is put on hold during the Civil War, though Lapham understands that he might have gotten the product "into government hands" and seen his fortunes soar. Instead, Lapham enlists, gets wounded, becomes a colonel, and survives. Returning home, he plunges into paint "like my own blood to me," lovingly labeling the various market brands with family names. He is soon shipping "to all parts of the world," admirably rewarded for his wartime sacrifice.[14]

Yet Lapham's conscience remains troubled because he was forced to fire a dishonest partner, Milton K. Rogers, who supplied the capital for his paint business. Lapham atones for his guilt by accepting Rogers's business proposition and is eventually ruined since it requires that Lapham sell land to shady investors at the expense of the community, which he won't do. In short, Lapham insists on fair dealing in a business world that increasingly privileges ruthlessness. Howells's idealized portrait of a successful businessman might even be called unrealistic by his own standards. In an 1891 essay "A Call for Realism," he proclaimed that fiction must "cease to lie about life; let it portray men and women as they are, actuated by the motives and the passions in the measure we all know."[15] An ambitious man of business like Lapham who makes a fortune in paint but finds the ultimate exploitation of his gains to be inconsistent with his Christian values is not impossible. But the plot never quite demonstrates *why* Lapham's sale of his land to Rogers's investors would be harmful to the community. What is essential for Howells is the either/or option: either Lapham sacrifices his wealth or his morality; under no circumstances can he preserve both.

The same rigid scheme prevails in the novel's love story, which is critical to its realism. Lapham's two daughters, Irene and Penelope, both love the same young man, Tom Corey, but Tom reciprocates only Penelope's love. Like the business plot, the love story is resolved by the necessity of sacrifice for the common good. Lapham must give up his wealth in order to preserve his virtue, and Irene must give up Tom Corey to Penelope, whose love is reciprocated. Both solutions honor a utilitarian morality: it is better that one person suffer than two or more. The difficulty of such a reading for the business theme is that it presumes Lapham's economic ruin is requisite to a sound conscience, which the novel fails to establish convincingly. The difficulty of such a reading for the love theme is that it presumes, in the manner of fairy tales, that once people are married—Tom and Penelope—their problems disappear, whereas it seems likely that both will continue to lament Irene's pain and their own role in it. All this complication of ready solutions suggests that the basis of Howells's realism is his interest in people's beliefs about what constitutes moral behavior. Howells's novel is realistic because it focuses on the ways in which people in the late nineteenth century groped toward resolutions to their predicaments that seemed to them upright and honest, whether or not they were (or could be).

It is not Howells who believes in the concluding decisions of his characters, but the characters themselves. He opts for uncertainty and open-endedness in suggesting that the outcomes of actions remain unpredictable, however moral they might presently appear. This makes Howells's attitude toward American business more consistent with a Norris or a Dreiser than with a Phelps, and it signals his receptiveness to modernity in all its forms.

Howells's *The Rise of Silas Lapham* directly inspired Abraham Cahan's *The Rise of David Levinsky* (1917), which echoes Howells's ambivalence toward his protagonist, emphasizing his vitality while doubting his rectitude in business and in love.[16] Both novelists highlight an ethos of sacrifice that persists within these stories of "making it" in America. Whether the Protestant Lapham or the Jew Levinsky, both characters believe that material success requires they forfeit something significant. Thus Levinsky's personal misery at the novel's end is understood as the price he pays for professional triumph. Poised on either side of a thirty-year history of literary representations of manufacturing, the novels reveal how much had changed in the business world from 1885 to 1917. Most striking among these was the increasingly central role of immigrants in the nation's key industries. Robert Herrick's *Memoirs of an American Citizen* (1905), for instance, which recounts the life of a penniless farm boy, Edward Van Harrington, who works his way up to become the head of the meat trust in Chicago, describes how he becomes successful through his recognition of the monopoly afforded by the market segmentation of kosher meat. Going into business with German Jews, Harrington secures a niche that eventually enables his full-scale expansion. Aided as well by John Carmichael, a "foul-mouthed Irishman," Herrick's "American Citizen" rides his way to fame and fortune with the help of smaller immigrant businessmen, who soon have their own dreams realized, as confirmed by David Levinsky's "rise."

Because Cahan approached American business as an outsider, keenly

FIGURE 21 :: Levinsky making a toast. Illustration by Jay Hambidge for the serialization of Abraham Cahan's *The Autobiography of a Jew: The Rise of David Levinsky*. From *McClure's Magazine*, July 1913.

aware of the unique opportunities it offered to maligned foreigners, he was less worried than Howells about its deleterious effects. Such optimism, however, was qualified by anxieties about the predicament of Jews in his adopted country, which grew during the novel's writing. *The Rise of David Levinsky* originated in a proposal from an editor at *McClure's* that Cahan contribute to a series on immigrants in business. Neither of them could have anticipated that in March 1913, a month before the appearance of Cahan's serialized novel, an associate editor, Burton J. Hendrick, would publish an essay entitled "The Jewish Invasion of America" (covering topics such as "Intensity of Jewish Competition," "Jews the Greatest Owners of Land," and "Jews as a Great Power in American Railroads"). Nor could they have known that Hendrick's essay would be the vehicle for announcing Cahan's forthcoming serialization. The effects of Hendrick's piece were reinforced by Jay Hambidge's illustrations for *Levinsky*, which contained offensive Jewish stereotypes (Figs. 21 and 22). These frames, together with the realism of Cahan's portrait, led to accusations that the author had betrayed his people. While Cahan's sympathies were clear, the subject of Jews in business inevitably raised stereotypical associations that were bound

FIGURE 22 :: Levinsky and well-dressed young ladies. Illustration by Jay Hambidge for the serialization of Abraham Cahan's *The Autobiography of a Jew: The Rise of David Levinsky*. From *McClure's Magazine*, July 1913.

to be controversial. Still, the faults of David Levinsky, the coat manufacturer who rises from rags in Russia to wealth and power in America, are a product of his author's respect. Given the opprobrium Cahan endured over *Levinsky*, it is ironic that he was haunted during its writing by the trial in Kiev, Ukraine, of Mendel Beilis—a Jew accused, and later acquitted, of murdering a Christian boy to use his blood for ritual purposes—and the case in Atlanta, Georgia, of Leo Frank, a Jew convicted of murdering a Christian girl and later lynched by a mob.[17]

Jewish persecution forms an important subtext for Cahan's novel, largely because the garment industry it featured was a direct beneficiary of the devastating Russian pogroms of 1881–82. The convergence of an influx of Russian tailors seeking refuge and the growing demand from American women for mass-produced overcoats, dresses, and suits galvanized clothing manufacture. And it resulted in the radical democratizing of fashion. In the words of Cahan's David Levinsky, "It was the Russian Jew who had introduced the factory-made gown, constantly perfecting it, and reducing the cost of its production. The ready-made silk dress which the American woman of small means now buys for a few dollars is of the very latest style and as tasteful in its lines, color scheme, and trimming as a high-class designer can make it. . . . The average American woman is the best-dressed average woman in the world, and the Russian Jew has had a good deal to do with making her one."[18] Cahan makes the story of clothing manufacture a multicultural story by detailing how Russian Jews establish an increasingly solid footing in this critical industry. This is due in part to the incomparable hospitality of American speculators willing to supply capital to Jewish businessmen whom they considered good risks. Far from being exclusionary, American financiers, according to Cahan, welcomed Jews as both manufacturers and salesmen in rapidly expanding urban markets.

The focus of American economic growth in the late nineteenth century was urban commerce, the specialty of Jewish immigrant entrepreneurs, who brought with them a history of experience with cosmopolitan consumers. Throughout the cities of Europe, skilled Jewish workers and merchants nearly monopolized the production of clothing and footwear. This was even true of Russian cities, until the 1880s when anti-Semitic sanctions ruined many merchants. The American marketplace offered a miraculous cessation of anti-Semitic restrictions on Jewish enterprise. Often starting out in America as peddlers, many Jews were able by the last decades of the nineteenth century to establish specialty and department stores. These included the Filenes of Boston; the Kaufmanns of Pittsburgh; the Lazaruses of Columbus; the Goldsmiths of Memphis; the Sangers of Dallas; the Spiegelbergs of New Mexico; the Goldwaters of Arizona; and the Meiers of Portland. While American observers typecast Jews as a people of business, they did little to hinder the development of what one writer for the *New York Tribune* dubbed disparagingly, a "Hebrew Hive of Industry."[19]

Cahan's contribution to American literature was his powerful fictionalization of these economic trends. Nor is his portrait confined to clothing manufacture; his hero's ambitions take him into other businesses, including New York real estate, where Jews again are a critical force. Cahan describes the Russian Jew as builder, emphasizing his magical transformation from quintessential wanderer to developer of land and neighborhoods. Such details reinforce Cahan's theme that America is "different" for the Jew. No other nation is more hospitable to his material ambitions; no other nation is more threatening to his spirituality and intellect.

"I was worth over a million, and my profits had reached enormous dimensions," David Levinsky confesses near the novel's end. "I had no creed. I knew of no ideals."[20] Levinsky falls in love with the daughter of a poet, who complains about America's materialism and spiritual impoverishment, but he is too assimilated for her. The novel closes on Levinsky's paralyzing nostalgia for himself as a penniless schoolboy poring over the Talmud. Professional achievement and personal satisfaction are mutually exclusive. Yet Cahan also suggests, recalling Antin, that immigration and Americanization are fundamentally isolating, religiously as well as humanly. Levinsky has reached, through his material triumphs, a tragic condition; his self-recognition as the one commodity he cannot sell. "In business I am said to know how to show my goods to their best advantage. Unfortunately, this instinct seems to desert me in private life. There I am apt to put my least attractive wares in the show-window."[21] Because Levinsky himself considers business degraded, he doubts what he has accomplished. He has pleasures; for instance, the pride he takes in mapping the growth of American commerce and the role of fellow Jews in this expansion. He enjoys the material comforts afforded by his success. But he would readily change places with the Jewish scholar, sculptor, or musician. Cahan leaves his clothing manufacturer lonely and insecure because he believes in a higher social office for his people. In contrast to Dreiser and Norris, he cannot see the poetry in a coat or a grain of wheat. The problem for Cahan lies not in the particular organization of the social economy but in the social preoccupation with material things.

What distinguishes Frank Norris's *The Octopus: A Story of California* (1901) from these other treatments, respectively, of the textile (Phelps), paint (Howells), and clothing (Cahan) industries is his profound aesthetic respect for the manufacture of wheat. This may explain why his novel provides the era's most idealistic portrait of a large industry. *The Octopus*, like *The Silent Partner*, drew inspiration from a historical incident, the Mussel Slough Massacre, and sought to expose a moral wrong identified with a specific industry, the railroad trust. Norris's approach to his subject recalls Phelps's: he was not interested in representing the event in historically precise terms but in building on its dramatic potential. In May of 1880 in the Mussel Slough district of California, federal deputies representing the railroads killed five ranchers participating in a mass demonstration against impending eviction from their lands. The Southern Pacific Railroad had invited ranchers to develop the land and promised to sell it to them subsequently at a nominal cost. When the railroad priced the land years later, however, they included its *new* rather than *original* value, essentially asking the ranchers to pay for their own improvements. The incident had already inspired one novel, *The Feud of Oakfield Creek* (1887), by the philosopher Josiah Royce, a native Californian. Norris did research at the Mechanics Institute Library in the San Joaquin Valley and interviewed railroad magnate Collis P. Huntington. He also spent a summer at the Santa Anita Rancho near Hollister, California, witnessing the process of modern wheat production, with one of the first combined harvesters and threshers.

It is important to recognize that the heroes of Norris's novel are capitalist ranchers with large investments in land and farming equipment, competing with the railroads for the great wealth afforded by wheat production. They have no particular love of the land; their purpose is to exploit its bounty. They respond to the railroad commission's critical decision against them by resolving to "buy" themselves a commissioner. The complexity of this portrait befits Norris, who was a member of the Anglo-Saxon elite: his mother, a descendant of old New England and Virginia families; his father, a wealthy self-made businessman. When he covered a 1902 mining strike in Pennsylvania, for example, his perspective was not particularly pro-labor.[22] But his father disinherited Norris when he divorced his mother in 1894, a circumstance that increased Norris's sympathies for the middle and working classes and also made him more ambitious to pursue the writing career his father opposed. Norris was heartened by the reception of *The Octopus*, a commercial as well as critical success. Doubleday advertised the novel well and succeeded in selling all 33,000 copies of the first printing, while a high-profile reviewer promised that the book would "quicken the conscience and awaken the moral sensibilities." Norris's title image of the railroad as "octopus," the monstrous "colossus" swallowing up everything in its wake, became notorious as an example of "shrill, anti-corporate rhetoric."[23] The novel's true demonic force, however, is neither technology nor the businessmen, whether railroad magnates or wealthy ranchers, who benefit from it, but Nature itself, which is always capitalized in Norris's works.

The Octopus: A Story of California was the first novel in Norris's "Trilogy of the Wheat," to be followed by *The Pit: A Story of Chicago* and *The Wolf: A Story of Europe*. *The Octopus* concerned production, *The Pit*, distribution, and *The Wolf*, consumption. Before beginning *The Wolf*, Norris died of appendicitis. His sprawling *Octopus* is framed by the story of a poet, Presley, who is ambitious to write the "Song of the West" but suffers from writer's block. Finally stirred by the circumstances of the farmers, Presley produces a "socialistic" poem, "The Toilers," which is a huge success. Presley becomes a celebrity: the people's champion against the railroad trust, as well as an item on the high-society dinner circuit. This doesn't prevent Presley from complaining to Shelgrim, the head tycoon himself, who denies every principle of modern manufacture in declaring that railroads grow themselves just like wheat. The novel is full of eccentrics, including the priest, Father Sarria, a latter-day St. Francis, who loves all creatures great and small but harbors a shameful passion for cockfighting. There is the tragic shepherd Vanamee, who meets his beloved nightly under a row of trees, only to arrive one night to find her ravaged and comatose. He is driven by grief to a nomad existence, but it is never clear whether he was himself the ravisher. And there is the rancher Annixter, obsessed with digestion, superhuman in his energy for intellection and physical work. Skilled at farm management, he proves equally adept in law when he challenges the railroad trust. Yet it is Annixter who admits that the methods of the western farmer are self-destructive; after failing to alternate crops, they bemoan hard times when the soil is exhausted.

The novel's central mythology is the law of Nature, the great force, bound to defeat the most carefully conceived human efforts: "Men were naught, death was naught, life was naught; FORCE only existed—FORCE that brought men into the world, FORCE that crowded them out of it to make way for the succeeding generation, FORCE that made the wheat grow, FORCE that garnered it from the soil to give place to the succeeding crop."[24] California wheat growers are Nature's select beneficiaries, the suppliers of the world, another myth that is qualified by the representation of wheat production as global. This is why every ranch office has a telegraph linked to Chicago, New York, and Liverpool, reporting worldwide stores, the latest prices, and weather in the remotest wheat-producing areas. Various local, national, and international factors impact the wheat dealers' price, from the expansion of production beyond worldwide consumption needs to the draining of profits by intermediaries—banks, warehouses, merchants, buyers, and above all, the railroad.

The watchword of the nineteenth-century economy was production; the watchword of the twentieth is consumption. This is the main argument of the novel's leading dealer, Cedarquist, who recognizes the necessity of creating markets. His vision spurs the ranchers to new dreams, "set free of the grip of Trust and ring and monopoly acting for themselves, selling their own wheat, organising into one gigantic trust, themselves, sending their agents to all the entry ports of China."[25] The rancher's prospective liberation from the railroad trust enables the wheat trust. The wheat trust, however, was not to be. As business historians have pointed out, only certain kinds of industries lent themselves to trusts: those that featured economies of scale (steel, oil, automobiles) and those that featured economies of scope (pharmaceuticals, trademarked snack foods). Products in technologically advanced industries able to link mass production to mass distribution had the best chance of surviving in cartel form. National Biscuit became a successful American trust at the turn of the century; National

Wheat did not. A certain degree of artificiality apparently was required to make it as a trust.[26]

It seems appropriate that the novel's dramatic ending features a revenge of the wheat through its live burial of the Jewish railroad agent, S. Behrman. He dies from curiosity, peering into a wheat chute that inhales him, leading to his suffocation. Behrman is the ultimate Jewish middleman, a capitalist agent par excellence, to be pitied, according to Abraham Cahan. As the front of the railroad's power, he is the ranchers' nemesis. A mediator among artificial things and therefore an affront to Nature, his death is appropriately brought about by productive force. Thus Norris gives the last word to Nature's abundance, with the acknowledgment that this was indeed to be the last word.

CAPITALISTS

No American realist writer was more drawn to the world of business than Samuel Clemens, who trademarked his own literary merchandise with the self-made pseudonym "Mark Twain" (a term meaning a depth of two fathoms in a river) in 1863. Twain was the son of John Marshall Clemens, a struggling lawyer and judge who failed at every business proposition he pursued, and Jane Lampton Clemens, who was widowed young. John Clemens left his family little else except 70,000 acres of Tennessee land, upon which everyone but Twain staked his hopes long after the claims had been invalidated. Twain, twelve when his father died, was raised in a Mississippi river town, Hannibal, Missouri. His life was bounded by a cosmic event, Haley's Comet (which appeared the year of his birth and again the year of his death), and his maturation and success coincided with the astonishing economic and technological expansion of the country. He seemed to have had his hand in every significant economic venture of the era. Fascinated by new technologies, he often speculated: The Paige Typesetter was the most notorious of these investments, which included a domestic still for desalinating water and a new steam generator for tugboats.[27] He also undertook the risky option of a partnership in a publishing company, which at its height produced best sellers like Grant's *Personal Memoirs*, but proved in the long run a financial misstep. A born salesman, intrigued by advertising, Twain launched one of the era's biggest bookselling campaigns for *Personal Memoirs* and also initiated the Lackawanna Railroad's successful promotion of its new passenger rail service between New York and Buffalo, with advertisements featuring Phoebe Snow.[28]

Twain's most significant connection to the business world was his close friendship with Henry H. Rogers, a director of the Standard Oil trust, who guided Twain in the 1890s from bankruptcy to the considerable wealth he enjoyed until his death. Rogers was an admirer of Twain's writings and learned of his financial troubles from mutual acquaintances. He described himself as "Capitalist" in his *Who's Who* entry and once told a government commission investigating Standard Oil that "we are not in business for our health, but are out for the dollar."[29] He made a point of patronizing the arts. Rogers took control over all of Twain's business investments, and they became so close that Twain would spend the day in Rogers's Standard Oil Building office reading and smoking while Rogers conducted business.[30] Twain also became intimate with Andrew Carnegie, who sent him cases of his special Scotch, and they referred to each other as "Saint Mark" and "Saint Andrew."[31] Twain lived on Fifth Avenue and spent summers at Tuxedo Park (an elite estate in Westchester County), vacationing in Palm Beach and Bermuda with the likes of Carnegie and Rogers (Fig. 23). In 1908, Twain made a speech at the Aldine Club before fifty magazine publishers in support of the Rockefellers. This was not so much Twain's betrayal of an earlier empathy for the underdog as an embrace of plutocratic leanings he had always had.[32] As he observed in a letter to his pastor, the Reverend Joseph Twichell, "Money-lust has always existed, but not in the history of the world was it ever a craze, a madness, until your time and mine."[33] Twain counted himself among the mad, but his paradoxical genius enabled him to recognize it as a moral and political failing. It was this guilt toward his own capitalist ambitions, his resistance to a world of business he was deeply attracted to and saw firsthand at its highest reaches, that makes him such an invaluable witness to his era.

Mark Twain once characterized Theodore Roosevelt as "the Tom Sawyer of the political world of the twentieth century," implying that the president was a show-off.[34] But the label also highlighted the Yankee ingenuity that both displayed. Twain wrote *The Adventures of Tom Sawyer* (1876) around the same time as *The Gilded Age* (1873, coauthored by Charles Dudley Warner), and the novels share an interest in inheritances, stockholding, and speculation. Twain later called *Tom Sawyer* "a hymn" to boyhood and initially assumed that its readers would be the adults for whom it was written.[35] Many of its paradigmatic scenes and details concern capital and its manipulation. Exchange makes the devout world of St. Petersburg go round, seeming to drive every social interaction. But Tom is the ultimate master, managing to one-up everyone, from Aunt Polly, who invariably fails to deliver his deserved punishment, to the friends he succeeds in keeping on Jackson's Island. Tom manages to remain sweet while stealing sugar, to

FIGURE 23 ::

Photograph of Mark
Twain (*right*) and
Henry Rogers sailing
together in Bermuda,
1907. Courtesy of the
Mark Twain Project,
The Bancroft Library.

appear genuine while showing off, to commandeer all the tickets for the
Sunday school prize Bible, though he is unfamiliar with the Good Book and
could not have cared less about it. The one boy who challenges Tom's
speculative supremacy is the "juvenile pariah of the village," Huckleberry
Finn, who falls outside the dominant economy.[36] Son of the town drunkard,
lawless, idle, and unwashed, Huckleberry Finn arouses the envy of other
boys for his ostensible "free will."[37] Huck, who gets the better of Tom in all
their trades, would never capitulate to Tom's ultimate business scheme: the
redefinition of fence-painting from a chore to a privileged activity. Forced
by Aunt Polly to whitewash her fence, Tom manages to make the task look
so inviting that other boys pay for the opportunity. By the end of the day,
Tom has succeeded in remaking himself as well, from a "poverty-stricken
boy in the morning" to one "rolling in wealth," a transformation that
anticipates the novel's ending. If Tom hadn't run out of paint, Twain observes, "he would have bankrupted every boy in the village."[38] Tom has
educated himself in a fundamental principle of capitalism: that value is
determined by the sacrifice required to attain it. The more people are made

to pay for something, the more they will covet it. It is no surprise to find Tom with a "prodigious" income at the novel's end, his fortune invested at 6 percent interest.[39] But it is a sign of Twain's idealism about money matters at this point in his career that the outsider Huck Finn is in the identical financial condition.

Though speculation and fortune building is an activity perfected by children in *The Adventures of Tom Sawyer*, there is nothing innocent about it. This is even more dramatically true of *The Gilded Age*, which is entirely populated by adults and set principally in the corrupt world of Washington politics. Subtitled *A Tale of To-Day*, the book succeeded in coining a phrase that would come to stand for the post–Civil War era in general: the Gilded Age. Significantly, it was the first and last novel Twain would set in the historical present. Writing about the greed and profiteering that he believed typified it could only make him want to escape to other times, as he did in all his subsequent works. In his "Revised Catechism," Twain wrote bitterly, "What is the chief end of man?—to get rich. In what way?—dishonestly if we can; honestly if we must. Who is God, the one only true? Money is God."[40] The bitterness extends to *The Gilded Age*, which expresses much of Twain's despair about the effects of unfettered capitalist development. The novel represents the collaboration of two Connecticut neighbors disgusted by the state of culture, reeling over the Beecher-Tilton trial (for adultery between the famed minister Henry Ward Beecher and Mrs. Theodore Tilton, the wife of an upstanding congregant), and convinced that American democracy would most likely be a failed experiment.

Neither Twain nor his coauthor, Warner, a newspaper editor, had ever written a novel. Twain had his own family's obsession with their father's Tennessee land to build on, while Warner could draw on his experience as a railroad surveyor in Missouri and a businessman in Philadelphia. Twain was responsible for the novel's satirical centerpiece, the Hawkinses' speculations on their Tennessee land, and for the sequences on Washington politics. Warner wrote the love story set in Philadelphia and also covered parts on the Missouri railroad surveyors. Together they wrote the sections on Laura Hawkins's career as a political lobbyist and her trial for murder. Twain and Warner found much to exploit in the contemporary scene: the Beecher affair; the Credit Mobilier scandal, involving charges of stealing from the U.S. Treasury against the Credit Mobilier Company, an offshoot of the Union Pacific Railroad, in which several U.S. congressmen were implicated in the corruption; and a Senate vote-buying prosecution involving Senator Samuel C. Pomeroy (the novel's Senator Dillworthy). "I think I can say, and say with pride, that we have some legislatures that bring higher prices than any in the world," Twain observed caustically in one of his speeches.[41] It was the point of this biting satire to present recognizable situations and personages. While the novel had a promising geographical design, sending one set of characters east in search of wealth, and the other west to pursue love and resolve questions of parentage, a surplus of personalities and plots continually threatened to overwhelm it. Indeed, it was typical of Twain that, in his major indictment of the era's capitalist ethos, the novel's charming speculator Colonel Beriah Sellers is the primary source of imaginative integrity. This was indicative of the continual slippage between Twain's moral outrage against capitalism and his admiration for its harnessing of human energies and passions, including his own. Reading audiences repaid Twain's ambivalence in kind, buying up 35,000 copies of the novel in the first two months and then pulling back purchases to almost nothing. Twain blamed the Panic of 1873, but he might have factored in his own deeply divided perspective.

Twain's novels and stories abound in pigs, frogs, dogs, coyotes, cats, horses, and cows; all of them carry moral weight, making demands on the conscience of his human characters. Twain's commitment to the law of nature complemented his understanding of market capitalism. His fiction often minimized free will; human beings were fallen creatures fulfilling their natures in competitive social economies. By providing the basic elements of what might be called a Darwinian aesthetic, Twain's writing offers an appropriate introduction to subsequent "naturalist" accounts of the worlds of business and economy.

Theodore Dreiser and Frank Norris extended Twain's vision by finding inspiration in the natural brutality of society. While a novel like Cahan's *The Rise of David Levinsky* undermined its protagonist's commercialism by favoring religious and cultural values, and Phelps's *The Silent Partner* and Howells's *The Rise of Silas Lapham* invoked ethics to counter the cruel rhythms of urban industries, Dreiser's novels are noteworthy for their indifference to such alternatives. Dreiser was unparalleled as a chronicler of the business world because of his almost innocent admiration for successful capitalists. In contrast to Gustavus Myers, whose critical investigations in *The History of the Great American Fortunes* (1907–10) he read in preparing his own portrait, Dreiser was dazzled by "the great financiers."[42] Myers stressed the ruthlessness and dishonesty of men like John D. Rockefeller, J. P. Morgan, and Collis P. Huntington, the combined result of character, harsh childhoods, and opportunity. Dreiser eliminated traits that Myers had presented as exemplary, in particular a puritanical austerity. Despite his experience of poverty in a cruel American economy and the developing political radicalism that would ultimately flower into socialism, Dreiser insisted that these figures were true artists. The individual who was made for finance, for whom speculation was a vocation, was as free of moral constraints as the poet or painter. Dreiser's Frank Algernon Cowperwood has a persistent and powerful sensuality. The son of a bank teller, possessed of a steely aptitude for speculative advantage, he knows exactly what to do with a windfall from an uncle, working it as collateral credit, enhancing its uses ten times beyond its actual worth. According to Dreiser, Cowperwood's moral immunity derives from his condition as an embodiment of natural law, a "Superman," or *ubermensch*. Asked in an interview after the publication of *The Financier* (1912) whether Cowperwood had the right to behave as he did, Dreiser replied that there was "in Nature no such thing as the right to do or the right not to do. . . . I am convinced that so-called vice and crime and destruction and so-called evil are as fully a part of the universal creative process as the so-called virtues, and do as much good."[43]

Dreiser's ethically neutral portrait of a capitalist nevertheless exposed one of the most significant results of the American Civil War: an event that *unmade* so many proved the *making* of many others. The first American war to produce mass numbers of casualties was also the first to yield vast fortunes. The war gives Dreiser's protagonist a major opportunity, the handling of a state loan, resulting in a substantial profit and an enhanced reputation. But the Great Chicago Fire of 1871 induces a panic in the stock market. Cowperwood, whose speculations have been typically bold, is the fall guy, in part because he is having an adulterous affair with Aileen Butler, the daughter of a well-connected boss. Sent to prison, Cowperwood characteristically excels there too, effortlessly mastering its Quaker regime (silence, solitude, self-scrutiny). Released just in time for the Panic of 1873, Cowperwood exploits its effects and manages to regain his fortune just before the novel's close. *The Financier* focuses on post–Civil War capitalist expansion and is the first of a trilogy loosely based on the life of businessman Charles Yerkes, including *The Titan* (1914), which follows Cowperwood's reemergence in Chicago and building of the street railway system there, and *The Stoic* (1947), which Dreiser left unfinished when he died in 1945.

Throughout *The Financier*, Dreiser emphasizes Cowperwood's auspicious compatibility with the principles of opportunism and risk that dominate the economy of his time. Cowperwood and John D. Rockefeller both have their first significant business ventures at age thirteen, and their deductions could easily have been the same: "The impression was gaining ground with me that it was a good thing to let the money be my slave and not make myself a slave to money."[44] Ever alert, Cowperwood happens by a wholesale auction and arranges on an intuition to buy seven cases of Castille soap, which he then sells at a net gain of $30 to the local grocer. Cowperwood lives up to his middle name, "Algernon," in his knack for seizing an opportunity. The transaction foreshadows a method of the post–Civil War economy that Cowperwood will come to manipulate expertly, the futures contract. The futures contract allowed a product to be bought and sold before delivery, to the advantage of both seller and buyer by ensuring against a price drop or rise, while allowing them to distribute the sale or purchase over a longer time. Its most significant effect was the creation of a new category of businessman, who stood between the producer and the buyer, never possessing or even desiring the commodity but enriching himself by way of it. In the soap exchange, the thirteen-year-old Cowperwood finds a specialized niche in the new commerce that, according to business historian Alfred Chandler, was devised in the 1850s and 1860s and institutionalized by 1870.[45] His father's response—"are you going to become a financier already?"—identifies his son as a man of his age.[46]

There is no moment in all of his writings that better captures Dreiser's sense of that age than the description of an even younger Frank Cowperwood watching a tank at the local fish store.

> One day he saw a squid and a lobster put in the tank, and in connection with them was witness to a tragedy which stayed with him all his life and cleared things up considerably intellectually. The lobster, it appeared from the talk of the idle bystanders, was offered no food, as the squid was considered his rightful prey. He lay at the bottom of the clear glass tank on the yellow sand, apparently seeing nothing—you could not tell in which way his beady, black buttons of eyes were looking—but apparently they were never off the body of the squid. The latter, pale and waxy in texture, looking very much like pork fat or jade, moved about in torpedo fashion; but his movements were apparently never out of the eyes of his enemy, for by degrees small portions of his body began to disappear, snapped off by the relentless claws of his pursuer. The lobster would leap like a catapult to where the squid was apparently idly dreaming, and the squid, very alert, would dart away, shooting out at the same time a cloud of ink, behind which it would disappear. . . . The incident made a great impression on him. It answered in a rough way that riddle which had been annoying him so much in the past: "How is life organized?" Things lived on each other—that was it.[47]

The scene foregrounds the survival-of-the-fittest philosophy and the analogy between the animal and human orders that were staples of Dreiser's fiction. Dreiser probably drew here on an essay he published in 1906 in *Popular Magazine* entitled "A Lesson from the Aquarium." *The Financier* is full of such lessons from the aquarium. This passage and the novel's closing depiction of the powerfully deceptive "Black Grouper" provide a pair of naturalist bookends introducing and concluding the ruthless but still magnificent career of his financier.[48] The young Cowperwood comes to the fish store daily, as if hypnotically drawn there, to stare in rapt wonderment at the stark drama of predation. Significantly, the boy *feels* nothing but gazes coldly on a process that he perceives as *the* answer, and Dreiser suggests that Cowperwood's sense of purpose is formed by this spectacle. But there is a deeper allegory here, beyond the budding financier, in the "idly dreaming" squid releasing his protective scribal ink clouds. While the squid can't prevent his inevitable demise, he manages to dream, nevertheless, and to prolong his life by darting and shooting. The drama is tragic, which reinforces its undeniable artistry. Despite his admiration for his lobster-identified financier, Dreiser's sympathies are with the ink-laden squid whose triumph is that there is any drama at all. Herein lies Dreiser's literary power: his aesthetic eloquence derives from his conviction of the brutal organization of life and his insistent pondering and reflecting upon it.

The Titan is an extended examination of the life of Frank Cowperwood following his relocation, with his new wife, Aileen Butler, to Chicago where he invests in the urban streetcar system. The novel is less character-driven than *The Financier* and has a more documentary focus. This is especially evident in the detailed portrait of Cowperwood's efforts to win a franchise for his streetcars, against claims for municipal control over systems like transportation and gas so critical to the fate of the community at large. *The Titan*'s powerful sense of place is also evident in its presentation of local and national politics. The novel offers a rich account, for instance, of William Jennings Bryan's campaign to establish legal parity between the value of gold and silver in order to ensure an ample money supply, beyond the control of central banks and the titans who ran them. Cowperwood's gift of a telescope to the University of Chicago (which recalls his stargazing at the Quaker penitentiary) is an attempt to establish credentials as a public benefactor, thus facilitating loans from reluctant Chicago banks. There are also the Irish ward bosses Kerrigan and Tiernan, whose resistance to Cowperwood in areas necessary to his expanding rails proves critical. Yet *The Titan* is a rather predictable sequel lacking the integrity and force of its predecessor. The problem here is not, as some critics have suggested, that finance is inherently abstract, lacking the reality and substance of paint or wheat and thus incapable of keeping readers interested over two long novels, because Dreiser speculates on the most vital social and aesthetic activities. Nor does Dreiser give more play in this novel to historical events because his financier absorbs him less. In *The Titan* Cowperwood is still a compelling figure, though split by multiple love interests, which contrasts with the intense polarization of wife and mistress in *The Financier*. Indeed, he remains a credible lover despite the increasing disparity between his age and that of the youthful women who attract him.

Instead, the novel's limitation is its focus on accumulation: of money, houses, and masterpieces. Cowperwood's relationship to these activities is dull, because Dreiser has made the case for his suitability to finance so well. Cowperwood lives and breathes speculation, divesting, investing, and dispensing money and the objects it buys. Speculating in romance is no substitute, since women cannot be administered in the same emotionless, exacting way as currency. He has little passion for the consumptive materialism afforded by his wealth. The one time in his life when Cowperwood appears relatively content being still is in prison, but there, significantly, he possesses nothing and derives pleasure from looking inward and upward at the stars. At the end of *The Titan*, Cowperwood has lost the agility of his speculating days and become an edifice, his own vast estate, a condition that is utterly at odds with the laws of his nature. His impending flight from Chicago to new foreign economic territory is, for Dreiser, an attempt to rekindle the animation and art of an earlier financier self. On this point, as with much else in Dreiser's free adaptation of the life of Charles Yerkes, fiction is kinder than fact. "After reducing the railway system of Chicago to chaos," Matthew Josephson reports, Yerkes "decamped forever to London."[49]

What made Chicago a place that could transform a financier into a titan, according to Dreiser, was the freedom of this "prairie metropolis" from the "unctuous respectability" of the urban East.[50] It was a place where a man like Frank Cowperwood could begin anew, without crossing the continent. Every industry seemed to thrive in that spacious, ever-expanding gateway between East and West that was Chicago, from stockyards and railroads, to real estate, hotels, and hardware. After streetcars, whose "vast manipulative life" forms a principal attraction for Cowperwood, he is drawn to the Chicago commodities exchange, specifically its dealings in wheat, corn, and other kinds of grain.[51]

Wheat deals on the Chicago Board of Trade were the subject of the other great American literary portrait of a financier, Frank Norris's *The Pit* (1903).[52] Published posthumously, the novel's prepublication orders were so great that two additional printings were ordered before the day of publication, and the first year's sales approached 95,000. The novel was not only widely and respectfully reviewed but commercially successful: made into a play in 1904, a silent film in 1917, and a Parker Brothers game based on the Chicago Board of Trade. *The Pit*, like *The Titan*, was part of a trilogy, but without a reappearing lead character. Norris's Wheat Trilogy was designed, he explained to William Dean Howells, "to keep the idea of this huge Niagara of wheat rolling from West to East."[53]

As he had done with *The Octopus*, Norris drew on history for his main plot: Joseph Leiter's cornering of the wheat market in 1897–98. Dubbed "King of the Wheat," Leiter drove up the price of the grain, managing to dominate the Chicago Board of Trade for a full six months before capitulating to the bears, led by Philip Armour of the meat trust (the novel's Calvin Crookes). In addition to spending time in Chicago, observing activities at its Board of Trade, Norris was tutored in the intricacies of market speculation by a young broker, who invented a game to help Norris grasp the fluctuations of a market run. Extending a wire from the radiator grate in the floor to a hook in the ceiling, he threaded a float through it, whose rise (from an influx of furnace heat) indicated a bull market, whereas its fall (in the absence of heat) indicated a bear market.[54]

Curtis Jadwin was also modeled on Norris's own father: his summers spent on Lake Geneva in Wisconsin; his Lake Michigan mansion near those of Marshall Field, George M. Pullman, and Philip D. Armour; his rural childhood and self-made fortune; his sponsorship of a Sunday school for poor children; and his marriage to a cultivated, histrionic woman who mystified him.[55] As befits their similarity to Norris's parents, Curtis and Laura Jadwin are respected dramatis personae, with few of the caricatured qualities of the characters in *McTeague*. Laura is passionate and beautiful; Jadwin is introduced in classic male terms, by what he is capable of doing. A bachelor when the story begins, who has made his fortune in real estate, he occasionally takes part in wheat or corn "deals," consulted by other financiers who respect his shrewdness. The narrative is recounted from the perspective of Laura Jadwin, which seems designed to enlarge its prospective readership, since women constituted a significant portion of the novel-buying public, whereas male readers might be appealed to on the grounds of Norris's topic alone. The novel's broad intent is also signaled by the foregrounding of predictable romantic situations accompanying its detailed portrait of modern economic trends. Chicago appears grimy but impressive, containing all the rich cultural and commercial opportunities that money can buy.

Women exercise a pervasive influence in *The Pit* because Norris believes they enable the operation of the business world at its center. The description of the Jadwins' wedding at an Episcopal church is reverential. "Not in the midst of all the pomp and ceremonial of the Easter service had the chancel and high altar disengaged a more compelling influence. . . . The whole world was suddenly removed, while the great moment in the lives of the Man and the Woman began."[56] Jadwin's unqualified pursuit of the market is enfolded in this virtuous bond. Women facilitate commercial activities precisely by their natural opposition to them. Thus, Jadwin's bachelorhood requires a careful equilibration of business and spiritual activity, exemplified by his sponsorship of a Sunday school for poor children. Jadwin's subsequent neglect of good works as a married man suggests that he is liberated from this responsibility by the behavior of his "better half."

In contrast to Dreiser's Cowperwood, Norris's financier is not ruthless. Jadwin is the people's champion, rehearsing their sufferings when a bear market drives down the price of wheat, visited by a gift-bearing deputation of wheat farmers after his bull market has driven the price up. But here, as in *The Octopus*, Norris emphasizes the global interconnectedness of economic events and the subjection of the most resourceful human agents. As the trading floor of a major exchange, the "Pit" has a "centrifugal power" that reverberates throughout the world with the force of Nature. This is supported by the convention of naturalizing the wheat pit, with its bulls and bears, by consistent suggestions that the wheat demonstrates independent principles of growth and by the characterization of the novel's financiers as "blooded to the game." Yet Nature also assumes a curiously miniaturized form in the novel, embodied in a cat that lingers in the Pit after all the traders have gone home. "The floor of the Board of Trade was deserted. Alone, on the edge of the abandoned Wheat Pit, in a spot where the sunlight fell warmest—an atom of life, lost in the immensity of the empty floor—the grey cat made her toilet, diligently licking the fur on the inside of her thigh, one leg, as if dislocated, thrust into the air above her head."[57] Her leg pointed straight upward, in mocking mimicry of the traders' bidding gesture, this domesticated creature provides a kinder, gentler variation on a more daunting principle of Nature.

For Norris the categories of Nature and artifice are interwoven: the most artificial things appear the most natural, and sometimes vice versa. This naturalizing appears in the novel as compensatory, designed to alleviate the anxiety generated by what Thorstein Veblen calls "a credit economy." The distinctive aspect of a credit economy is the primacy of the businessman, who does not direct the production of real commodities but manipulates their value by way of investments and markets, thus initiating a ceaseless process of valuation and revaluation. Noting that post–Civil War America featured increasingly an economy dominated by credit and controlled by financiers, Veblen focused on the devastating cycles of prosperity and depression caused in part by competition among speculators. In the credit economy that was especially dominant after the 1880s, all value seems unsettled. While *The Pit* registers admiration for the great financier, it ultimately shares Veblen's wariness about his impact, although not in the name of the socialism Veblen endorsed. Instead Norris's decision to destroy his financier together with his speculative impulse at the end of *The Pit*, returning him to a purer, agrarian lifestyle, can be seen as a form of qualified populism.[58]

Preoccupied with the consequences of speculative finance, Norris employs religion, culture, and femininity to counterbalance it. A traditionalist at heart, despite his conviction that value was relative, he worried about the human effects of market economics. Tellingly, the one novelist Curtis Jadwin admires is William Dean Howells, whose Silas Lapham elicits "all his sympathy."[59] Jadwin's drowning at the novel's end in a deluge of his own unmaking is, fortunately for him, financial rather than ultimate. For Jadwin, unlike Behrman the Jew, is no scapegoat; a broad economic community shares his loss. And his domestic sanctuary is enriched, the clear beneficiary of his commercial ruin. The Jadwins' relocation out West is a spiritual rebirth; bankrupt, they anticipate a new beginning built on stronger foundations. Their backward glance on "the Board of Trade building, black, monolithic, crouching on its foundations like a monstrous sphinx," is a glance on behalf of the nation as a whole.[60] From Norris's nostalgic posthumous perspective, Americans were eager to put the speculative beast behind them. He did not live to realize that they had only just begun.

TITANS

By 1905, American big business was securely in place. It had triumphed in the post–Civil War years because it proved the most efficient method for organizing production and finance in a country that valued material progress above all things. This was Henry Adams's perception as he contemplated the great world's fairs set successively in major Midwestern cities (Chicago, in 1893; St. Louis, in 1904): his nation had fully realized its ultimate faith in machines, materialism, and industrial capitalism. Henry Blake Fuller's *The Cliff Dwellers* (1893) and Henry James's *The Golden Bowl* (1904) encompass this critical period. While Fuller sets his novel in Chicago, joining many other literary chroniclers of business and finance, James chooses London, with ongoing references to "American City," the anonymous (Midwestern) hometown of the novel's titan, who ultimately returns there.[61] These novels and the works of social analysis discussed in what follows understand big business as an established social and economic fact. The corporate mind is less a focus of moral scrutiny, as it is in Norris and Howells, or a natural phenomenon to be explained, as it is in Dreiser. It is, for Fuller and James, Thorstein Veblen, Ida Tarbell, and Andrew Carnegie, a consolidated and determining fixture of the culture. Taking a long view, they assess the place of American corporate culture in world history, recognizing the sign of institutionalization in identifiable rituals, which they set out to catalog. How will these ritualized economic practices be understood years' hence (Fuller, Veblen)? What are the parallels between ancient gift exchange and charitable contributions in contemporary corporate culture, and what do they reveal about continuities between primitives and moderns (James)? Will the turn-of-the-century titan be seen by future generations as benefactor or outlaw (Carnegie, Rockefeller, Tarbell, Henry Demarest Lloyd)?

The Cliff Dwellers is a story of greed and social mobility featuring members of the Chicago elite who work at "the Clifton," the eighteen-story office building that serves as the novel's central gathering place. These latter-day "cliff dwellers" constitute a "tribe" distinguished by various rituals, including occasional recourse to a "pipe of peace."[62] However significant by their own estimations, these cliff dwellers are as precariously situated as any primitive tribe, one among many social orders that has passed away over time. The result of Fuller's ethnographic approach to Chicago's business world is inevitably satirical. George Ogden, the novel's hero, is a New Englander trying to make his way in more expansive commercial territory. Regional dissonance thus helps to intensify the narrative's already distanced perspective. "In the public conveyances," he detects "a range of human types completely unknown to his past experience; yet it soon came to seem possible that all these different elements might be scheduled, classified, brought into a sort of *catalogue raisonne* which should give every feature its proper place—skulls, foreheads, gaits, odors, facial angles, ears." Forced by a rainstorm into the public library's main reading room, Ogden feels surrounded by a "cataract of conflicting nationalities," united in his view by a shared mortality.[63] This is Ogden's preoccupation; over the course of the novel he loses every relation. Burying his wife and tiny daughter, he discovers that wealthy Chicagoans fight as aggressively for favorable cemetery space as for they do for the best real estate. He reflects accordingly on epidemic rates of insanity and suicide, on how society's "fine-spun meshes bind us and strangle us."[64] It is a sign of just how enmeshed he is that

Ogden's means of retreat at the novel's end is marriage to the disaffected daughter of a villainous bank president. The final pages offer a ritualized image of foundation sacrifice through a character whose need for lavish jewels has required the debilitating fees charged by her architect husband. "It is for such a woman that one man builds a Clifton and that a hundred others are martyred in it."[65] Aligning the habits of wealthy turn-of-the-century Chicagoans with the ritual practices of any number of extinct "tribes," Fuller predicts their imminent demise.

The Golden Bowl (1904), considered by James and many critics to be his best work, provides a more intricate ethnographic approach to turn-of-the-century capitalism. The novel's central subject is exchange: both the exchange of men and women across the genealogical boundaries that is marriage and the exchange of commodities like the Golden Bowl itself. The novel is set primarily in London and features a handsome Italian prince, Amerigo, from a family that has lost its wealth; an American man of enterprise, Adam Verver, who has everything but Amerigo's celebrated ancestry; Maggie Verver, Adam's daughter, who has been given everything money can buy, including remarkable innocence; and Charlotte Stant, an admired older friend of Maggie's from boarding school. The novel's plot, which begins with preparations for the marriage of the prince and Maggie, is built on a few simple details. Maggie's mother has died long ago, and Maggie worries about leaving her father when she marries. Though their relationship is barely altered by her marriage, Maggie conceives a plan to marry her father to Charlotte. Charlotte and the prince have had a brief but intense love affair that ended with a mutual recognition of its impossibility, given their mutual poverty. The Ververs know nothing about this affair, nor do they sense its lingering aftereffects, in part because they are preoccupied with their own intense father-daughter bond, the novel's "open secret."

Everything in James's novel—from princes, friends, husbands, fathers, and daughters, to tiles, precious art, dinner invitations, sex, and love—is subject to exchange. The Golden Bowl is preoccupied with the condition of the Anglo-American empire and the social and sexual form considered crucial to its preservation—heterosexual marriage. Yet marriage, as figured in the bowl itself, is slightly damaged, cracked. Vended by a mildly "sinister" Jew, who keeps it ceremonially apart from the other bric-a-brac in his shop, the bowl seems to bind the novel's social and racial plot (centered on the empire's perilous condition and the social aliens who threaten it) with the novel's familial plot (centered on the curious arrangements—incestuous, adulterous—of the novel's principal foursome). The novel features not one but two Jewish merchants, each of whom presides over an exchange preceding a marriage: the unnamed antique dealer, and the tile merchant, Mr. Gutterman-Seuss, whose progeny, "eleven little brown clear faces, yet with such impersonal old eyes astride of such impersonal old noses," contrasts menacingly with the one-child families of Adam Verver (Maggie) and Prince Amerigo (the *principino*).[66] Each exchange, the transfer of merchandise across race (Jewish was at this time a racial category), introduces a bride exchange, of Maggie and Charlotte, respectively. The economic prominence and formally pivotal roles of these stereotyped outsiders signals a potentially dangerous assimilation of alien rites and people that is foreshadowed by the marriage of the prince's brother to a woman "of Hebrew race."[67] The implication here that marrying Jewish wealth is a family trait highlights the question of James's attitude toward Jews in general, as well as their particular symbolic relationship to the novel's pivotal action—adultery.

The novel's characters contemplate ancient exchange rituals (the prince's early ruminations about marriage, the image of the bowl vendor displaying "the touch of some mystic rite of old Jewry") in terms that anticipate Marcel Mauss's *The Gift* (1925).[68] Mauss believed his gift theory to be "one of the human foundations on which our societies are built" that enabled one to come to conclusions of a moral nature "concerning certain problems posed by the crisis in our own law and economic organization."[69] He emphasized continuity between archaic and modern systems of exchange: "A considerable part of our morality and our lives themselves are still permeated with this same atmosphere of the gift, where obligation and liberty intermingle." Thus, "things sold still had a soul"; unreciprocated gifts still established the inferiority of the recipient; charity was still wounding; and traces of ancient aristocratic potlatches still evoked the "basic imperialism" of human relations.[70] Mauss's theory was a plea for moderation in the name of the durability of ancient principles. He criticized upper-class extravagance and urged limitation on "the rewards of speculation and interest." And he commended "social security, the solicitude arising from reciprocity and cooperation," which he deemed far superior to "capitalist saving."[71] In *The Golden Bowl*, James intuited what social scientists of his time had come to recognize as the commonalities between gift and commodity, between the spirit of reciprocity that ruled the world of the gift and the profit-oriented, calculating spirit that ruled the world of commodity.

Adam Verver in *The Golden Bowl* is the agent of that unification, a figure that stages the continuities between capitalist self-interest and primitive exchange. Giving is for him a way of keeping. A gift that is not matched by a counter-gift creates a lasting bond, restricting the debtor's freedom; one of the ways of "holding" someone is to keep up a lasting asymmetrical relationship of indebtedness. Verver's museum in American City has "all the sanctions of civilization . . . a house from whose open doors and windows, open to grateful, to thirsty millions, the higher, the highest knowledge would shine out to bless the land. In this house, designed as a gift, primarily, to the people of his adoptive city and native State . . . his spirit today almost altogether lived, making up, as he would have said, for lost time and haunting the portico in anticipation of the final rites."[72] Verver's power lies in his ability to give, a power that in turn allows for unlimited acquisition. The world appears to him as a sea of things to be appropriated, especially those most beloved. Thus his daughter recalls, some "slim draped 'antique' of Vatican or Capitoline halls, late and refined, rare as a note." And Verver regards his new grandson, the *principino*, "in the way of precious small pieces he had handled."[73] While there is no record of James's having had an intimacy on the order of Mark Twain's with American business titans, his brother William, who was deeply impressed by John D. Rockefeller, treated Henry to detailed descriptions. William's letter to Henry of January 1904 may resonate in the portrait of Adam Verver. "A man 10 stories deep, and to me quite unfathomable . . . flexible, cunning, quakerish, superficially suggestive of naught but goodness and conscientiousness, yet accused of being the greatest villain in business whom our country has produced." Yet Henry himself also admired Ida Tarbell and noted of her *History of Standard Oil*, "Miss Tarbell has done a great work, that is, it seems to me she has done a real work. She has a shining personality." However mystified the term "real" here, James's remark undeniably conveys approbation.[74]

By marrying Maggie Verver to Prince Amerigo and Adam Verver to Charlotte Stant, as James does in book 1, "The Prince," he makes giftgiving, the sharing of one's fortune with "the poor," the basis of marriage and identifies marriage as the most typical method of exchange. Marriage is also linked irrevocably to social aliens, who play critical roles in the novel's major transactions. The memorable, bilingual Jew (who eavesdrops on the Italian conversation of Charlotte and Amerigo) subsequently sells the same bowl to Maggie for her father's birthday present. The dealer is aligned with the prince as an Italian speaker and also through their respective conversions in book 2. The prince rededicates himself to marriage, while the dealer informs Maggie of the bowl's crack, acting "on a scruple rare enough in vendors of any class, and almost unprecedented in the thrifty children of Israel."[75] This slur on the bowl dealer is consistent with the representation of the tile vender. The stereotypes of *The Golden Bowl* argue for the shifting kaleidoscope of Jewish identity in James's time: the standing of Jews in

England and America as an antique group that was also extraordinarily amenable to capital and modernity.

This striking duality in Jewish identity is captured by a contemporaneous advertisement for Sapolio soap (see Fig. 11 in Chapter 5). The ad employs Hebrew script to promote the ritual purity—certifiably kosher—of Sapolio soap, whose benefits as an agent of health and cleanliness are supported by its appeal to this highly traditional people. Moreover, by invoking Jews as the spur to a sale, the ad draws implicitly on a presumed Jewish facility for commerce. Henry James and E. Morgan's Sons (the manufacturer of Sapolio) together build on a presumed Jewish knack for survival and adaptation: the culture has endured since ancient times and yet is readily identified with modern economic exchange.

James's portrayal of Jews, then, is hardly innocent. Indeed, what Jews seem to stand for in his novel, above all, is a threatening modernity, which is understood as both inevitable and problematic. In this way, their position vis-à-vis society is exactly analogous to James's understanding of adultery in marriage. The plot of *The Golden Bowl* yields the following postulate: Jews are to society (Anglo-Saxons) as adultery is to marriage—transgressive, distasteful, yet necessary. By implying that the prince's infidelity has enabled the preservation of his marriage to the princess, and by portraying complex Jewish aliens as essential participants in the exchange rites necessary to marriage, James lent his support to theories emphasizing continuities between primitives and moderns.

Such assumptions were basic to the thought of Thorstein Veblen, a contemporary who shared James's distaste for great American businessmen with, at the same time, a tendency to become profoundly absorbed by them. Veblen wrote his searing critique of the captains of industry while ensconced as a professor at the University of Chicago, the direct heir of John D. Rockefeller's philanthropy. It was a sign of Veblen's own iconoclastic refusal to be bought that he denounced the university's president, William Rainey Harper, as "a captain of erudition," the intelligentsia's variation on the robber baron.[76] Identified by *Fortune Magazine* as "America's most brilliant and influential critic of modern business and the values of a business civilization," Veblen's originality derived from his ability to take a long view of turn-of-the-century incorporation combined with the perspective of a cultural outsider.[77] Here was the brilliant son of Norwegian farmers assuming a mantle previously held by Brahmins like Henry Adams. Veblen's most renowned contribution to social theory was *The Theory of the Leisure Class* (1899), in which he single-handedly defined a new social class, detailing its attributes, its relationship to other classes, and its impact on society as a whole. The leisure class was characterized by its exemption from industrial toil and its possession of wealth sufficient to its lavish exhibition. What made "prestige behavior" so significant socially was the way it served as the glue uniting upper-class hierarchies everywhere, facilitating a coordination of interests ranging from intraelite marriages to executive corporate decisions.[78]

Veblen was born in 1857 in rural Wisconsin to an artisan farmer. His parents were well-educated populists who taught their precocious son Greek, Latin, and German. Because Norwegian was spoken at home and English was a late acquisition, Veblen mumbled well into adulthood, which didn't prevent his excelling at Carleton College, where he encountered one of the era's greatest economists, John Bates Clark. Following graduate work at Johns Hopkins and Yale (where he earned a Ph.D. in philosophy), Veblen couldn't get an academic job because of his atheism. Returning home, he read socialist theory and was inspired by Edward Bellamy's utopian nationalism, serving as a regular reviewer for the *Journal of Political Economy*. In 1891, in succession, Veblen was hired and fired, first by the University of Chicago's economics department, and then by Stanford's. While these dismissals were attributed to affairs with female students, they were also undoubtedly related to his unorthodox views. Veblen's disenchantment with the early twentieth-century academy was expressed in *The Higher Learning: A Memorandum on the Conduct of Universities by Business* (1918), whose original subtitle, *A Study in Total Depravity*, highlighted its argument. At the University of Missouri, Veblen was more productive, if not more successful institutionally, and managed to write a number of books while on the faculty there, including *The Instinct of Workmanship* (1914), *Imperial Germany* (1915), and *The Nature of Peace* (1917). During World War I, Veblen worked at the Food Administration, and he got a job at the New School for Social Research in New York after the war. Later returning to Stanford to live in a shack in the woods near the campus, he died in 1929.

The Theory of the Leisure Class is properly understood as ethnography on his own society. Here he transformed various social standards—"pecuniary emulation"; "conspicuous leisure and consumption"; "the belief in luck"— into objects of ritual analysis.[79] Veblen's method was evolutionary, tracing the development of the human species from the period of savagery, the longest and most peaceful in human history, where the dominant concern was group survival and the foremost value workmanship. The creation of tools facilitated the production of surpluses and wealth, which in turn led to class distinctions and exploitation. A predatory hunter-warrior class gave way to a feudal elite, the precursors to the owners and managers of modern industry. Modern industrial society emphasized consumption as the ultimate indicator of class status. Veblen was the first to recognize how the obligation to consume urged upon the citizens of a modern capitalist society actually intensified class distinctions and conflicts. While other economists believed that increased access to consumer goods would minimize class-consciousness, Veblen believed that it would become the major avenue for expressing class differences. He hoped that such invidious distinctions would lead to the overthrow of the class system and its eventual replacement by socialism. Veblen seized on evidence of countermovements, the value of innovation in industry, the overall importance of machines and scientific culture, and the challenges of the New Women movement to prophesy the end of leisure-class mores. Yet his own account of how ably consumer society generated states of false consciousness belied such hopes. Moreover, it is important to recognize that the leisure class described by Veblen was only part of an upper class whose most elite and powerful element cultivated *inconspicuousness*. The higher and more secure the social status of a group or individual, the more subtle and reserved they could be.

Upward social mobility, however, required being noticed. This was the cardinal principle of one of the era's most notorious titans, Andrew Carnegie, who elevated a personal craving for attention (understandable for a man who stood five feet, three inches tall, full grown, four inches below the current national average) into a creed. He emphasized the importance of keeping the attention focused, of being devoted single-mindedly to a particular business endeavor. The maxim with which he became identified was "Put all your eggs in one basket, and then watch that basket."[80] A classic Horatio Alger type, Carnegie also meant attracting the attention of benevolent superiors eager to discover a resource in their office boy or janitor. "The rising man must do something exceptional," Carnegie wrote, "HE MUST ATTRACT ATTENTION," teaching his employer "that he has not a mere hireling in his service . . . but one who devotes his spare hours and constant thoughts to the business."[81]

On his own road to wealth, Carnegie succeeded in impressing employers like his crucial mentor, Thomas A. Scott, who hired Carnegie as office manager of the western division of the Pennsylvania Railroad. Referred to in the company as "Mr. Scott's Andy," Carnegie, who was only seventeen when they met, worshipped Scott and received critical aid from him, including money for his first significant business investment, which made Carnegie's subsequent treatment of Scott, to some, indicative of ruthlessness. During the Panic of 1873, while he was senior vice president of the

Pennsylvania Railroad, Scott solicited Carnegie, who had expanded his steel business considerably due to the panic and had previously aided Scott, for another loan. Carnegie staunchly refused, despite anguished pleas from both Scott and his supporters.[82]

Born in 1835, Carnegie was the eldest child of a Scottish weaver, a Chartist, whose craft was tragically displaced by the advent of steam-powered weaving mills. Immigrating to America, the family settled in the bleak environment of Allegheny-Pittsburgh nicknamed "slabtown" by inhabitants. Carnegie took to it with zeal, determined to make good: from his first job at thirteen as bobbin boy in a textile mill for $1.20 per week, by the age of fifty-six he had amassed over $300 million. Rising through the ranks at the mills, Carnegie's big break was a job as telegraph office manager for the Pennsylvania Railroad, which led to a promotion in railroad administration, where he began to invest in railroads and other enterprises. By 1868, with help from the Civil War, the thirty-three-year-old Carnegie was worth $400,000. Carnegie's recognition that "steel was destined to change the material basis of civilization" launched him into the upper ranks of multimillionaires.[83] The 1856 discovery of an expeditious means of removing impurities from pig iron opened the way to large-scale steel manufacturing. Access to additional raw materials—iron ore, limestone, and coke—necessary for production sealed the prospect. By 1881, Carnegie had hired an expert German chemist and teamed up with leading coke manufacturer Henry Clay Frick, and his empire was underway. Carnegie's achievement depended on the following principles: keep the steel mills running; hire top engineers to design the original plants (thus avoiding expensive industrial accidents); spend what is needed to maintain low operating costs; the larger the scale of operation, the cheaper the product; the larger the market, the greater the competitive advantage.

Throughout the essays he wrote for popular journals, Carnegie offered a pragmatic view of self-development. Like his admirer Booker T. Washington, Carnegie repudiated college education, classical education in particular, advocating in their place direct vocational experience. Carnegie extolled poverty as a crucial means of getting individuals fired up with ambition, but he stretched his advantage with the preposterous claim that "you can scarcely name a great invention, or a great discovery . . . a great picture, or a great statue, a great song or a great story" that "has not been produced by an individual born poor."[84] Abolish poverty, Carnegie concludes, and all progress would cease. Carnegie's suspicion of inherited wealth enhanced an instinctive passion for charity; as he wrote, "the man who dies thus rich dies disgraced."[85] From the late 1880s to the end of his life, Carnegie threw his energies into endowments, ensuring his reputation as one of the world's great benefactors. John D. Rockefeller admired Carnegie's bequests, in particular the deliberate orchestration of gifts (Carnegie's focus on cultural institutions), which he emulated in focusing himself on science and medical research.

Carnegie might well have preserved a comparatively untarnished reputation if not for crises like the Homestead Strike in July of 1892. Previously considered a friend of labor, which was unusual for an ambitious manufacturer (he opposed, for instance, the use of "scabs" to break strikes), Carnegie was confronted with a strike at his own mill, spurred by dissatisfaction with wage cuts and workers' demands that mill owners acknowledge their union. Henry Frick, Carnegie's partner and executive manager, who was antiunion and uncompromising, arranged to shift major orders to a different mill and hired three hundred Pinkerton detectives and a force of armed guards. Following a four-month standoff, one of the bloodiest confrontations between capital and labor in history erupted, with hundreds wounded and ten killed. When the conflict was over, the union was crushed and the workers returned to work. The handling of the strike went against every tenet of Carnegie's avowed views on capital-labor relations. The sign that Carnegie perhaps recognized this was his decision to leave Frick alone to oversee the mill's long siege against labor. Frick kept Carnegie posted, reporting with pride that though their economic losses from the strike were heavy, the company showed profits of $4 million immediately afterward. Carnegie's response came by telegram from vacation in Italy: "Congratulations all around—life worth living again—how pretty Italia."[86]

By 1913 John D. Rockefeller's net worth was approximately $900 million (federal spending that year was $713 million), twice that of Andrew Carnegie's. Rockefeller's supremacy was founded in part on his ability to outmaneuver Carnegie on his own turf. Anticipating the value of iron ore (a product critical to steel production), Rockefeller managed to secure a monopoly on it, forcing Carnegie to deal with him for a material essential to his own industry. While both titans profited from their alliance, Rockefeller profited most. Likewise, while Carnegie blazed the path with his charitable donations ($350 million in his lifetime), Rockefeller's philanthropy far surpassed Carnegie's ($530 million before he died, $1.25 billion through his descendants).[87] As befit the ambition that led them to amass great fortunes and then invest much of them in philanthropic institutions bearing their names, both Carnegie and Rockefeller were deeply concerned for their personal reputations. This was especially true of Rockefeller, the subject of sustained and increasingly visceral attacks from the 1880s on, which culminated in his prosecution for monopoly, conspiracy, and price fixing. Through all of this, Rockefeller remained enormously sensitive to criticism and preoccupied with how his life and works would be read by posterity.

In 1917, when he agreed to an interview with his authorized biographer, William O. Inglis, Rockefeller suggested that the best way to revive those all-important years between 1865 and 1878 when he was establishing his company, Standard Oil, was to return to the books on that era by his two nemeses.[88] In *Wealth against Commonwealth* (1894) and *The History of the Standard Oil Company* (1904, serialized in *McClure's Magazine*, 1902–4), Henry Demarest Lloyd and Ida Tarbell, respectively, memorialized the greatest struggles and triumphs of Rockefeller's career. It was telling that Rockefeller, an astute reader of his own life, believed these books indispensable to an appraisal of it. The controversy generated by Standard Oil attached to everyone connected with it, including critics. One hundred years after the publication of Tarbell's 406-page book, readers disagree about its ultimate opinion of the titan and his works. It seems clear that while Tarbell evidently followed the legendary advice given her by Henry James, "cherish your contempt," she also felt admiration for her robber baron subject.[89] The complexity of her response suggests that the more one knew, the more difficult it was to maintain an unequivocal attitude toward the nation-defining events of this critical time in American history and culture.[90] The best prospects for cultural history remain, therefore, immersion in the most informed sources of the time, particularly those that aroused controversy and were respected by people of various political persuasions.

Prior to the mid-nineteenth century in America, few recognized the commercial possibilities of the petroleum oil buried deep below the surface of the earth in states such as Kentucky, West Virginia, Ohio, and, principally, Pennsylvania. People knew the dark smelly substance as a nuisance, discovered while drilling for the salt-water essential to salt production. It was not until members of the new Pennsylvania Rock-Oil Company sent a specimen off for testing to a Yale chemist, Benjamin Silliman, that the commercial properties of this oil became widely known. "Your company have in their possession a raw material from which, by simple and not expensive process, they may manufacture very valuable products," was the succinct conclusion of the report, a model of scientific and literary precision prized for its commercial facts.[91] By August 1859, oil was being pumped out of the ground in Pennsylvania at the rate of 25 barrels a day; within two years, it was 2,000 to 4,000 a day, and the price per barrel had dropped from $20 to 10¢. Related manufactories arose to accommodate this rushing substance: drills to ensure a steady stream of oil; barrels to hold it, first wooden, then iron, to be replaced gradually by oil pipelines; road, water, and rail services to transport the barrels; industries for refining the oil. In an ongoing cycle of hope, elation, and despair, fortunes were made and lost in the ruthless hit or miss expansion of the oil industry. At the end of the Civil War, thousands poured into the region: in the words of Tarbell, "this little corner of Pennsylvania absorbed a larger portion of men probably than any other spot in the United States." She might have said "larger and more varied," for it was possible to hear seemingly *any* language spoken in this region—a multicultural labor force matched by the multiculturalism of the product's markets. By 1872, oil was being shipped from rural Pennsylvania to forty European ports, the Middle East, the West Indies, and the East Indies. Through the 1880s, no one grasped the value of one of oil's chief waste products, gasoline, which was usually discarded unconscionably, allowed to run into nearby rivers, making them dangerously flammable. In the 1890s a method was devised to "crack" petroleum, enabling a greater yield of gasoline, just in time for the first Ford two-cylinder automobile.[92]

Early setbacks (Robert E. Lee's invasion of Pennsylvania; Civil War taxes; the 1870 Franco-Prussian War foiling foreign exports; fluctuations in the price of oil) never deterred the industry pioneers, who in ten years, according to Tarbell, had established an oil enterprise that was efficient as well as lucrative. The future looked bright for these self-reliant businessmen, including Tarbell's father, until "a big hand reached out from nobody knew where, to steal their conquest and throttle their future."[93] That hand belonged to John D. Rockefeller. What Rockefeller did was brazen and simple: step-by-step he built a monopoly of one of the world's most crucial resources. Together with Jay Gould and James Fisk of the Erie Railroad, Thomas Scott of the Pennsylvania Railroad, and Cornelius Vanderbilt of the New York Railroad, and his co-owners, William Andrews and Henry Flagler, Rockefeller created the South Improvement Company, which amounted to a unique collaboration between the freshly incorporated Standard Oil Company and the railroads. Standard Oil provided incentives to the railroads (e.g., assuming legal liability for fires or accidents; sixty free carloads of refined oil per day), while the railroads provided Standard Oil with rebates on the cost of its oil shipments at the same time they were doubling the rates paid by its competitors. With most competitors destroyed by uneven freight rates, Rockefeller proceeded to buy out the survivors, offering them stock in Standard Oil in exchange for their refineries. In case after case, floundering companies were presented with offers they could not refuse. Rockefeller himself never saw his pursuit of a monopoly as anything but a rational and even idealistic effort to introduce order into an industry that had become self-destructively overdeveloped. His son, John D. Rockefeller Jr., summed up his thinking in a 1902 address at Brown University, a statement that Tarbell used as an epigraph to her *History*: "The American Beauty Rose can be produced in its splendor and fragrance only by sacrificing the early buds which grow up around it."[94]

John D. Rockefeller Sr. was born in 1839 in Richford, New York, and raised in nearby Moravia, small upstate towns in the center of what was called "the Burned-Over District," a region marked by the fires of Protestant evangelicalism. From boyhood, Rockefeller proved an astute student of finance, with an affinity for math soon complemented by a love of bookkeeping. Even as a boy, he kept a book, which he called "Ledger A," where he recorded dutifully every cent earned, spent, and given to charity. His sobriety issued from the strict regime of his mother, who treated her eldest son as a small patriarch when his father was away from home, which was often. The only subject that absorbed Rockefeller, who was an indifferent pupil at the Owego Academy, was the principal's weekly report on new business inventions. Like other tycoons, ranging from Andrew Carnegie to Bill Gates, Rockefeller eschewed a college degree for a three-month course at a business college. Rockefeller's legacy from his mother was a devout Baptist faith. While hers was a democratic creed that emphasized potential reformation for all, free will, and self-scrutiny, Eliza Rockefeller forbade smoking, drinking, dancing, card-playing, and theatergoing and encouraged thrift and good works. It is hardly surprising that her famous son, in his own words, "never had a craving for anything."[95]

Rockefeller's paternal legacy could not have been more different. A charlatan as well as charmer, sometime peddler, cure doctor, lumberman, and eventual bigamist (even indicted for rape), William Rockefeller was undoubtedly responsible for his eldest son's distrust of passion. His recurrent absences and irregular work patterns spelled perpetual financial insecurity. At the same time, the elder Rockefeller had an incurable, indeed a deep and sensual love, for money. As one contemporary recalled, "The old man had a passion for money that amounted almost to a craze," and another remembered the four-gallon pail brimming with gold pieces that William kept at home during his solvent periods. While John D. Rockefeller minimized such testimonies, his memory of his own first look at a significant banknote, and the way he locked and unlocked the safe over the course of the day at his bookkeeping job just to gaze upon the bill, parallels the accounts of his father, not to mention pivotal moments in Dreiser's *Sister Carrie* and Norris's *McTeague*.[96] Rockefeller's yearning makes him both a chip off the old block and highly representative of his age. Like many other ambitious young men, he bought his way out of Civil War conscription with money for a substitute and subsequent annual contributions. His Cleveland food and farm implement business profited greatly from the conflict, with annual earnings ($17,000) four times larger than before the war. In 1863, Rockefeller (with his partner) invested $4,000 in an oil-refining venture and almost immediately recognized the prospects of the emerging industry. By 1865 he was owner of Cleveland's largest oil refinery.[97]

John D. Rockefeller once remarked of his oil empire, "It was right before me and my God. If I had it to do tomorrow I would do it again the same way."[98] It was left to Henry Demarest Lloyd and Ida Tarbell, individuals with strong moral and civic impulses of their own, to assess his legacy. Lloyd was born in 1847 to a poor Calvinist minister who became a bookseller after the family moved to New York City to live near his wife's wealthy relatives. Lloyd's childhood of genteel poverty (his mother pawned inherited silver to buy overshoes for Henry, who was later a scholarship student at Columbia), together with his developing preference for worldly Christianity, disposed him toward civic reform. Following law school at Columbia, he worked for the Free-Trade Association, editing their magazine advocating laissez-faire liberalism and railing against governmental corruption. Soon after marrying into the wealthy family that co-owned the *Chicago Tribune*, Lloyd landed a job there. His eventual home at the *Tribune* was a "Money and Commerce" column in which he took stands on economic issues: from abolishing grain corners at the Chicago Board of Trade, to stiffer regulatory oversight of the nation's railroads following the Great Railroad Strike of 1878, which resulted in more than a hundred deaths, thousands of injuries, and incalculable loss of property.[99]

Like the main ideas of Henry George's *Progress and Poverty*, those of Lloyd's *Wealth against Commonwealth* received a trial run in essay form before they were expanded into a book. In contrast to George's modestly circulated pamphlet, Lloyd's essay, "The Story of a Great Monopoly," was published in the *Atlantic Monthly*, whose editor, William Dean Howells, predicted its sensational success. In a mere sixteen pages, "The Story of a Great Monopoly" (which drove the March 1881 issue of the *Atlantic* to six reprintings) managed to grant Standard Oil its "legitimate greatness," while deploring its unscrupulousness, citing a web of bribery so thick that it seemed the company had "done everything with the Pennsylvania legislature except refine it."[100] Posing as a friend of the consumer, Lloyd adopted the position that Americans were perilously innocent of the dangers threatened by corporate monopolies. Thirteen years later, Lloyd, who counted Booker T. Washington, Jane Addams, and Robert Louis Stevenson as friends, sought out Mark Twain's publishing company for his book-length version of the story. When Twain refused *Wealth against Commonwealth* in deference to his friendship with Henry H. Rogers, Howells again stepped in, helping Lloyd secure a contract with Harper and Brothers.[101]

Though he characterized himself during the writing of *Wealth against Commonwealth* as "a socialist-anarchist-communist-individualist-collectivist-cooperative-aristocrat-democrat," Lloyd's allegiances placed him securely in the camp of Progressivism.[102] Rockefeller, to whom he referred elsewhere as "the most selfish usurper that ever lived," was the central figure of the book, but Lloyd avoided direct references to preclude prosecution for libel.[103] Lloyd's depersonalized narrative also enhanced his claim for the wider implications of his study, which he conceived as a general indictment of America's commercial civilization. He displayed a fascination with the conspiratorial rituals and language of the oil business that made the book extraordinarily revealing of its era and subject matter. And he showed that he had an eye for the suspenseful theatrics of investigating committees, detailing how agents grilled a series of Standard Oil men into revealing the meaning of an oft-repeated phrase, "to turn another screw" (to press a reluctant victim into compliance). Lloyd appreciated the inherent drama of his story and allowed its subjects to speak on their own behalf. Thus he centered his case against the oil monopoly upon the life histories of four particular casualties of the Rockefeller empire: a poor widow; an aged inventor; a small manufacturer; and a would-be saboteur, bested by people more devious than he.[104]

The fates of these individuals fed directly into Lloyd's conclusion, where he adopted, like Henry George, an antimodernist stance, arguing the superiority of a time when hardworking innovators could earn good livings without threat of absorption by monopolies. America, he suggested, had bargained with the devil and sold its vocational birthright for a pittance— ever more affordable heaps of commodities. Lloyd's solution—government ownership of the trusts—was consistent with the historical trajectory of his analysis, the inexorable drive toward combination. He argued that regulatory commissions were inadequate to contend with the excesses of monopoly capitalism, which required more vigorous socialist measures. Lloyd conceived of a major role for the rational managerial methods of the new social sciences. "It is not a verbal accident," he wrote, "that science is the substance of the word conscience." Led by the intelligentsia and a new professional managerial class, these social reforms would result in the replacement of "the profit-hunting Captain of Industry" by "the public-serving Captain of Industry."[105] But Lloyd's vision was not to be. Though his book sold well and was reprinted four times in its first year of publication, he recognized dejectedly that "the trust is virtually supreme in the United States."[106]

Less politically radical, though no more enamored of monopolies, Ida Tarbell was prepared to assume Lloyd's mantle of literary trust-busting. In 1900, the editors of *McClure's Magazine* sought to make a splash in the highly competitive journalistic market by running a series on corporate trusts, destined in their view to succeed silver as *the* national topic in the first decade of the new century. Ida Tarbell, the magazine's managing editor and ace author, who had won both popular and professional acclaim for her profiles of Napoleon and Abraham Lincoln, settled on Standard Oil after considering the beef, sugar, and steel trusts. In part, her choice was personal. Raised in the oil region, she had seen her father and many others put out of business by Rockefeller's company. Even more important was the paper trail on the company's history (not surprising, given its founder's devotion to bookkeeping), comparable, she suggested, to archives of the Civil War or the French Revolution. The availability of records covering congressional probes of the company (1872, 1876) and state investigations (1879, 1891) further bolstered the prospects for high-profile journalistic treatment. There was one glitch: a critical piece of documentary evidence had gone missing. A pamphlet entitled "The Rise and Fall of the South Improvement Company" proved as difficult to locate as the Willa Cather biography of Mary Baker Eddy, for the same reason—its subjects and their followers had purchased and destroyed most extant copies. When Tarbell finally tracked one down, she had proof of the crucial link between the illegal activities of the South Improvement Company and Rockefeller's Standard Oil.[107]

Ida Minerva Tarbell was the most renowned of Samuel McClure's distinguished staff of writers, which included Ray Stannard Baker (whose articles on union abuses and on U.S. Steel were celebrated), Lincoln Steffens (famed investigator of municipal corruption), and Finley Peter Dunne (author of the Mr. Dooley stories). Born in 1857 into a family with ties to the *Mayflower*, Ida Tarbell moved at the age of three to the heart of the Pennsylvania oil region, where her father hoped to prosper. A devout Methodist, Franklin Tarbell's career in oil provides a history in miniature of the industry's evolution: first barrel manufacturing in Rouseville, then oil drilling, and finally ownership of a refinery in Titusville. Tarbell was fifteen years old when her father became one of the first victims of the South Improvement Company, his profits nullified by a 100 percent hike in railroad shipping rates.

Tarbell was a brilliant girl, a voluminous reader filled with intellectual curiosity and a determination that led her to pursue evolutionary science, despite its irreconcilability with her Methodist upbringing, and to reject conventional expectations of women. Graduating from the Methodist-affiliated Allegheny College, she took a job as editor of the *Chautauquan*, helping the magazine's circulation grow from 15,000 in 1880 to 50,000 by the mid-1880s. This was largely owing to Tarbell's enlargement of its scope to include the major economic concerns of the day, from violent capital-labor conflict to battles over protective tariffs.

Syndicate publishing, so fruitfully exploited by her future boss, Samuel McClure, liberated Tarbell from the claustrophobia of the Pennsylvania oil region. It occurred to her that she might write articles in an exotic place like Paris and offer them for syndicate publication across the United States. In 1891, Tarbell relocated to Paris and proceeded to do just that, until the appearance of Samuel McClure. He had recognized in Tarbell's syndicated piece "The Paving of Paris" certain qualities of scientific precision and dramatic flair that he coveted for the magazine he had just begun in New York. By 1894 she was ready to accept his offer of a full-time position as an editor. Tarbell was an immediate success at *McClure's*, where her serial biographies of famous men dramatically raised the magazine's circulation. Never one to rest on her laurels, she began research in 1900 on a serial that was destined to become one of the most important pieces of journalism in American history. Tarbell researched, reviewed, and cross-referenced sources and employed an assistant to explore areas she couldn't reach herself so that her claims would be supported by hard evidence. She submitted drafts to expert economists John R. Commons of the University of Wisconsin and John Bates Clark of Carleton College, hired by McClure to ensure the consistency of her arguments. Senior editor John S. Phillips and McClure himself also scrutinized Tarbell's manuscripts. Given a significant and gripping subject, a writer and researcher of Tarbell's talent, and experts and editors supporting her in this fashion, the serial's impact was assured. The serial's second installment (December 1902) spelled the beginning of the end for Rockefeller's reputation, by providing proof of his role in the ruthless and unlawful tactics of the South Improvement Company. "Mr. Rockefeller has systematically played with loaded dice," Tarbell observed in her conclusion, "and it is doubtful if there has ever been a time since 1872 when he has run a race with a competitor and started fair."[108]

Though Tarbell once wrote that the editors at *McClure's* were not "trying to reform the world," she was delighted to receive praise from President Theodore Roosevelt and to learn that her series was responsible for forcing Roosevelt's hand on the issue of trusts (Republicans in the House under his leadership voted half a million dollars to the attorney general's office for the prosecution of trusts).[109] In May of 1911, seven years after the publication of Tarbell's serial in two-volume book form, the U.S. Supreme Court ordered the dissolution of Standard Oil. Significantly, with the exception of his recorded interview with William Inglis, which was consigned to the archives along with the prospective biography, John D. Rockefeller never responded to the charges leveled by Tarbell in her *History*. According to his most recent biographer, Ron Chernow, Rockefeller remained silent because he could not have repudiated some of the charges without acknowledging, tacitly, the justice of others.[110]

Tarbell's exposé was celebrated in her own time and ever since as an example of a free press triumphing over a major threat to national democratic ideals. Yet it was a sign of the profundity of corporate power in America that Standard Oil was able to rise like a phoenix from its ashes in World War I, when called upon by the government to assist the war effort. With the president of Standard Oil of New Jersey serving as its chairman, a Petroleum War Service Committee was formed to pool production and coordinate resources.[111] Though the great oil anaconda had been chopped into pieces by the Supreme Court decision, these pieces apparently retained the magical capacity to reconstitute themselves as a single corporate body. To Ida Tarbell and other observers of this model trust, it might have seemed that it had never been disturbed.

AMERICAN UTOPIAS

It is well known that one of the most popular works of American literary utopianism, Edward Bellamy's *Looking Backward* (1888), was written in the era of capitalist expansion; less familiar is the extraordinary outpouring of utopian novels that appeared between *Looking Backward* and Charlotte Perkins Gilman's *Herland* (1915). From the late 1880s to the turn of the century alone, more than 150 utopian novels were published in the United States, a figure unequalled in any other country or historical period.[1] It may seem paradoxical, from the perspective of literary history, to find a vogue of utopian art and thought in a culture renowned for its practicality and materialism. But it is precisely the intensity and pace of capitalist development that helps to explain the appeal of utopianism. The utopian novelistic form afforded writers a distance that facilitated an engagement with the economic and social developments that both dazzled and disturbed them. In work after work, narrators and characters tested the institutionalization of extreme principles, sometimes radically enlightened ones, as in William Dean Howells's *A Traveller from Altruria* (1894), and sometimes dangerously pessimistic ones, as in Ignatius Donnelly's *Caesar's Column* (1890). They imagined inventions and scientific advances beyond the ken of contemporaries, as in Alvarado Fuller's *A.D. 2000* (1890) and Arthur Bird's *Looking Forward* (1899). Or, as in *Unveiling a Parallel* (1893) by Alice Jones and Ella Merchant, they conceived of societies where probable but still remote political changes—women's right to vote and occupational parity with men— had been realized.

American utopian novels written from the 1880s to the beginning of

World War I represented a cultural form that emerged in tandem with economic and industrial expansion and helped to express the mood of Progressive Era reform. Utopian novelists took a variety of positions on the major political issues of the day, from the rise of big corporations and the growing chasm between rich and poor, to immigration and women's rights. Some utopian authors were themselves businessmen: King Gillette, inventor of the Gillette razor and author of *The Human Drift* (1894); Bradford Peck, owner of one of the largest department stores in New England and author of *The World a Department Store* (1900); and L. Frank Baum, traveling salesman with expertise in advertising and author of *The Wonderful Wizard of Oz* (1900). This convergence between the apparently antithetical fields of business and utopianism does more than confirm the popularity of the utopian novel (even businessmen wrote them). It also confirms one of its central purposes—to reconcile the harsh effects of capitalist expansion. Authors like Gillette and Peck argued that the values of innovation and enterprise needed to be reconciled with humanistic and spiritual values. Many utopian novelists were concerned with the renovation of religious ideals they believed essential to alleviating social ills. Bellamy's *Looking Backward* registers the influence of his father, a Baptist minister; Donnelly's *Caesar's Column* parodies upper-class Protestantism in the name of a more just Christianity; Howells's *A Traveller from Altruria* outlines an ideal Christian Socialism; and Baum's *The Wonderful Wizard of Oz* reflects his faith in theosophy, which decreed, "God is Nature; Nature, God." These authors sought a religion free of sectarian quarreling, readily applicable to ordinary experience, and open to Darwinian science.

The preoccupation with reproduction, ethnicity, and race in utopian novels was even more pronounced. It reveals how the genre helped to express the distress generated by rising levels of social heterogeneity (with immigration rates unrivalled by those of any previous or subsequent time in the nation's history). What makes utopian novels a critical point of reference here is the cultural range of their authors and subjects, which included, for instance, African Americans (e.g., Sutton E. Griggs, *Imperium in Imperio*, 1899), Jews (e.g., Solomon Schindler, *Young West*, 1894), and Irish (e.g., Ignatius Donnelly, *Caesar's Column*). Through its obligatory account of a traveler entering an unknown and wondrous region, confronted with people and customs both alien and familiar, the utopian novel offered a literary laboratory for probing the nature of cultural difference. Utopian novels typically featured an American or group of Americans as time travelers, most commonly projected forward, like Bellamy's Julian West, or projected backward, like Twain's Connecticut Yankee, whose experiences represented direct reversals of both the colonial and the immigrant situations. Transported to new worlds, sometimes their native lands transformed, whose norms and rituals seem counterintuitive even if preferable to those left behind, these travelers became captives of the new worlds and often captivated, through sustained education and retraining, by their dominant values.

Many of the most important novelists of this generation, from William Dean Howells and Mark Twain to Jack London and Charlotte Perkins Gilman, contributed to the genre. And the genre's high points represent some of *the* most significant literary confrontations with capitalism in any form at the time. Novels such as Bellamy's *Looking Backward* and Gilman's *Herland* are regarded, deservedly, as models of the genre, but others, such as Donnelly's *Caesar's Column*, were just as eagerly embraced by reading audiences. Like the characters in their literary utopias who carried their own distinctive traits of personality and culture wherever they went, Twain, Howells, and Gilman retained their signature styles and concerns in, respectively, *A Connecticut Yankee at King Arthur's Court* (1889), *A Traveller from Altruria*, and *Herland*. But in helping to formulate the unique type of utopianism that flourished in their lifetimes, they also demonstrated a powerful aesthetic and political breadth.

PERFECTING MANUFACTURE

As a work that sought solutions to the gravest social and economic problems, *Looking Backward: 2000–1887* deserves to be read alongside classic social theory, such as Plato's *Republic* and More's *Utopia*, and along with nineteenth-century writings by Owen and Fourier. The novel expressed Bellamy's attraction to militarism and socialism and his sympathy for the women's rights movement. And it reflected his disdain for a society that squandered its valuable resources by exploiting labor, allowing factories to remain idle, and countenancing routine cycles of inflation and depression. Bellamy believed that the root of these ills lay not in technology and innovation but in the increasing power of plutocrats. The novel sold nearly half a million copies and was a worldwide best seller. Translated into many languages, it spawned a national social reform movement and influenced seemingly every significant American intellectual of the time. Dozens of sequels appeared in the 1890s, yet another sign of the extraordinary capacity of this son of a Baptist minister to inspire. Bellamy, who recalled vividly in his journals accompanying his father to evangelical camp meetings, possessed a moral fervor that was especially suited to a late nineteenth-century society marred by scandal and corruption. Bellamy's answer to this national malaise was, in Mark Twain's words, to make "heaven paltry by inventing a better one on earth."[2]

Twain's rhetoric located *Looking Backward* squarely in the arena of religion, which represented not only a shrewd appraisal of its deepest methods and ideas but also an understanding of its political limitations. Bellamy deliberately invoked the term "Nationalism" in all of his writings, to distinguish his agenda from the socialism that it resembled in key respects. Socialism, Bellamy wrote Howells in 1888, is a term he "never could well stomach. . . . In the first place it is a foreign word in itself and equally foreign in all its suggestions. It smells to the average American of petroleum, suggests the red flag, with all manner of sexual novelties, and an abusive tone about God and religion, which in this country we at least treat with decent respect."[3] The hint of physical revulsion at the thought of a term at once "foreign" and incendiary is reinforced by the social purity of Bellamy's utopia. The paradox of Bellamy's novel is that utopia exists at the expense of social heterogeneity, invention, and innovation; that is, all the things that made technological advance and economic expansion possible in the first place. And the novel's very success was partly due to its blandness and restraint. In a manner similar to Henry George's in *Progress and Poverty*, a work he admired, Bellamy in *Looking Backward* drew adherents to his radical agenda because his own deep convictions were commonplace, sometimes prejudicially so.

Like no other form of social protest in the late nineteenth century, Bellamy's *Looking Backward* supplied a rudder for a sea of discontent. By 1890 there were 162 Bellamy Clubs in twenty-seven states, and the *Nationalist*, a Boston-based magazine, became the official voice of a movement composed of professionals and intellectuals. In 1891 Bellamy launched his own magazine, *New Nation*, whose purpose was to outline a plan of practical reform, which featured government ownership of all critical industries from coal mines and steel mills to telegraph companies and railroads. In 1891, a new Nationalist Party, founded on Bellamy's ideas, sponsored a slate of candidates in New England and joined forces with the People's Party (home to another famous utopian author, Ignatius Donnelly) in the Midwest, a region where Bellamy was especially admired. Bellamy's political work fell off after 1893 due to poor health, and he again threw his political energies into novel writing. His sequel to *Looking Backward*, *Equality* (1897), published the year before he died of tuberculosis, was neither a popular nor a critical success, primarily because it was set exclusively in a golden age. Bellamy's best fiction thrived on the tension between society as it was (beset with flagrant inequalities, misery amid abundance), and society as it might be (where human rationality and benevolence prevail).[4]

Bellamy was born in Chicopee Falls, Massachusetts, in 1850 and raised in a religious household marked as much by his mother's forbidding Calvinism as by his father's Baptist faith. Like many industrial towns of the era, Chicopee was full of immigrant families working long hours for low wages and subject to constant capital-labor conflict. Because the town was relatively small, its crowded tenements, frequently hazardous factories, strikes, and epidemics were visible to all and made a strong impression on Bellamy. Following graduation from Union College and study in Germany (law and socialist theory), Bellamy worked in New York as a reporter on William Cullen Bryant's *Evening Post* and later for Theodore Tilden's radical paper, *Golden Age*. Such articles as "Riches and Rottenness," "Overworked Children in Our Mills," and "Wastes and Burdens of Society" for his own paper, the *Springfield Penny News*, helped prepare him for *Looking Backward*. Equally beneficial was the fiction Bellamy managed to write (four novels and twenty-three short stories) and place in the best magazines (e.g., *Atlantic Monthly* and *Century*) while working as a journalist.

The protagonist of *Looking Backward*, Julian West, is a neurasthenic upper-class Bostonian awaiting construction of his new house and subsequent marriage, a prospect delayed by labor strikes as chronic, apparently, as West's insomnia. West relies on unorthodox methods to alleviate his sleep problem: mesmerism and nightly retreat to an underground vault that replicates "the silence of the tomb." Falling into an especially deep sleep one night, he awakens 113 years later in Utopian America, 2000. Dr. Leete, his wife, and his daughter, Edith, whom West marries at the novel's end, guide him through the ideal particulars of this new society. Bellamy finds various means of providing soapboxes so his characters can recite the wrongs of late nineteenth-century America and the superiority of its utopian version. For early twenty-first-century readers, *Looking Backward*'s utopia is satisfyingly prophetic with its shopping malls, credit cards (Edith Leete is an avid shopper), and telephonic radios prefiguring television. The novel even anticipates the Internet-based religious worship of the twenty-first century with its image of a preacher, Mr. Barton, who sermonizes by telephone, reaching audiences of 150,000. All of this under an equitable democratic regime: for the centralized utopian economy is designed to eliminate the excess and inefficiency of laissez-faire capitalism. Production and distribution are organized; everyone works until the age of forty-five, and each individual receives the same annual income. Women's work outside the home remains defined by their traditional work within it, but they enjoy equal pay. The symbol for the mass-produced abundance made uniformly available to all is the system of mechanical umbrellas covering all the sidewalks of Boston during rainstorms.

The rigid class and material distinctions of America 1887 have been eradicated at the expense of its multicultural variety, for America 2000 is unequivocally homogeneous. Indeed, the virtual absence of characters in the novel suggests Bellamy's difficulty in conceptualizing the human types amenable to the kinds of reforms he imagines. He emphasizes systematic changes, while minimizing the human factors that complicate them. Thus Bellamy fails to *represent* the transformed social relations—conversational forms, habits, collective rituals, and emotional behaviors—that assist and express a general accommodation of utopia. The potential success of the utopian society Bellamy delineates in his novel is belied by his inability to depict its human dimensions. As in many utopian works, the most pressing and engaging question of the novel becomes the nature of predictability itself: can the consequences of change, the future, be predicted?

Hence the importance of religion to the novel's deepest vision. From a religious perspective, the future is fundamentally predictable. They "still have Sundays and sermons in utopia," for the sake of Bellamy's late nineteenth-century audience, which requires *some* mechanism of belief.[5] Bellamy's own recourse to this mechanism is consistent throughout his career, which from beginning to end confirms the depth of his prophetic commitment to America. "Let us bear in mind," Bellamy wrote, "that, if [America] be a failure, it will be a final failure. There can be no more new worlds to be discovered, no fresh continents to offer virgin fields for new ventures."[6] Bellamy's biblical typology—America as the New Israel—builds on a Puritan legacy, to convert the crises of the Gilded Age into prophecies of the Millennium. This is made explicit in the first of the narrative's many tutorials, between the all-knowing host, Dr. Leete, and the innocent pilgrim, Julian West. As Leete observes, half-questioningly: "You must, at least, have realized . . . [these crises,] the general misery of mankind, were portents of great changes of some sort."[7] Equally important is the framing of West's embrace of the utopian perspective in the unmistakable terms of religious conversion. The profoundly spiritualized underpinnings of West's odyssey are especially evident in his nightmare late in the novel. Returning to late nineteenth-century America, he tries to preach to the unconverted but finds them hopelessly unresponsive. Bellamy's comparison of utopian conversion to a religious conversion is utopian in its own right. If only human minds were as open to conversion on socioeconomic grounds as they were on spiritual ones.

The problem of how to change beliefs is fundamental to utopian novels. There was no novelist more deeply interested in this problem than Mark Twain, who made it the central concern of his greatest works and grasped its particular relevance to utopianism. Twain had an almost scientific appreciation for how ideas are instilled and adhered to. For Twain the human-machine analogy was reciprocal; one might work back from machines to new conceptualizations of the human minds that created them. What better circumstance for testing the wondrous mental powers of humans than the traveler to utopia, a stranger in a strange land. More than any other novel by Twain, *A Connecticut Yankee at King Arthur's Court* fired the late nineteenth-century American popular imagination. The idea of an entrepreneurial mechanic transported to sixth-century England appealed to readers because it combined the attributes of the historical novel with modern values of innovation and industry. In staging his clash of civilizations, Twain drew on the striking transformations he had witnessed during his lifetime. Raised in the slave South, Twain saw firsthand the effects of emancipation. He experienced the revolution in transportation, from the stagecoach and steamboat to the railroad, and the advent of full-fledged industrialization enabled by technological innovations and constantly changing modes of production. Twain's sense of time was equally informed by intellectual transformations initiated by major thinkers like Charles Darwin, a devotee of Twain's fiction, whom Twain visited in 1879.

Connecticut Yankee's vivid dramatization of historical and intellectual dislocation resulted in Twain's most politically radical work. The novel depicts material progress as the paradoxical route to "a new Dark Ages," and the Yankee, Hank Morgan, characterizes institutions as "civilisation-factories" and "man-factories" to express his view of industrialization as inevitably dehumanizing.[8] These assumptions were supported by the controversial illustrations of Daniel Beard, which identified Twain's narrative with Henry George's single tax plan, among other anticapitalist measures. The most infamous of Beard's drawings was "The Slave Driver," whip in hand, foot on the breast of a prostrate woman, the unmistakable image of railroad titan Jay Gould. Twain expressed his approval in an 1889 letter to Beard: "Hold me under everlasting obligations. There are a hundred artists who could have illustrated any other of my books, but only one who could illustrate this one." As Beard reported in his autobiography, the illustrations that so impressed Twain "grievously offended some big advertisers" and were therefore removed from future editions of the novel.[9]

Connecticut Yankee is a powerful novel because its elaborate political and economic concerns are integral to the humanity of its characters, especially the protagonist-narrator, who for all his energy and enterprise retains a capacity for wonder. "It was a soft, reposeful, summer landscape, as lovely as a dream, and as lonesome as Sunday," Hank Morgan recounts in the novel's opening. "The air was full of the smell of flowers, and the buzzing of insects, and the twittering of birds, and there were no people, no wagons, there was no stir of life, nothing going on."[10] Like Huckleberry Finn's, Hank's narrative is full of sensual detail, suggesting the goodness of a natural world devoid of human elements. The opening contrasts with a novelistic society whose barbarism and cruelty is unequivocally manmade. Hank Morgan is a Huck Finn with distinct Tom Sawyer elements: Huck's gentle reflectivity combined with Tom's entrepreneurial greed.

The dominant paradigm in *Connecticut Yankee* is that of progress. Have Americans discovered in the nineteenth century an idea so powerful that it can simply be transferred to Arthurian England and, through the ingenuity of an energized Yankee, instituted there? It takes little time for Hank Morgan to establish a variety of nineteenth-century innovations. And by the narrative's end, the Connecticut Yankee has managed to modernize, single-handedly, the sixth century. There are schools, colleges, newspapers; authorship is a profession, slavery is abolished, all are equal before the law. There are telegraphs, telephones, phonographs, typewriters, sewing machines, and a stock exchange. They even have baseball. Of all the innovations that Hank Morgan introduces in Camelot, none in his view holds greater potential for collective transformation than soap and its marketing. The benign tolerance of the populace for Morgan's modern manipulations confirms the impact of an exceptionally tyrannical regime. And the very ease of his efforts suggests a troubling compatibility between modern innovation and traditional hierarchy. The chief difference between the final massacre, initiated by Morgan (utilizing all the fruits of progress), and Old World barbarisms is the degree of slaughter afforded by new technologies. Yet he makes continual distinctions between medieval-style oppression and more recent forms, to the credit of the latter. There is no question in his mind that his native Connecticut, where power, however corruptible, resides ultimately in the people, is preferable to what he witnesses in King Arthur's court.

In its contradictoriness, the political vision of *Connecticut Yankee* is most reflective of conditions in nineteenth-century America. Morgan's orchestration of a clash between civilizations succeeds in staging, above all, the tension between tradition and modernity in American society. To what extent were Americans capable of adapting to the social, economic, political, and spiritual upheavals of their time, and what would be the result if too many people were left in the wake of these transformations? And most important from Twain's perspective, how did human minds accommodate change—from the most concrete (changing modes of transportation; changing commodities, from bulk to brand) to the most cerebral (Darwinian versus biblical explanations for human origins)? By attempting to introduce enlightenment on a grand scale to the most superstitious of peoples, Morgan embarks on a deep exploration of the tenacity of belief. This is why he concentrates from the outset on invention and discovery, from the patents that secure one's property in creative products, to the schooling that provides the ideas and tools for innovations, to the newspaper that allows for the dissemination of new information. The Yankee ponders continually his all-powerful purpose: the transformation, bit by bit, of the Arthurian collective mentality. History intrudes on utopia in the form of the Interdict. In banning electric light, the Church threatens the very foundations of Morgan's empire. While he is able to enlist boys for an armed resistance, most of Camelot's adults capitulate. There follows a confrontation between Morgan's small band and the Church with its knights. Morgan is convinced he will triumph, a conviction fulfilled by the electrocution of the vast enemy force in a scene of utter devastation. But Morgan is finally also a casualty of this spectacle of mass death, succumbing in its aftermath.

Given the proximity of Twain's utmost obsession with the Paige Typesetter and his writing of *Connecticut Yankee* (from 1884 to 1889), it is not surprising to find traces of that ill-conceived investment in the novel's apocalyptic ending. Twain's typesetter was made at the same Fire Arms Manufacturing Company in Hartford, Connecticut, that turned out Gatling guns, the weapon of choice for Morgan's army at the novel's end. The technology that produced magically rapid print was intimately linked to the technology that produced magically rapid gunfire. This was not the first time that Twain had linked literary firepower to the deadlier kind, as in the epigraph to *Huckleberry Finn*. Twain's disastrous experience with the Paige Typesetter was only one of nearly a hundred new inventions that drew his apparently boundless enthusiasm for innovation. In *Connecticut Yankee*, Twain seems prepared to contemplate those enthusiasms from a distance, through the hapless persona of his protagonist-narrator. Utopias, Twain recognized, required the things that human beings believed they needed in addition to those that were good for them.

While critics have read this ending as a sign of Twain's deep disenchantment with his own era of progress, it is also a characteristically bleak commentary on humankind in general. "Human ideas are a curious thing, and interesting to observe and examine," Morgan comments. "I had mine, the King and his people had theirs. In both cases they flowed in ruts worn deep by time and habit, and the man who should have proposed to divert them by reason and argument would have had a long contract on his hands."[11] Talk is itself one of the biggest impediments: where there is incessant, air-filling monologue, there is little room for thought, for challenge, for renovation. Moreover, the limitation on any individual experience creates an enormous barrier. Genuine empathy for unfamiliar suffering is in equally short supply in nineteenth-century America and in Arthurian England.

In keeping with the complexity and elusiveness of its main ideas, Twain's novel has eluded generic definitions, seeming as much an idiosyncratic apocalyptic romance as a bona fide utopian novel. But the novel is preoccupied with utopia and with the possibility that the future might represent utopia to the past—the very basis of the myth of progress. *Connecticut Yankee* is more a commentary on the utopian novel than a concerted attempt to be one. Twain's novel reverses the typical utopian scenario, where a guide who translates the terms of the superior (or inferior) society befriends the protagonist, a confused alien in another world. In making his time traveler the expert among a dim populace of medieval souls, introducing a modernity that is historically inevitable, Twain distorts the classic utopian message. Despite its author's proclaimed appreciation for Bellamy, Twain's utopian-dystopian novel reads as a grim disavowal of the peddlers of perfection. Utopias always fail, Twain implies, not because human beings are essentially flawed but because any system of reformation bent on perfecting the work of higher powers is bound to go terribly wrong. This was not an argument for submission to Christianity, which he bitterly parodied in the novel, but rather Twain's pessimistic insistence that malicious forces beyond human beings always get the last word. Twain gives us the most skilled practical agent in Hank Morgan, and still his utopia goes awry.

From this perspective, King Camp Gillette's counterintuitive argument in *The Human Drift* (1894) is directly relevant to Twain's portrait: Gillette claims that businessmen are the only appropriate crafters of utopia. Though Gillette's worldwide renown, which persists to this day, is based on his razor blades, his fame in his own time was due equally to the social reorganization schemes that seemed so much at odds with the purposes of a major manufacturer. At the start of *The Human Drift*, Gillette asserts that the tycoon is the consummate source of reform, because he understands the power of capital. He may lack motivation, but his rationality will ultimately prevail, allowing him to grasp the irreversible trend, or "drift," toward concentration and the inevitability that such consolidated power will in time have to be more equitably distributed along with resources themselves. Only a social system based on what he called the "united intelligence and material equality" was capable of realizing the potential of modern American invention and industry.[12] Gillette's argument was similar to that set forth in any number of contemporary utopian works, many of them with greater formal claims to cultural significance. His book is important because of the attention that it received in its time and because it remains a curiosity. How could an ambitious businessman produce a work notable for the purity of its idealism, a mere year before he invented a product that would earn him international celebrity in addition to a fortune? While many business titans became identified with visionary enterprises of different sorts, some of them more practical than others (John D. Rockefeller's funding of cutting-edge medical research vis-à-vis Andrew Carnegie's quest for "world peace"), these efforts *followed* their amassing of millions and were the appropriate charitable consequences of self-enrichment.[13] Gillette was unusual in that his idealism preceded (and survived) his business triumphs.

The Human Drift offers 150 pages of impassioned political argument, historical analysis, poetry, and architectural designs to plead for a just allotment of modern industrial wealth. It was due to the openness of the utopian novel form as such that *The Human Drift* could be thus classified. For Gillette's art was his architecture. Like Howells, who drew inspiration for *A Traveller from Altruria* from the same source, Gillette was influenced by the "White City" of the Chicago world's fair in conceiving a city space defined by the harmonizing of diverse elements. The most revolutionary aspect of his plan, both aesthetically and socially, was the configuration of his apartments: spiraling high-rises with vast indoor as well as outdoor public spaces. Combinations of steel, brick, porcelain, and glass, with foliage, grass, and flowers, these aesthetically stunning buildings facilitated maximum durability and efficiency. Urbanites in Gillette's utopia enjoyed the sophistication and intensity of urban life, without forfeiting nature. Rural America was restructured to facilitate large-scale production and give rural inhabitants access to thoroughly equipped and modernized facilities (libraries, theaters, restaurants, schools). Gillette's vast metropolis accommodated the whole of North America, 70 million people in 40,000 skyscrapers, each of them built around gorgeous, plant-filled atriums crowned by skylights and bordered on their outer rings by rural areas that fed the urban populations inside. While every building and apartment was the same in terms of size and quality, parity did not equal monotony. Every building in his vast metropolis, he insisted, was a distinct work of art.

There was little in Gillette's background to explain his reconciliation of commercial ambition and utopian idealism. In contrast to many other utopian authors, religion did not play a significant role in his upbringing or in his adult life. Born in Wisconsin in 1855, to a family of modest means with seven children, Gillette was the son of a small businessman who liked to tinker with new inventions and a housewife who published a best-selling cookbook. After the family relocated to Chicago, where Gillette's father owned a hardware supply business, they lost everything in the Great Chicago Fire of 1871. Gillette began work at the age of seventeen, first selling hardware and later bottle-stops and Sapolio soap. Like his father, Gillette liked to experiment and was particularly drawn to disposable commodities, taking a hint from a successful employer to think of a throwaway item that required constant repurchasing. According to company legend, Gillette scoured the alphabet, in search of some need he might fulfill with an invention. One morning in 1895, while shaving, he conceived the disposable safety blade. While the idea may have come instantly, it took six years for Gillette and his partner, an MIT engineer, to form the American Safety Razor Company and another two to begin full-scale production with the financial backing of an Irish immigrant brewer.[14]

As suggested by his trust in a disposable product—what business historians call "planned obsolescence"—Gillette proved a savvy manufacturer. In 1903, he paid $200 for the first advertisement featuring his razors, and as his company grew, ad campaigns became increasingly ambitious. Because Gillette's image invariably appeared in product advertisements and the multimillion-dollar business had great success in a global market, Gillette's face was soon familiar worldwide (he once described being mobbed by Egyptians excitedly simulating with their fingers the movement of razors across their cheeks, during travels in the Middle East).[15] With so much ingenuity dedicated to the fine points of commerce, where did Gillette find room in his mind for the altogether different intellectual demands of social renovation? For the utopian dreaming of his 1894 book, *The Human Drift*, extended over the course of his commercial career. And what was truly distinctive about Gillette's vision was its combination of social radicalism—a system of material equalization and collective control that, despite his caveats, would require a complete dismantling of the status quo—and commonsensical business methods. Gillette's capacity to balance seemingly incompatible purposes promised the practical success of his utopian measures, which had a direct influence on urban planners in the twentieth century.

Like King Camp Gillette, Bradford Peck was a successful businessman who brought his commercial experience to bear in conceptualizing utopian alternatives. Peck took his utopia further than Gillette, both by testing it in corporate terms and by imagining it in more satisfying fictions. The year before he published his 1900 novel, *The World a Department Store*, Peck launched the "Cooperative Association of America" in Lewiston, Maine, a business partnership between producers and consumers that eliminated middlemen—bankers, speculators, advertisers—who, Peck believed, drove up costs artificially. The Cooperative membership was primarily upper-class, Anglo-Saxon, Protestant and focused on gradual social change. Peck was convinced that his utopian scheme, which included a cooperative res-taurant, a cooperative grocery store, and a cooperative electric light com-pany, was so compelling that it would be reproduced nationally. *The World a Department Store*, Peck's only novel, was designed to generate support for his social model. Peck shared Gillette's combination of business practicality and utopian idealism, privileging efficiency over competition, in the name of progress. He differed from Gillette, and joined other utopian authors like Baum and Donnelly, in his embrace of religion. Peck's business utopia promoted a thoroughly Christianized commerce.[16]

Peck was born in 1853 and raised in a home where work, of necessity, was emphasized over education. A cash boy at a department store at age twelve, he looked forward, in classic Horatio Alger terms, to one day having his own store. He worked his way up the ladder of retail, eventually opening a department store in Lewiston, Maine, which he built into the largest in New England, outside of Boston. Peck's rise from "rags to riches" and the ongoing success of his commercial ventures (in real estate, dry goods, etc.) prompt the same question raised by Gillette's career. What motivated this triumphant capitalist to pursue utopian schemes for social reorganization? In Peck's case the answer was lifelong devotion to Christianity, which he considered inimical to the competitive practices and Darwinian principles of modern capitalism.

The World a Department Store registers the influence of *Looking Backward* by depicting a hero who awakens in a utopia twenty-five years hence that has righted all the wrongs of turn-of-the-century America. The hero's inno-cence of his new world and competing memories of his past society yield plentiful opportunities for detailed social comparisons. As in Bellamy and Gillette, there are no kitchens, and food acquisition, preparation, and ser-vice are professionalized. The family as a child-rearing institution has disap-peared; child development experts raise offspring in groups. There is no use of liquor, except for medicinal purposes. Yet most social hierarchies (specifi-cally those of class, gender, and race) remain. Society is strictly Christian; there are no alternative faiths. And the only nonwhite faces appear in a schoolroom display of past human types. The homogeneity of Peck's utopia is confirmed by the neat symmetry of the novel's romances; dark-haired male mates with blonde female, blond male with dark-haired female, in a careful balancing of attributes. The predictability of romance is matched by the predictability of the novel's chief activity—shopping. No longer challenging or enervating, no bargains, no lines at checkout, no crowds. Above all, there is no advertising, which Peck portrays as a key source of inflation in the modern marketplace.

What cooperation meant to Peck was a system organized in the interest of the efficient manufacturer and the upper classes. Middlemen who threatened the manufacturer's profits were eliminated, as were the non-Anglo-Saxons, non-Christians, and working classes who threatened social harmony. Peck's utopia was not designed to improve the lot of competitive capitalism's primary victims but to eliminate the victims themselves. Though his vision failed to accommodate a Christianity open to all animal- and humankind, Peck's interpretation of Christianity made it readily reconcilable with his business practices. Christianity, according to Peck, flourished in societies that were conducive to the most rational and profitable methods. In *The World a Department Store*, turn-of-the-century Christianity is presented as bad business: a system of warring creeds, competing for members and resources. In Peck's utopia, Christianity has become standardized; indeed, it looks very much like a Christian trust. This is borne out by Peck's closing celebration of none other than John D. Rockefeller and Standard Oil. Adopting a familiar corporate defense, Peck applauded the company's cooperative organizational methods. Apparently, Peck's "Cooperative" had more in common with private corporations than was recognized by those who feared its socialistic ambitions. To readers of *The World a Department Store*, it all made perfect sense.

The career of L. Frank Baum, the most famous utopian author of the era next to Bellamy, has something in common with each of the previous examples. Baum had Mark Twain's boundless enthusiasm for inventions and showmanship and even went bankrupt due to the grandiose ventures he pursued following his greatest success. Baum was highly spiritual, like Bellamy and Peck, though he was less moralistic, preferring his religion mysterious and playful. Baum also shared Gillette's knack for business, pursuing a variety of professions and always landing on his feet. In 1900, Baum published two books that were intimately related: *The Art of Decorating Dry Goods Windows and Interiors* and *The Wonderful Wizard of Oz*. The first reflected his work advising midwestern store owners on their window displays in the rural towns he visited as a traveling salesman. As founder of the National Association of Window Trimmers of America, he had accumulated enough material on the subject to put together the small book, which he sold by subscription. The title confirmed Baum's view of advertising, particularly the highly personable and immediate form in shop windows, as an entertainment art. Window displays were narrative enactments designed to entrance potential consumers as if they were spectators at a theater. Because people were naturally curious about mechanical contrivances and would inevitably stop to contemplate a moving object, Baum considered them especially valuable. Capturing the interest of potential consumers was more than half way to the sale.

Baum's passion for invention and exhibition, his advertising skill and desire to captivate, came to fruition in his world-famous novel. When asked about his inspiration for *The Wonderful Wizard of Oz*, Baum replied that he was a mere "instrument" of "the Great Author," echoing statements by many pious novelists from the previous century.[17] Baum's reply was indicative of the importance of his faith—a blend of theosophy (nature religion), mysticism, spiritualism, and renovated Christianity—to his best-selling novel. Those beliefs derived from his Methodist upbringing, the intense evangelicalism of his native region, and the growing liberalism and religious uncertainty of his era. Baum was so confident of the book's likely success that he reportedly framed the pencil (now a stub) with which he had written it. He did not wait long for the realization of his expectations: within weeks of publication, 10,000 copies were gone and the second and third printings were in press. Contemporary critics were lavish: pronouncing it "the best children's story-book of the century" (*Minneapolis Journal*) and the start of a new era of writing for children (*New York Times*).[18]

Lyman Frank Baum was born in 1856 in Chittenango, New York, a small town upstate. After the elder Baum, a barrel manufacturer, struck oil in Titusville, Pennsylvania, he built a country estate just outside of Syracuse, New York, where Baum and four siblings were raised. The family's wealth and indifference to formal education liberated Baum to pursue other activities, such as editing and printing magazines with his own press and operating a fowl-breeding business. The latter led to national recognition in the field and his first publication, *The Book of the Hamburgs* (1886). The restless, multitalented Baum then turned to local theatricals, appearing in amateur productions and writing plays for a Syracuse troupe. In the fall of 1882, Baum married Maud Gage, daughter of a prominent feminist, Matilda Joslyn Gage, a participant in the Seneca Falls Women's Rights Convention, and subsequently entered his family's oil business to ensure adequate support for his wife and child. It was Baum's wife, Maud, who engineered their move to Dakota Territory, where she had relatives. In Aberdeen, South

Dakota, Baum discovered his avocation for journalism, editing the *Aberdeen Saturday Pioneer*, whose opinion columns he used to explore topics such as feminism and Indian-white conflict.[19]

Baum sided with the Dakota pioneers, repudiating all claims of the original inhabitants. Indeed, after the 1890 massacre of Indians at Wounded Knee, Baum openly endorsed the extermination of the remaining Indians, fearing they would seek vengeance. General unrest and economic depression resulted in a mass exodus of settlers in the early 1890s, which the Baums joined, relocating to Chicago, where Baum became a traveling salesman for a wholesale china firm. The Baum family now had four sons, and Baum prized the domestic intervals when he would create stories for them. His first children's book, *Mother Goose in Prose*, with illustrations by Maxfield Parrish, was published in 1897. Then came *By the Candelabra's Glare* (1898) and *Father Goose: His Book* (1899), a best seller that was greatly admired by Howells and Twain.

Like these earlier books, *The Wonderful Wizard of Oz* was a departure in children's literature visually, with bold, original color illustrations by William Denslow that combined Art Nouveau with the linear clarity of Japanese painting. In narrative terms, the novel eschewed didacticism and sentimentality for plainness and economy. Over his writing desk Baum kept a plaque with lines from 1 Corinthians 13:11: "When I was a child I spake as a child, I understood as a child, I thought as a child." A gentle democratic spirit rules Dorothy's world, where the bark even of witches is worse than their bite. Dorothy is a brave and resourceful product of midwestern pioneer culture, a young orphan on a Bunyan-like journey. She succeeds in rescuing not only herself but also the friends she makes along the way, overcoming terrific odds, and propelling herself toward her goal without conventional forms of male assistance. Dorothy's companions, the Scarecrow, the Tin-man, and the Lion, represent, among other things, the three kingdoms of nature—vegetable, mineral, and animal—in addition to the three personal faculties that each seeks: intelligence, love, and courage. They can also be seen as emblems of contemporary social movements or developments: agrarianism (Scarecrow), industrialization (Tin-man), back-to-nature (Lion). The novel leaves little doubt that Dorothy and her companions already possess the things they seek. The emphasis on self-discovery, on overcoming a series of trials to locate the power within, is as universal as it is specifically American.

The novel's most emphatically American type is the "Wizard" himself, unmasked at the end as a "humbug," whose true occupations are ventriloquism and ballooning. The wizard recalls any number of nineteenth-century showmen and charlatans. But he is also the capitalist par excellence, instructing visitors who come to request favors in the basic laws of exchange. Supplicants must pay dearly for the use of his miraculous powers. The wizard's Emerald City bears comparison to the White City of Chicago's 1893 Columbian Exposition, the brainchild of American business leaders. Despite his fraudulence, the wizard is no villain, and his portrait conveys the same respect for deceivers Baum once expressed in an editorial: "Barnum was right when he declared that the American people liked to be deceived."[20] Baum's theories on window dressing depended on the same pleasure in deception. Yet still more powerful in Baum's famous novel is an ideal of directness and honesty. The principles he sanctioned in the various business enterprises he pursued so avidly were somewhat at odds with the pragmatic and childlike world he created in his most memorable fiction.

> The sun had baked the plowed land into a gray mass, with little cracks running through it. Even the grass was not green, for the sun had burned the tops of the long blades until they were the same gray color to be seen everywhere. Once the house had been painted, but the sun blistered the paint and the rains washed it away, and now the house was as dull and gray as everything else.
> When Aunt Em came there to live she was a young, pretty wife. The sun and wind had changed her, too. They had taken the sparkle from her eyes and left them a sober gray; they had taken the red from her cheeks and lips, and they were gray also. She was thin and gaunt, and never smiled, now. When Dorothy, who was an orphan, first came to her, Aunt Em had been so startled by the child's laughter that she would scream and press her hand upon her heart whenever Dorothy's merry voice reached her ears; and she still looked at the little girl with wonder that she could find anything to laugh at . . . It was Toto that made Dorothy laugh, and saved her from growing as gray as her other surroundings. Toto was not gray; he was a little black dog, with long, silky hair and small black eyes that twinkled merrily on either side of his funny, wee nose. Toto played all day long, and Dorothy played with him, and loved him dearly.[21]

Baum stages a classic struggle here between things that make experience bleak (from drought and want to dullness) and those that enliven it (the instinctive humor and happiness of children and their pets). The scene reveals the contradictory power of nature: draining life of color while rejuvenating it via children and animals. There is simply no way for an adult in this landscape to escape being gray. Children and animals, however, retain an inherent, untouchable vitality so alien to this world that it strains the heart. The passage endorses variety by omission: the variety of human, animal, and vegetable existence, the potential variety of worlds unknown that may exist undetected in the little cracks of the land.

Baum's emerald utopia is everything that Kansas is not. It is a sea of colorful beings, most of them alternative *kinds*: Munchkins, walking scarecrows, talking dishes, witches, Winkies, and Winged Monkeys. This is not to suggest that a writer who supported the annihilation of the South Dakota Indians was at heart a defender of multiculturalism but to affirm a critical cliché: that novels can convey messages unbeknownst to their authors. Moreover, such sentiments *are* consistent with Baum's liberal openness to different religions. He was drawn to esoteric faiths such as Kabbalism and Rosicrucianism, as well as to Eastern ideas of reincarnation and karma. He engaged in assorted religious practices, conducting séances, participating in spiritualist groups, and remaining alert to psychic events, such as the haunting of his Chicago house. Faith, for him, was imaginative, intuitive, flexible, and synthetic as befitted an era of novelty and invention.

Most of all, Baum believed that modern science afforded a view of a more (not less) spiritualized universe. An editorial he wrote on the subject reads like a philosophical appendage to *The Wonderful Wizard of Oz*. "Scientists have educated the world to the knowledge that no part of the universe, however infinitesimal, is uninhabited. Every bit of wood, every drop of liquid, every grain of sand or portion of rock has its myriads of inhabitants —creatures deriving their origin from and rendering involuntary allegiance to a common Creator."[22] Such a faith, one could argue, amounted to an ultimate form of multiculturalism. It was perhaps owing to its author's diverse and supple belief system that *The Wonderful Wizard of Oz* had a more extensive afterlife than any other novel of this period. A musical and "fairylogue" (moving pictures accompanied by orchestra and lecture) in Baum's . time, it became one of the most popular films in American cultural history. Through these different media, the novel's multicreature utopia became familiar, indeed integral to the imaginative life of every subsequent generation. And in this way, however inadvertently, it helped to ensure greater tolerance for the growing multiculturalism of nonutopian America.

REINVENTING RACE AND CLASS

In American utopian novels of the late nineteenth century there was no single social issue that received more consistent attention than racial and ethnic differences. Written mainly by authors of Anglo-Saxon, Protestant descent, these novels pictured ideal worlds devoid of the troubling cultural variety that increasingly marked their society. However radical the social organizations of these utopias might be in political and economic terms, they were more often than not eugenicist breeding grounds for a purified citizenry. Thus, in Alexander Craig's *Ionia* (1898), Jews are forbidden to marry each other, and any Jew who commits a crime is immediately sterilized. In Arthur Vinton's *Looking Further Backward* (1890) and John Bachelder's *A.D. 2050* (1890), evil Chinese populations launch unprovoked attacks on the United States. Frona Colburn dedicates her *Yermah the Dorado* (1897) to "WHITE KNIGHTS of all times," who are exemplified by her idealized Aryan hero. Black Americans and Native Americans are rarely mentioned in these utopias, except where, as in Walter McDougall's *The Hidden City* (1891), their absence is highlighted as evidence of their inability to accommodate a superior civilization. Benjamin Rush Davenport's *Anglo-Saxons, Onward!: A Romance of the Future* (1898) and Stanley Waterloo's *Armageddon: A Tale of Love, War, and Invention* (1898) predict the victory of Anglo-Saxon armies in global wars of the twentieth century, whose result is the annihilation of all inferior races.[23]

An alternative to these genocidal impulses was a strain of racial pluralism introduced by utopian authors with roots in different cultural communities. Dr. Sutton E. Griggs, an African American author whose utopian novel *Imperium in Imperio* (1899) circulated more widely among other African Americans than works by Charles W. Chesnutt and Paul Laurence Dunbar, conceived a separate state in America where blacks would fulfill their distinct destiny. Jewish author David Lubin in *Let There Be Light* (1900) staged a series of dialogues in which his hero, a Jewish laborer named Ezra, imagines a utopian harmony of classes and races. Others sought to dramatize this pluralistic agenda that was increasingly popular among intellectuals such as Horace Kallen and Charles Eastman, who urged the acceptance of America's multicultural character. Thus in Charlotte Perkins Gilman's *Herland* (1915), where care has been taken "to breed out, when possible, the lowest types," race remains a prominent differentiation, while ideal variety becomes the general aim: "Celis was a blue-and-gold-and-rose person; Alima, black-and-white-and-red . . . Ellador was brown: hair dark and soft like a seal coat; clear brown skin with a healthy red in it."[24] The shared purpose in these examples was the commitment to improving prevailing methods of social and racial reproduction so as to alleviate what all these authors perceived to be unhealthy, heterogeneous patterns. Utopian authors trained their sights persistently on matters of race and culture, it seems obvious in retrospect, because the spectacle of cultural difference was omnipresent, and the subject was a constant source of political controversy and intellectual debate. By reinventing race, these authors paved the way for the renovation of a social system built on punishing disparities between rich and poor. Mitigating the racial distinctions that fragmented their society, many utopian authors believed, would give everyone a greater stake in a just social order. Greater homogeneity, these utopian works assert, leads naturally to a stronger sense of collective welfare.

Ignatius Donnelly's *Caesar's Column: A Story of the Twentieth Century* (1890), a best seller published under the pseudonym Edmund Boisgilbert, M.D., has long been notorious for its anti-Semitic elements. Featuring a Jewish villain, Jacob Isaacs, known as Prince Cabano (the Italian title purchased by his wealthy father), the prince is the most reptilian of ruling-class exploiters. Corpulent and big-nosed, with "a Hebraic cast of countenance," he is a brutal tyrant, responsible for the misery of millions.[25] He also has an insatiable appetite for gorgeous virgins, whom he buys in a white slave market of his own making and keeps in the harem on his estate. Donnelly's Jewish villains cover both ends of the political spectrum, for the other unnamed but equally diabolical Jew is part Shylock, part Bolshevik. A hooked-nosed Russian cripple, this Jew robs the "Brotherhood" he has served and flees to Judea, where he seeks to "re-establish the glories of Solomon, and revive the ancient splendors of the Jewish race."[26]

The son of Irish immigrants, Ignatius Donnelly, born in Philadelphia in 1831, knew the experience of being a foreigner in America, one generation removed. His father was an American-educated doctor, and Donnelly himself attended public schools, received legal training, and was admitted to the Pennsylvania bar in 1853. Married to Katharine McCaffrey in 1853, they moved out West, where he invested heavily in a Minnesota town called Niniger that he hoped might eventually rival Chicago as a midwestern center of commerce. The investments failed, partly due to the Panic of 1857, and Donnelly turned to politics, where his oratorical talents led to two terms as lieutenant governor and then to Congress, where he became known as a defender of the people's rights against corporate interests. Returning to Minnesota in 1874 to serve in the state senate, Donnelly started a newspaper called the *Anti-Monopolist*. Journalism whet his appetite for writing, and over the next decade, he published five utopian novels and a book arguing for Francis Bacon's authorship of Shakespeare's plays. Donnelly's vast and learned first novel *Atlantis: The Antediluvian World* (1882) sought to prove the existence of Atlantis, its role as the source of ancient mythology, and its destruction in a single natural disaster. The book was a critical and commercial success, but the string of utopian novels that followed, leading up to *Caesar's Column*, while similar in scope, were largely ignored.

Given Donnelly's prominence as a politician—he helped found the Populist Party in 1892 and was the party's candidate for vice president in 1900—one might have expected his writing to be subordinated, but his extraordinary fund of energy ensured his parallel pursuit of both vocations. Donnelly's political activity and literary work were mutually reinforcing. As a politician, Donnelly was as ambitious and idealistic as his novels, known particularly for his support of public education, and the speeches of his characters often sounded like Populist Party platforms. No novel of Donnelly's expressed his political views more accurately than *Caesar's Column*, the most enduring of his works. Donnelly drew on two previous literary best sellers for inspiration: Bellamy's *Looking Backward* and John Hay's *The Bread-Winners*, whose notoriety as an anonymous book may have influenced Donnelly's decision to adopt a pseudonym. The first publisher Donnelly submitted the novel to (A. C. McClurg) found it incendiary, but the second (Frances J. Schulte) read it as a cautionary jeremiad.

Indeed, despite the heated politics of its author, *Caesar's Column* is a sustained argument against extremism. The narrative consists of letters from the novel's hero, Gabriel Weltstein, to his brother Heinrich back home in Uganda. A Dantesque wayfarer in America circa 1988, Gabriel is a humanitarian, overwhelmed by the brutal intensity of both the ruling class and the insurgent Brotherhood stirring the masses as the revolution draws near. Donnelly's turbulent society displays elements of utopia. Liquor, for instance, is outlawed, though rulers imbibe freely, and the improvement in the health of those who can afford the luxuries of scientific consumption has dramatically increased longevity, as has the air quality in all the places frequented by the rich. The novel's plot is set in motion when its three principals collide in a street accident: Gabriel; Maximilian (Max) Petion, a former member of the elite, now a leader in the Brotherhood; and Estella Washington, the beautiful descendant of George Washington who is a new (and still virginal) concubine of the evil Prince Cabano. Max takes Gabriel on a tour of the Under-World, where he sees masses of Americans living in squalor, the end result of late nineteenth-century economic policy. Meanwhile the elites (many of them "Israelites") enjoy resplendent luxury, insulated by their complete control of the government, military, and media.[27] The lone gap in this tight and intricate machinery is the (inexplicable) perpetuation of a public education system, which manages to keep the otherwise wretched working classes well educated, filling their ranks with learned and eloquent leaders.

The solution advanced by Donnelly's hero in a chapter entitled "Gabriel's Utopia" is an instrumental Christianity designed to extend the fruits of innovation and industry to all, in the name of its originator. It is left to the religion's true devotees to "take possession of the *governments* of the world and enforce *justice!*"[28] Social improvement, according to *Caesar's Column*, depends on the fulfillment of Christianity's foundational principles. Donnelly's example of fallen Christians is a congregation of lavishly attired women who listen to a sermon on the necessity of suffering while entertained by dancers in earth goddess costumes wet with blood. This grossly sensual, perverse Christianity leads straight to the inevitable holocaust at the novel's end.

En route to this devastation, Caesar Lomellini, the leader of the Brotherhood, manages to triumph over the evil plutocracy, and the world is turned upside down. Mob rule is even more appalling than anticipated. At the head of the mob stands Caesar, "so black with dust and blood that he looked like a negro . . . his mat of hair rose like a wild beast's mane . . . his eyes were wild and rolling."[29] Bodies fill the streets, making them impassable, so Caesar orders that a column be built of the dead, in tribute to his power. From their electric airship, Gabriel, Estella, and Max, with his new Anglo-Saxon, Protestant bride, espy a horrific effigy atop Caesar's column: the leader's head. Murdering the leader, Max explains, is the first instinct of mobs. Returning to Uganda, Gabriel and his party fortify their island against potential aggressions from abroad. Within five years their small mountainous country has become an idyll where excessive wealth and poverty are unknown. Like so many other utopian communities, theirs is safe from "the dark and terrible throngs" of urban America.[30] How Donnelly reconciled this purified idyll with his own Irish Catholic background remains a mystery. Secure in the bounty of their rural retreat, Donnelly's homogeneous island community is free to realize Christ's message on earth. True to its author's populism, *Caesar's Column* endorses an agrarian democratic ideal against a modern pluralism ultimately devastating to rich and poor alike.

The setting of Charlotte Perkins Gilman's women's utopia in *Herland* (1915) is equally pastoral and remote. And the exclusive method of single-sex reproduction ensures more control with a perfected result. Gilman's novel anticipates a recurring fantasy in utopian novels by women: a world without men. In suggesting that simply by eliminating whole categories of people certain social problems might be solved, Gilman was typical of the era's utopian novelists. Still, utopia in the hands of a seasoned author was different from utopia in the hands of a Lane or Donnelly. Though Gilman raised similar questions about race, reproduction, and social organization, she explored the issues with greater complexity. Moreover, her theoretical interests were more carefully woven into the novel's form. *Herland* has characters with contradictory tendencies, a suspenseful plot with surprising twists, an imaginatively detailed setting, and a philosophy that reflects deliberate reading and reflection. When Gilman offers renovated ideas about gender, they are presented convincingly through characters likely to contemplate such matters. What made Gilman's novel especially noteworthy in the canon of American utopian fiction was the depth of its immersion in contemporary intellectual debates.

By the time she wrote *Herland*, Gilman was an international celebrity, known for her fiction, her polemical writings, and her lectures.[31] A coveted speaker, Gilman had published 8 novels, 171 short stories, 9 nonfiction books, and more than 1,000 essays. Gilman was also editor of her own magazine, *Forerunner*, where much of her writing appeared. Her most popular story, "The Yellow Wall-Paper" (1892), was as controversial as it was widely read.[32] In "Why I Wrote 'The Yellow Wall-Paper'" (1913), she explained that the story was inspired by her ordeal as a patient of the famous Dr. S. Weir Mitchell, an effort to persuade him of "the error of his ways."[33] Gilman drew on her own depression both before and after her daughter's birth for her story, which shows how any experience of maternity that is less than ideal is treated as pathological. The protagonist-narrator is consigned to a rest cure by her physician husband, an eminently rational character, and forbidden to engage in work of any kind, which drives her further into madness. The story makes clear that this apparent "insanity" is, in fact, a displaced form of rage. The protagonist's only mental rudder is the story itself, which she records in a secret diary.

The construction of motherhood in *Herland* is a direct response to the heroine's trials in "The Yellow Wallpaper." The novel features three male explorers: Van, a student of sociology; Terry, a wealthy man of enterprise; and Jeff, who is trained as a doctor. Young and adventurous, they join a "scientific expedition" to a mountainous, forested region unrecorded on maps featuring dialects unknown to civilized man. Persistent allusions from their guides to a Country of Women that has never been visited piques their curiosity, and the trio breaks off from the expedition in search of it. *Herland* is the story of what they find.

Gilman's utopia institutionalizes her own innovative solutions to prevailing social problems. The effort to reconcile scientific reason with feminist idealism is built into the structure of *Herland*, which is narrated by Van, the social scientist. The novel's deepest implications are that all the tendencies that impede rational behavior are male traits projected onto women. Hence the primary purpose of Van's retrospective narrative: the recollection by a male consciousness of how he comes to accept a counterintuitive and disconcerting reality. Throughout, Van conveys his newfound loyalty to the civilization of Herland and his sense of wonder at discovering a country from which men have been absent for two thousand years. Because the women of Herland intend to keep it that way, Van has been deprived of his meticulous records and drawings and must write from memory. But his enthusiasm—"the world needs to know about that country"—works against them.[34] Van's narrative consistently contrasts his own barbaric impulses (shared by his fellow male travelers) with the restrained civility of his women hosts. Van's early response to Herland, "why, this is a *civilized* country! There must be men," ironic at his own expense, reveals how much he has to learn: For the novel's main point is that Herland is the most civilized country on earth precisely because there are none.[35] Through Van's descriptions of his homeland to eager audiences of Herlanders, the illogic of contemporary American society is exposed by its contrast with the logic of Herland.

Herland is a nonhierarchical matriarchy whose social model is the welfare state. All citizens benefit from a maternalistic government and enjoy equal access to the bounty afforded by the intelligent cultivation of national resources. The only form of reproduction is parthenogenesis, regulated with a strictness that Francis Galton would have envied. The rigorous control of human reproduction informs all other kinds of production—animal, agricultural, artificial. Child rearing is the revered work of experts, there is neither competition nor poverty, crime is unheard of, and even sickness is so radically minimized that the profession of medicine is "a lost art."[36] The key to this ideal social order is the eradication of sexuality, which has been bred and trained out of the "race." "An endlessly beautiful undiscovered country" has replaced a modern Western sexual tradition that exaggerates "femininity."[37] The only normative passion in *Herland* is maternal, with filial and sisterly devotion regarded as acceptable outgrowths. So fierce is this maternal feeling that Herland women grow pale at the thought of modern American production procedures that rob the cow of her calf, and the calf of its natural sustenance.

Free to fulfill their instincts, the women of Herland flourish, creating a world without vice. Feminine weaknesses—"submissive monotony," "pettiness," "jealousy," "hysteria"—turn out to be "mere reflected masculinity."[38] Gilman anticipated her novel's agenda in a 1913 essay, "New Mothers of a New World," where she attributed the majority of social problems to male engendering and concluded fervently, "we will work together, the women of the race, for a higher human type."[39] According to Gilman, it was the male partner that inhibited the creation of a perfected citizenry of the type represented in *Herland*. Parthenogenesis (ovular development without fertilization) was the highest form of reproductive purity, the only kind that could absolutely control genetic inheritance. As recognized by groups that defined kinship through matrilineal descent, the maternal body that contained and nurtured the egg and then the fetus, delivering it up after maturation, was the only infallible source of parental identity. According to Gilman, whose portrait, however male-averse, would have appealed, theoretically, to contemporary sociologists, nature was the wild card in transmission, while socialized traits were fully susceptible to control. They likewise would have approved of Gilman's view of sexuality and desire as disempowering to women, recalling a Victorian ethos that viewed ideal women as devoid of physical passion. Finally, they would have accepted the presentation of mothering as the primary and ultimate form of pleasure and power in Gilman's utopia, which almost made the novel a corrective to her own personal experience.

Despite this contradiction, Gilman's ingenious narrative achieves a complete reversal of the terms of encounter. Where the male visitors have everything on their side that would sustain a judgment of their superiority —civilization, science, modernity, progress, Western education, firsthand knowledge of the world—all of these advantages are found to be more finely tuned in the isolated society of women, who have been cut off from the rest of the world for over two thousand years. What makes this credible, in Gilman's scheme, is women's inherent possession of all of these qualities. Civilization, rationality, modernity, a thirst for knowledge, wisdom, *Herland* suggests, are as natural to women as mother's milk. If allowed to develop, unimpeded by male prerogatives such as patriotism, competition, sexual desire, and conquest, the result would be utopia.

While racial and reproductive solutions to social problems were pervasive in realist utopias, their authors (as we have seen) were no less attentive to the need for socioeconomic renovation. Indeed, racial purification was often viewed as the precondition for radical economic change; a homogeneous culture was the first step toward a more equitable society. The majority of utopian authors advocated a transformation of the current capitalist system to achieve a more cooperative and centralized economy and a more even distribution of wealth. While most, like Edward Bellamy, stopped short of truly radical plans for social reorganization, rejecting bona fide socialism, others, like William Dean Howells and Jack London, embraced it, convinced that the nation's expanding monopolistic capitalism, which allowed the concentration of wealth in the hands of ever smaller numbers, was creating a permanent underclass. Howells and London worried that a growing gap between rich and poor would spell the end of the American middle class.

In his renowned proletarian utopian novel *The Iron Heel* (1908), London conceived a dystopian nightmare with the mass of Americans confined to poverty under plutocratic rule and revolutionary violence looming. *The Iron Heel* anticipated science fiction disaster films of the late twentieth century that predicted the state of the world after an unchecked capitalist-industrial system had reached its ill-fated end. The novel was London's message to his contemporaries that there was no time to lose; America circa 1908 was on the verge of Armageddon. The narrative's central conceit is the discovery of a manuscript by a futurist historian, Anthony Meredith, from the utopian era "419 B.O.M.," seven centuries hence. The Everhard Manuscript is a firsthand account of the period between 1912 and 1932, when the proletariat challenged the vicious ruling oligarchy repeatedly, each time with disastrous results. The manuscript represents the recollections of Avis Everhard, the devoted wife of Ernest Everhard, the primary leader of the revolution. Thus the narrative combines a personal defense of socialist revolution from the perspective of its chief architect's wife, with a running catalog of notes on the early decades of the twentieth century by a historian writing from utopia. Anthony Meredith's notes present eye-opening history lessons on the first decades of the twentieth century. Focused on corporate developments, such as the rise of Rockefeller's Standard Oil, they provide an ongoing rationale for socialism. Yet Meredith also qualifies the glowing presentation of revolution and revolutionaries in Avis Everhard's narrative. For his main claim is that the revolutionaries were poor readers of history, failing to consider that the fascist boot of the Iron Heel might be a more likely outgrowth than socialism of an exploitative capitalism.

The Everhard Manuscript portrays Ernest Everhard as a proletarian *ubermensch*, that is, a typical London hero. Much of the narrative is devoted to his animated diatribes lovingly introduced by Avis, who never fails to describe how he looks delivering his speeches. As befits the novel's utopianism, Everhard is a full-blown radical theoretician from the start, however contradictory his agenda, a blend of Nietzschean philosophy, Darwinism, socialism, and democratic idealism. As "a natural aristocrat," Everhard exhibits the usual antagonism of London's protagonists, who are always superior to their working-class roots, however much they champion and idealize them.[40] Nor has Everhard's mind developed at the expense of his body, for his overpowering intellect is matched by a superb physique. His physical and mental powers fortify each other in cerebral debates that are portrayed as combat. Everhard's intellectual dominance of the elite depends on the assurance that he can pound them into insensibility.

The symbolic violence of these exchanges where Everhard is invariably masterful and castigating is not simply for the pleasure of his wealthy wife, who falls promptly in love after noting, "I had never been so brutally treated in my life." The triumphant dynamics of the novel's love plot are exactly reversed in the novel's political plot, where the working class is smashed to bits by the fascist Iron Heel, which, in an oft-repeated phrase, is destined to "walk upon [their] faces."[41] Despite the persuasiveness of Everhard's rhetoric, and the self-evidence of his facts, the narrative progresses to its inexorable devastating conclusion: the obliteration of the middle and working classes in a holocaust that leaves the streets carpeted with corpses.

No class in *The Iron Heel* holds a corner on brutality, though the upper classes come close. Perhaps the most memorable image in the novel is that of the mill hand, Jackson, who is denied compensation after his arm is shredded by a machine at work. The rule of the novel's oligarchy is everywhere, silencing the pulpit and the press, suppressing dissent at the universities, swallowing up the middle classes, making deals with the labor unions at the expense of most workers, packing both houses of the Congress with their loyalists, and swelling the coffers of the major trusts. There are fleeting moments of hope: Everhard's Socialists win in a landslide in the 1912 elections, though they find themselves powerless when they arrive in Congress, and they manage to avert a war with Germany through an alliance between American and German workers, who refuse to fight each other "for the benefit of their capitalist masters." These proletarian victories, however, are blips on a horizon of ruin, as the novel winds down with chapter titles such as, "The Beginning of the End," "Last Days," and "The Roaring Abysmal Beast." The end result of this dystopian class war is the transformation of humans into beasts.[42]

The voice that speaks through Avis Everhard is the voice of Jack London, the believer, who could declare in a 1906 lecture at Yale University, "We Socialists will wrest power from the present rulers. By war, if necessary. Stop us if you can." So stirred were the students present that a group of them launched soon after it a Yale chapter of the Intercollegiate Socialist Society.[43] Yet the debacle that closes *The Iron Heel* affirms a more sober attitude London articulated in a 1901 letter: "I should much prefer to wake tomorrow in a smoothly-running socialistic state; but I know I shall not."[44]

Had London survived to the 1930s, he would have seen his novel enshrined as a socialist cult object, widely viewed among keepers of the red flame as a powerful articulation of socialist principles in the face of a fascist enemy.

Though both were on the same political side, as proponents of socialism, William Dean Howells's gentle utopia in his Altruria trilogy could not have been further from the violent dystopia of Jack London's *The Iron Heel.* Similarly, the fierce and aggressive rhetoric of London's Ernest Everhard is replaced by the sweet reasonableness of Aristides Homos, the traveler from Altruria, in confirmation of the fact that theoretical bedfellows could be utter aliens when it came to method. Howells's utopian imaginings provide an appropriate culmination to his career as a major realist writer, influential editor, generous supporter of literary apprentices, and spokesman for humanitarian political causes. As an author who accomplished more in practical cultural affairs than any American writer of his time, Howells's professional activities were also marked by an incomparable idealism. He was drawn to Bellamy's "Nationalism" as well as to Christian Socialism, and in addition to supporting the accused anarchists in the Haymarket Affair, expressed dismay over the treatment of the strikers at the Carnegie Iron and Steel Company in Homestead, Pennsylvania. Between 1889 and 1891 when he lived in Boston, Howells frequented Bellamy's Nationalist meetings and Edward Everett Hale's Tolstoy Group, and he endorsed Hamlin Garland's efforts to combine cultural practice and social protest. Throughout this period, his concerns about the social effects of an American plutocracy and the need for sweeping change were increasingly focused on the prospects of Christian Socialism. Howells wrote approvingly of Leo Tolstoy's radical Christianity in an 1888 review of *What to Do?*, arguing that a system in which a small elite amasses wealth while the majority lives in poverty is necessarily short-lived. Howells's traveler from Altruria directly echoed the review in observing that the last straw in his country was the appalling greed of the wealthy, whose accumulations simply became intolerable.

The Altrurian narratives originated in a request from John Brisben Walker, a successful businessman who had bought *Cosmopolitan* in 1889, that Howells write some "sociological essays" in support of the Christian Socialist creed they shared. Howells preferred the term "altruism" to "socialism," a concept he introduced in his final "Editor's Study" column for *Harper's Monthly* in 1892, where he described an imaginary society founded on this principle. Altruria, Howells explained, was "an outlandish region inhabited by people of heart, a sort of economic *Pays du Tendre.*"[45] Howells's Altrurian narratives sought to dramatize the possibilities of altruism,

were it to become the driving force in a society, as a "national polity."
Altrurians live *"for* each other," Howells wrote, in contrast to Americans
who live *"upon* each other."[46]

The first book of the projected utopian trilogy, *A Traveller from Altruria:
A Romance* (1894, serialized in *Cosmopolitan,* 1892–94) features Aristides
Homos, a traveler from the utopia of Altruria to America in the early 1890s,
who is troubled by a society in which "4,000 American millionaires" are
"richer than all the other Americans put together."[47] Such terrible inequities recall the traveler's Altruria before its evolution into a benevolent
social order. The traveler's guide, also the novel's narrator, is a thoughtful
but naïve member of the elite, who struggles to rationalize prevailing
customs, but in doing so finds himself entangled in the contradictions
between American ideals and social reality. The group of friends he assem-
bles to meet the traveler, which includes a professor, a doctor, a lawyer, a
minister, a banker, and a manufacturer, are equally self-satisfied and close-
minded, incapable of understanding any social order but their own. The
obvious irony at their expense is the traveler's deep understanding of their
civilization, his multiple sympathies for its various members, and his overriding conviction that it is nothing short of "savage." Much of the novel's
dramatic energy is invested in the narrator's gradual abandonment of his
own views in favor of the traveler's. For this reason, their relationship is
compelling, marked by the narrator's ambivalence toward the source of his
destabilization, whose humanity he sometimes questions. As he gazes upon
the traveler in one scene, for instance, the narrator wonders, "Was he really
a man, a human entity, a personality like ourselves, or was he merely a sort
of spiritual solvent?"[48]

The Altrurians' distinction between their worlds captures the gulf separating the two men. "If you could imagine an Altruria where the millennium had never yet come, you would have some conception of America."[49]
Altruria, as described by the traveler in ongoing comparisons with America,
is a Christian Socialist society where everyone lives in small, intimate communities, travels to urban centers for entertainment, and makes use of
resources that are uniformly available to all. There is no money, no one
works for anyone else; everyone does his share of labor and shares equally
in the social wealth. Moreover, chance has been entirely eradicated from
economic life. Nor is there hurry, for now that people have stopped competing against one another, there is no need to rush. Recalling William Morris's *News from Nowhere* in critical respects (the professor responds to one of
the Altrurian's descriptions, "He has got *that* out of William Morris"),
Howells's utopia honors craftsmanship and is designed to restore the dig-

nity of labor: mass production is gone, and the work ethic once again prevails.[50] As these examples demonstrate, Howells's utopia betrayed nostalgia for a preindustrial, agrarian social order that he believed characterized the Midwest of his childhood. The Altrurian's message is above all a Christian message; contemporary America is the scene of Christ's suffering upon the cross, so that he might be known in a future world like Altruria.

Howells's serial tapped common sentiments, and he reported that it was more enthusiastically received than anything he had written in years, with letters coming from all over the country and from all kinds of people. Among admirers of the serial was Edward Bellamy, who applauded Howells's stirring critique of contemporary America. The response of the book's publisher, Harper and Brothers, was more tepid, and they refused to publish the second serial, "Letters of an Altrurian Traveller" (serialized in *Cosmopolitan*, 1893–94, partly incorporated into his novel *Through the Eye of the Needle*, 1907), in book form. A review of *A Traveller from Altruria* in the *New York Daily Herald* entitled "Poets Become Socialists Too: Howells Champions Socialism," suggests why.[51] Howells was too politic not to attempt to assuage the concerns of his publishers, who were famously allergic to political controversy. Indeed, during his editorship of *Harper's Monthly* (which continued until his death in 1920), Howells reported himself always prepared to hear "the tinkle of the little bell" signaling a visit from owner J. W. Harper, when his columns expressed opinions that could irk the magazine's conservative readership. The fact that the bell never rang was a sign of how successfully he had internalized its chime.[52]

This was perhaps why Howells, for the final book of his utopian trilogy, *Through the Eye of the Needle* (1907), decided to embrace the term "Romance" in the subtitle, providing as the novel's centerpiece a love affair between the Altrurian and an upper-class American. Eveleth Strange, the young widow of a wealthy man, is beset with an exceptionally active social conscience. Anticipating the women of Gilman's Herland, Eveleth lacks the flirtatiousness typical of the women the Altrurian meets and is also fiercely independent and outspoken. While she has engaged in continuous charity work, she is frustrated by its obvious limitations. Overwhelmed by the social misery she is incapable of ignoring and convinced that nothing other than complete social reorganization will do, she is drawn to the fair-minded utopian traveler. Eveleth's instinctive altruism is the fruit of the maternal relation. Her mother, with whom she lives, is a devout Christian who takes the teachings to heart and compares the American present to the American past with the same intensity expressed by the Altrurian in his social comparisons. Howells struggles to preserve the complexity of this romance between people of two worlds, insisting that however idealistic, Eveleth is a product of her environment, wedded to a world of status and luxury. Part 1 of *Through the Eye of the Needle: A Romance*, set in America and narrated by the Altrurian, ends with his forcing Eveleth to choose between her love and her money, a choice he fears will preclude their marriage. Part 2, set in Altruria and narrated by the blissfully happy bride, dissolves all doubt. The remainder of *Through the Eye of the Needle* is Eveleth's cheerful recounting of life in Altruria, which her mother (whom she has convinced to accompany her) deems just like the America of her childhood. Although some critics noted that the Altruria recalled by the traveler in the recollections of *A Traveller from Altruria* (1894) looked more inviting than its firsthand rendition in *Through the Eye of the Needle* (1907), the novel was respectfully reviewed.

Despite his commitment to social justice and genuine sympathy for socialist agendas, Howells remained temperamentally a moralist, who found the task of reconciling his idealism with the unvoiced constraints imposed by Harper and Brothers relatively congenial. His comments in a 1907 letter reveal that his appraisal of utopia, and of social reorganization in general, was always more ambivalent than his zealous fellow travelers were capable of recognizing. Howells could not help discovering, he noted, "imperfections even in Utopia."[53] This did not make his vision any less courageous or complete. Like that of writers of comparable stature, Howells's utopia reflected his own ongoing interests in the nature of social obligations and the role of sympathy in collective life. By contrast, Jack London's *The Iron Heel* expressed his passion for class politics and became a cult work whose rhetorical fervor inspired subsequent generations of socialists. The charming originality of Baum's *The Wonderful Wizard of Oz* managed to extend spiritual meaning into unfamiliar territory. Charlotte Perkins Gilman's powerful engagement with major social problems and theories in *Herland* grew out of her role as a public intellectual. Finally, the imaginative brilliance of Twain's *A Connecticut Yankee at King Arthur's Court*, which incorporated so much of philosophical, economic, political, and religious significance into its formal structure, demonstrated the unique range of its author.

Perhaps what was most distinctive about all of these writers was what their utopian designs resisted. None of them embraced the racial and ethnic stereotypes or purification schemes that yielded cultural homogeneity in the ideal communities of writers like Peck and Donnelly and so many others. Gilman came closest with her method of parthenogenetic reproduction, but the society of *Herland* was resolutely pluralistic, indeed it celebrated people of color. Howells, London, Gilman, Baum, and Twain seemed to recognize that even in utopia history had to be reckoned with. They grasped implicitly that a utopia in which cultural differences stood in the way of social welfare was utopia in name alone. Though they viewed this fact with varying degrees of trepidation, they understood that America would endure in the future as *the* multicultural nation among the nations of the world.

AFTERWORD

I have argued in this book that America became a multicultural nation between 1865 and 1915 and that this happened in large part because all the engines of modern capitalist development were in place to assist it. Whether observers invoked the term "cultural pluralism" or "melting pot," or predicted according to nativist principles that most "aliens" would eventually die out or go "home," they acknowledged that the debate over cultural variety had become an American ritual. This recognition, I argue further, was the work of print culture: of literary writers, journalists, photographers, social reformers, intellectuals, and advertisers whose productions confirmed how fully integral people from various cultural backgrounds had become to American society.

In making this argument, I have advanced two claims that may seem surprising or counterintuitive. First, I locate the category of multiculturalism in late nineteenth-century America, identifying the origins of the debates ongoing today in that relatively early historical moment. The term "multiculturalism" belongs in this period because it is the first moment of profound and widespread cultural awareness of America's identity as a nation composed of many cultures. However much mixing occurred, however successfully schools and other institutions "Americanized" social strangers, however eagerly the "strangers" themselves sought to embrace mainstream American values, the recognition that diversity was here to stay was irrefutable, in part because it seemed increasingly *to be* the mainstream. This did not occur without lament, strife, and violence, but it assumed an air of inevitability as the forces of capital conspired to integrate indispensable populations of workers, professionals, and intellectuals into its ever-widening circle of consumption and prosperity.

As this last point suggests, my study demonstrates, secondly, that the crucial forces underlying America's development into a multicultural nation were economic—specifically, the forces of full-scale consumer capitalism. To identify this historical period as the moment of the nation's multicultural becoming is not to overlook the remarkable heterogeneity of colonial America, nor is it to ignore previous waves of immigration in American history.[1] To be sure, subsequent periods in American history, the years immediately following World War I for instance, were more notorious for virulent opposition to cultural variation and immigration, which was codified in anti-immigrant legislation.[2] But the period between the Civil War and World War I was distinctive in that an unrivaled expansion of the economy coincided with rising rates of immigration and migration, making economic forms and institutions singularly receptive to these mobile populations. At the same time a developing print culture flourished through its incorporation and representation of this diversity. These methods of incorporation and representation were not always flattering to alien cultures (even when issuing from representatives of alien cultures themselves) nor were they always optimistic about their chances. But these novels and advertisements, photographs and essays, magazines and newspapers initiated a process of coming to terms with social multiplicity that has been underway now for a century and a half.

To identify the years between 1865 and 1915 as the crucial ground of American multiculturalism is to provide a historical perspective and understanding that is often missing from our contemporary debates about race, ethnicity, and immigration. It is to recuperate a legacy with the potential both to invigorate current battle lines and highlight points of reconciliation. And it is to avail ourselves of a past that, however remote or strange, remains vibrantly as well as peculiarly American.

NOTES

Introduction

1 *Mark Twain: Collected Tales, Sketches, Speeches and Essays, 1891–1910* (New York: Library of America, 1992), 362. The essay was published in *Harper's Monthly*, one of the era's most prominent magazines.

2 Twain's essay predated by only a few years Max Weber's famous study, *The Protestant Ethic and the Spirit of Capitalism* (1905), which used a familiar American, Benjamin Franklin, to stand for the capitalist prototype. Weber's book, published in German, was not translated into English until 1930, but it was widely read in America. Werner Sombart's *The Jews and Modern Capitalism* (1911) was translated into English in 1913.

3 W. E. B. Du Bois, *The Negro in Business* (Atlanta University Publications, 1899; reprint, New York: Arno, 1968), 15; see also 7–39, which show how the refusal of whites to bury black people provided blacks with a business exclusive. Du Bois also notes that the taboo was not always observed in reverse: some whites engaged black undertakers, thus enabling the further enrichment of blacks in this industry. His points are echoed by sociologists St. Clair Drake and Horace Cayton in their 1945 study, *Black Metropolis: A Study of Negro Life in a Northern City* (New York: Harcourt, Brace), 456–67, and also by Douglas S. Massey and Nancy A. Denton in their 1993 study, *American Apartheid: Segregation and the Making of the Underclass* (Cambridge, Mass.: Harvard University Press), esp. 40.

4 Michael Schudson, *Advertising, the Uneasy Persuasion: Its Dubious Impact on American Society* (New York: Basic Books, 1984), 232. Capitalism involves private property, entrepreneurial opportunity, technological innovation, respect for contracts, widespread use of money, and the availability of credit. Above all, capitalism is future-oriented—an economic drama of aspiration and struggle.

As Joseph Schumpeter pointed out, "Stabilized capitalism is a contradiction in terms." See Thomas K. McCraw, ed., *Creating Modern Capitalism: How Entrepreneurs, Companies, and Countries Triumphed in Three Industrial Revolutions* (Cambridge, Mass.: Harvard University Press, 1999), 2–7.

5 The two ads are analyzed in chapters 5 and 7, respectively.

6 McCraw, *Creating Modern Capitalism*, 306–7. McCraw points out that by the start of the twentieth century, "most Americans were either nonwhite, immigrants, or the children of at least one immigrant parent." The "notable exception" in terms of other countries with comparable rates of immigration was "the multicultural makeup of the business community in London. But even so, only 6 percent of London's total population in 1890 had come from outside the British Isles. By contrast, 80 percent of New York's citizens were immigrants or the children of immigrants, 87 percent of Chicago's, and 84 percent of Detroit's and Milwaukee's. By 1900 there were more people of Italian descent in New York than in any Italian city except Rome, and probably more Jews than in any other city anywhere" (307).

7 There were additional distinctive features: North America's extraordinarily rich natural resources, the deliberate diversification of the national economy away from agriculture and toward manufacturing, mining, and services, and a government unusually supportive of entrepreneurial risk-taking.

8 See John Higham, *Strangers in the Land: Patterns of American Nativism, 1860–1925* (New York: Athenaeum, 1966); Alan Trachtenberg, *The Incorporation of America: Culture and Society in the Gilded Age* (New York: Hill and Wang, 1982); and McCraw, *Creating Modern Capitalism*.

9 See Werner Sollors, ed., *Multilingual America: Transnationalism, Ethnicity, and the Languages of American Literature* (New York: New York University Press, 1998).

10 James's letter is reproduced in *Henry James: A Life in Letters*, ed. Philip Horne (New York: Penguin, 1999), 162; see also 177, 228.

11 In making this claim, I draw on Talal Asad's suggestion that "political supremacy . . . works effectively through institutionalized differences." "Neither the invention of an expressive culture," Asad goes on to point out, "nor the making of hybrid cultural forms . . . holds any anxieties for defenders of the status quo. On the contrary, such developments are comfortably accommodated by urban consumer capitalism." Talal Asad, *Genealogies of Religion: Discipline and Reasons of Power in Christianity and Islam* (Baltimore: Johns Hopkins University Press, 1993), 263–64. While Asad's powerful polemic focuses on "multiculturalism" in late twentieth-century Britain, his theoretical assertions are, I believe, relevant to the specific period and culture, and the debates surrounding it, with which I am concerned.

12 However, according to some historians, America's veritable multiculturalism extends at least as far back as the eighteenth century. For an argument along these lines, see Alan Taylor, *American Colonies: Penguin History of the United States* (New York: Penguin, 2001). And see also Allan Nevins and Henry Steele

Commager, *A Pocket History of the United States* (New York: Pocket, 1974); and Higham, *Strangers in the Land*.

13 Moreover, I seek to highlight the long prehistory that can precede the coinage of a term for any given phenomenon; "capitalism", for instance, did not come into widespread use until the 1850s, though British capitalism itself predated the term by at least half a century.

14 Werner Sollors recounts how the period from 1910 to 1950 provided the United States with a new vocabulary that was needed for "the multiethnic re-imagining of the country." His point is that it was not until after World War II and the Holocaust that modern democratic societies began to define themselves "against the fascist trajectory from racist stereotype to genocide." American multiculturalism developed accordingly, and he notes as an early use of the term "multicultural" an obscure novel by Edward F. Haskell, *Lance: A Novel about Multicultural Men* (1941). See Sollors's analysis of this genealogy in "Ethnic Modernism, 1910–1950," *American Literary History* 15 (Spring 2003): 74–75. See also his valuable account of debates on pluralism and multiculturalism, "The Multicultural Debate as Cultural Context," in *Beyond Pluralism: The Conception of Groups and Group Identities in America*, ed. Wendy F. Katkin, Ned Landsman, and Andrea Tyree (Urbana: University of Illinois Press, 1998), 63–104.

15 The complicated issue of American immigrant racial hierarchies, which has been written about extensively, is of obvious importance here. Immigrants from western Europe assimilated more readily than those from southern and eastern Europe. But it is important to emphasize how extreme anti-Irish sentiments were in this period and to recognize that all immigrants faced some discrimination. For two perspectives on this, see Matthew Frye Jacobson, *Whiteness of a Different Color: European Immigrants and the Alchemy of Race* (Cambridge, Mass.: Harvard University Press, 1998); and Stanley Lieberson, *A Piece of the Pie: Blacks and White Immigrants since 1880* (Berkeley: University of California Press, 1980).

16 For a book that draws direct parallels between the Haymarket trial and the Sacco and Vanzetti trial, see Vito Marcantonio, *Labor's Martyrs: Haymarket 1887, Sacco and Vanzetti 1927* (New York: Workers Library Press, 1937). Consider also the notorious 1895 Maria Barbella case, only recently discovered, in which a southern Italian woman was tried and nearly executed for murdering a lover who wouldn't marry her. According to Thomas Ferraro, "Maria Barbella threatened the American public because she was the bearer of an alternative culture with different traditions of conflict resolution, self-assertion, and guilt attribution (part fact, part legend), which were put to risky use across the Atlantic and almost earned her a truly barbaric American death. The tribulations of Maria Barbella in the United States occurred only because of *changed* circumstances . . . a sensationalist media fanning the flames of an already-prejudicial courtroom, a legal system focused on the genderless appraisal of utterly gendered circumstances and behavior, a death sentence designed to be

a lesson to the hot-blooded multitudes." *Feeling Italian: The Art of Ethnicity in America* (New York: New York University Press, 2005), 27. Ferraro's inspired and inspiring study covers some of the Italian American cultural history that falls outside of my purview here.

17 Simon Patten, *The Theory of Social Forces* (Philadelphia: American Academy of Political and Social Science, 1895), 143.

18 One observer declared a general "mania for magazine starting." Quoted in Frank Luther Mott, *A History of American Magazines, 1865–1885* (Cambridge, Mass.: Harvard University Press, Belknap Press, 1957), 5. According to Mott, between 1865 and 1885, the number of officially registered periodicals rose from about 700 to 3,300 (5–6). Speaking of the period between 1885 and 1905, Mott notes, "of all the agencies of popular information, none experienced a more spectacular enlargement and increase in effectiveness than the magazines. . . . But when the price of excellent, well-illustrated, general magazines was broken to fifteen and even ten cents, conditions changed radically. Editors locked up their ivory towers and came down into the market place." *A History of American Magazines, 1885–1905* (Cambridge, Mass.: Harvard University Press, Belknap Press, 1957), 2.

19 W. E. B. Du Bois, *The Souls of Black Folk*, in *Three Negro Classics*, ed. John Hope Franklin (New York: Avon, 1965), 238.

20 Ibid., 284.

21 For more on this aspect of Du Bois's thought, see Eric Sundquist's *To Wake the Nations: Race in the Making of American Literature* (Cambridge, Mass.: Harvard University Press, Belknap Press, 1993); and my own book, *The Science of Sacrifice: American Literature and Modern Social Theory* (Princeton, N.J.: Princeton University Press, 1998).

22 This was affirmed years later when the New Deal welfare programs of Franklin Delano Roosevelt were made politically feasible by their systematic exclusion of blacks. For this argument see Ira Katznelson's study, *When Affirmative Action Was White: An Untold History of Racial Inequality in Twentieth-Century America* (New York: Norton, 2005); and Jill Quadagno, *The Color of Welfare: How Racism Undermined the War on Poverty* (New York: Oxford University Press, 1994). Much has been written in recent years on the fate of European and Scandinavian welfare states as these countries become increasingly multicultural and the people benefiting from their social services are increasingly immigrants or children of immigrants. For a brief analysis along these lines, see Christopher Caldwell, "Islam on the Outskirts of the Welfare State," *New York Times Magazine*, February 5, 2006, 55–59. Noting the notorious contradictions of capitalism, Caldwell concludes that the welfare state "has its cultural contradictions too. It rests on consensus, which is another way of saying a lack of cultural variety. The stronger the consensus, the more room a welfare state has to grow. But as consensus strengthens, so does a certain naiveté, a belief

that your own idiosyncratic habits are something that no one else could fail to find irresistibly seductive" (59).

Chapter 1

1 Quoted in Brooks D. Simpson, *America's Civil War* (Wheeling, Ill.: Harlan Davidson, 1996), 135. For more on the Civil War book industry, see Alice Fahs, *The Imagined Civil War: Popular Literature of the North and South, 1861–1865* (Chapel Hill: University of North Carolina Press, 2001); Lyde Cullen Sizer, *The Political Work of Northern Women Writers and the Civil War, 1850–1872* (Chapel Hill: University of North Carolina Press, 2000); and Elizabeth Young, *Disarming the Nation: Women's Writing and the American Civil War* (Chicago: University of Chicago Press, 1999).

2 Tony Horwitz, *Confederates in the Attic: Dispatches from the Unfinished Civil War* (New York: Vintage, 1998).

3 On these developments, see, among others, Alfred Chandler, *The Visible Hand: The Managerial Revolution in American Business* (Cambridge, Mass.: Harvard University Press, 1977); David F. Noble, *America by Design: Science, Technology, and the Rise of Corporate Capitalism* (New York: Knopf, 1977); David Hounshell, *From the American System to Mass Production, 1800–1932: The Development of Manufacturing Technology in the United States* (Baltimore: Johns Hopkins University Press, 1984); Glenn Porter, *The Rise of Big Business, 1860–1920* (Arlington Heights, Ill.: Harlan Davidson, 1992); Thomas K. McCraw, *Creating Modern Capitalism: How Entrepreneurs, Companies, and Countries Triumphed in Three Industrial Revolutions* (Cambridge, Mass.: Harvard University Press, 1999).

4 Douglass and Grant quoted in Simpson, *America's Civil War*, 70, 127.

5 This is not to deny the ambitious effort on the part of northern cultural elites in the post–Civil war period to forge a national *culture* on par with a national economy and government. For an elaboration of this effort and the role of women writers in it, see Nomi Z. Sofer, *Making the America of Art: Cultural Nationalism and Nineteenth-Century Women Writers* (Columbus: Ohio State University Press, 2005), esp. chapter 5. I focus here on the ambivalence that many writers, elite and subordinate, displayed toward this project. Sofer notes, "As members of the educated cultural elite who believed in the necessity of producing a uniquely American culture, and well-respected writers whose work had broad popular appeal, Phelps, Alcott, and Woolson were insiders, uniquely suited to both produce the nation's high culture and advocate for its importance; as women, who had not fought in the Civil War, who did not enjoy the same educational opportunities as their male peers, and whose access to the highest circles of cultural authority was limited, they were outsiders, whose commitment to the cultural nationalism project was tempered by their understanding of the masculine bias and elitism at its core" (179).

6　Henry James, *Hawthorne: A Critical Essay on the Man and His Times* (1879; reprint, New York: Collier, 1966), 124–25.

7　See Alan Trachtenberg, *Reading American Photographs: Images as History, Matthew Brady to Walker Evans* (New York: Hill and Wang, 1989). Throughout this section on photography, and especially in the reading of Gardner's "The Burial Party," I am indebted to Trachtenberg's book as well as to Mark D. Katz, *Witness to an Era: The Life and Photographs of Alexander Gardner, the Civil War, Lincoln, and the West* (New York: Viking Studio Books, 1991).

8　Review of "Incidents of the War," *New York Times*, July 21, 1862.

9　These ideas are discussed at length in chapter 2. For a recent play that takes a retrospective look at these connections, see Suzan-Lori Parks, "The America Play," in *The America Play and Other Works* (New York: Theatre Communications Group, 1995). And see my essay, "Neighbors, Strangers, Corpses: Death and Sympathy in the Early Writings of W. E. B. Du Bois," in *Centuries Ends, Narrative Means*, ed. Robert Newman (Palo Alto: Stanford University Press, 1995), 191–211.

10　Stephen Crane, *The Red Badge of Courage and Other Stories* (New York: Penguin Classics, 1991), 175–76.

11　Ibid., 141.

12　Judge Thomas Mellon quoted by Matthew Josephson, in *The Robber Barons: The Great American Capitalists, 1861–1901* (New York: Harcourt, Brace, 1934), 50. On the demographic composition of Civil War troops and the practice of hiring substitutes, which was one cause of the New York Draft Riots in 1863, see Eugene C. Murdock, *One Million Men: The Civil War Draft in the North* (Westport, Conn.: Greenwood, 1980); W. J. Rorabaugh, "Who Fought for the North in the Civil War?: Concord, Massachusetts, Enlistments," *Journal of American History* 73, no. 1 (December 1986): 695–701; Reid Mitchell, *Civil War Soldiers: Their Expectations and Their Experiences* (New York: Viking, 1988); Philip Shaw Paludan, *"A People's Contest": The Union and Civil War, 1861–1865* (New York: Harper and Row, 1988); James I. Robertson Jr., *Soldiers Blue and Gray* (Columbia: University of South Carolina Press, 1988); and Maris A. Vinovskis, "Have Social Historians Lost the Civil War?: Some Preliminary Demographic Speculations," *Journal of American History* 76 (June 1989): 34–58.

13　Crane, *Red Badge of Courage*, 110, 116, 114.

14　For more on the role of ritual sacrifice in Anglo-American culture during this time, see my *Science of Sacrifice: American Literature and Modern Social Theory* (Princeton, N.J.: Princeton University Press, 1998).

15　Roland Barthes, "Myth Today," in *A Barthes Reader*, ed. Susan Sontag (New York: Hill and Wang, 1982), 130–31.

16　Crane, *Red Badge of Courage*, 84–85, 88.

17　See Elaine Scarry, *The Body in Pain: The Making and Unmaking of the World* (New York: Oxford University Press, 1984), 83 and chapter 2 as a whole.

18　On the contemporary context of *Red Badge of Courage*, see Terry Mulcaire,

"Progressive Visions of War in *The Red Badge of Courage* and *Principles of Scientific Management*," *American Quarterly* 43 (1991): 46–72. Mulcaire discusses at length Frederick Winslow Taylor's 1911 book, *The Principles of Scientific Management*, in terms of *The Red Badge of Courage*.

19 In other works both Phelps and Alcott explored these alternative terrains. Alcott's short story "My Contraband," for instance, published in the *Atlantic Monthly* in 1863 and set in a Civil War hospital, concerns the tension between two brothers, a wounded Confederate soldier and his mulatto half brother, and a former slave, whom the story's protagonist, a nurse, deeply desires. While more restrained in confronting race, Phelps fictionalizes the war more directly in her 1877 novel, *The Story of Avis*, which explores the life of a woman painter.

20 Anna E. Dickinson, *What Answer* (1868; reprint, Freeport, N.Y.: Books for Libraries, 1972), 238.

21 The death of a young beau in the Civil War probably assisted her decision to remain unmarried as long as she did.

22 Nina Baym quotes Phelps's autobiography in her introduction to *Three Spiritualist Novels*, by Elizabeth Stuart Phelps (Urbana: University of Illinois Press, 2000), xvi.

23 It is worth emphasizing, however, that some in the contemporary religious establishment missed her reformist effort. Frank Luther Mott quotes from a February 28, 1874, review in *Publishers' Weekly*: "Heresy was her crime, and atrocity her name. She had outraged the church; she had blasphemed its sanctities." *A History of American Magazines, 1865–1885* (Cambridge, Mass.: Harvard University Press, Belknap Press, 1957), 247.

24 Gail Smith makes this point and cites reviews in "From the Seminary to the Parlor: The Popularization of Hermeneutics in *The Gates Ajar*," *Arizona Quarterly* 54 (1998): 99–133.

25 Phelps, *The Gates Ajar*, in *Three Spiritualist Novels*, 133.

26 Ibid., 127.

27 See William Mumler, *The Personal Experiences of William H. Mumler in Spirit-Photography, Written by Himself* (Boston: Colby and Rich, 1875), and "Occultism and Photography," in *The Oxford Companion to the Photograph*, ed. Robin Lenman (New York: Oxford University Press, 2005), 455.

28 Burroughs and Whitman quoted in David W. Blight, *Race and Reunion: The Civil War in American Memory* (Cambridge, Mass.: Harvard University Press, 2001), 23, 18. My study largely complements Blight's persuasive account of these postwar years.

29 Alcott's biographer, Madeleine B. Stern, remarks of Alcott's enlistment as a nurse, "The time had come for Father [Bronson Alcott] to send his only son to war." *Louisa May Alcott: From Blood and Thunder to Hearth and Home* (Boston: Northeastern University Press, 1998), 112.

30 Louisa May Alcott, *Hospital Sketches*, in *Alternative Alcott*, ed. Elaine Showalter (New Brunswick, N.J.: Rutgers University Press, 1988), 58.

31 Ibid., 65.

32 Quoted by Madelon Bedell in the introduction to *Little Women*, by Louisa May Alcott (New York: Modern Library, 1983), ix–x.

33 Ibid., 108.

34 Ibid., 535.

35 Ibid., 597.

36 Ulysses S. Grant, *Personal Memoirs of U.S. Grant, Selected Letters, 1839–1865* (New York: Library of America, 1990), 779. The notes and chronology by Mary Drake McFeely and William S. McFeely provide a valuable guide to the book's publishing history.

37 Ibid., 773, 774.

38 *Nation* 24, no. 128 (March 1, 1877). Quoted in Mott, *History of American Magazines, 1865–1885*, 286.

39 This is the judgment of Grant's biographer, Brooks D. Simpson, in *America's Civil War*, 214. See also Simpson's *Let Us Have Peace: Ulysses S. Grant and the Politics of War and Reconstruction, 1861–1868* (Chapel Hill: University of North Carolina Press, 1991).

40 Maria Amparo Ruiz de Burton, *Who Would Have Thought It?*, ed. and introd. Rosaura Sanchez and Beatrice Pita, Recovering the U.S. Hispanic Literary Heritage Project (Houston, Tex.: Arte Publico, 1995), 287.

41 This phrase comes from the classic theory on this subject elaborated by Adrienne Rich in the essay "Compulsory Heterosexuality and Lesbian Existence," *Signs* 5, no. 4 (Summer 1980): 631–60.

42 Henry James, *The Bostonians* (New York: Penguin, 1978), 56, 108.

43 Ibid., 55.

44 Ibid., 31.

45 Ibid., 163, 318.

46 Ibid., 129.

47 Ibid., 389.

48 Henry James, "Alphonse Daudet," in *Henry James: Literary Criticism, Volume 2: French Writers, Other European Writers, Prefaces to the New York Edition* (New York: Library of America, 1984), 223.

49 Grant, *Personal Memoirs*, 778–79.

50 Quoted in Mott, *History of American Magazines, 1865–1885*, 157–58.

51 These included Mark Twain, Charles Dudley Warner, Helen Hunt Jackson, Henry James, William Dean Howells, and Constance Woolson, among others.

52 Quoted by Lyndall Gordon in her superb biography, *A Private Life of Henry James: Two Women and His Art* (New York: Norton, 1998), 257.

53 Ibid., 164.

54 Grant, *Personal Memoirs*, 149.

55 Ellen Glasgow, *The Battle-Ground* (New York: Doubleday, Page, 1902), 323.

56 For a fine account of Dunbar's literary career that features his work in the

theater, see Nancy Bentley, *Literary Forms and Mass Culture, 1870–1920* (Philadelphia: University of Pennsylvania Press, forthcoming)

57 William Dean Howells, introduction to *Lyrics of Lowly Life*, in *The Complete Poems of Paul Laurence Dunbar* (New York: Dodd, Mead, 1913), viii.

58 Philip Fisher, *Hard Facts: Setting and Form in the American Novel* (New York: Oxford University Press, 1985), 87.

Chapter 2

1 Excerpts from Jacobs's book were published anonymously as "Letter from a Fugitive Slave," in the *New York Tribune*, 1853.

2 This term is from Orlando Patterson's classic comparative analysis of slavery, *Slavery and Social Death: A Comparative Study* (Cambridge, Mass.: Harvard University Press, 1982). I understand Jacobs's book as a striking confirmation of Patterson's theories.

3 The extremity of Jacobs's book inspired early readers to doubt its authenticity; but this is to misunderstand its main claim. Gothic excess, according to Jacobs, is the only means to a realist account of slavery. Historically speaking, American slavery is the gothic made real. This claim finds support in the Works Projects Administration interviews with surviving slaves in the 1930s. John Blassingame's skeptical response to Jacobs's narrative is cited in Harriet Jacobs, *Incidents in the Life of a Slave Girl: Written by Herself*, ed. Jean Fagan Yellin (1861; reprint, Cambridge, Mass.: Harvard University Press, 1987), 256. Orlando Patterson cites interviews with ex-slaves in the 1930s in *Slavery and Social Death*, 365.

4 W. E. B. Du Bois, "The Economics of Negro Emancipation in the United States," *Sociological Review* 4 (1911): 310–11.

5 Douglass's 1862 comments are quoted by Eric Sundquist in *To Wake the Nations: Race in the Making of American Literature* (Cambridge, Mass.: Harvard University Press, Belknap Press, 1993), 242.

6 Indeed, *The Negro in Business* (1899), the third volume of the monumental multivolume analysis of black life in America, the Atlanta University Studies, was the first under the direct editorship of Du Bois, who went on to edit all subsequent volumes.

7 Larry Tye, *Rising from the Rails: Pullman Porters and the Making of the Black Middle Class* (New York: Henry Holt, 2004), 3, 2.

8 "Competitive" is the term used to characterize this postemancipation period by George Fredrickson, *The Black Image in the White Mind: The Debate on Afro-American Character and Destiny, 1817–1914* (Middletown, Conn:: Wesleyan University Press, 1971), 255.

9 These ideas are elaborated at length in chapter 4 of my *Science of Sacrifice: American Literature and Modern Social Theory* (Princeton, N.J.: Princeton University Press, 1998), 269–366.

10 For two superb studies of the institutionalization of racism in turn-of-the-century America, see Douglas S. Massey and Nancy A. Denton, *American Apartheid: Segregation and the Making of the Underclass* (Cambridge, Mass.: Harvard University Press, 1993); and Stanley Lieberson, *A Piece of the Pie: Blacks and White Immigrants since 1880* (Berkeley: University of California Press, 1980).

11 W. E. B. Du Bois quoted in "Discussion of the Paper by Alfred Holt Stone, 'Is Race Friction between Blacks and Whites in the United States Growing and Inevitable?,' " *American Journal of Sociology* 13 (May 1908): 835.

12 It is no accident that both Stetson and Bruce were published by major eastern publishers, George Ellis in Boston and Putnam's in New York, respectively.

13 George Stetson, *The Southern Negro as He Is* (Boston: George Ellis, 1877), 20; and Charles Ellwood, review of *The Color Line*, by William Benjamin Smith, *American Journal of Sociology* 11 (January 1906): 574.

14 See, for instance, Alfred Hart Bushnell's admiring review of Cutler's *Lynch Law* in *American Historical Review* 11 (January 1906): 425–28.

15 "Discussion of the Paper," 822.

16 Ibid., 824.

17 Ibid., 837, 838. The southerner quoted in Walter White, *Rope and Faggot* (1929; reprint, New York: Arno Press, 1969), 27.

18 Albion Winegar Tourgée quoted in a May 18, 1897, interview in the *Jamestown (N.Y.) Journal*, cited by Otto H. Olsen, *Carpetbagger's Crusade: The Life of Albion Winegar Tourgée* (Baltimore: Johns Hopkins University Press, 1965), 57.

19 Tourgée's wife, Emma, quoted in Olsen, *Carpetbagger's Crusade*, 351; NAACP memorial described, 352.

20 Ibid., 260.

21 Harriet Beecher Stowe, *A Key to Uncle Tom's Cabin: Presenting the Original Facts and Documents upon Which the Story Is Founded, together with Corroborative Statements Verifying the Truth of the Work* (Boston: Jewett, 1853).

22 Albion Tourgée, "The South as a Field for Fiction," *Forum*, no. 6 (December 1888): 404–13.

23 See Olsen, *Carpetbagger's Crusade*, 327, on the railroads' preference for integrated seating; and 330, for Supreme Court opinions.

24 Tourgée's brief quoted in Sundquist, *To Wake the Nations*, 247, which is followed by extensive analysis of this highly contradictory sticking point.

25 Otto Olsen refers to Wells-Barnett's notation on the copy of the booklet in the Tourgée Papers, in *Carpetbagger's Crusade*, 320.

26 Ibid., 350.

27 Ida Wells-Barnett, "How Enfranchisement Stops Lynching," *Original Rights Magazine* (1910).

28 Quoted in Eric Sundquist's introduction to *The Marrow of Tradition* (1901), by Charles Chesnutt (New York: Penguin, 1993), xii.

29 Ibid., x.

30 Du Bois, in "Economics of Negro Emancipation," suggests that capitalism is

the cause and racial oppression the outcome. Jim Crow and lynch laws conceal deeper designs: "Under the flame of this outward noise went the more subtle and dangerous work"—the systematic subordination of black labor. The extent of northern investments in the South both confirmed and ensured their complicity with southern outrages. Add to this the profound fatalism "toward the possibility of real advance on the part of the darker nations." The economic complexity of America's race problem, Du Bois concludes, "is but a local phase" of a vaster dilemma. "How far is the world composed of an aristocracy of races, unalterable and unmovable, by which certain people have a right to vote and exploit all others" (311–13).

31 W. E. B. Du Bois, *The Souls of Black Folk*, in *Three Negro Classics* (New York: Avon, 1985), 322.

32 Ibid., 350.

33 Quoted in *Health and Physique of the Negro American*, ed. W. E. B. Du Bois (Atlanta: Atlanta University Press, 1906), 16.

34 Kenneth Burke, *The Philosophy of Literary Form* (Berkeley: University of California Press, 1973), 1.

35 For a broad exploration of this cultural phenomenon, see my *Power of Historical Knowledge: Narrating the Past in Hawthorne, James, and Dreiser* (Princeton, N.J.: Princeton University Press, 1988). See also Leonard Green, Jonathan Culler, and Richard Klein, "Interview with Frederic Jameson," *Diacritics* (Fall 1982): 72; and Hayden White, "Getting Out of History," *Diacritics* (Fall 1982): 2–13.

36 Mark Twain, *The Adventures of Huckleberry Finn* (New York: Penguin Classics, 1986), 7.

37 Toni Morrison, *Beloved* (New York: New American Library, 1987), 89.

38 Twain, *Adventures of Huckleberry Finn*, 154–55.

39 On the basis of his own hairy arms and chest, Jim prophesies his likely wealth. His first speculations in stock involve "live stock," which "up 'n' died" and put him off further investments of this particular kind. The small amount that he recovers from this foiled venture (from his scrappy sale of the tallow and hide) is put in a bank run by another slave (which is subsequently robbed, in an allusion to the Freedmen's Bureau Bank scandal) and a remaining portion goes to a slave named Balum, who donates it to charity, because the return sounds promising ("whoever give to de po' len' to de Lord, en boun' to git his money back a hund'd times"). Ibid., 19, 50–52.

40 Ibid., 52.

41 Ibid., 320.

42 Ibid., 30–31, 321. This is true of criticism early and late. See, for example, *New Essays on Adventures of Huckleberry Finn*, ed. Louis J. Budd (Cambridge: Cambridge University Press, 1985); and *Adventures of Huckleberry Finn: A Case Study in Critical Controversy*, ed. Gerald Graff and James Phelan (Boston: Bedford, 1985).

43 Richard Ohmann, *Selling Culture: Magazines, Markets, and Class at the Turn of the Century* (London: Verso, 1996), 161–64.

44 In describing the distinctiveness of the African American case relative to other disadvantaged groups, immigrant minorities in particular, David Hollinger highlights the prohibitions on black-white marriage through the mid-twentieth century that "ensured that the color line would long remain to a very large extent a property line. Hence the dynamics of *race* formation and the dynamics of *class* formation were . . . largely the same." Hollinger refers subsequently to "the specific claims of African Americans on the national conscience" given their "multi-century legacy of group-specific enslavement and hypodescent racialization long carried out under constitutional authority in the United States. . . . Black immigrants from the Caribbean and their descendants are more likely than the American-born heirs of the Jim Crow system to advance in education and employment and to marry outside their natal community. So too are black immigrants from Africa, as the public has recently been reminded by the remarkable career of Illinois politician Barack Obama, elected to the U.S. Senate in 2004." *Cosmopolitanism and Solidarity: Studies in Ethnoracial, Religious, and Professional Affiliation in the United States* (Madison: University of Wisconsin Press, 2006), 24–25, 50, 53.

45 As Leon Litwack reports in James Allen et al., *Without Sanctuary: Lynching Photography in America* (Santa Fe, N.M.: Twin Palms, 2000), "Many photographs of lynching and burnings (such as the burning of Sam Hose) would reappear as popular picture post-cards and trade cards to commemorate the event." A Unitarian minister in New York, John H. Holmes found in his mail one day a postcard picturing a lynched black man. The postcard included a note that read, "will put you on our regular mailing list. Expect one a month on the average" (11).

Chapter 3

1 For two historical accounts of American immigration that explore the late nineteenth century with contemporary developments in mind, see Nancy Foner, *From Ellis Island to JFK: New York's Two Great Waves of Immigration* (New Haven: Yale University Press, 2000); and Mae Ngai, *Impossible Subjects: Illegal Aliens and the Making of Modern America* (Princeton, N.J.: Princeton University Press, 2004).

2 Howells and Marx are quoted by Tom Lutz in *Cosmopolitan Vistas: American Regionalism and Literary Value* (Ithaca, N.Y.: Cornell University Press, 2004), 23; see also 49–58, esp. 53, which offers a valuable summary of relevant theories. Lutz cites the common Enlightenment definition of "cosmopolitanism" as the valuation of a world citizenry over and against ethnic or national allegiances but goes on to show how the term has increasingly come to incorporate, in the words of Arnold Krupat, the "recognition and legitimation of heterogeneity" (52). According to David Hollinger, cosmopolitanism, as distinct from univer-

salism, regards the diversity of humankind as fact and opportunity, respecting "the honest difficulties that even the most humane and generous people have in achieving solidarity with persons they perceive as very different from themselves." But it is, in contrast to pluralism, oriented to the individual, assuming that "individuals will be simultaneously affiliated with a number of groups, including civic and religious communities, as well as communities of descent." David Hollinger, *Cosmopolitanism and Solidarity: Studies in Ethnoracial, Religious, and Professional Affiliation in the United States* (Madison: University of Wisconsin Press, 2006), xix. Anthony Appiah highlights two strains of cosmopolitanism: the notion that our obligations to others transcend the limits of "kith and kin" and the valuation of the particular and different practices and beliefs that make other lives significant. According to Appiah, "The one thought that cosmopolitans share is that no local loyalty can ever justify forgetting that each human being has responsibilities to every other." *Cosmopolitanism: Ethics in a World of Strangers* (New York: Norton, 2006), xv–xvi. Finally, consider the outlines of the "new cosmopolitans" defined in *New Cosmopolitanisms: South Asians in the U.S.*, ed. Gita Rajan and Shailja Sharma (Stanford: Stanford University Press, 2006), as "people who blur the edges of home and abroad by continuously moving physically, culturally, and socially, and by selectively using globalized forms of travel, communication, languages, and technology to position themselves in motion between at least two homes, sometimes even through dual forms of citizenship, but always in multiple locations." Rajan and Sharma point out that these new cosmopolitans cross class identifications, to include well-educated, technologically versed elites, working classes, and also an "expendable," usually illegal workforce without access to citizenship that nevertheless manages to inhabit "the hybridized, overdetermined, multicultural, and multiracial spaces of urban America" (2–4). Kirin Desai offers a powerful fictional portrait of this last group in her novel, *The Inheritance of Loss* (New York: Grove, 2006). I want to suggest that the American landscape of the late nineteenth and early twentieth centuries represents an early incarnation of the spaces described by Rajan and Sharma.

3 The phrase is Edmund Wilson's, quoted in Amy Kaplan, *The Social Construction of American Realism* (Chicago: University of Chicago Press, 1988), 78.

4 For more on the novel's portrait of consumption and spectacle, see especially, Wai Chee Dimock, "Debasing Exchange: Edith Wharton's 'House of Mirth,'" *PMLA* (October 1985): 783–91; Kaplan, *Social Construction of American Realism*, 88–103; and Ruth Bernard Yeazell, "The Conspicuous Wasting of Lily Bart," *English Literary History* (Fall 1992): 713–34.

5 See Jean Strouse, *Alice James: A Biography* (Boston: Houghton Mifflin, 1980), still a valuable source of information on the James family as a whole.

6 Quoted in the introduction to Abraham Cahan's *The Rise of David Levinsky*, ed. Jules Chametzky (New York: Penguin, 1995), x.

7 I refer to Nathanael West's 1930 novel of the same name, which might well have been inspired by this spectacle of immigrant grief that was well known to Jewish New Yorkers like West.

8 For more on social scientists' accounts of women's reproduction and its impact on women's roles in this period, see my "Reproducing Women in *The Awkward Age*," *Representations* (Spring 1992), 107–36.

9 The Norton edition of Norris's novel *McTeague* includes the *San Francisco Examiner* articles on the Collins murder as well as details on the popularity of Cesare Lombroso's theories of criminal atavism in turn-of-the-twentieth-century America and Norris's likely knowledge of them. See William Dean Howells, "A Case in Point," in Frank Norris, *McTeague: A Norton Critical Edition* (New York: Norton, 1977), 325–26.

10 Pierre Bourdieu's account of the class differences that govern consumption habits in French society in his classic study *Distinction* (New York: Basic Books, 1985) provides a valuable register for Norris's portrayal of eating habits in *McTeague*. Equally illuminating is Carol Adams's striking study, *The Sexual Politics of Meat: A Feminist-Vegetarian Critical Theory* (New York: Continuum, 1990).

11 Albion Small, quoted in Harry Elmer Barnes, *Introduction to the History of Sociology* (Chicago: University of Chicago Press, 1948), 787.

12 Another acquaintance of Twain's, Charles Dudley Warner, characterized Keller as "the purest-minded human being in existence." *Harper's Magazine*, 1896, quoted in Helen Keller, *The Story of My Life*, ed. Roger Shattuck and Dorothy Hermann (New York: Norton, 2003), 228.

13 This idea was confirmed, for instance, by Charles Darwin's 1872 study, *The Expression of the Emotions in Man and Animals* (reprint, New York: Dover, 2007).

14 Helen Keller, *The Story of My Life: With Her Letters (1887–1901) and a Supplementary Account of Her Education, including Passages from the Reports and Letters of Her Teacher, Anne Mansfield Sullivan, by John Albert Macy* (New York: Grosset and Dunlap, 1905), 72.

15 Ibid., 425.

16 Ibid.,

17 Ralph Barton Perry, quoted in F. O. Matthiessen, *The James Family: A Group Biography* (New York: Vintage, 1980), 210.

18 "Frederic Myers' Services to Psychology," in *A William James Reader*, ed. Gay Wilson Allen (Boston: Houghton Mifflin, 1975), 162.

19 The book began as lectures for the distinguished "Gifford Lectures" series at the University of Edinburgh.

20 William James, *The Varieties of Religious Experience* (New York: Macmillan, 1961), 42.

21 Ibid., 407.

22 John Dewey, quoted in Matthiessen, *James Family*, 587.

23 Ibid., 590.

24 See William James's 1902 letter in Henry James, *The Wings of the Dove: A Norton Critical Edition* (New York: Norton, 1978), 458; and Henry James to Mrs. Cadwalader James, in ibid., 453. Max Beerbohm captured James's predicament in a famous drawing of the master—massive head and tiny body. Artistic authority, according to Beerbohm's James, required domination of the physical.

25 Walter Benjamin, "The Storyteller," in *Illuminations*, ed. Hannah Arendt (New York: Schocken, 1969), 101.

26 Elizabeth Stuart Phelps, *The Gates Between* (Boston: Houghton Mifflin, 1887), 223.

27 Serialized in *Harper's Monthly*, December 1907–January 1908, *Captain Stormfield* was one of the earliest books Twain wrote (a manuscript exists from the early 1870s) and the last book he published (it was issued as a Christmas gift book by Harper and Brothers, six months before Twain's death, in 1909). Twain supposedly waited to publish the book until the death of his wife, Olivia (a great fan of the Phelps series), but it's also likely that he was never entirely satisfied that it was done.

28 Mark Twain, *Extract from Captain Stormfield's Visit to Heaven* (reprint, New York: Oxford University Press, 1996), 33–34.

29 *Christian Science* was excerpted in *Cosmopolitan Magazine*, October 1899, and the *North American Review*, December 1902, prior to its publication as a book.

30 Mark Twain, *Christian Science* (reprint, New York: Oxford University Press, 1996), 284.

31 Ibid., 201.

32 Willa Cather and Georgine Milmine, *The Life of Mary Baker G. Eddy* (Lincoln: University of Nebraska Press, 1993), 45.

33 Ibid., 191.

34 Ibid., 192.

35 Ibid., 194.

36 Ibid., 209.

37 Ibid., 370.

38 Twain, *Christian Science*, 68, xxxii.

Chapter 4

1 I draw these quotations from Peter Nabokov, ed., *Native American Testimony: A Chronicle of Indian-White Relations from Prophecy to the Present, 1492–2000* (New York: Penguin, 1999), xvii, 233, 256–57.

2 Ibid., 256–57.

3 Arthur C. Parker, commenting at the society's third annual meeting in Denver, Colorado, quoted in ibid., 276. Parker edited an "Executive Council Report" on the proceedings (ibid., 487) and also wrote about them, in "The League of Peace," *Southern Workman*, October 1911. This journal was published at the Hampton Institute, and Parker, along with such prominent figures as James

Weldon Johnson, Rabbi Stephen Wise, and W. E. B. Du Bois, was a regular contributor.

4 My analysis here is consistent with Alan Trachtenberg's account in *Shades of Hiawatha: Staging Indians, Making Americans, 1880–1930* (New York: Hill and Wang, 2004) of the double role played by Indians in this period, as the ultimate authentic Americans, possessed of heroic bloodlines and a link to the dwindling frontier, as well as an idealism that opposed the most pernicious effects of capitalist expansion, and at the same time, as a natural impediment (among others, such as mountains, trees, etc.) to national expansion and industrial development.

5 Arthur C. Parker, *The Life of General Ely S. Parker* (Buffalo, N.Y.: Buffalo Historical Society, 1919), 52.

6 This is confirmed in personal narratives such as Sara Winnemucca Hopkins's *Life among the Piutes: Their Wrongs and Claims*, ed. and introd. Mrs. Horace Mann (Boston: G. P. Putnam's Sons, 1883); and Carl Sweezy's *The Arapaho Way: A Memoir of an Indian Boyhood* (New York: C. N. Potter, 1966).

7 Parker worked in the law office of Angel and Rice in Ellicotville, Cattaraugus County. During his three years as a clerk, he read law, drew up forms, prepared arguments, and attended court proceedings, which would have earned him admission to the bar had he been an American citizen. Parker, *Life of General Parker*, 79.

8 Parker took "a short elementary course" at the Rensselaer Polytechnic Institute in Troy, New York, and then went to work on improvements to the Erie Canal. One of Grant's soldiers, J. T. Lockwood of White Plains, New York, reported that an officer on Grant's staff, "whom we always called 'the Indian,' . . . did much of the engineering work. . . . We always supposed 'the Indian' was one of Grant's chief engineers" (ibid., 113–14).

9 Frank H. Severance, preface to *Life of General Parker*, xi. All subsequent references to this work will be included parenthetically in the text.

10 For a brilliant anthropological analysis of how Christianity, as the ultimate synthetic religion, always exists uneasily beside the indigenous beliefs it seeks to displace, see Eytan Bercovitch, "The Altar of Sin: Social Multiplicity and Christian Conversion among a New Guinea People," in *Religion and Cultural Studies*, ed. Susan L. Mizruchi (Princeton, N.J.: Princeton University Press, 2001), 211–35.

11 Parker remained throughout his life a reader, as apt to quote, in letters and speeches, from philosophy, law, and the classics, as from Harriet Beecher Stowe's *Uncle Tom's Cabin*.

12 Details of the council meeting were reported in the *Buffalo Courier*. Parker, *Life of General Parker*, 236–37.

13 Arthur C. Parker adds that "the Parker home was in a measure the spot where a new American science was born." *Life of General Parker*, 89. My account of Morgan and Parker is also indebted to Gillian Feeley-Harnik, " 'The Mystery of

Life in All Its Forms': Religious Dimensions of Culture in Early American Anthropology," in Mizruchi, *Religion and Cultural Studies*, 140–91. See also by Feeley-Harnik, " 'Communities of Blood': The Natural History of Kinship in Nineteenth-Century America," *Comparative Studies in Society and History* 41 (1999): 215–68.

14 Quoted in Elisabeth Tooker's indispensable study, *Lewis H. Morgan on Iroquois Material Culture* (Tucson: University of Arizona Press, 1994), 45.

15 See ibid., esp. 9–15, on Morgan's understanding of material culture.

16 Parker would have had meals with Lincoln during the winter of 1864–65 when the president visited Grant's regiment frequently and dined with the general and his officers. Parker, *Life of General Parker*, 119–20.

17 General Horace Porter, *Campaigning with Grant*, quoted in Parker, *Life of General Parker*, 115.

18 This observation was General Porter's, quoted in ibid., 133.

19 Parker's role in these procedures is confirmed by documents reproduced in Parker, *Life of General Parker*, 130–41.

20 I draw on Feeley-Harnik, "Mystery of Life," 155, for this interpretation of how Morgan saw the Iroquois.

21 Feeley-Harnik reproduces "a graphic image of the vacant wilderness that most New Yorkers saw themselves entering" from *A Gazeteer of the State of New York* (1843). "Mystery of Life," 153.

22 Quoted from *League of the Ho-dé-no-sau-nee, or Iroquois*, by Morgan and Parker, in Trachtenberg, *Shades of Hiawatha*, 18.

23 Trachtenberg discusses this aspect of Morgan's arguments and their attractiveness to Friedrich Engels, in his brief treatment of Morgan in *Shades of Hiawatha*, 18–19.

24 Parker, *Life of General Parker*, 176. This comment from Parker's correspondence with Mrs. Harriet Maxwell Converse, from the late 1880s, is filled with criticism of Christianity and Christians, which Parker never quite separates.

25 According to Thomas R. Trautmann, Marx took copious notes on Morgan's book during the winter of 1880–81, and for Engels, it was "a kind of scientific Rousseau." But Morgan "would have been alarmed at this appropriation of his ideas for socialist ends," and his attraction for Marx lay partly in his status as a solid "yankee Republican." *Lewis Henry Morgan and the Invention of Kinship* (Berkeley: University of California Press, 1987), 251–55.

26 The most elaborate theoretical account of this contribution to anthropology is Meyer Fortes, *Kinship and the Social Order: The Legacy of Lewis Henry Morgan* (New Brunswick, N.J.: Transaction, 2006, originally published in 1969). Fortes argues that Morgan's discoveries and methods of analysis provide the basis for structural theory in social anthropology, and furthermore, that "the distinction Morgan drew in exact and rigorous terms between classificatory and descriptive systems of terminology was and remains the linchpin of his and of subsequent kinship theory" (18–19).

27 Trautmann, *Morgan and the Invention of Kinship*, 3.

28 Morgan's reflections on his first serious explorations of Indian culture are quoted in ibid., 41.

29 In his chapter on Morgan, Arthur C. Parker quotes a friend of Morgan's who notes that Parker "was an invaluable find for Morgan." *Life of General Parker*, 80.

30 Ibid., 75.

31 Feeley-Harnik makes this point in "Mystery of Life," 157–58.

32 This is among the most important claims in ibid., 154.

33 This summary is from Trautmann, *Morgan and the Invention of Kinship*, 50–57.

34 Ibid., 40.

35 See Feeley-Harnik, "Mystery of Life," 178–79. In his address at Morgan's funeral, lifelong friend Reverend Dr. Joshua Hall McIlvaine relayed Morgan's last word on religion: "I do not claim to have freed my mind from all skeptical doubts, but my heart is with the Christian religion." Trautmann, *Morgan and the Invention of Kinship*, 63. Both Feeley-Harnik and Trautmann emphasize the importance of family tragedy—the death of his two young daughters from scarlet fever—as an emotional backdrop to Morgan's work on the Iroquois and his major anthropological studies.

36 Feeley-Harnik, "Mystery of Life," 172–79; Trautmann, *Morgan and the Invention of Kinship*, 19–25.

37 Feeley-Harnik, "Mystery of Life," 178.

38 The quoted phrase is Morgan's. In his "biography" of Morgan's kinship book, Thomas Trautmann discusses Morgan's contributions to the decade that launched "the public discourse of kinship." *Morgan and the Invention of Kinship*, ix, xi, 3.

39 Lewis H. Morgan, *Ancient Society; or, Researches in the Lines of Human Progress from Savagery through Barbarism to Civilization*, ed. Eleanor Burke Leacock (New York: Meridian, 1963), 561–63.

40 Trautmann, *Morgan and the Invention of Kinship*, 9; Henry Sumner Maine, *Ancient Law: Its Connection with the Early History of Society and Its Relation to Modern Ideas* (1861); John F. McLennan, *Primitive Marriage: An Inquiry into the Origin of the Form of Capture in Marriage Ceremonies* (1865); Johann Bachofen, *Das Mutterrecht* (1861).

41 Tooker, *Morgan on Iroquois Material Culture*, 11.

42 This is the implication of Morgan's foremost analysts, Thomas Trautmann, Elisabeth Tooker, and Gillian Feeley-Harnik.

43 In his study of Indian autobiography, David J. Carlson warns against the problematic assumption that dominant and subordinate cultures are ever pure or stationary, whether before or after contact, and notes as well the limits of a critical method that depends on notions of authenticity and inauthenticity. He suggests instead that "an ongoing process of engagement with identity-defining discourses might produce lasting effects on a writer's rhetoric, politics, and

worldview" such that questions of what is "authentic" for a particular individual or community become meaningless. *Sovereign Selves: American Indian Autobiography and the Law* (Urbana: University of Illinois Press, 2006), 19.

44 Hopkins, *Life among the Piutes*, 5.

45 Eastman quoted in Raymond Wilson, *Ohiyesa: Charles Eastman, Santee Sioux* (Urbana: University of Illinois Press, 1983), 41.

46 Quotations are from Ronald Niezen, *Spirit Wars: Native North American Religions in the Age of Nation Building* (Berkeley: University of California Press, 2000), 130–36; and Wilson, *Ohiyesa*, 52–62. While their accounts differ in minor respects, they concur on most points and draw together on James Mooney's report, "The Ghost Dance Religion and the Sioux Outbreak of 1890," *Fourteenth Annual Report of the Bureau of American Ethnology* (Washington, D.C.: Government Printing Office, 1896), which is based on firsthand testimonies.

47 Wilson, *Ohiyesa*, 61.

48 Though the marriage was for the most part a rocky one, Elaine Goodale Eastman was devoted to Indian causes and, by all reports, to her husband's career. She helped Eastman as editor on all of his books and often handled his correspondence and publicity. She worked hard on the summer camp for boys and girls, "the School of the Woods" advertised as "The Summer Camp with a Difference" that the couple ran in New Hampshire. The Eastmans' had six children together, five girls and a boy, and remained married for thirty years, separating in 1921. See ibid., 52, 62, 67, 81, 83, 151–52, 163–65, 191.

49 Ibid., 126–28.

50 The book was serialized in *St. Nicholas: An Illustrated Magazine for Young Folks*, December 1893–May 1894. Like other popular literature of the time, Twain's *Adventures of Tom Sawyer* (1876) or Hamlin Garland's *Boy Life on the Prairie* (1899), *Indian Boyhood* was marketed as a book for children but soon found an adult audience.

51 Charles Alexander Eastman, *Indian Boyhood* (1902; reprint, New York: Dover, 1971), 3. Eastman wrote a book specifically for the Scouts, *Indian Scout Talks: A Guide for Boy Scouts and Camp Fire Girls* (Boston: Little, Brown, 1914), and also worked for the Boy Scouts from 1910 to the end of his life, assisting them in their use of the Indian lifestyle as their prototype. See Wilson, *Ohiyesa*, 135, 150–51, 189, 190.

52 Eastman, *Indian Boyhood*, 108.

53 Wilson, *Ohiyesa*, 143.

54 Eastman, *Indian Boyhood*, 288.

55 Charles Alexander Eastman, *From the Deep Woods to Civilization: Chapters in the Autobiography of an Indian* (Boston: Little, Brown, 1916), 143.

56 Eastman, *Deep Woods*, 192, 57.

57 Ibid., 195. Eastman's criticism of America fits the paradigm of the jeremiad as analyzed by Sacvan Bercovitch in his classic study, *The American Jeremiad* (Madi-

son: University of Wisconsin Press, 1978), which sees such ritualized censure as a type of national loyalty.

58 It is worth noting that Zitkala-Ša's sense of the injustice and suffering of her own people made her more attuned to the injustice and suffering of others. Thus she courageously defended Sacco and Vanzetti in an article entitled "Has President Lowell Courage?" published in the *Lantern*, April–June 1929, 17–18.

59 Zitkala-Ša, or Red Bird, also known as Gertrude Simmons Bonnin, was born at the Yankton Sioux Agency in South Dakota in 1876, the daughter of a full-blooded Sioux and a white father who died before she was born.

60 For more on turn-of-the-century theories of cultural pluralism, see Werner Sollors, "A Critique of Pure Pluralism," in *Reconstructing American Literary History*, ed. Sacvan Bercovitch (Cambridge, Mass.: Harvard University Press, 1986), 250–79.

61 Helen Hunt Jackson, quoted in Kate Phillips, *Helen Hunt Jackson: A Literary Life* (Berkeley: University of California Press, 2003), 222. I draw throughout my account of Jackson on this splendid biography.

62 Helen Hunt Jackson, "Author's Note," in *A Century of Dishonor: A Sketch of the United States Government's Dealings with Some of the Indian Tribes* (New York: Harper and Brothers, 1881; reprint, Norman: University of Oklahoma Press, 1995).

63 *Ramona* was serialized in the *Christian Union*, May 15–November 6, 1884, before its 1884 publication by Roberts Brothers. The novel's publishers reported in 1936 that total sales to date were about 537,800 and commented that "we have never had a novel which has had such a continuously large sale in regular and higher priced editions over a long period." Phillips, *Helen Hunt Jackson*, 31.

64 Phillips, *Helen Hunt Jackson*, 226.

65 Ibid., 19.

66 Ibid., 20–23.

67 Ibid., 168, 170.

68 Ibid., 177.

69 See ibid., 225–29, on the complexity of both Helen's and William's views on race. Each of them could be extraordinarily liberal and generous on the rights and claims of racial others, at the same time that each also expressed views on blacks and Indians that were quite the opposite.

70 Phillips, *Helen Hunt Jackson*, 115.

71 Ibid., 39.

72 Epigraph in Helen Hunt Jackson, *Ramona* (1884; reprint, New Yor: Signet, 1988).

73 This is the insight of Jackson's biographer, Kate Phillips, *Helen Hunt Jackson*, 39.

74 There have been seven reissues of the book, including, most recently, a 1995 edition published by the University of Oklahoma Press.

75 Jackson, *Century of Dishonor*, 1–2, 16, 17, 29.

76 Ibid., 337–38.

77 Phillips, *Helen Hunt Jackson*, 252.

78 Quoted in Michael Dorris, introduction to *Ramona*, by Helen Hunt Jackson (New York: Signet, 1988), v. Tourgée's review appeared in the *North American Review*, September 1886, and in fact ranked *Ramona* higher than *Uncle Tom's Cabin*, calling it "unquestionably the best novel yet produced by an American woman."

79 Advised by Edward Everett Hale, she read Jesuit histories by Miguel Venegas and Francisco Javier Alegre; *Personal Narrative of Explorations in Texas, New Mexico, California, Sonora, and Chihuahua*, by J. Russell Bartlett (a founder of the American Ethnological Society); and Hale's own account of California history in his contribution to William Cullen Bryant's *Popular History of the United States* (1876–1880). Phillips, *Helen Hunt Jackson*, 236–37.

80 Phillips, *Helen Hunt Jackson*, 179–80.

81 Jackson, *Ramona*, 13–14.

82 According to Jackson's biographer, so much profit was accruing from Ramona fervor that at a certain point "local Indians also asserted their right to share in the profits from Jackson's novel." Phillips, *Helen Hunt Jackson*, 276.

83 Ibid., 1–3.

84 Rosaura Sanchez and Beatrice Pita provide valuable biographical information about Ruiz de Burton in their introductions to two of her novels for the Recovering the U.S. Hispanic Literary Heritage series by the University of Houston's Arte Publico Press.

85 Samuel Carson and Co. published *The Squatter and the Don* in San Francisco in 1885. The novel appeared in its own day under a pseudonym, C. Loyal, or "loyal citizen," a conventional form for concluding a letter in official Mexican correspondence. In addition to disguising Ruiz de Burton's identity and gender, the pseudonym provided ironic commentary on the unheeded loyalty (despite their unjust treatment) of the Mexican American citizenry. The novel was largely ignored when published and has only recently begun to receive some attention through its 1992 republication in the Recovering the U.S. Hispanic Literary Heritage series.

86 Quoted in the introduction to the Penguin Classics edition of Owen Wister, *The Virginian*, ed. John Seelye (New York, 1988), ix.

87 For more on this reading of the Western, see Jane Tompkins, *West of Everything: The Inner Life of Westerns* (New York: Oxford University Press, 1992).

88 Wister is quoted by Richard Slotkin in *Gunfighter Nation: The Myth of the Frontier in Twentieth-Century America* (New York: Macmillan, 1992), 159–60.

89 Wister quoted in the introduction to the Penguin edition of Wister, *The Virginian*, xv.

90 Ibid., 392.

91 The book was serialized in *Field and Stream*, January 1912–July 1913.

92 Patrick Gray, "Getting into Six Figures," *Bookman*, 1924, quoted in Thomas H.

Pauly, *Zane Grey: His Life, His Adventures, His Women* (Urbana: University of Illinois Press, 2005), 195.

93 These facts on Grey's sales, etc. are from Jean Karr, *Zane Grey: Man of the West* (New York: Greenberg, 1949), x, xii, xiii. See Pauly, *Zane Grey*, 269, on the marlin displayed in the Museum of Natural History.

94 Grey's first publication, "A Day on the Delaware," came out in *Recreation* in 1902. Five years later "A Night in the Jungle" was published in the prestigious *Field and Stream*, which became a regular vehicle for Grey's travel pieces and serialized with great fanfare his "Roping Lions in the Grand Canyon" beginning in January 1909. After he became famous, Grey was able to serialize his novels in magazines that paid him enormous fees; for instance, $20,000 for *The Vanishing American* from *Ladies Home Journal* in 1922 and $40,000 for *Nevada* from *American Magazine* in 1926. See Pauly, *Zane Grey*, 47–48, 67, 255–56.

95 Pauly, *Zane Grey*, chapter 5, "Moviemaking and Button Fish: 1915–19."

96 Zane Grey, "Death Valley," *Harper's Magazine*, April 1920, quoted in Stephen J. May, *Maverick Heart: The Further Adventures of Zane Grey* (Athens: University of Ohio Press, 2000), 128.

97 Zane Grey, *The Rainbow Trail* (1915; reprint, Lincoln: University of Nebraska Press, 1995), 344.

98 Karr, *Zane Grey*, 111. John Wanamaker was also the 1896 founder, by way of his New York store, of *Everybody's Magazine*, discussed below in chapter 5. Wanamaker seems to have had little to do with the magazine's content.

99 See Alan Trachtenberg's account of Dixon and Wanamaker, in *Shades of Hiawatha*, chapter 5, "Wanamaker Indians."

Chapter 5

1 John Updike, "Speech to the National Arts Club" (1984), quoted in James O. Twitchell, *Adcult U.S.A.: The Triumph of Advertising in American Culture* (New York: Pantheon, 1996), vii.

2 Stephen Fox, *The Mirror Makers: A History of American Advertising and Its Creators* (Urbana: University of Illinois Press, 1997), 39.

3 Amelie Rives's novel, *The Quick or the Dead*, serialized in *Lippincott's Magazine* in 1888, cited by Ellen Gruber Garvey, *The Adman in the Parlor: Magazines and the Gendering of Consumer Culture, 1880s to 1910* (New York: Oxford University Press, 1996), 87–88.

4 Among other works serialized in leading magazines (some elite, some popular) prior to their publication in book form were Helen Keller's *The Story of My Life* (*Ladies Home Journal*), Henry James's *The Bostonians* (*Century*) and *The Ambassadors* (*North American Review*), Booker T. Washington's *Up from Slavery* (*Outlook*), Abraham Cahan's *The Rise of David Levinsky* (*McClure's*), Willa Cather and Georgine Milmine's *The Life of Mary Baker G. Eddy* (*McClure's*), Frank Norris's *The Pit* (*Saturday Evening Post*), William Dean Howells's *A*

Modern Instance (*Century*) and *A Hazard of New Fortunes* (*Harper's Weekly*), S. S. McClure's *My Autobiography* (*McClure's*), Jack London's *Martin Eden* (*Pacific Monthly*), and Robert Herrick's *Memoirs of an American Citizen* (*Saturday Evening Post*).

5 Twain had long kept a file of autobiographical pieces framed around significant exchanges or events: his relationship with Ulysses S. Grant, his world tour, the death of his beloved daughter Susie. When George Harvey praised the pieces that Twain shared with him and offered $30,000 to publish them in his *North American Review*, Twain began work in earnest. While Twain displays concern for many subjects personal and public, the autobiography seems above all an exercise in literary salesmanship. See Mark Twain, *Chapters from My Autobiography* (New York: Oxford University Press, 1996).

6 Dana Estes of the Boston publishing house of Estes, Lauriat & Co., quoted in Frank Luther Mott, *A History of American Magazines, 1885–1905* (Cambridge, Mass.: Harvard University Press, Belknap Press, 1957), 41–42. Mott's unsurpassed five-volume study runs from 1741 to 1930.

7 See Judith Williamson, *Decoding Advertisements: Ideology and Meaning in Advertising* (London: Boyars, 1978), for an invaluable model for analyzing advertisements.

8 See Pamela Walker Laird, *Advertising Progress: American Business and the Rise of Consumer Marketing* (Baltimore: Johns Hopkins University Press, 1998) for more on these developments.

9 See Wolfgang Schivelbusch, *Disenchanted Night: The Industrialization of Light in the Nineteenth Century* (Berkeley: University of California Press, 1988); and Carolyn Marvin, *When Old Technologies Were New: Thinking about Electric Communication in the Late Nineteenth Century* (New York: Oxford University Press, 1988).

10 By 1880, the American illiteracy rate had dropped to 17 percent, largely attributable to a public education system that was free and compulsory. Between 1880 and 1900 the volume of advertising grew from $200 to $542 million. See Juliann Sivulka, *Soap, Sex, and Cigarettes: A Cultural History of American Advertising* (New York: Wadsworth, 1998), 46–47, for these details and more discussed in these paragraphs.

11 Ibid., 55.

12 During this period many enduring trademarks were coined, among them figures such as: the curly-headed boy of Hires' Root Beer; the boy-in-slicker of Uneeda Biscuit; the cod fisherman of Omega Oil; the Cream of Wheat chef; Aunt Jemima; and Sunny Jim of Force Cereal. Frank Presbrey devotes a chapter to Powers, in which he discusses "Powerisms" and trademarks. See chapter 34 in *The History and Development of Advertising* (New York: Doubleday, 1929), esp. 366–74.

13 "Although substantially all men are readers of advertisements," Fowler wrote, "and are directed by advertising argument, an advertisement has not one

twentieth the weight with a man than it has with a woman of equal intelligence and the same social status." Fowler began as a journalist and wrote a series of books in the 1880s, including *Advertising and Printing, Building Business*, and the encyclopedic *Fowler's Publicity*. See Presbrey, *History and Development*, 315–18. The quotation is on 317.

14 See Jackson Lears, *Fables of Abundance: A Cultural History of Advertising in America* (New York: Basic Books, 1994); Sivulka, *Soap, Sex, and Cigarettes*, 36–42; and Presbrey, *History and Development*, esp. 296–98.

15 Presbrey, *History and Development*, 341. See also 296–98.

16 Ibid., 337–43. For a superb account of the role of immigrants, Jews in particular, in consumption trends of the period, see Andrew Heinze, *Adapting to Abundance: Jewish Immigrants, Mass Consumption, and the Search for American Identity* (New York: Columbia University Press, 1990).

17 According to Pamela Laird, magazines came into this period of transformation with a tradition of addressing the "better classes." J. Walter Thompson had helped to convince national advertisers of the advantages of magazines precisely because of their differential appeal. This included the magazines that aimed for the prosperous literati, who began pursuing the advertising they had spurned before the 1880s, in order to defray the costs of competing with new magazines on the market and also to pay writers and artists whose fees had greatly increased. As magazines became prominent through the 1890s, their numbers actually declined dramatically, paralleling the bankruptcies and consolidations that were taking place in business overall. See Laird, *Advertising Progress*. Richard Ohmann notes how the *Atlantic* claimed to reach "persons of highest cultivation." The *Forum* sought readers of "culture, taste, enterprise, and the means to gratify their many wants," while *Frank Leslie's Popular Monthly* and *Women's Argosy* aimed at "the great masses" and "the people," respectively. *Selling Culture: Magazines, Markets, and Class at the Turn of the Century* (London: Verso, 1996), 114.

18 Laird, *Advertising Progress*, section 1.

19 Walter Dill Scott noted, for instance, that sympathy operated in terms of ideals. "If I am ambitious to be a well-dressed man, I feel sympathetically toward those who are well dressed." *The Psychology of Advertising* (Boston: Small, Maynard, 1908), 40. Scott's first book, *The Theory of Advertising* (Boston: Small, Maynard, 1903), was published serially in *Mahin's Magazine*, prior to its publication in book form, which allowed Scott to include in the complete work some account of the advertising community's response to his suggestions. *Effective Magazine Advertising: 508 Essays about 111 Advertisements*, ed. and with an introduction, "On the Science of Advertising Copy," by Francis Bellamy (New York: Kennerley, 1909), originally published in *Everybody's Magazine*, November 1907.

20 Deas's *The Voyageurs* (1845) pictures an American father with his Indian wife and their four "half-blood" children. Miller's *The Trapper's Bride* (1850) pictures

the intermarriage of an Indian and a white trapper. See *The West as America: Reinterpreting Images of the Frontier, 1820–1920*, ed. William H. Truettner (Washington, D.C.: Smithsonian Institution Press, 1991), 176–78. On "White Indians" see Philip J. DeLoria, *Playing Indian* (New Haven: Yale University Press, 1998).

21 "I am told that my commendation of Pears's Soap has opened for it a large market in the U.S.," Beecher noted. Quoted in James D. Norris, *Advertising and the Transformation of American Society, 1865–1920* (New York: Greenwood, 1990), 56.

22 See Donald S. Tull, "A Re-Examination of the Causes of Decline in Sales of Sapolio," *Journal of Business* 28.2 (1955), 128–37; and Presbrey, *History and Development*, 374–95.

23 In highlighting the sophistication of these advertisements, my analysis concurs with the conclusions of Richard Ohmann in *Selling Culture*: that characteristics typically identified with advertising from the 1920s forward can be found in the late nineteenth century. As he observes, "visual extravagance, personalization, social status, and communicative magic, called into play by corporate needs . . . permeated brand advertising at the outset" (218).

24 This is confirmed by the major studies of advertising. See, among others, Sivulka, *Soap, Sex, and Cigarettes*, 70–73; Presbrey, *History and Development*, 390–95; and Fox, *Mirror Makers*, 23–25.

25 Scott anticipates Michael Schudson's characterization of advertising as "capitalism's way of saying 'I love you' to itself," in *Advertising, the Uneasy Persuasion: Its Dubious Impact on American Society* (New York: Basic Books, 1984), 232.

26 Bellamy's book was excerpted in *Everybody's Magazine*, November 1907. The magazine offered ten prizes of $25 each for the best essays on the topic, "Which is the most effective advertisement in the November issue of *Everybody's Magazine* and why?" The contest went on to specify a series of questions: does the ad catch one's attention; "please the eye"; inspire thorough reading; cultivate true interest; imprint itself on the memory. Bellamy notes that the magazine was circulated among an audience of half a million, that 950 essays were received, and that it "reached a very intelligent class of readers, of comfortable incomes" (*Effective Magazine Advertising*, iii). *Everybody's Magazine* was begun by John Wanamaker in 1896 as a muted supporter of American business, but it turned to muckraking in 1903. Its most notorious series was the twenty-month-long "Frenzied Finance," which exposed "the tigerishly-cruel system" of American industry, replete with a terrifying tiger on the cover. The series began in July 1904, and in the contradictory way of American political life helped to catapult sales, so that by 1911 the magazine had a circulation of half a million and the highest volume of advertising of any American monthly. See Frank Luther Mott, *A History of American Magazines, 1905–1930* (Cambridge, Mass.: Harvard University Press, Belknap Press, 1957), 72–87. The tiger cover appears on 77. The magazine's literary contributors included Mary Wilkins Freeman, Rudyard Kipling, O. Henry, and Frank Norris.

27 The savvy of consumers at this point in American history is barely acknowl-

edged in recent studies (by Sivulka, Fox, Laird, Ohmann, etc.) of marketing and consumption during this period.

28 This advertising logic recalls Robert Frost's preferred poetic subjects, "common in experience but uncommon in books . . . it should have happened to everyone but it should have occurred to no one before as material." Frost, who was intrigued by advertising language and sometimes incorporated its familiar rhetoric in his poems, made this comment in a letter to L. W. Payne Jr., quoted in Richard Poirier, *Robert Frost: The Work of Knowing* (New York: Oxford University Press, 1977), 151. For more on Frost and advertising, see ibid., 256–61.

29 According to Bellamy, people "understand that the advertisements make their favorite magazines possible." Moreover, they take advertising seriously in its own right, and he supports this contention with quotations from the *Everybody's Magazine* contest: "I always read the magazine advertisements; beginning at the last page, I run through the pages hurriedly, stopping to read only those which are exceptionally attractive, and waiting for a spare moment to examine the others more carefully." "When I need merchandise of any kind the first thing I do is to consult the index to advertisers in this magazine." "It is my habit to look through the advertisements in this magazine every month to keep posted about the new and pretty things." See Bellamy, *Effective Magazine Advertising*, 5–14.

30 For instance, one of the most resistant journals, the *Atlantic Monthly*, had just 14 pages of ads in its December 1865 issue. As the "beneficiary of a kind of divine election to leadership in American letters . . . for a large section of the American public, whatever the *Atlantic* printed was literature." Frank Luther Mott, *A History of American Magazines, 1850–1865* (Cambridge, Mass.: Harvard University Press, Belknap Press, 1957), 13, 492–93. By December 1891, the *Atlantic* had 101 pages of advertising and was commanding $100 per page. By 1905 *McClure's* was printing 165 pages of ads in each issue at $400 per page. Mott, *History of American Magazines, 1885–1905*, 21.

31 See Lears, *Fables of Abundance*, 274–81, 358–59, on Dreiser and Anderson; and Sivulka, *Sex, Soap and Cigarettes*, 70, 105, on Hart Crane, Parrish, Wyeth, and Rockwell.

32 Thomas Townsend Taber, *The Delaware, Lackawanna and Western Railroad: The Road of Anthracite in the Twentieth Century, 1899–1960, Part Two* (Williamsport, Pa.: T. T. Taber III, 1981), esp. 395.

33 French artists, such as Eugene Grasset, and Anglo-American artists, such as Aubrey Beardsley and William H. Bradley, designed these covers. See Sivulka, *Soap, Sex, and Cigarettes*, 84–89.

34 Ibid., 96–97.

35 As a writer for the *Journalist* declared in 1889, "The rapidity with which magazines are started in this country is equaled only by the suddenness of their disappearance. Periodicals of all sorts and kinds and devoted to the interest of everything under the heavens . . . come and go. . . . By far the greater number

either fail or ruin their proprietors." Quoted in Mott, *History of American Magazines, 1885–1905,* 11.

36 Quoted in Laird, *Advertising Progress,* 223.

37 Robert Bonner of the *Ledger* paid Fern $100 per column in 1855 and Beecher the fixed sum. Mott, *History of American Magazines, 1850–1865,* 23–24.

38 Howells had a $10,000 per year contract with Osgood and a more complex contract with Harper's. These facts are covered in the chronology provided by Susan Goodman and Carl Dawson in their biography, *William Dean Howells: A Writer's Life* (Berkeley: University of California Press, 2005), xxi–xxvi. See also 212, 265–66.

39 Serialized in the *North American Review* from 1902 to 1903, *The Ambassadors* accompanied such pieces as Mark Twain on Christian Science, Hamlin Garland on "Sanity in Fiction," Edith Wharton on reading, and William Dean Howells on Chicago fiction. See "Project of Novel by Henry James," describing his plans for serialization, in *The Ambassadors* (New York: Norton, 1994), 377–404. That James's serializing efforts were not altogether successful was confirmed by a rejection he received prior to its acceptance by the *North American Review.* An editor at *Harper's New Monthly Magazine* wrote of "Project of Novel" in 1900, "The scenario is interesting but it does not promise a popular novel. The tissue of it are too subtly fine for general appreciation. It is subjective, fold within fold of a complex mental web, in which the reader is lost if his much-wearied attention falters. . . . [I] do not advise acceptance. We ought to do better" (quoted in James, *Ambassadors,* 415).

40 Howells's fee was an improvement of $200 on *Scribner's* offer. See Michael Anesko, *"Friction with the Market": Henry James and the Profession of Authorship* (New York: Oxford University Press, 1986), 41.

41 James, *Ambassadors,* 385, 47, 341.

42 Samuel McClure, *My Autobiography* (New York: Frederick Stokes, 1914), 234.

43 Ibid., 222.

44 *McClure's Magazine* serialized McClure's *Autobiography* from 1913 to 1914.

45 McClure, *My Autobiography,* 130–31.

46 The magazine was later incorporated into *Outing* but always offered an array of cycling pieces. See Mott, *History of American Magazines, 1885–1905,* 377–80, 633–34.

47 The appeal for James in particular was the *Sun's* 150,000 readers and the thousands more reached by syndication in the other papers. See Anesko, *"Friction with the Market,"* 86–87.

48 Review quoted in Mott, *History of American Magazines, 1885–1905,* 596.

49 McClure quoted in ibid., 597.

50 Ibid., 607.

51 Quotations and figures are from W. E. B. Du Bois, *Dusk of Dawn,* in *Writings: W. E. B. Du Bois* (New York: Library of America, 1986), 621, 719–21, 743. *Dusk of Dawn,* Du Bois's autobiography, was originally published in 1940.

52 Quoted in David Levering Lewis, *W. E. B. Du Bois: Biography of a Race, 1868–1919* (New York: Henry Holt, 1993), 409.

53 Advertising was purchased by Madame E. Toussaint's Conservatory of Art and Music—"The Foremost Female Artist of the Race"; Real Estate Broker Philip A. Payton—"New York's Pioneer Negro Real Estate Agents"; L. C. Smith and Bros. Typewriters of Syracuse, New York; the Henry Phipps Model Tenements for Colored Families; Marshall's Hotel on West Fifty-third Street; "The Leading Colored Restaurant in America"; and the Nyanza Pharmacy—"the only colored Drug Store in New York City." With the magazine's growing success, these advertisers were joined by major black colleges and universities—Atlanta, Fisk, Howard, Shaw, Virginia Union, Wilberforce—and by leading publishers of black writers. Ibid., 411.

54 Du Bois, *Dusk of Dawn*, 734.

55 Quoted in Lewis, *W. E. B. Du Bois*, 426.

56 Du Bois, *Dusk of Dawn*, 783.

57 Anesko, *"Friction with the Market,"* 34, 163–64. James attended the 1883 meeting of the American Copyright League, and a U.S. senator used a letter by James in legislative efforts to pass the 1891 Copyright Act.

58 The agent's efforts on behalf of this novel were unsuccessful. Anesko, *"Friction with the Market,"* 169. But in fact Pinker, whose clients included H. G. Wells, Arnold Bennett, Joseph Conrad, and Rudyard Kipling, also helped James secure solid fees for all his work. See Leon Edel, *Henry James: The Treacherous Years, 1895–1901* (New York: Avon, 1969), 337–39.

59 Anesko, *"Friction with the Market,"* 47.

60 James's first two published books, *A Passionate Pilgrim* and *Transatlantic Sketches*, published in 1875 by the American James R. Osgood, earned him royalties of s 88.20 and $196.80, respectively. By contrast, James was paid $1,350 in 1876 by the *Atlantic Monthly* for its serialization of *The American*. Anesko, *"Friction with the Market,"* 32–34.

61 James, like other family members, received a regular sum from the family's Syracuse, New York, properties, but the sum was not significant before 1893. See Anesko, *"Friction with the Market,"* 172, 223.

62 James's brother William, for instance, noted, "For gleams and innuendos and felicitous verbal insinuations you are unapproachable, but the *core* of literature is solid. Give it to us *once* again! The bare perfume of things will not support existence, and the effect of solidity you reach is but perfume and simulacrum." One reader bragged of her ability to read James "in the original." And another reader recommended James not "put the tail of his sentences where the head belongs and the head where the body should be or the body where one naturally expects to see the tail." Quotations from Leon Edel, *Henry James: The Master, 1901–1916* (New York: Avon, 1972), 301–2.

63 The phrase comes from James's essay on Turgenev. See *Henry James: Literary Criticism, Volume 2: French Writers, Other European Writers, Prefaces to the New*

York Edition (New York: Library of America, 1984), 975. Edel suggests that James grew distressed with the process of registering as an "alien" in his English village during the war. Edel, *Henry James*, 529–33.

64 Henry James, *Hawthorne: A Critical Essay on the Man and His Times* (New York: Macmillan, 1966), 25.

65 James's elaborate responses to these different literary traditions, American, English, and European, are contained in the two-volume Library of America collection of his criticism. *Henry James: Literary Criticism, Volume 1: Essays on Literature, American Writers, English Writers* (New York: Library of America, 1984).

66 Edel, *Henry James*, 433–34.

67 Ibid., 476–78.

68 Quoted in Goodman and Dawson, *William Dean Howells*, xiii–xiv, 22, 409–10.

69 Richard Brodhead, *The School of Hawthorne* (New York: Oxford University Press, 1986), 87.

70 The novel was serialized in *Century Magazine* from 1881 to 1882, before its publication by James R. Osgood in 1882.

71 Goodman and Dawson, *William Dean Howells*, 21, 35–40.

72 Ibid., 48–50.

73 Ibid., 61–71.

74 Ibid., 83–85.

75 Howells earned $3,500, and later $5,000, per year at the *Atlantic*. According to Richard Brodhead, he was the first American author to make "authorship practicable as a specialized career" that allowed "him to live in a handsome display of style." *The School of Hawthorne* (New York: Oxford University Press, 1986), 87.

76 Goodman and Dawson, *William Dean Howells*, 140–47.

77 Ibid., 234.

78 Howells quoted in Edwin Cady, introduction to *A Modern Instance*, by William Dean Howells (New York: Penguin, 1988), ix.

79 These details are from William Gibson, introduction to *A Modern Instance*, by William Dean Howells (Boston: Houghton, Mifflin, 1957).

80 Goodman and Dawson, *William Dean Howells*, 234–37.

81 Ibid., 287, 429–30.

82 Joseph R. Urgo, "Willa Cather's Political Apprenticeship at *McClure's* Magazine," in *Willa Cather's New York: New Essays on Cather in the City*, ed. Merrill MaGuire Skaggs (Cranberry, N.J.: Associated University Presses, 2000), 61.

83 The Eddy biography was serialized in *McClure's* from January 1907 through June 1908. Cather confirmed in a 1922 letter that she wrote the whole book, with the exception of chapter 1. Janis P. Stout, *Willa Cather: The Writer and Her World* (Charlottesville: University Press of Virginia, 2000), 98–99, 327.

84 Urgo, "Willa Cather's Political Apprenticeship," 65–70.

85 Cather quoted in the appendix to Willa Cather, *O Pioneers!* (New York: Oxford World's Classics, 1999), 172.

86 The novel was dedicated to Jewett. Marilee Lindemann, introduction to Cather, *O Pioneers!*, xvii.

87 Stout, *Willa Cather*, 8–13.

88 Ibid., 32–39.

89 These reviews, written between 1895 and 1900, are collected in *Willa Cather: Stories, Poems, and Other Writings* (New York: Library of America, 1992), 889, 892, 920, 905.

90 Stout, *Willa Cather*, 107, 88.

91 The phrase "migratory consciousness" is from Joseph Urgo, *Willa Cather and the Myth of Migration* (Urbana: University of Illinois Press, 1995), 26. See also 17, 21, for Sargeant quotes. Susan Rosowski on Cather and immigrants in American literature is quoted in Stout, *Willa Cather*, 151.

92 Stout, *Willa Cather*, 151–55.

93 Ibid., 161.

94 Willa Cather, *The Song of the Lark* (New York: Penguin, 1999), 434.

95 Quoted by Sherrill Harbison in introduction to Cather, *Song of the Lark*, xviii, xx.

96 Quoted by Harbison, ibid., xxiv.

97 Jerome Loving, *The Last Titan: A Life of Theodore Dreiser* (Berkeley: University of California Press, 205), 76–84.

98 Ibid., 122–23.

99 Ibid., 1–75.

100 Dreiser was listed as "Journalist—author . . . contributed prose and verse to various periodicals. Author: Studies of Contemporary Celebrities; Poems." F. O. Matthiessen, *Theodore Dreiser* (New York: William Sloane, 1951), 48.

101 See "The Real Howells," *Ainslee's* (March 1900), 137–42; "Curious Shifts of the Poor," *Demorest's Family Magazine* 36 (November 1899), 22–26; and Loving, *Last Titan*, 125–28.

102 Dreiser's only royalty check from Doubleday was for $68.40. Loving, *Last Titan*, 152–59.

103 Ibid., 187–99.

104 Ibid., 257.

105 Matthiessen, *Dreiser*, 63, 166–69.

106 Theodore Dreiser, *"The Genius"* (New York: Meridian, 1984), 403.

107 Howells, from his admiring review of Tolstoy's *What to Do?*, quoted by Clara and Rudolph Kirk, in introduction to William Dean Howells, *The Altrurian Romances* (Bloomington: Indiana University Press, 1968), xvii.

Chapter 6

1 David Montgomery, *Workers' Control in America: Studies in the History of Work, Technology, and Labor Struggles* (New York: Cambridge University Press, 1979), 2.

2 Mass production of pocket watches by the American Watch Company in

Waltham, Massachusetts, began during the Civil War. Daniel T. Rodgers, *The Work Ethic in Industrial America, 1850–1920* (Chicago: University of Chicago Press, 1978), 18.

3 Montgomery, *Workers' Control*, 13.

4 Ira Katznelson, *City Trenches: Urban Politics and the Patterning of Class in the United States* (Chicago: University of Chicago Press, 1982), 16.

5 Rodgers, *Work Ethic*, 36.

6 *The Jungle* was serialized in the Socialist magazine *Appeal to Reason*, February–November 1905. Five publishers turned down the book before Doubleday Page accepted it, with first editions appearing in 1906. Ronald Gottesman, introduction to *The Jungle*, by Upton Sinclair (New York: Penguin Classics, 1985), xvii–xxii.

7 Sinclair, *Jungle* (Penguin edition), 42, 44–45.

8 Despite his own southern aristocrat background and sympathy for the Confederacy, Sinclair modeled his novel on *Uncle Tom's Cabin*, though he insisted that Stowe's task was far easier than his own. "The life of the modern wage-slave is so much more mechanical and so much less picturesque than that of the chattel-slave of fifty years ago." See Sinclair's 1906 *Cosmopolitan* essay, "What Life Means to Me," in *The Jungle* (New York: Norton, 2003), 350.

9 Richard A. Epstein, "Animals as Objects, or Subjects, of Rights," in Cass R. Sunstein and Martha C. Nussbaum, eds., *Animal Rights: Current Debates and New Directions* (New York: Oxford University Press, 2004), 153.

10 For two classic essays on the historical context of Stowe's representation of the suffering slave, see Elizabeth B. Clark, "Pain, Sympathy, and the Culture of Individual Rights," *Journal of American History* 82, no. 2 (September 1995); and Thomas Haskell, "Capitalism and the Origins of the Humanitarian Sensibility," Parts 1 and 2, *American Historical Review* 90 (April 1985): 339–61, (June 1985): 547–66.

11 Sinclair, *Jungle* (Penguin edition) 152, 350.

12 Ibid., xxii–xxiii.

13 Roosevelt added that Sinclair's socialism was "pathetic," suggesting that its implementation would destroy, morally and physically (death by starvation and epidemic) the very classes it sought to save. Ibid., xxiii–xiv.

14 The novel was first serialized in *Harper's New Monthly Magazine*, 1900–1901. Freeman was one of the era's most respected authors, highlighted consistently in lists of the most distinguished and renowned writers. See, for example, Frank Luther Mott, *A History of American Magazines, 1885–1905* (Cambridge, Mass.: Harvard University Press, Belknap Press, 1957), 544, 769.

15 Mary Wilkins Freeman, *The Portion of Labor* (New York: Harper and Brothers, 1901; reprint, Ridgewood, N.J.: Gregg, 1967), 17–18.

16 Ibid., 75.

17 Ibid., 165.

18 The novel was serialized anonymously in *Century* magazine, 1883–84, prior to

its publication by Harper and Brothers (1884). The serial aroused much speculation about its author, and some proposed it was Howells, though his politics directly opposed those of his friend John Hay.

19 Hay quoted in introduction to 1911 edition of John Hay, *The Bread-Winners* (New York: Harper and Brothers).

20 John Hay, *The Bread-Winners* (New York: Harper and Brothers, 1884), 5–6.

21 Ibid., 246.

22 Friedman's novels included *Poor People* (1900), about Chicago tenement life; *By Bread Alone* (1901), on the 1892 strike at the Carnegie Steel Mills in Homestead, Pennsylvania; *The Autobiography of a Beggar* (1903); and *The Radical* (1907), the story of a man's rise from delivery boy to United States senator. They were all published by mainstream presses, including McClure and Phillips; Appleton; Houghton, Mifflin; and Small, Maynard. And they were reviewed in major journals, including the *New York Times Book Review*.

23 Isaac Kahn Friedman, *Poor People* (Boston: Houghton, Mifflin, 1900), 135.

24 Ibid., 224.

25 I draw in this paragraph on Daniel T. Rodgers's discussion of Addams in *Work Ethic*, 81–90.

26 Jane Addams, *Twenty Years at Hull-House; with Autobiographical Notes*, illustrations by Norah Hamilton (New York: Macmillan, 1910), serialized in *American Magazine* and one chapter excerpted in *McClure's*.

27 Addams, *Twenty Years at Hull-House*, 310.

28 Ibid., 255–56.

29 Addams quoted by Daphne Spain, *How Women Saved the City* (Minneapolis: University of Minnesota Press, 2001), 26. I draw here on Spain's study.

30 For more on the participation of women in municipal reform, see Seth Koven and Sonya Michel, *Mothers of a New World: Maternalist Politics and the Origins of Welfare States* (New York: Routledge, 1993); Theda Skocpol, *Protecting Soldiers and Mothers: The Political Origins of Social Policy in the United States* (Cambridge, Mass.: Harvard University Press, 1992); and my "Reproducing Women in *The Awkward Age*," *Representations* (Spring 1992), 101–30. As Daniel Rodgers points out, however, the number of women with significant leisure time on their hands was most likely less than 5 percent of the total population of women. *Work Ethic*, 202–3.

31 See my "Reproducing Women in *The Awkward Age*" for more on the eugenics movement of the time and its impact on women and work.

32 Quoted in Rodgers, *Work Ethic*, 190, 200.

33 For a superb study of Stein that succeeds in reconciling her scientific interests in cognition and language with her keen social awareness, see Steven Meyer, *Irresistible Dictation: Gertrude Stein and the Correlations of Writing and Science* (Stanford: Stanford University Press, 2001).

34 See Eugene E. Miller, "Richard Wright and Gertrude Stein," *Black American Literature Forum* 16, no. 3 (Autumn 1982): 107–12.

35 From James's preface to the New York Edition of *In the Cage*, quoted in *Henry James: Eight Tales from the Major Phase* (New York: Norton, 1969), 6.

36 See Morton Zabel, introduction to *Henry James: Eight Tales*, 6–7.

37 Appleton finally accepted the book with the proviso that George pay the cost of plates.

38 Quoted in the introduction to Henry George, *Progress and Poverty* (New York: Sterling, 1879).

39 Published in the *New York Tribune*, May 1, 1869, and quoted in John L. Thomas, *Alternative America: Henry George, Edward Bellamy, Henry Demarest Lloyd, and the Adversary Tradition* (Cambridge, Mass.: Harvard University Press, 1983), 62–63. Thomas also describes here his reply to William Lloyd Garrison Jr.

40 Du Bois's emphasis on the economic threat posed by blacks in this era is supported by recent research, which likewise treats race as a secondary cause. "The racial emphasis resulted from the use of the most obvious feature of the group," argues Stanley Lieberson, "to support the intergroup conflict generated by a fear of blacks based on their threat as economic competitors." *A Piece of the Pie: Blacks and White Immigrants since 1880* (Cambridge, Mass.: Harvard University Press, 1980), 382–83. Du Bois and Lieberson concur that blacks' progress (rather than alleged morbidity) complicates their social success in part by motivating attempts to limit it.

41 W. E. B. Du Bois, *The Philadelphia Negro* (Philadelphia: University of Pennsylvania Publications, 1899), 126, 128.

42 Ibid., 10–11.

43 Ibid., 359–67.

44 Ibid., 397.

45 The book was reprinted twice in its first year of publication.

46 John Spargo, *The Bitter Cry of the Children* (New York: Macmillan, 1906), 8.

47 Ibid., 141.

48 Ibid., 198–200.

49 Ibid., 142–45.

50 Ibid., 164–65.

51 Ibid., 264–69.

52 Quoted by David Leviatin, introduction to Jacob Riis, *How the Other Half Lives* (New York: Bedford, 1996), 8. I draw on this introduction for facts presented above.

53 Riis, *How the Other Half Lives*, 73.

54 Lenin quoted by George Meany, introduction to Samuel Gompers, *Seventy Years of Life and Labor: An Autobiography* (New York: Dutton, 1957), 6.

55 Quoted in Rodgers, *Work Ethic*, 160.

56 Max Weber, *The Protestant Ethic and the Spirit of Capitalism* (trans. Talcott Parsons, New York: Scribners, 1930) was first published in the *Arciv fur Sozialwissenschaft und Sozialpolitik* 20 (1904), 21 (1905). The book was widely read in the United States, though the first English translation did not appear until 1930.

Invoking Franklin throughout, Weber observes, "At this point it will suffice for our purpose to call attention to the fact that without doubt, in the country of Benjamin Franklin's birth (Massachusetts), the spirit of capitalism . . . was present before the capitalistic order" (55).

57 Rodgers, *Work Ethic*, esp. 8–9.

58 Louis Harlan's *Booker T. Washington: The Making of a Black Leader, 1856–1901* (New York: Oxford University Press, 1972) and *Booker T. Washington: The Wizard of Tuskegee, 1901–1915* (New York: Oxford University Press, 1983) are invaluable guides to Washington's life.

59 Booker T. Washington, *Up from Slavery*, in John Hope Franklin, ed., *Three Negro Classics* (New York: Avon, 1965), 181–82.

60 Washington's Atlanta Exposition Address, September 18, 1895, quoted in Franklin, *Three Negro Classics*, 159.

61 The book was serialized in *Outlook*, November 3, 1900–February 23, 1901, before its publication by Doubleday.

62 W. E. B. Du Bois, review of *Up from Slavery*, by Booker T. Washington, *Dial*, July 16, 1901. Washington's assistant on this book was Max Bennet Thraser, a journalist.

63 Quoted in David Levering Lewis, *W. E. B. Du Bois: Biography of a Race* (New York: Henry Holt, 1993), 274.

64 Franklin, *Three Negro Classics*, 37.

65 Ibid., 50.

66 Ibid., 162.

67 Ibid., 182.

68 Ibid., 38.

69 Quoted by Werner Sollors in the introduction to Mary Antin, *The Promised Land* (New York: Penguin, 1997), xxxviii–xxxix. The *New York Sun* reported of Antin's book in 1912 that it "led all the rest" among "the books most called-for at the various libraries." Quoted in ibid., xxxii. I draw here on Sollors's introduction.

70 Antin, *Promised Land*, 280.

71 Ibid., 157–59.

72 Ibid., 74.

73 Ibid., 146, 196–97.

74 For anthropologists, food is central to boundary making, a universal means of distinguishing kinship and confirming acceptance. The mass production of American ethnic foods—Mexican tamales, Jewish bagels—signals, however partially, a group's assimilation. Certain prized foods—coffee, tea, sugar, and salt—figured prominently in previous centuries in the international trade that confirmed national borders. While the cultivation of global appetites for a country's leading commodity is certain to undermine its identity as such, that original association is key to its value. See Gillian Feeley-Harnik, *The Lord's*

Table: Eucharist and Passover in Early Christianity (Philadelphia: University of Pennsylvania, 1981).

75 Antin, *Promised Land*, 26.

76 Ibid., 201.

77 From 1869 to 1877 Alger lived in the Seligmann home tutoring their sons in preparation for college and subsequently worked for the Cardozos. Richard Polenberg, *The World of Benjamin Cardozo: Personal Values and the Judicial Process* (Cambridge, Mass.: Harvard University Press, 1997), 18–24.

78 See Rodgers, *Work Ethic*, 140–43; John G. Cawelti, *Apostles of the Self-Made Man: Changing Concepts of Success in America* (Chicago: University of Chicago Press, 1965), chap. 4; and Michael Moon, "The Gentle Boy from the Dangerous Classes: Pederasty, Domesticity, and Capitalism in Horatio Alger," in Philip Fisher, ed., *The New American Studies: Essays from Representations* (Berkeley: University of California, 1991), 260–83.

79 This happens, for instance, in *Ragged Dick, Tattered Tom, Luck and Pluck*, and *Brave and Bold*.

80 Henry James Sr. informed Henry Jr. of Alger's self-characterization in a letter, quoted in introduction to Horatio Alger, *Ragged Dick and Struggling Upward* (New York: Penguin, 1985), xv.

81 The book was serialized in *Student and Schoolmate* in 1867 prior to publication.

82 Alger, *Ragged Dick and Struggling Upward*, 4–5, 49.

83 Ibid., 250–54.

Chapter 7

1 Quoted in Thomas K. McCraw, ed., *Creating Modern Capitalism: How Entrepreneurs, Companies, and Countries Triumphed in Three Industrial Revolutions* (Cambridge, Mass.: Harvard University Press, 1999), 17.

2 Ibid., 319.

3 Some of these details are based on Allan Nevins and Henry Steele Commager, *A Pocket History of the United States* (New York: Washington Square, 1974), 256, 292–94, 319–20.

4 McCraw, *Creating Modern Capitalism*, 315–21.

5 Matthew Josephson, *The Robber Barons: The Great American Capitalists, 1861–1901* (New York: Harvest, 1934), vi.

6 Elizabeth Stuart Phelps, *Chapters from a Life* (Boston: Houghton, Mifflin, 1896), 90.

7 Ibid., 259, 262.

8 Elizabeth Stuart Phelps, *The Silent Partner* (Old Westbury, N.Y.: Feminist Press, 1983), 45–46.

9 Ibid., 20.

10 Ibid., 278.

11 Ibid., 287–88.

12 The book was serialized in *Century Magazine*, 1884–85.

13 William Dean Howells, *The Rise of Silas Lapham* (New York: Oxford University Press, 1996), xxviii, 65.

14 Ibid., 16–18.

15 "A Call for Realism," in *Criticism and Fiction* (New York: Harper, 1891), excerpted in William Dean Howells, *The Rise of Silas Lapham* (New York: Norton Critical Edition, 1982), 500.

16 Cahan's *The Rise of David Levinsky* was serialized in *McClure's Magazine* with the added title *Autobiography of a Jew* in 1913, beginning with the April issue and continuing through May, June, and July.

17 For more on the reception of the Beilis case in America, see Albert S. Lindemann, *The Jew Accused: Three Anti-Semitic Affairs (Dreyfus, Beilis, Frank), 1894–1915* (Cambridge: Cambridge University Press, 1991); and my essay, "The Place of Ritual in Our Time," in my edited collection *Religion and Cultural Studies* (Princeton: Princeton University Press, 2001), 56–79.

18 Abraham Cahan, *The Rise of David Levinsky* (New York: Penguin, 1995), 443–44.

19 *Tribune* writer quoted in Andrew R. Heinze, *Adapting to Abundance: Jewish Immigrants, Mass Consumption, and the Search for American Identity* (New York: Columbia University Press, 1990), 186. The department stores are listed on 183. Cahan's novel provides its own detailed history of Jewish business in America; Heinze's study complements it.

20 Cahan, *Rise of David Levinsky*, 380.

21 Ibid., 468.

22 Frank Norris, "Life in the Mining Regions," *Everybody's Magazine*, September 1902, 251–58.

23 Reviews quoted by Franklin Walker in *Frank Norris: A Biography* (New York: Doubleday, 1932), 273–74.

24 Frank Norris, *The Octopus* in *Frank Norris: Novels and Essays* (New York: Library of America, 1986), 1084.

25 Ibid., 830.

26 McCraw, *Creating Modern Capitalism*, 323–24.

27 For facts in the passage above, see Eric Sundquist, introduction to *Mark Twain: A Collection of Critical Essays* (Englewood Cliffs, N.J.: Prentice Hall, 1994).

28 On the Grant campaign see Walter A. Friedman, *Birth of a Salesman: The Transformation of Selling in America* (Cambridge, Mass.: Harvard University Press, 2004), 34–55. On Twain and the Lackawanna, see chapter 5 above.

29 Quoted in Josephson, *Robber Barons*, 279–80. Rogers's *Who's Who* listing cited in Justin Kaplan, *Mr. Clemens and Mark Twain: A Biography* (New York: Simon and Schuster, 1966), 322.

30 See Ron Chernow, *Titan: The Life of John D. Rockefeller, Sr.* (New York: Vintage, 1998), esp. 381–82. I draw on this superb cultural history in this section and the next.

31 Kaplan, *Mr. Clemens and Mark Twain*, 384.

32 Chernow, *Titan*, 534–35.

33 Quoted in Kaplan, *Mr. Clemens and Mark Twain*, 384.

34 Quoted in ibid., 363.

35 Quoted in ibid., 197.

36 Mark Twain, *The Adventures of Tom Sawyer* (New York: Oxford University Press, 1993), 51.

37 Ibid., 52.

38 Ibid., 22–23.

39 Ibid., 241.

40 *New York Tribune*, September 27, 1871, cited in Kaplan, *Mr. Clemens and Mark Twain*, 95–96.

41 Twain quoted in Kaplan, *Mr. Clemens and Mark Twain*, 162.

42 See F. O. Matthiessen, *Theodore Dreiser* (New York: William Sloane, 1951), 129–30.

43 Quoted in ibid., 132–33.

44 Rockefeller quoted by Ida B. Tarbell, *The History of the Standard Oil Company*, 2 vols. (New York: McClure, Phillips, 1904), 1:40.

45 Alfred Chandler, *The Visible Hand: The Managerial Revolution in American Business* (Cambridge, Mass.: Harvard University Press, Belknap Press, 1997), 211–14.

46 Theodore Dreiser, *The Financier* (New York: New American Library, 1981), 19.

47 Ibid., 7–8.

48 Ibid., 446–47.

49 Josephson, *Robber Barons*, 386.

50 Theodore Dreiser, *The Titan* (New York: Signet, 1965), 10.

51 Ibid., 12.

52 The novel was serialized in the *Saturday Evening Post*, September 20, 1902–January 31, 1903.

53 Quoted in introduction to Frank Norris, *The Pit* (New York: Penguin, 1994), xii. See this introduction for details in the passage above.

54 Walker, *Frank Norris*, 277.

55 Ibid., 13–15.

56 Norris, *Pit*, 162.

57 Ibid., 96.

58 Thorstein Veblen, *The Theory of Business Enterprise* (1904; reprint, New Brunswick, N.J.: Transaction Books, 1978), 150–54. See Howard Horwitz, " 'To Find the Value of X': *The Pit* as a Renunciation of Romance," in Eric Sundquist, ed., *American Realism: New Essays* (Baltimore: Johns Hopkins University Press, 1982), 215–37.

59 Norris, *Pit*, 190.

60 Ibid., 369.

61 Fuller noted of Chicago in an 1895 letter to William Dean Howells, "Really I write about this town, neither because I like it or hate it, but because I can't

escape it and because I am so ashamed of it. If you are condemned to residence on a muckheap wouldn't you too edit it? Wouldn't you want to give it some credit, some standing (*as* a muckheap) by ordering, formulating, characterizing its various delectabilities? No—I am only devoting Chicago to literary manipulation . . . to raise this dirt pile to some dignity. . . by annexing it to the principality of literature." Quoted by Daniel Aaron in introduction to Robert Herrick, *Memoirs of an American Citizen* (Cambridge, Mass.: Harvard University Press, Belknap Press, 1963), xi.

62 Henry Blake Fuller, *The Cliff Dwellers* (Ridgewood, N.J.: Gregg, 1963), 4–5.

63 Ibid., 54.

64 Ibid., 296.

65 Ibid., 324.

66 Henry James, *The Golden Bowl* (1904; reprint, New York: Penguin, 1973; text from first English edition, 1905), 171.

67 Ibid., 39.

68 Ibid., 173.

69 Marcel Mauss, *The Gift*, trans. W. D. Halls (New York: Norton, 1990), 4.

70 Ibid., 65. Mauss defines "potlatch" as "to feed," "to consume." It is "a continual festival of feasts, fairs, and markets" in which "the principle of rivalry and hostility" prevails. Mauss's contemporary example is a village family in Lorraine, which had "contented itself with living very frugally," but beset by the need to "act the 'great lord' " "ruined itself for the sake of its guests on saints days, and at weddings, first communions, or funerals" (6–7, 66).

71 Ibid., 69.

72 James, *Golden Bowl*, 124–25.

73 Ibid., 153, 126.

74 William James quoted in Chernow, *Titan*, 412–13. Henry James quoted in Kathleen Brady, *Ida Tarbell: Portrait of a Muckraker* (New York: Seaview, Putnam, 1984), 166.

75 James, *Golden Bowl*, 449.

76 Quoted in Chernow, *Titan*, 318.

77 Epigraph in Thorstein Veblen, *The Theory of the Leisure Class* (New York: Mentor, 1953).

78 The phrase is from C. Wright Mills's introduction to Veblen, *Theory of the Leisure Class*, xvi.

79 Ibid., esp. 34, 80–81.

80 Andrew Carnegie, *The Empire of Business* (New York: Doubleday, Page, 1902), 17. Chapters were published previously in the *North American Review*, February 1889 and June 1891; *Forum*, March 1895; *New York Evening Post*, January 12, 1901; *New York Tribune*, April 13, 1890; *Iron Age*, 1898; *New York Journal*, 1900; *Youth's Companion*, September 1900; *Contemporary Review of Britain*, September 1894; *Nineteenth Century of Britain*, February 1898; and *Macmillan's Magazine*, January 1885.

81　Carnegie, *Empire of Business*, 12.

82　For more on this episode and Carnegie's rise, see Richard Tedlow, *Giants of Enterprise: Seven Business Innovators and the Empires They Built* (New York: HarperBusiness, 2001), 43–51.

83　Ibid., 56.

84　Carnegie, *Empire of Business*, 89.

85　Quoted in Chernow, *Titan*, 313.

86　Quoted in Josephson, *Robber Barons*, 371–72.

87　Chernow, *Titan*, 393, 566.

88　Ibid., xix–xx.

89　Quoted in Brady, *Ida Tarbell*, 167.

90　Richard Ohmann, for instance, in his 1994 analysis of the American culture industry of this era, *Selling Culture: Magazines, Markets, and Class at the Turn of the Century* (London: Verso, 1996), argues that Tarbell's portrait exonerates Rockefeller, in part by suggesting that illegal business practices were widespread: that was just the way the game was played. Moreover, Rockefeller is portrayed as a powerful intelligence, with great imagination, drive, and sense of purpose. Writers like Tarbell, Ohmann concludes, celebrated the methods of their subjects as the most admirably "rational" means of organizing society and labor. In contrast, Ron Chernow, author of a 1998 biography of Rockefeller, insists that far from admiring, "Tarbarrel," as Rockefeller referred to her in private, was relentless and damning: "although Tarbell pretended to apply her scalpel to Standard Oil with surgical objectivity, she was never neutral." *Titan*, 439.

91　Tarbell, *History of Standard Oil*, appendix, 1:266, 273–75. Quotation is on 275.

92　Ibid., 1:30–31; Chernow, *Titan*, 335.

93　Tarbell, *History of Standard Oil*, 1:35–37. Quotation is on 37.

94　Ibid., 1:v.

95　Rockefeller quoted in Chernow, *Titan*, 48.

96　William Rockefeller described and John D. Rockefeller quoted in ibid., 24, 48.

97　Ibid., 68–72.

98　Ibid., 137.

99　See John L. Thomas, *Alternative America: Henry George, Edward Bellamy, and the Adversary Tradition* (Cambridge, Mass.: Harvard University Press, Belknap Press, 1983), 4, 58, 77–79, 82, on Lloyd's ambivalent reactions to the Great Railroad Strike.

100　Quoted in Chernow, *Titan*, 266.

101　Howells recommended the book warmly to Harper and Brothers, commenting to Lloyd, "the monstrous iniquity whose story you tell so powerfully . . . is so astounding, so infuriating, that I have to stop from chapter to chapter, and take breath." Quoted in Chernow, *Titan*, 341.

102　Ibid., 339.

103　Quoted in ibid., 340.

104 Henry Demarest Lloyd, *Wealth against Commonwealth* (New York: Harper and Brothers, 1894), 213–14.

105 Ibid., 534–35.

106 Quoted in Thomas, *Alternative America*, 344.

107 See Brady, *Ida Tarbell*, 123–24, 136–38.

108 Tarbell, *History of Standard Oil*, 2:288.

109 Tarbell's 1933 letter quoted in Brady, *Ida Tarbell*, 139. See 140–43 on repercussions of Tarbell's *History of Standard Oil*.

110 Chernow, *Titan*, 615–19.

111 See Brady, *Ida Tarbell*, 159, on Standard Oil's reconstitution during wartime.

Chapter 8

1 Kenneth M. Roemer, *The Obsolete Necessity: America in Utopian Writings, 1888–1900* (Kent State University Press, 1976), which I draw on where relevant, covers some of this territory.

2 Twain quoted in John Kasson, *Civilizing the Machine: Technology and Republican Values in America, 1776–1900* (New York: Penguin, 1999), 202.

3 Quoted in ibid., 201.

4 This paragraph and the following depend for facts on Cecelia Tichi's introduction to Edward Bellamy, *Looking Backward* (New York: Penguin, 1982).

5 Bellamy, *Looking Backward*, 193.

6 "Letter to the People's Party," *New Nation* (1892), quoted in Roemer, *Obsolete Necessity*, 1.

7 Bellamy, *Looking Backward*, 62.

8 See Justin Kaplan's introduction to *A Connecticut Yankee at King Arthur's Court* (New York: Penguin, 1971).

9 Daniel Carter Beard, *Hardly a Man Is Now Alive: The Autobiography of Dan Beard* (New York: Doubleday, Doran, 1939), 338; Twain quoted in Norton Critical Edition of *A Connecticut Yankee at King Arthur's Court* (New York: Norton, 1982), 308.

10 Twain, *Connecticut Yankee* (Penguin ed.), 41.

11 Ibid., 88.

12 King Camp Gillette, *The Human Drift* (Delmar, N.Y.: Scholars' Facsimiles, 1976), 4.

13 Another fascinating example is Milton Hershey's attempt to make his company town of Hershey, Pennsylvania, into a utopia. See Michael D'Antonio, *Hershey: Milton S. Hershey's Extraordinary Life of Wealth, Empire, and Utopian Dreams* (New York: Simon and Schuster, 2006).

14 Kenneth Roemer, introduction to Gillette, *Human Drift*, xiv–xv.

15 Ibid., xii.

16 For facts in this paragraph and the following, see the introduction to Bradford

Peck, *The World a Department Store: A Story of Life under a Cooperative System* (Lewiston, Maine: B. Peck, 1900).

17 Quoted in Michael Patrick Hearn's introduction to L. Frank Baum, *The Annotated Wizard of Oz* (New York: Norton, 2000), xcv. See the detailed notes and introduction by Hearn in this superb edition of the novel.

18 Quoted in ibid., xlv–xlvi.

19 See also Susan Wolstenholme's introduction to L. Frank Baum, *The Wonderful Wizard of Oz* (New York: Oxford World's Classics, 1997) for facts in this paragraph and the following.

20 Quoted in Baum, *Annotated Wizard*, 260.

21 Ibid., 18–20.

22 Ibid., xci.

23 Roemer, *Obsolete Necessity*, esp. 70–71.

24 Charlotte Perkins Gilman, *"Herland," "The Yellow Wall-Paper," and Selected Writings* (New York: Penguin, 1999), 92.

25 Ignatius Donnelly, *Caesar's Column: A Story of the Twentieth Century* (Cambridge, Mass.: Harvard University Press, Belknap Press, 1960), 117.

26 Ibid., 283.

27 Ibid., 97–98.

28 Ibid., 169.

29 Ibid., 272.

30 Ibid., 312.

31 The novel was serialized in *Forerunner*, 1915, prior to its publication.

32 The story appeared in the *New England Magazine*, January 1892.

33 Charlotte Perkins Gilman, "Why I Wrote 'The Yellow Wall-Paper,'" *Forerunner*, October 1913, 271. Quoted in Denise D. Knight's introduction to Gilman, *"Herland" and Other Writings*, xviii.

34 Gilman, *"Herland" and Other Writings*, 3.

35 Ibid., 13.

36 Ibid., 72.

37 Ibid., 128.

38 Ibid., 82, 60.

39 The essay was published in *Forerunner*, June 1913, 149.

40 *The Iron Heel*, in *Jack London: Novels and Social Writings* (New York: Library of America, 1982), 326.

41 Ibid., 348, 384.

42 Ibid., 459, 463, 471, 517.

43 London quoted in Francis Shor, "Power, Gender, and Ideological Discourse in 'The Iron Heel,'" in *Rereading Jack London*, ed. Leonard Cassuto and Jeanne Campbell Reesman (Stanford: Stanford University Press, 1996), 75, 247.

44 London quoted in Cassuto and Reesman, *Rereading Jack London*, 85.

45 Quoted in Clara and Rudolf Kirk's introduction to William Dean Howells, *The*

Altrurian Romances (Bloomington: Indiana University Press, 1968), xiv–xv. I draw here and in the previous paragraph on the Kirks' introduction and notes.

46 Ibid., xxi, 154.

47 Ibid., 71.

48 Ibid., 99.

49 William Dean Howells, *Letters of an Altrurian Traveller*, in *Altrurian Romances*, 183.

50 Howells, *Traveller from Altruria*, 157.

51 *New York Daily Herald*, 23 September 1894, cited in introduction to Howells, *Altrurian Romances*, xxv.

52 Quoted in introduction to Howells, *Altrurian Romances*, xvii.

53 Quoted in ibid., xxxii.

Afterword

1 See, for example, Alan Taylor, *American Colonies: Penguin History of the United States* (New York: Penguin, 2001), for a comprehensive account of colonial society with its significant populations of Germans, Dutch, French, and Scotch Irish, as well as smaller but notable populations of Swedes, Finns, Italians, and Jews. The classic source on American immigration is John Higham, *Strangers in the Land: Patterns of American Nativism, 1860–1925* (New York: Athaneum, 1966). Consider also Ronald Takaki's observation that "America has been racially diverse since our very beginning on the Virginia shore." *A Different Mirror: A History of Multicultural America* (Boston: Little, Brown, 1993), 2.

2 Walter Michaels explores American nativism during the 1920s from the perspective of literary authors in *Our America: Nativism, Modernism, and Pluralism* (Chicago: University of Chicago Press, 1995).

INDEX

Alger, Horatio, Jr.: life, 204, 209–12, 245, 325 (nn. 77, 80)
—writings: *Ragged Dick*, 204, 210–11, 325 (nn. 79, 81); *Struggling Upward*, 211–12
Allegheny College, 254
American Alliance for Labor and Democracy, 192
American Federation of Labor, 4, 202–4
American Journal of Sociology, 48, 51, 78
American Revolution, 105
American Safety Razor Company, 267
American Tobacco Company, 214
Amherst College, 124
Anagnos, Michael, 90
Anderson, Sherwood, 156
Andover Seminary, 22
Andrews, William, 249
Animals, 68, 179–80, 231, 272–73
Anthony, Susan B., 41, 57
Anti-Monopolist, 275
Antin, Frieda, 208–9
Antin, Mary: life, 204, 207–9
—writings: *The Promised Land*, 177, 204, 207–9, 324 (n. 69); *They Who Knock at Our Gates*, 208
Appeal to Reason, 321 (n. 6)
Appiah, Anthony, 302–3 (n. 2)
Appleton's Journal, 35
Appomattox, Va., 4, 10, 15, 29–30, 39, 53, 105, 109; Indian mistaken for black at Appomattox, 109
Armour, Philip, 18, 236
Arnold, Matthew, 121
Art Nouveau, 156, 271
Arts and Crafts Movement, 156
Asad, Talal, 292 (n. 11)
Atlanta, Ga., 63–64
The Atlanta University Publications, 63–65, 291 (n. 3), 299 (n. 6)
Atlantic Monthly: advertising, 6, 10, 58, 125, 145–47, 146 (fig. 6), 147, 314 (n. 17), 316 (n. 30); Alcott in, 26; Bellamy in, 260; Cahan in, 6; Henry James in,

158, 318 (n. 60); Howells in, 157–58, 166, 167, 319 (n. 75); Jackson in, 125; Lloyd in, 251; Phelps in, 216; Zitkala-Ša in, 122
Austen, Jane: *Northanger Abbey*, 139
Authorship, 2–3, 4–6, 163–75, 314 (n. 17), 316 (n. 30), 318 (nn. 57, 60), 319 (n. 75); and women, 20–28, 30–32, 35–39, 40–43, 57–58, 70–71, 122–29, 168–71, 207–9, 216–18, 277–80, 295 (n. 5), 321 (n. 14). See also individual authors

Bachelder, John: *A.D. 2050*, 274
Bacon, Francis, 275
Baker, Mark, 99
Baker, Ray Stannard, 152 (fig. 11), 161, 253
Balzac, Honoré de, 7
Bancroft, Edgar A., 121
Bancroft Library, 127
Barbella, Maria, 293–94 (n. 16)
Barber, Max, 162
Barnet, Ferdinand L., 57
Barnum, P. T., 272
Barthes, Roland, 19
Baum, L. Frank: early children's books, 271; on Indians, 271, 273; life, 269–73
—writings: *The Art of Decorating Dry Goods Windows and Interiors*, 269, 270, 272 *The Book of the Hamburg*, 270; *The Wonderful Wizard of Oz*, 257, 268, 269–73, 286, 287
Beard, Daniel, 262
Beecher, Henry Ward, 147, 157, 230, 315 (n. 21)
Beecher-Tilton Trial, 230
Beerbohm, Max, 305 (n. 24)
Beilis, Mendel, 222
Bell, Alexander Graham, 11, 41, 90
Bellamy, Edward: and Howells, 174, 259, 283, 285; influence, 186, 244, 257, 269; life, 258–61; militarism, 257; national-ism, 174, 259, 283; and religion, 257–61, 269; and socialism, 257, 259, 280;

—writings: "Bintel Brief," column, 84–85; *The Imported Bridegroom*, 84; *The Rise of David Levinsky*, 84, 218, 220–24, 221 (fig. 21), 222 (fig. 22), 231, 326 (n. 16); *Yekl*, 84–85

Caldwell, Christopher, 294–95 (n. 22)

Capitalism: American distinguished from British and European, 2–3, 8, 176, 223–24; defined, 291–2 (n. 4), 293 (n. 13); expansion of, in U.S., 213–55, 292 (n. 7); and labor, 176–204, 247, 254; and multiculturalism, 1–2, 178, 220–24, 225–27, 240–43, 288–89; and possessions as constitutive of self, 240–43; and race, 1–2, 45, 46, 61–62, 69–75, 178, 191–92, 204–7, 240–43, 300–301 (n. 30), 323 (n. 40); and social conflict, 4–5; and utopianism, 256, 257, 258. *See also* Business; Industry; Titans of business; Trusts

Cardozo, Albert, 209, 325 (n. 77)

Cardozo, Benjamin, 209, 325 (n. 77)

Carleton College, 244, 254

Carlson, David J., 308–9 (n. 43)

Carnegie, Andrew: life, 4, 171, 213, 228, 245–47, 250, 266

—writings: *The Empire of Business*, 245–47, 328 (n. 80)

Carnegie Hall, 72

Cather, Willa: and Dreiser, 171, 173; on Henry James, 170; honored by American Academy of Arts and Letters, 171; on Howells, 170; and immigrants, 169–71, 174–75; and Indians, 169, 174–75; as journalist, 159, 161; life, 166, 168–71; on Norris, 170; sexuality of, 169–71; and travel, 170, 175; on Twain, 169–70; on women, 86, 169–71

—writings: *Alexander's Bridge*, 170; *The Life of Mary Baker G. Eddy and the History of Christian Science* (co-author), 98–101, 169, 319 (n. 83); *My Auto-*

biography (co-author with Samuel S. McClure), 168–69; *O Pioneers*, 169, 170; *The Song of the Lark*, 170–71

Cayuga Academy, 106, 107

Central Pacific Railroad Company, 130

Century Magazine (formerly *Scribner's Monthly*), 6, 28, 32, 65, 123, 127, 147, 149 (fig. 8), 152 (fig. 11), 158, 167–68, 260, 319 (n. 70), 321–22 (n. 18)

Chandler, Alfred, 233

Charles L. Webster & Co. (Twain's publishing house): and Grant's *Memoirs*, 28, 227

Chautauquan, 254

Chernow, Ron, 255, 329 (n. 90)

Cherokee people, 103, 124, 126

Chesnutt, Charles Waddell: life, 58, 274; lynching in work of, 60; and passing, 58–60; sacrifice theme, 59–60

—writings: *The House behind the Cedars*, 58–59; *The Marrow of Tradition*, 58–60

Cheyenne people, 126

Chicago: Board of Trade, 235–38; Fire of 1871, 232, 267; *Daily Globe*, 172; *Globe Democrat*, 172; and Hull House, 184–86; streetcar system, 234–35; *Tribune*, 251; University of, 234, 243, 244

Chicopee Falls, Mass., 260

Child, Lydia Maria, 44

—writings: *Romance of the Republic*, 21

Children's Aid Society, 210

Chinese immigrants, 190

Chippewa people, 103

Chittenango, N.Y., 270

Chopin, Kate: life, 86

—writings: *The Awakening*, 86–87

Christian Science, 67, 92, 97–101, 174, 319 (n. 83)

Christian Union, 123, 310 (n. 63)

Churchill, Winston, 180

Cincinnati Gazette, 167

Civil War, 10–43; and advertising, 138, 142–43; Alcott's novels on, 11–12, 20–

Delaware people, 110, 126

Delineator, 173

Denslow, William, 271

Depressions, economic, 160, 214–15, 231, 232, 245

Desai, Kirin, 302–3 (n. 2)

Dewey, John, 93

Dial Magazine, 49, 205, 324 (n. 62)

Dickinson, Anna: *What Answer*, 21

Diversity. *See* Multiculturalism

Dixon, John K., 137

Donnelly, Ignatius: life, 8, 259, 275–77
—writings: *Atlantis*, 275; *Caesar's Column*, 256, 257, 258, 268, 275–77, 286

Doolittle Report (1867), 102

Doubleday Co., 173, 225, 320 (n. 102), 321 (n. 6)

Douglass, Frederick, 12, 39, 44, 45, 53, 56, 58, 103, 162

Doyle, Arthur Conan, 160

Draft Riots (New York), 21

Draper, John William, 16

Dreiser, John Paul, 172

Dreiser, Theodore: advertising, 156; on business, 216, 232–35; on capitalism, 171–74, 232–35; and Cather, 171, 173; censorship and suppression, 171, 172, 173, 320 (n. 102); on class, 171–74, 188–89; on communism (and socialism), 172, 173, 174, 175; on desire, 189; as editor, 172–74; and Howells, 172–73, 220; as journalist, 171–74; life and family, 171–74, 188; and materialism, 171–74; and Norris, 173, 220, 231; published in journals, 171, 320 (n. 100); and religion, 98, 172–74; on survival of the fittest, 231–35; on working women, 188–89
—writings: *An American Tragedy*, 189, 212; "Curious Shifts of the Poor," 172–73; *Dreiser Looks at Russia*, 174–75; *The Financier*, 218, 232–35; *The "Genius,"* 98, 173–74; *Jennie Gerhardt*, 177, 188–89; "A Lesson from the Aquarium," 234; *Newspaper Days*, 172; *Sister Carrie*, 172, 173, 189, 250; *The Stoic* (unfinished), 232; *The Titan*, 232, 234–35

Drummond, Henry, 160

Du Bois, Burghardt, 62–63

Du Bois, W. E. B.: on blacks' status, 2, 7, 46, 74; on capitalism, 2, 45, 46, 61–62, 74, 191–92, 291 (n. 3), 300–301 (n. 30), 323 (n. 40); on double consciousness, 58; as editor, 6, 161–63, 299 (n. 6), 318 (n. 53); and Henry James, 62; Hull House lecture, 185; on labor, 45, 46, 61, 64, 177, 178, 191–92, 300–301 (n. 30), 323 (n. 40); life, 61–65, 70; on lynching, 52, 162; and NAACP, 161, 162; and Pauline Hopkins, 71; political agenda, 42, 52, 60–65, 161–63, 189, 191–92; on racial identity, 61–62, 64–65, 191–92, 323 (n. 40); and racist pseudo-science, 47–48, 49, 50, 52, 63–65, 192; range of work, 60–62, 64–65, 299 (n. 6); and sacrifice, 7, 62–63, 209; tribute to Howells, 168; and Washington, 205–6, 324 (n. 62); and William James, 62
—writings: Atlanta University Publications, 63–65, 291 (n. 3), 299 (n. 6); "Economics of Negro Emancipation," 300–301 (n. 30); "The Negroes of Farmville," 61; *The Philadelphia Negro*, 177, 178, 189, 191–92, 323 (n. 40); *The Souls of Black Folk*, 7, 60–63

Dumas, Alexandre, 7

Dunbar, Paul Laurence: Civil War writing, 11, 39–40, 42; and Douglass, 39; and Howells, 39, 136; life, 39–40, 274; published in magazines, 6, 39
—writings: *The Fanatics*, 12, 39–40; *Lyrics of a Lowly Life*, 39; *Majors and Minor*, 39; *Oak and Ivy*, 39

Franklin, Benjamin, 2–4, 204, 206, 291
   (n. 2), 323–24 (n. 56)
—writings: *Autobiography*, 206
Frederic, Harold, 98
Fredericksburg, Va., 25
Freedmen's Bureau, 1, 95, 110, 112, 113,
   301 (n. 39)
Freeman, Mary Wilkins: as prominent
   author, 173, 321 (n. 14); published in
   magazines, 6, 321 (n. 14)
—writings: *The Portion of Labor*, 177,
   181–82, 321 (n. 14)
Freemasons, 107, 108
Free Speech, 56
Free Trade Association, 251
Fremsted, Olive, 170–71
Freud, Sigmund, 82, 151
Frick, Henry Clay, 246, 247
Friedman, Isaac Kahn: *Poor People*, 183–
   84, 322 (n. 22)
Frost, Robert, 173, 316 (n. 28)
Fruitlands community, 26
Fugitive Slave Law (1850), 29
Fuller, Alvarado: *A.D. 2000*, 256
Fuller, Henry Blake: *The Cliff Dwellers*,
   218, 238–40
Futures contract, 233

Gage, Matilda Jocelyn, 270
Gage, Maud, 270
Galton, Francis, 279
Gardner, Alexander, 13–18; "The Burial
   Party," 16 (fig. 1)
Garfield, James, 54
Garland, Hamlin, 119, 283
Garrison, William Lloyd, Jr., 41, 53, 162
Gates, Bill, 250
George, Henry: life, 177, 190–91
—writings: *Progress and Poverty*, 189,
   190–91, 251, 252, 259
German immigrants, 4, 50, 88, 132, 136–
   37, 169, 170, 172, 173, 184, 187, 220, 246
Ghost Dances (Sioux), 103, 118, 119

Gift, concept of, 240–43, 328 (n. 70)
Gillette, King Camp: Gillette razors,
   257, 265–67; life, 265–68, 269
—writings: *The Human Drift*, 257, 265–
   67, 268
Gilman, Charlotte Perkins: edits *Forerunner*, 278; life, 277–80; and multiculturalism, 274, 277–80; political
   agenda, 86, 186–87, 274, 277–80; and
   reproduction, 186, 274, 277–80; rest
   cure, 278; on Sinclair's *The Jungle*,
   180; and utopianism, 5, 8, 256, 258,
   274, 277–80, 285, 286, 287
—writings: *Herland*, 5, 256, 258, 274,
   277–80, 285, 286, 287, 331 (n. 31);
   "New Mothers of a New World,"
   279–80; "Why I Wrote The Yellow
   Wallpaper," 278; *Women and Economics*, 177, 186–87; "The Yellow
   Wallpaper," 278
Gladden, Washington, 168
Glasgow, Ellen, 11, 37–38, 42
—writings: *The Battle-Ground*, 38–39
Glasgow Sentinel, 14
Glassmaking industry, 177
The Golden Age, 260
Gompers, Samuel, 4, 177, 189, 192, 202–4
—writings: *Seventy Years of Life and
   Labor*, 203–4
Gould, Jay, 18, 169, 249, 262
Grabau, Amadeus, 208
Grant, Ulysses S.: and Civil War, 12, 28–
   31, 38; and Indians, 102, 104–5, 108–10;
   and Parker, 4, 104–5, 108–10; on
   travel, 35
—writings: *Personal Memoirs*, 11, 28–30,
   313 (n. 5)
Grey, Zane: life and early writings, 133–
   37, 312 (n. 94), 166; on Indians, 103,
   104, 133–37
—writings: *The Border Legion*, 134; *The
   Heritage of the Desert*, 134; *The Rainbow Trail*, 134–35; *Riders of the Purple*,

Howells, William Dean: and Baum, 271; and Bellamy, 174, 259, 283, 285; on business, 166–68, 215, 216, 218–20; and Cahan, 84, 166, 220; and Cather, 166, 170; and Chesnutt, 166; and class, 6, 157–58, 166–68; and commercialization of culture, 139, 157–58, 166–68; and Crane, 166; and Dreiser, 172–73, 174, 220; Du Bois tribute, 168; and Dunbar, 39, 166; as editor, 157–58, 166–68, 283, 285, 286, 317 (n. 38); ethical dilemmas in, 168; and finances, 157–58, 166–68, 317 (n. 38), 319 (n. 75); and Harte, 166; and Hay, 321–22 (n. 18); and Henry James, 158, 166; and Herrick, 327–28 (n. 61); and Jewett, 166; journalism, 166–68; and Keller, 90; life, 166–68; and Lloyd, 251–52, 329 (n. 101); multiculturalism, 39, 40, 167–68; and Norris, 87, 166, 220, 236, 238; and religion, 283–86; sacrifice in, 218–20; and socialism, 168, 280–81, 283–86, 320 (n. 107); and syndication, 160; and Tolstoy, 283, 320 (n. 107); and Twain, 166; and utopianism, 280–81, 283–87; on travel, 76; work published in magazines, 6, 139, 160, 166–68, 319 (n. 70)

—writings: "A Call for Realism," 219; "The Editor's Easy Chair," 157; "The Editor's Study," 157, 283, 285, 286; *A Hazard of New Fortunes,* 157–58; *An Imperative Duty,* 168; "Letters of an Altrurian Traveler," 285; Lincoln campaign biography, 166; *A Modern Instance,* 160, 166–68, 218–19, 319 (n. 70); *The Rise of Silas Lapham,* 84, 216, 218–20, 238, 326 (n. 12); *Through the Eye of the Needle,* 285, 286; *A Traveler from Altruria,* 84, 256, 257, 258, 266, 283–86

Hull, Charles J., 185

Hull House (Chicago), 57, 184–85

Hunt, Edward, 124

Hunt, Rennie, 124

Huntington, Collis P., 130, 224–25, 231

Immigrants: and advertising, 2, 6, 144, 147–50, 149 (fig. 8), 152–54, 152 (fig. 11), 153 (fig. 12), 154 (fig. 13), 243; Antin as, 207–9; and assimilation, 2, 50, 137, 152–55, 152 (fig. 11), 154 (fig. 13), 207–9, 288–89; blacks as, 206, 302 (n. 44); class consciousness, 159–61, 207–9, 243–47; as consumers, 83–85, 137, 180, 289; and cultural legacy, 83–85, 184–86, 207–9, 220, 224; economic role, 77–78, 159–61, 213–14, 220–24, 243–47, 288–89; and food, 206, 209, 324–25 (n. 74); labor, 77–78, 178–89, 194–204, 196 (fig. 14), 197 (fig. 15), 198 (fig. 16), 199 (fig. 17), 200 (fig. 18), 201 (fig. 19), 202 (fig. 20), 243–47; narratives by, 4, 83–85, 159, 160, 194–203, 207–9, 220–24, 243–47; nativist hostility toward, 76, 79–82, 85–86, 87–88, 132, 133, 190, 293 (n. 16); novels on, 76, 79–82, 183–84, 187, 207–9, 220–24; numbers, 77–78, 289, 292 (n. 6); and philanthropists, 184–86, 204–7; and racial attitudes, 185, 293 (n. 15); as readers, 3, 83–85; social conditions, 178, 189, 194–202, 196 (fig. 14), 197 (fig. 15), 198 (fig. 16), 199 (fig. 17), 200 (fig. 18), 201 (fig. 19), 202 (fig. 20); social scientists on, 78, 85–86; stereotypes of, 2, 4, 131, 152–55, 154 (fig. 13), 183–84, 207, 221–24, 221 (fig. 21), 222 (fig. 22), 238, 240–43; successes of, 4, 159–61, 194–203, 202–4, 245–47, 288–89; and unions, 202–4; and utopianism, 8–9, 257–58, 261, 268–69, 272–80; and women reformers, 184–86. *See also individual ethnicities and nationalities*

The Independent, 123

Indians: assimilation, 105–10, 117–22,

modity, 5–6, 294 (n. 18), 314 (n. 17), 317 (nn. 40, 47), 318 (nn. 58, 60); muckraking, 159–61, 248–55, 315 (n. 26); numbers, 144, 162, 294 (n. 18), 314 (n. 17), 316–17 (n. 35); serialization of novels, 5–6, 32, 138–42, 157–61, 163–64, 167–68, 221–22, 248, 284, 305 (n. 27), 310 (n. 63), 311 (n. 85), 313 (n. 6), 317 (nn. 39, 40), 319 (n. 70), 321–22 (nn. 6, 14, 18), 326 (nn. 12, 16), 331 (n. 31). *See also individual titles, authors, and advertising*

Julian, Sophia, 203

Jung, Carl Gustav, 151

Kallen, Horace, 207, 274

Katznelson, Ira, 176

Keller, Helen, 89, 90, 304 (n. 12)

—writings: *The Story of My Life*, 90–92

Kent, James, 126

Khayyam, Omar, 91

Kinship, 111–15, 280, 302–3 (n. 2), 307 (n. 26), 324–25 (n. 74)

Knox College, 121, 160

Kodak camera, 74–75, 143, 205

Krupat, Arnold, 302–3 (n. 2)

Ku Klux Klan, 53–55, 68

Labor, 176–212; and Addams, 184–86; and blacks, 15–17, 19–20, 45–46, 50, 61, 64, 191–92, 204–7, 300–301 (n. 30), 323 (n. 40); Booker T. Washington on, 204–7; child, 192–94; class versus ethnic consciousness, 144–47, 145 (fig. 5), 146 (fig. 6), 152–55, 154 (fig. 13), 176–78, 180–81, 187, 321 (n. 8); commission report, 180; eight-hour work day, 203; organization, 4, 84, 202–4; reformers, 184–86, 189–204, 321 (nn. 8, 13); unrest, 183, 247, 254; and women, 184–86, 216–18, 322 (n. 30). *See also* Blacks: labor; Immigrants: labor; Women: labor

Lackawanna Railroad, 193; advertisement, 156

Ladies Home Journal, 90, 136, 169, 311 (n. 85)

Laird, Pamela, 314 (n. 17)

Lane, Mary, 277

Lasky, Jesse, 136

Lee, Robert E.: invasion of Pennsylvania, 249; mistakes Ely S. Parker for black at Appomattox, 109; surrender at Appomattox, 4, 10, 15, 29–30, 39, 53, 105, 109

Legal decisions and cases: *Brown v. Board of Education*, 56; Dawes Act (1887), 102–3; 1891 Act for the Relief of the Mission Indians, 123; Emancipation Proclamation, 12, 31, 45, 300–301 (n. 30); Fugitive Slave Law (1850), 29; Homestead Act (1862), 11; Indian Citizenship Act, 102; International Copyright Act (1891), 3, 318 (n. 57); Meat Inspection Act, 180; National Banking Act, 11; Pacific Railway Act, 11; *Plessy v. Ferguson*, 53, 56, 58; Pure Food and Drug Inspection Act, 180; Sherman Antitrust Law (1890), 215; *U.S. v. Kagema*, 102. *See also individual decisions and cases*

Leiter, Joseph, 236

Lenin, Vladimir, 202

Lesbianism, 32–35, 170–71

Leslie's Illustrated Weekly Newspaper, 147

Lewis, Edith, 99

Lewiston, Maine, 268

Lieberson, Stanley, 323 (n. 40)

Lincoln, Abraham: in books and journals, 20, 31, 160–61, 167, 253; and Civil War, 11–12, 14, 31; and Indians, 102, 109, 307 (n. 16)

Literacy, 3, 142, 313 (n. 10)

Lithuanian immigrants, 178, 179

Litwack, Leon, 302 (n. 45)

Mobility, social, 177, 181–82, 188–89, 204–12, 220–24, 245–47; and advertising, 152–55, 154 (fig. 13), 314 (nn. 17, 19); and Civil War, 35; immigrants, 152–55, 154 (fig. 13); and internal migration, 2, 39–42, 51–52, 58
Montgomery, David, 176
The Moon, 161
Mooney, James, 118
More, Thomas: Utopia, 258
Morgan, Henry Lewis: and Ely S. Parker, 4, 104, 107–8, 110–13, 116, 306 (n. 13); on Indians, 103, 104, 105, 107–8, 110–16, 132, 308 (n. 35); kinship theory, 16, 111–14, 305 (n. 38), 307 (n. 26)
—writings: The American Beaver and His Works, 114; Ancient Society, 111, 115, 307 (n. 25); Houses and House-Life of the American Aborigines, 111; The League of the Ho-de-nosau-nee, or Iroquois, 4, 107, 111, 113, 114; Systems of Consanguinuity and Affinity of the Human Family, 111–12, 114–15
Morgan, J. P., 231
Morgan, Mary Elizabeth Steele, 114
Morgan, Thomas Jefferson, 118
Mormons, 135, 152 (fig. 11)
Morris, William: News from Nowhere, 284
Morrison, Toni: Beloved, 68
Morse, Samuel F. B., 14
Mott, Frank Luther, 294 (n. 18), 313 (n. 6), 315 (n. 26), 316 (n. 30), 316–17 (n. 35), 317 (n. 46), 321 (n. 14)
Mount Auburn Cemetery, 83
Muckraking journalism, 159–61, 248–55, 315 (n. 26)
Multiculturalism: and advertising, 2, 5–6, 7–8, 143–55, 145 (fig. 5), 146 (fig. 6), 149 (fig. 8), 152 (fig. 11), 153 (fig. 12), 154 (fig. 13), 243, 288–89; and capitalism, 207–9, 213–14, 220–24, 221 (fig. 21), 222 (fig. 22), 225–27, 240–43, 288–89; impact on welfare, 176–78, 273–

80, 286–87, 294 (n. 22); social conflict, 4–5, 257–58, 261; use of term discussed, 3–4, 302–3 (n. 2). See also Utopianism: and multiculturalism
Mumler, William, 24
Munsey's Magazine, 138
Museum of Natural History, 133
Mussel Slough Massacre, 224
Myers, Frederic, 92
Myers, Gustavus, 231
Myrdal, Gunnar, 48

NAACP (National Association for the Advancement of Colored People), 58, 161
Napoleon, 90, 160, 253
The Nation, 29, 167, 173
National Association of Window Trimmers of America, 269
National Citizens Rights Association, 53
Nationalism, 174, 259
Nationalist Party, 259
Nationalist, 259
Nativism, 76, 79–82, 85–86, 87–88, 132, 133, 170, 190
Navajo people, 135
Nebraska: literary culture of, 169; and Nebraska State Journal, 169
"Nell Meeting," 51, 52
New Nation, 259
New York: New School for Social Research, 244; New York City Tenement-House Commission (1884), 194; New York State Board of Regents, 107; New York State Museum, 108
—journalism in: Daily Herald, 285; Golden Age, 260; New York Evening Post, 63, 124, 162, 260; New York Times, 14–15, 270; New York Times Book Review, 169, 322 (n. 22); New York World, 84; Sun, 160, 194, 317 (n. 47), 324 (n. 69); Tribune, 194
Nez Perce people, 126